*Understanding and Teaching
the Vietnam War*

The Harvey Goldberg Series
for Understanding and Teaching History

The Harvey Goldberg Series for Understanding and Teaching History gives college and secondary history instructors a deeper understanding of the past as well as the tools to help them teach it creatively and effectively. Each volume focuses on a specific historical topic and offers a wealth of content and resources, providing concrete examples of how teachers can approach the subject in the classroom. Named for Harvey Goldberg, a professor renowned for his history teaching at Oberlin College, Ohio State University, and the University of Wisconsin from the 1960s to the 1980s, the series reflects Goldberg's commitment to helping students think critically about the past with the goal of creating a better future. For more information, please visit www.GoldbergSeries.org.

Series Editors

John Day Tully is an associate professor of history at Central Connecticut State University and was the founding director of the Harvey Goldberg Center for Excellence in Teaching at Ohio State University.

Matthew Masur is an associate professor of history at Saint Anselm College, where he is codirector of the Father Guerin Center for Teaching Excellence. He is a member of the Teaching Committee of the Society for Historians of American Foreign Relations and writes on American-Vietnamese relations.

Brad Austin is a professor of history at Salem State University. He has served as chair of the American Historical Association's Teaching Prize Committee and has worked with hundreds of secondary school teachers as the academic coordinator of many Teaching American History grants.

Advisory Board

Kevin Boyle   Ohio State University
Ross Dunn   Professor Emeritus, San Diego State University
Leon Fink   UIC Distinguished Professor of History, University of Illinois at Chicago
Kimberly Ibach   Ben L. Smith High School, Greensboro, North Carolina
Alfred W. McCoy   J.R.W. Smail Professor of History, Director, Harvey Goldberg Center for the Study of Contemporary History, University of Wisconsin–Madison
David J. Staley   Director, Harvey Goldberg Center for Excellence in Teaching, Ohio State University
Maggie Tran   McLean High School, McLean, Virginia
Sam Wineburg   Margaret Jacks Professor of Education and (by courtesy) of History, Director, Stanford History Education Group, Stanford University

Understanding and Teaching the Vietnam War

Edited by

JOHN DAY TULLY

MATTHEW MASUR

BRAD AUSTIN

The University of Wisconsin Press

The University of Wisconsin Press
1930 Monroe Street, 3rd Floor
Madison, Wisconsin 53711-2059
uwpress.wisc.edu

3 Henrietta Street
London WC2E 8LU, England
eurospanbookstore.com

Printed in the United States of America

Library of Congress Cataloging-in-Publication Data

Understanding and teaching the Vietnam War / edited by John Day Tully,
Matthew Masur, and Brad Austin.
p.   cm.—(The Harvey Goldberg series for understanding and teaching history)
Includes bibliographical references and index.
ISBN 978-0-299-29414-4 (pbk.: alk. paper)
ISBN 978-0-299-29413-7 (e-book)
1. Vietnam War, 1961–1975—Study and teaching—United States.
I. Tully, John Day.   II. Masur, Matthew.   III. Austin, Brad, 1972–
IV. Series: Harvey Goldberg series for understanding and teaching history.
DS557.74.U53   2013
959.704'3071—dc23
2012040084

For

NANCY

JENN

LAGINA

Contents

**Part Three: Understanding and
Teaching Specific Content**

Contents

Preface

Our inspiration for this project began with the career of an amazing teacher and prolific scholar, Harvey Goldberg. Born in New Jersey in 1922, he earned both his undergraduate degree and his PhD in history from the University of Wisconsin–Madison, completing his dissertation on the life and contributions of the French socialist Jean Juarès. He published widely, producing not only a monograph biography of Juarès but also numerous academic articles intended to advance scholarly debates and essays in popular magazines designed to engage and inform the public.

The dual desire to bring scholarly insights to the people and to bring the pressing concerns of the real world to the ivory tower manifested themselves in his teaching as well. The combination of his passion, intellect, and compelling stage presence made Goldberg one of the most effective and influential educators of his age.

After a brief stint at Oberlin College, Professor Goldberg taught at both Ohio State University and the University of Wisconsin–Madison for many decades. Although the editors of this volume never had the honor of working directly with Professor Goldberg, his influence and legacy were all around us. While graduate students at Ohio State, we had the opportunity to work on various projects through the Department of History's Harvey Goldberg Center for Excellence in Teaching, which grew out of the desire of many of Goldberg's former students to honor him, his teaching, and his positive influence on their lives. As graduate students, we were honored to work on publishing projects designed to improve the quality of teaching in American history survey classes, on grant projects with local secondary teachers, and on continuing efforts within the department itself to improve the quality of the undergraduate classroom experience. We also were able to meet and talk with many of Goldberg's former students, who, even many years later, recounted with emotion and genuine appreciation how Harvey's teaching helped them to become critical thinkers and engaged citizens. We became better teachers because of this experience and inspiration.

The mark of a great teacher is an ability to change students' lives. Perhaps the mark of a truly great teacher is that such a gift influences generations of students, who in turn carry forward the legacy. The existence and prominence of the Ohio State Harvey Goldberg Center for Excellence in Teaching and the University of Wisconsin's Harvey Goldberg Center offer testimony to the power of his influence on his legions of admirers and students.

Harvey taught these students that the "appeal of history" is "not chronology, and it is not archaeology, and it is not computers, and it is not the memory bank, and it is not really getting on some kind of cards every little *lopin* of land in a French province in 1702." Instead, he proclaimed, the purpose of history is "to go back and to find the useable past. That is all that is interesting to me." His desire to make students realize how much power comes from understanding the past is still valid today. He was able to live that truth in his teaching; this book and the Harvey Goldberg Series for Understanding and Teaching History are designed to help teachers make such a belief a reality in their own classrooms.

Acknowledgments

This book would not have been possible without the contributions of Harvey Goldberg's former students, who have generously contributed time and money to sustain his legacy at both the University of Wisconsin and Ohio State University. The three of us all worked in the Harvey Goldberg Center for Excellence in Teaching (then the Harvey Goldberg Program) while graduate students at OSU. It gave us a chance to learn about Harvey Goldberg and what he meant to his students. It also gave us the opportunity to work with OSU faculty members and fellow graduate students to become better teachers. We extend our thanks to the department chairs and professors who helped create and sustain the Goldberg Program: Michael Hogan, Leila Rupp, Kenneth Andrien, Peter Hahn, Steven Conn, Saul Cornell, Tim Gregory, Mark Grimsley, Margaret Newell, Carla Pestana, and David Stebenne.

The staff and faculty board at the University of Wisconsin Press have been advocates for this book since we first proposed it. We would especially like to thank Gwen Walker, Andrea Christofferson, and Sheila Leary for their comments, advice, and support. This is a better book because of them. We also wish to thank Adam Mehring, Marian Halls, Matthew Cosby, and Logan Middleton. Gwen deserves credit for suggesting that this book could be part of a series in honor of Harvey Goldberg. We are very glad she had such foresight.

We also want to acknowledge the essential contributions made by the talented teachers and scholars who contributed essays for this volume. As is the case with most edited collections, the authors' diversity of interests, experiences, and expertise has made this a more complete and complex volume than any one author could have produced. We especially want to thank the authors for their willingness to weave discussions of content and pedagogy together in ways that most had not done before. Their thoughtfulness and eagerness to write to our intended audience of university and high school teachers made this a much stronger volume.

We are thankful for the support of the Harvey Goldberg Series Advisory Board: Kevin Boyle, Ross Dunn, Leon Fink, Kimberly Ibach, Alfred McCoy, David Staley, Maggie Tran, and Sam Wineburg. We look forward to working with them as the series takes shape. The reviewers who read this manuscript offered a host of suggestions that helped us refine our approach and make the volume more informative and useful to teachers. We thank them for the time and care they took to improve each draft.

Our respective colleges and universities offered support along the way. John was on a sabbatical leave from his teaching duties at Central Connecticut State University when he first thought of a book on teaching the Vietnam War. His colleagues in the Department of History offered valuable advice on both the book and the series. Matthew was inspired by the many great teachers at Saint Anselm College, especially his colleagues in the history department. He is grateful for the financial support he received from Father Augustine Kelly, dean of the college. Brad benefited from generous travel funding provided by his department at Salem State University and the College of Arts and Sciences and from the countless conversations about what constitutes good teaching that he has had with colleagues, students, and practicing teachers.

Miriam Hauss Cunningham, David Ryan, Emily Strange, Sarah Thelen, Chia Youyee Vang, the University of Kentucky Alumni Association, the University Press of Kentucky, the Vietnam Center and Archive at Texas Tech University, the Eugene McDermott Library at the University of Texas at Dallas, the Associated Press, and the Formosa Fountain and Engineering Company of Fullerton, California, gave us permission to reprint images. We are grateful for their generosity.

Most important, we thank our families. Our wives and children were patient with us while we interrupted meals, family outings, and parties to talk about teaching in general and this project specifically. None of this would be possible without their love and support.

Understanding and Teaching
the Vietnam War

Introduction

Key Questions and Enduring Debates

JOHN DAY TULLY, MATTHEW MASUR, and
BRAD AUSTIN

Any teacher who has taught the Vietnam War (or student who has learned about it) will recognize certain inherent challenges in defining the conflict. For example, how do we identify the beginning and end points? Did it start, as many Americans believe, when US Marines arrived in Danang in 1965? If so, what does that mean for the first American combat fatalities, which were suffered in 1959? Others might argue that the Vietnam War began in 1954, or perhaps in 1946, or maybe when Ho Chi Minh declared Vietnam's independence in 1945. The ending is more certain: the withdrawal of American forces in 1973. Unless it was the collapse of South Vietnam in 1975, or the creation of the Socialist Republic of Vietnam in 1976, or the end of Vietnam's occupation of Cambodia in the late 1980s . . .

And this is only the beginning. Students may have the general idea that the United States was defending South Vietnam from North Vietnamese aggression. In reality the United States was working with the South Vietnamese government to defeat a combination of southern insurgents and North Vietnamese soldiers. Many students will undoubtedly be familiar with the term Viet Cong, or VC, to describe America's enemy, but some historians avoid the term, finding it imprecise and somewhat pejorative. Rather, they might refer to the National Liberation Front and the People's Liberation Armed Forces (PLAF), along with their northern allies, the People's Army of Vietnam (PAVN). And some historians question whether it is appropriate to use the terms *South Vietnam* and *North Vietnam* because these suggest a conflict between two nations when in fact the Geneva Agreements stipulated a temporary division, which was not to be construed as a national border.

It is no surprise, then, that even the term used to describe the conflict is contested. The most common name Americans use is Vietnam War. Some historians, however, consider American involvement to be one part of three connected but distinct Indochina Wars. The First Indochina War (sometimes called the French Indochina War) began in 1946 when France went to war against the Viet Minh and ended in 1954 with the Battle of Dien Bien Phu and the Geneva Agreements. The Second Indochina War pitted the United States and the Republic of Vietnam against the National Liberation Front and the Democratic Republic of Vietnam. The Third Indochina War began in late 1978 when the Socialist Republic of Vietnam invaded Cambodia; a few months later China joined the fray by attacking across Vietnam's northern border. But even this does not tell the entire story. In Vietnam the Second Indochina War (America's "Vietnam War") is officially known as the War of National Salvation against the Americans, sometimes abbreviated as the American War. These various terms illuminate the many meanings the war had for its participants. It was a war between Vietnamese for the future of their nation and a war among Americans about the role of the United States in the world. And it is a war whose legacy and lessons are still being debated in political arenas, classrooms, and living rooms today.

This volume uses the singular Vietnam War because it is the standard usage in the United States. We do not intend the terminology to elide the multiple understandings of and perspectives on the war that teachers need to consider when preparing to teach. The American military participation in Vietnam took place within the historical context of the Cold War, growing nationalist and decolonization movements in Asia and Africa, and the intense national debates in the 1960s about American identity and ideals. Understanding these and other frameworks for discussing the war and deciding which or what combination of them to present to students are the first tasks facing teachers. This book's goal is to help with those decisions and provide specific ways to carry them into the classroom.

For all of these reasons, the Vietnam War presents a unique challenge to all teachers. For the past four decades, the war's influence and legacy have shaped much of the nation's policy debates and our understanding of America's role in the world. Well-known images of the war have defined our culture and remain as artifacts of public memory that have influenced what most Americans know and remember about the war and its meaning. This is particularly true for students who were born years after the war's conclusion; any understanding they may have is heavily shaped by politicized narratives and media images meant to serve contemporary policy debates or sell movie tickets. The consequence is that students rarely understand the underlying issues or national and international contexts that drove the United States into Vietnam. Nor do they grasp the war's development over time or its enduring legacy.

Teaching the Vietnam War requires exploring myriad trouble spots enmeshed within national memory and purpose, confronting cultural touchstones and myths, and considering current political debates. Dedicated teachers will want to incorporate the latest interpretations and insights in their lessons, but the sheer amount of historical literature on the war and its meanings is overwhelming. Even those scholars dedicated to the subject find it difficult to remain up to date. Adding to the complexity of teachers' tasks is the growing availability of primary sources and other pedagogical tools, all of which can open up wonderful teaching possibilities but can also overload even the best teachers with their volume.

Understanding and Teaching the Vietnam War offers a road map for navigating these scholarly and teaching challenges by providing educators succinct summaries of the most recent literature on the war and its legacy along with some thought-provoking reflections from the most accomplished teacher-scholars of the war. This volume also presents teachers with practical and proven classroom strategies that will enliven discussions and give students challenging and engaging ways to learn. Whether you are a new teacher or a seasoned educator well versed in the challenges of teaching the Vietnam War, whether you teach specialized courses at the university level or cover the war only in your high school world or American history classes, you will find that this book offers a variety of effective thematic and methodological frameworks from which the war can be presented and discussed.

The genesis of this book, and the series it inaugurates, began with the career of an amazing teacher, Harvey Goldberg. Professor Goldberg taught at both Ohio State University and the University of Wisconsin–Madison for many decades. While graduate students at Ohio State, we had the opportunity to work on various projects through the Department of History's Harvey Goldberg Center for Excellence in Teaching, which grew out of the desire of many of Goldberg's former students to honor him, his teaching, and his positive influence on their lives.

In the 1960s and 1970s, Goldberg incorporated the Vietnam War into his courses. Always an activist, he urged his students to see the war as an important milestone that grew out of past actions and decisions and stressed that only by understanding that past from multiple perspectives could one take hold of the future. On January 16, 1974, he told one of his classes:

> What I'm asking you to do about any problem of the world is to understand that the people who are involved in that problem have a history. And that, when they come upon you, in your history, it is as a moment. And that history, after all, of their own is the one that defines their problem. It was a magnificent Vietnamese, a Vietnamese who was in the Vietnamese delegation for the North Vietnamese at Paris who took me aside and said, "You know what I most criticize you Americans about? That you came into Vietnam never having been in our history, knowing nothing about our history, never having even had travelers there of note, and, see, you seek to define our destiny. Our destiny is rooted in all that we have fought for and all that we have defined by ourselves." And, so even though it is a tedious thing, it is important, after all, to go back into the history of a people and to define the problem as it emerges at that moment of contact with your own country and with its particular foreign policy.[1]

This comment goes to the heart of what we all struggle with daily as educators: how do we motivate our students to appreciate, grapple with, and consider the power of the past? This book seeks to answer that question within the context of teaching the Vietnam War. We do so with the help of excellent teachers, at all levels, some practicing Vietnam War specialists and some not, who share how they frame and work out such challenges in their own classrooms.

Our goal for this volume is to have it offer teachers information, resources, and strategies that will help them address the enduring debates and key questions that naturally arise any time classes focus on the Vietnam War. While there are certainly others, we have framed these debates and questions in this way.

1. What are the necessary contexts for understanding the American diplomatic and military involvement in Vietnam?
2. What explains the nature of that involvement? Preconceptions? Ideology? Inertia? Domestic concerns?
3. How did the Vietnam War affect the American home front, and vice versa?
4. What are the lasting political, cultural, military, and diplomatic legacies of the war?

Of course, it is entirely possible to modify this list extensively, add questions, and revisit our phrasing. We hope, however, that readers will see these as a reasonable way to structure an extended conversation about ways to understand and teach the Vietnam War.

As the historiography of the Vietnam War vividly demonstrates, we are joining a conversation that is well under way. We recognize that some teachers may be reluctant to discuss historiography in their classes, and they have good reasons to feel that way. The term alone can be intimidating for students who are unfamiliar with the concept. It is difficult for busy teachers to keep up with the voluminous scholarship on the war and the changing historiographic schools and interpretations, and many teachers might feel that their students are not equipped to understand historiography until they have shown some mastery of the content knowledge.

Nevertheless, the Vietnam War lends itself well to historiographic discussions. The scholarship on the war follows a relatively clear and understandable progression. Some of the central issues in the historiography—America's decision to go to war and the reasons for its defeat—will likely to be familiar to students; at least the questions might be, if not the answers. From a wider perspective, the historiography of the Vietnam War highlights some of the political and cultural divisions that have characterized American society since the 1960s. Whether they realize it or not, students have been exposed to the popular and public manifestations of these historiographic debates in films, television shows, political debates, or even family discussions.[2]

Lyndon Johnson's decision to send ground troops to Vietnam in March 1965 sparked a vigorous public debate about American policy. Historians, both those with a background in Vietnam or American foreign policy and those in other fields, played a prominent role in these discussions. Historians were actively involved in the teach-ins on college campuses that explored the roots of American involvement in Southeast Asia. The president of the Organization of American Historians referenced the escalation in his presidential address in April 1965.[3] By the end of the year, Bernard Fall and Marcus Raskin had published a collection of documents tracing the growing American commitment to South Vietnam, including the decisions in spring and summer 1965 that Americanized the conflict.[4] While there were exceptions, these early comments criticized American policy and looked skeptically on American motives.

Harvey Goldberg and other historians at the University of Wisconsin were active participants in these initial debates about America's intervention in Vietnam. Most prominent among them was William Appleman Williams, an influential diplomatic historian and leading figure of the "Wisconsin School" of left-wing historians. He and many of his graduate students argued that the Vietnam War was an exercise in American neo-imperialism.[5] While Goldberg was not a specialist on Vietnam or American foreign relations, he discussed the Vietnam War in his courses, connecting it to France's colonial history, other anti-colonial movements in the twentieth century, and Marxist theory.

By the early 1970s, historians had published numerous important studies about American involvement in Vietnam. These works, often described as the "orthodox" school of Vietnam historiography, tended to echo and amplify the earlier critiques of American policy. Some orthodox historians, such as George Kahin and John W. Lewis, questioned the connection between the National Liberation Front and the North Vietnamese government, thus undermining the rationale for American involvement. Arthur Schlesinger Jr. depicted the Vietnam War as the unfortunate and unintended outcome of a series of understandable, if mistaken, incremental actions. Frances FitzGerald criticized American policy makers for failing to understand Vietnamese society and culture and thus failing to see the futility of military intervention.

While the specifics of these works varied, some themes were common in the orthodox school. Orthodox historians saw the American intervention as unwarranted. They questioned whether South Vietnam was strategically important to the United States. They believed that American policy makers had failed to heed the warning of the French experience in Vietnam. They characterized American actions as misguided at best or belligerent at worst. Finally, they doubted that the United States could achieve military victory in the conflict.

The initial interpretation soon prompted a revisionist response. By the early 1980s a number of writers were challenging the orthodox critiques of the war. Norman Podhoretz, for example, justified America's efforts to stop the spread of communism, describing it as a worthwhile and laudable goal. Military historian Harry Summers criticized American policy makers for failing to implement the military and political strategies that would have brought victory. Finally, some writers blamed the media for misrepresenting conditions in Vietnam, fueling public opposition and disillusionment with the conflict.[6]

The emergence of revisionist historiography coincided with Ronald Reagan's presidency, a period when the Cold War intensified and Americans seemed intent on reasserting the nation's strength and moral authority. "Morning in America" was not just a call to look forward to a better time but also an effort to reimagine the events of the recent past. Basking in American greatness required a reappraisal of the Vietnam War, widely seen up to that point as an American failure. Reagan himself described the Vietnam War as a "noble cause," a phrase that echoed the conclusions of some revisionist historians.

In some ways, the orthodox/revisionist debate continues to define the contours of Vietnam War historiography. Historians are still focused on the key questions of the roots of American involvement and the reasons for America's defeat. But the back-and-forth that characterized the first decade or so of historical writing has largely been resolved. Revisionist conclusions may have been popular with a segment of the population tired of national self-criticism and self-doubt, but they never gained a foothold in the wider historical profession. Historians have dismissed revisionist works, such as Mark Moyar's *Triumph Forsaken*, as deeply flawed and poorly executed—much like the war he is trying to rehabilitate. The consensus among historians is not far from the views of the orthodox writers who questioned the wisdom of the Vietnam War and the likelihood of an American victory.[7]

The roots of American involvement in Vietnam and the reasons for America's defeat still loom large in the historiography, and twenty-first-century historians have raised important new questions about the war.[8] One of the most significant developments is growing attention to Vietnamese perspectives on the war. This trend was spurred in part by the growing availability of governmental and nongovernmental sources from the Republic of Vietnam (South Vietnam) and the Democratic Republic of Vietnam (North Vietnam).[9] It also parallels the larger trend of "decentering" the study of American foreign relations, or balancing the coverage of America and the countries with which it interacts. Under this rationale, Vietnam, which by most measures might appear to have been eclipsed by American strength, should not be subordinated in accounts of the war. Indeed, the Vietnam War is a powerful argument for the validity of this approach; in spite of all the apparent advantages of the United States, it was unable to dictate the outcome of the war.

Other historians have extended the geographic or chronological boundaries of the war. They have challenged the common view that the Vietnam War is best understood as a conflict between the United States (with its Vietnamese allies) and the North Vietnamese (with its allies in the National Liberation Front) from about 1965 to 1973. These historians have demonstrated that the roots of the war lie further in the past, during the French Indochina War or even earlier.[10] Similarly, even when the United States withdrew in 1973 and official hostilities ended two years later, the divisions at the heart of the conflict persisted.[11] Other historians have demonstrated that the Vietnam War was global in scope. While students may be vaguely aware that the French, Chinese, and Soviets were involved in the conflict to varying degrees, they may be less familiar with the role of Great Britain, Cambodia, South Korea, Canada, Japan, and Australia.[12]

Finally, historians have examined the social, cultural, and economic consequences of the war, whether individuals, communities, or entire countries felt these effects. Vietnam and the Vietnamese experienced some of the most profound changes, ranging from the environmental damage wrought by Agent Orange to the civilian suffering during the war and the political repression after the country was reunified.[13] Americans, too, had diverse experiences with the war, some as combatants, some as journalists, some as domestic supporters, and some as dissenters. In the case of Americans and Vietnamese, their experiences during the war were often expressed through literature, music, movies, and other cultural forms, and historians have come to pay close attention to these public reflections on the war.

This is not an exhaustive summary of the historiography, but it highlights the important trends. To maximize its utility to teachers, this volume touches on both the basic questions that drove the initial historiography and the new themes and issues that have broadened and expanded our understanding of the war.

The book's organization reflects our desire to contribute to larger and ongoing conversations about how teachers at all levels might understand and teach the key questions and debates about the Vietnam War. As historians ourselves, we thought that it would be useful to learn how two titans of Vietnam War historiography brought their scholarship to their classes and how their classes influenced their thinking about the war over several decades. In engaging and reflective essays in "Part One: Reflections on Teaching the Vietnam War," George C. Herring and Marilyn B. Young share their experiences of teaching the Vietnam War and its legacies to multiple generations of students who brought the changing national discussions and popular culture understandings of the war to their classroom discussions. Young's "Teaching the Vietnam War: A Life History" and Herring's "Teaching the Vietnam War: Recollections and Reflections from More than Thirty Years" are intrinsically interesting in their own right, and these essays serve the volume's larger purpose by providing concrete examples of how effective teachers address not only the "what" but also the "why" and "why should we care" questions that students might not articulate but always bring to our classes.

In order to make the volume most accessible and immediately useful to the teachers who consult it, we have divided the rest of the essays into two broad categories. Building on the Herring and Young essays, "Part Two: Methods and Resources" includes a sequence of essays that introduce readers to specific techniques and materials they can immediately start using in their classes. These essays will be especially useful to teachers who are already quite comfortable with the content they must cover when teaching about the Vietnam War but who are looking for new, effective approaches and materials they can use to grab their students' attention and spark engaged and informed discussions.

Part two begins with Kevin O'Reilly's "Putting Students in 'Their Shoes': A Decision-Making Approach to Teaching the Vietnam War." A two-time national high school teacher of the year, O'Reilly structures his classes around exercises that provide students with only the information available at the time to the historical actors who made key decisions. This essay explains his approach and provides readers with examples and materials that they can immediately implement in their own classrooms, pushing students to read materials carefully, ask the right types of questions, and get a visceral sense and understanding of how and why American policy developed as it did.

Hugo A. Keesing's "Understanding the Vietnam Era through Music" appears next and draws on Keesing's extensive experience collecting, categorizing, and writing about the music of the era. Teachers looking to add audio elements to their classes will especially appreciate Keesing's identification and explanation of the most useful songs for classroom use in a variety of categories. For example, if you're looking for the best songs from a Vietnamese point of view, songs written by soldiers while "in-country," songs that protest or support the war, songs by women, or songs in several other categories, Keesing's essay will give you the information and strategies you need to select songs for classroom use.

Mitchell B. Lerner's "'We Must Bear a Good Deal of Responsibility for It': The White House Tapes and the War in Vietnam" provides a fascinating overview of the history of White House recording systems before offering suggestions for how teachers can use specific excerpts to teach about the decisions to escalate and the role of the media and domestic politics in presidential-level decision making. These tapes open a virtually unprecedented window into Vietnam policy making at the highest levels, and Lerner's essay introduces teachers to their key characteristics and strategies for featuring the most valuable discussions in classroom activities.

Readers will note that Lerner's comments about the promises and pitfalls of teaching with recordings of conversations are paralleled nicely in Scott Laderman's "Movies and the Vietnam War." Laderman's essay explores the ways teachers can use Hollywood films to teach the Vietnam War and its aftermath. It examines some of the most popular and important films about the war, paying particular attention to the social context in which they originated, their major themes, their popular and critical reception, and their role in creating or sustaining certain narratives about the war. It offers direct aid to teachers by highlighting specific movie scenes that can be used in the classroom, and it suggests ways that these movie clips can prompt students to discuss changing attitudes about the United States and Vietnam. In short, this essay shows how films can be used to engage students while also encouraging new ways of thinking about historical sources.

Much like Laderman's chapter on movies, Maureen Ryan's "The Books We Carry: Teaching the Vietnam War through Literature" will appeal especially to teachers who want to adopt interdisciplinary approaches to teaching the Vietnam War. With its explanation of the variety of types of writings about the war, its identification of the most appropriate books and passages for students to read, and its suggestions for classroom use of these resources, Ryan's essay will prompt history, English, and American studies teachers to rethink their reading lists and approaches to the war.

If teachers can feel overwhelmed by the number and variety of books that discuss the Vietnam War, then they are surely numbed by the incredible volume of websites and resources available through the Internet. Richard Hume Werking and Brian C. Etheridge's "Teaching the Vietnam War in the Internet Age: Libraries, Websites, and Information Literacy" can help teachers navigate their way through the available resources and help their students do the same. Recognizing that any list of "the best" websites becomes obsolete almost immediately, Etheridge and Werking have avoided providing only a list of essential sites (although they have done that as well) and have focused on wider issues of information literacy that will help teachers provide meaningful and useful research tools to students.

The final essay in part two is Andrew Darien's "Hearts, Minds, and Voices: The Vietnam War and Oral History," which can help teachers in several related and important ways. First, it introduces a variety of collections of published and digital oral histories, highlighting the focus and strengths of each one. Second, it reminds teachers to have their students ask specific questions of the oral histories they are considering, offering practical suggestions about how to discuss historiography and source criticism with students. Finally, Darien draws on his own classroom experiences to offer concrete advice about preparing students to conduct their own interviews with veterans and others who lived through the Vietnam War era. Darien persuasively argues that oral histories offer some of the best opportunities for teachers to teach specific content about the Vietnam War while also helping students to hone their historical thinking skills, and his essay will assist teachers wanting to utilize existing resources or inaugurate their own oral history projects.

Our last group of essays, located in "Part Three: Understanding and Teaching Specific Content," offers concise summaries of many events and topics that are critical for teachers and students to understand when studying this conflict and its legacies. Unlike the essays available in other Vietnam War topical collections, however, all the essays in part three balance their explanations of the topics and events under consideration with suggestions and strategies for how teachers can translate this material into effective lesson plans and activities.

For example, readers will benefit from the way Matthew Masur's "Nationalism, Communism, and the Vietnam War" outlines the different ways in which historians and teachers have understood and explained the Vietnam War(s). As any teacher knows, the "big" themes and "essential" questions we choose for a class influence everything else we do in those courses. In this essay, Masur explains different ways to frame the conflicts in world and American history classes, and he offers teachers ideas about how they can use the biography of Ho Chi Minh as an effective device for helping students consider the often conflicting goals and experiences of the Vietnamese people as they tried to navigate and survive a constellation of national, regional, and international debates and conflicts.

For both faculty and students, the story of American involvement in Vietnam usually begins in the 1960s, with a brief overview of earlier American experiences there. Often missing from this narrative is the French experience. Kathryn C. Statler's "From the French to the Americans" will help teachers avoid this myopic presentation of the Vietnam War and will provide them with a clear and concise explanation of how American leaders became willing to support, and then take over, the French effort to recolonize and subdue Vietnam. Statler highlights the many similarities and differences between the French and American experiences in Vietnam, emphasizing that many American decisions made in the 1960s and 1970s can only be understood within the context of the First Indochina War. Like Masur, she covers the intersection of Cold War and colonial concerns while also addressing the role of public opinion, Dien Bien Phu as a case study of the dangers of underestimating the enemy, the possible internationalization of the war, the breakdown of Franco-American cooperation, and attempts to settle the conflicts. The essay features specific advice about how teachers can address and teach these subjects within the scope of American and world history surveys.

David Steigerwald's "Teaching the Antiwar Movement: Confronting Popular Myths, Teaching Complexity" offers an effective overview of the complexity of the antiwar movement, providing teachers with numerous and specific ways to complicate their students' preconceptions about the types of people who protested the war and why they did so. Steigerwald's candid discussion of his own teaching goals and strategies, his descriptions of central antiwar organizations and figures, and his identification of key passages and documents for classroom use, all make this essay an essential resource for teachers looking to discuss the American domestic environment with their students while also getting them to question the stereotypes they have formed based on popular culture representations of the antiwar movement.

Tuan Hoang's "The Vietnamese Sides of the 'American' War" will immediately help those teachers who know they should be more conversant about the Vietnamese perspectives on the war but have had neither the time nor the resources to explore the emerging scholarship in this area. Hoang's essay provides an accessible and appropriate starting place for teachers new to this vital topic. The essay explains the divisions among many Vietnamese groups and offers multiple ideas about ways to address and explain these differences in the classroom.

The diversity of the Southeast Asian experience is also manifest in the essays by Chia Youyee Vang and Karín Aguilar-San Juan, both of whom outline the effects of the war on Southeast Asian populations and can help teachers understand the migrations of many of those peoples to the United States. Vang's "'America's Most Loyal Allies': The Hmong and the War" will be especially useful for teachers hoping to relate course content to their region's significant Hmong populations. Aguilar-San Juan's "Vietnamese Americans in the Context of the Vietnam War" is a fantastic resource for anyone hoping to understand and teach more effectively the challenges and successes of these groups in the context of the continuing domestic effects of the war.

While Vang's and Aguilar-San Juan's essays focus on topics that some teachers might not feature in their general survey coverage of the war, Andrew Wiest's "The Tet Offensive in the Classroom" provides a narrative overview of a topic that most teachers will need to cover, along with specific pedagogical suggestions that all teachers will appreciate. His discussion of how teachers can understand and teach both sides' general strategies, the specific military engagements, and the role of the media in shaping public perceptions of the offensive and the war itself will benefit teachers at all levels.

Near the end of the book, David Fitzgerald and David Ryan reflect on the lasting impact of the war on culture and politics. In "Teaching the Collective Memory and Lessons of the Vietnam War," Fitzgerald and Ryan present a short review of the latest research on collective memory and an analysis of how the collective memory of the Vietnam War has evolved over the years. They provide a clear explanation of how collective memory is created and sustained, then later challenged and revised in light of new situations. Specifically, the essay explores how debates about the prospect of foreign military activities in the years after 1975 led to renewed examinations of the war years and to an ever-changing assessment of the "lessons" of the war. These are exactly the types of issues that our current students will have to resolve as they take on the roles of citizens.

Finally, in "Teaching the Vietnam War in Secondary Schools and Survey Classrooms," Stephen Armstrong, the president of the National Council for the Social Studies, offers high school teachers specific ideas on engaging juniors and seniors in survey and advanced placement classes. The essay includes analysis of various textbook accounts of the war and a discussion of integrating the teaching of the war into Common Core and state standards. Armstrong also includes specific ideas on websites, music, and literature, giving secondary teachers a wealth of ideas to use directly or as springboards for other assignments.

The Vietnam War did not end for the United States in 1973 when American combat troops left or in 1975 when South Vietnam fell. The war had such a deep and abiding effect on the nation, on our evolving understanding of America's mission and role in the world, and on our culture that it fits William Faulkner's observation that that past is never dead and is not even the past. Our efforts to understand what happened and why, and to help students explore the sources and grow in their own understanding of the war, will continue for many decades. We hope this book helps that process.

NOTES

1. Harvey Goldberg, "The History of Other Peoples," lecture given on January 16, 1974, audio and transcript, http://history.wisc.edu/goldberg/goldberg.htm.

2. For earlier overviews of Vietnam War historiography, see David Anderson, "Why Vietnam? Postrevisionist Answers and a Neorealist Suggestion," *Diplomatic History* 13 (Summer 1989): 419–29; Robert Divine, "Vietnam Reconsidered," *Diplomatic History* 12 (Winter 1988): 79–93; and Gary Hess, "Historians and the Vietnam War," in *America and the World: The Historiography of American Foreign Relations since 1941*, ed. Michael J. Hogan (Cambridge: Cambridge University Press, 1995), 358–94.

3. See John W. Caughey, "Our Chosen Destiny," *Journal of American History* 52 (September 1965): 239–51.

4. Marcus G. Raskin and Bernard B. Fall, eds., The *Viet-Nam Reader: Articles and Documents on American Foreign Policy and the Viet-Nam Crisis* (New York: Random House, 1965).

5. Along with Williams, the Wisconsin School critics included Walter LaFeber, Thomas McCormick, and Lloyd Gardner, all of whom would become respected historians in their own right. Long after the war they collaborated on a primary source reader about the Vietnam War. See William Appleman Williams et al., eds., *America in Vietnam: A Documentary History* (New York: W. W. Norton, 1989).

6. Norman Podhoretz, *Why We Were in Vietnam* (New York: Simon and Schuster, 1982); Harry G. Summers Jr., *On Strategy: A Critical Analysis of the Vietnam War* (New York: Dell, 1984); Peter Braestrup, *Big Story* (New Haven: Yale University Press, 1983).

7. Mark Moyar, *Triumph Forsaken: The Vietnam War, 1954–1965* (Cambridge: Cambridge University Press, 2006).

8. For discussions of these developments in the historiography, see Kendrick Oliver, "Towards a New Moral History of the Vietnam War?," *Historical Journal* 47 (September 2004): 757–74; and Christopher T. Fisher, "Nation Building and the Vietnam War: A Historiography," *Pacific Historical Review* 74 (August 2005): 441–56.

9. Matthew Masur and Edward Miller, "Saigon Revisited: Researching South Vietnam's Republican Era (1954–1975) at Archives and Libraries in Ho Chi Minh City," Cold War International History Project, Woodrow Wilson International Center for Scholars, http://www.wilsoncenter.org/sites/default/files/Saigon-Masur_Miller.pdf.

10. Mark Philip Bradley, *Imagining Vietnam and America: The Making of Postcolonial Vietnam, 1919–1950* (Chapel Hill: University of North Carolina Press,

2000); Kathryn C. Statler, *Replacing France: The Origins of American Intervention in Vietnam* (Lexington: University Press of Kentucky, 2007).

11. Bradley, *Imagining Vietnam and America*; Scott Laderman, *Tours of Vietnam: War, Travel Guides, and Memory* (Durham, NC: Duke University Press, 2009); Edwin A. Martini, *Invisible Enemies: The American War on Vietnam, 1975–2000* (Amherst: University of Massachusetts Press, 2007).

12. Heonik Kwon, *After the Massacre: Commemoration and Consolation in Ha My and My Lai* (Berkeley: University of California Press, 2006); Mark Atwood Lawrence, *Assuming the Burden: Europe and the American Commitment to War in Vietnam* (Berkeley: University of California Press, 2005); Qiang Zhai, *China and the Vietnam Wars, 1950–1975* (Chapel Hill: University of North Carolina Press, 2000).

13. David Elliott, *The Vietnamese War: Revolution and Social Change in the Mekong Delta, 1930–1975* (Armonk, NY: M. E. Sharpe, 2003); David Hunt, *Vietnam's Southern Revolution: From Peasant Insurrection to Total War, 1959–1968* (Amherst: University of Massachusetts Press, 2008).

PART ONE

Reflections on Teaching the Vietnam War

Teaching the Vietnam War

A Life History

MARILYN B. YOUNG

I began teaching about Vietnam and its wars in 1969, in the Residential College at the University of Michigan, Ann Arbor. We, the students and faculty, were living through the war together, though only the young men in the college had to fear being sent to fight in it. The students and faculty went to the same local demonstrations, rode the same buses to Washington for the biannual protest marches, and listened to the same antiwar music. As President Richard Nixon expanded the war in Vietnam and reversed course in China, my course expanded its range to include Laos and Cambodia and the meaning of the China card. When the Paris Peace Accords were signed we studied their terms, tracked violations on both sides, and were relieved rather than joyful when it was all over on April 30, 1975.

For the next four years, students who enrolled in my courses had lived through the latter part of the war as high school students. It took no effort on my part to explain its importance. They wanted to know what I too wished to understand: how it happened that the United States had fought so destructive a war over a country whose importance to US national security was so slight. We spent considerable time analyzing the shifting justifications that had been offered to explain why over fifty-eight thousand Americans and two to three million Vietnamese had died: the importance of Indochina to the Japanese economy, the threat of Communist China, the nature of dominoes. At the end of one such course, a young man whose way was being paid by Reserve Officers' Training Corps told me that he was leaving the university because he could no longer tolerate being part of ROTC but could afford to attend university no other way. I began to try to dissuade him, but his look of surprise at my apparent lack of principle stopped me.

Why the United States had fought in Vietnam continued to be the subject of fierce debate, so that its representations, in movies, novels, memoirs, on television, in political speeches, and in scholarly works, were tensely contradictory. The flood of representations of the Vietnam War during the first decade after the war ended gave many Americans the illusion that they had been to Vietnam. When I asked students what their images of Vietnam were, they answered in terms of sensory perceptions—the heat, noise, dust, and smell that none of them had ever in fact experienced.

Though in a sense they *had* been to the war in Vietnam. They had little difficulty inserting themselves into *Apocalypse Now* or *Platoon* because, like most of the novels and memoirs, Vietnam, the Movie, was populated mainly or mostly by Americans at war with an unseen enemy. Often that enemy turned out to be the Americans themselves: "We didn't fight the enemy in Vietnam," the hero of *Platoon* declares at the movie's end, "we fought ourselves." On television and in the movies, Vietnam was a generic jungle stage set, a faraway place where bad things happened to Americans who were forced, by circumstance, to do bad things in turn.

I became increasingly impatient with students whose approach to studying the war was relentlessly focused on the United States. After I started teaching at New York University, a colleague and I launched a new course titled Vietnam, Its History, Culture, and Wars, in which the American War put in a late and, as far as the students were concerned, too brief an appearance. Polite through most of the course, the students came fully awake only when we got to the American story. For the general public—and some students—the nature of the American story itself changed over time, focusing less on what happened in Vietnam than on a variety of domestic issues, such as the treatment of veterans and the behavior of the press, Congress, and the antiwar movement.

Teaching the history of the war from the Reagan presidency on required teaching the history of the uses to which it had been put politically. And it was possible to assess the accuracy of those politicized renderings of the war on the basis of a new range of historical sources, from translations of Vietnamese novels and documents to Vietnamese movie representations of the war to a flood of American documents and memoirs, the latter including those of the architects of the war,

Marilyn B. Young speaking at the National History Center. (photo by Miriam Hauss Cunningham, courtesy of the National History Center)

such as Robert S. McNamara, who had disowned their handiwork. Vietnam as a country as well as a war became marginally more real.

With students born in the 1980s, the main task I faced as a teacher was to enable them to understand why the Vietnam War continued to haunt the body politic. Most believed it all had to do with the way the country had mistreated returning veterans, and they vowed to support the troops in any future war—though not necessarily to join them. I thought that if they failed to understand more deeply how the lost war figured in the new wars through which they were living they could understand neither the present nor the past. Thus the courses on the history of the war I have taught from 1991 on have all incorporated the significance of Vietnam for current purposes. Uneasiness about America's new wars, from Desert Storm through the conflict in Afghanistan, all, without exception, drew on the example of Vietnam. Vietnam, said those who urged the withdrawal of American troops from whatever foreign country in which they were fighting, had been a quagmire, and Iraq (I and II), Somalia, Kosovo, and Afghanistan would be quagmires, too, unwinnable wars that should end as soon as possible. Similarly, those who supported these later wars pointed out the ways in which they differed from Vietnam, or, more commonly, the ways in which they corrected the mistakes that had been made in that war. To enable students to sift through contemporary arguments that utilize Vietnam, it helps if they understand what happened the first time out.

For teaching purposes, Gulf War I, in its two phases, Desert Shield and Desert Storm, was an ideal example of how a particular interpretation of the Vietnam War shaped contemporary policy. The military, recovering from the demoralization of the Vietnam War, had set about building an all-volunteer, professional army and devising a new doctrine for its use. The Weinberger/Powell Doctrine was like an insurance policy against all they saw as having gone wrong tactically in Vietnam: strong public support would be mobilized before any war began; force would be used massively rather than incrementally; and goals would be limited, the exit clearly marked, and a declaration of victory thus assured. Finally, there was no possibility of draft resistance with an all-volunteer, professional army.

Perhaps more important as a counter-model was the extent to which Desert Storm brutalities were almost entirely invisible as opposed to their relative visibility in Vietnam. Control of the press was absolute; there was no Iraqi body count, and the only acknowledged civilian deaths were due to Saddam Hussein's cynical use of an air raid shelter for military purposes. This was a clean war, epitomized by the endlessly repeated image of the crosshairs of an allegedly precision missile as it fell (but whose impact went unrecorded) or by the charred remains of vehicles (but not bodies on the Highway of Death out of Kuwait). A British reporter arriving the day after a battle between the US First Infantry Division and an estimated eight thousand entrenched Iraqi soldiers asked the press officer in charge where the bodies were. "What bodies?," the major replied. In every particular, Desert Storm was *not* Vietnam, enabling President George H. W. Bush to announce at its quick and relatively casualty free (on the US side) end that the country had, at long last, kicked the Vietnam syndrome.

By "Vietnam syndrome," Bush meant the reluctance of the American public to condone the use of US troops abroad for purposes not obviously related to the direct security of the country, and in a limited way he was right. Memories or historical arguments about Vietnam were no obstacle to the tendency of Americans to rally around the flag whenever a president planted it overseas. But should that flag fail to "win," and win quickly, support rapidly waned and the old Vietnam tropes reappeared in force.

For our students, Vietnam is as long ago as World War I was for me when I was a student, and 1975 feels as remote to them as 1919 did to me. What they want to know is why it mattered so passionately to their grandparents. In the absence of a social movement, they have little sense of the possibility of mass protest, and to most the Occupy Wall Street movement feels irrelevant. My students are barely surprised that American troops commit war crimes and not at all surprised that no one goes to jail for either executing or ordering them. After all, no one has.

I most often teach Vietnam as part of a course called American Wars Past and Present, which runs (quickly) from Korea through Afghanistan. To my surprise, the Vietnam War barely touches them, so eager are they to get to the present. It took twenty years after President George H. W. Bush said it would happen, but perhaps the United States really has kicked the Vietnam syndrome. Maybe, given the length of the war in Afghanistan, that is the syndrome the country will be battling in the future.

Even in our discussions of current wars, my students remain remarkably detached. Really, as Andrew Bacevich has insisted, the separation between the military and civilians has never been wider—a yawning gap that virtually none of my students tries very hard to cross. I cannot now imagine a current student who had decided to enlist—like that young ROTC recruit in Ann Arbor—changing his mind because of what I've taught. Indeed, one student told me he was trying to transfer to West Point and asked if I would please write him a letter.

These days, I think part of the task of teaching the Vietnam War is to recall a time when most Americans believed what their government told them and expected American troops to behave with utmost rectitude. And then we must move with them, thinking forward from the late 1950s as they learn how that changed and what the changes meant for the country.

My courses on Vietnam usually end where they began, with the question "Why Vietnam?" and a set of sober answers: because the American political elite is indifferent to the suffering it causes abroad, as well as to the uses to which it puts its young people—draftee or volunteer; because America cannot be allowed to lose a war or the myth crumbles; because the United States is a country like any other, neither more virtuous nor more vicious, exceptional only in its military force and its readiness to use it.

Teaching the Vietnam War

Recollections and Reflections
from More than Thirty Years

GEORGE C. HERRING

From the time I started teaching, the Vietnam War was center stage. I began my first job at Ohio University in September 1965, just two months after President Lyndon Baines Johnson had announced a major increase in US forces in Vietnam and their assumption of a combat role. Domestic protest against the war was rising, especially on campuses. Like most universities at that time, OU had gone through a huge expansion in enrollment in the 1960s. It was a very lively place. Student activism was growing. Vietnam was increasingly on the students' minds. During the fall of 1965, I taught for the first time a course in US diplomatic history. Even in that semester, when we covered the period to 1898, discussions on many different topics often turned to Vietnam.

At about this time, the sixties came to Ohio University with a vengeance. In the early spring of 1967, through a curious chain of events, the same National Guard unit that was at Kent State University in 1970, commanded by the same commander and dispatched by the same governor, was on the Athens County Fairgrounds, just off the OU campus. A Sunday night rampage by frat boys, resulting in property damage in downtown Athens, somehow morphed into a full-fledged student revolt with a long list of demands and an impossibly short deadline for meeting them. The only thing that spared further campus upheaval and possible National Guard intervention was a midweek flooding of the Hocking River that left much of the town and campus under water and students and National Guard troops frantically filling sandbags. Campus antiwar protest rose dramatically during those years, and the stalemated war in Vietnam was a daily topic of conversation. In 1968 campus demonstrations followed the assassination of Dr. Martin Luther King Jr.

As a result of student interest and my own growing curiosity, I sought to educate myself on the subject of the Vietnam War so I could better deal with the questions that inevitably arose. Two people were instrumental in this process. The first was Professor John F. Cady, a longtime, distinguished member of the OU faculty. John was one of a handful of people in the United States at that time who could legitimately be called an expert on Southeast Asia. He had written extensively on the region, spent considerable time there, and knew it firsthand. He had served as an analyst in the Office of Strategic Services during World War II and in the State Department from 1945 to 1949. John was a splendid teacher, a truly wonderful mentor and academic role model, and an engaging conversationalist. In private discussions in his office and impromptu "seminars" in the faculty club, he provided the sort of local background to the steadily expanding war in Indochina that could not be found in the popular press. He offered a totally different perspective on events in Vietnam. Indeed, knowing even a little bit about the origins of the war in the 1945 revolution against France made it impossible to accept the position being set forth by US policy makers. The other source of my early education was a graduate student in my research seminar in 1966–67. This student wanted to write a paper on US involvement with Vietnam from the end of World War II to the Geneva Conference. I approved the topic with some reluctance because of skepticism about adequate primary sources. It turned out to be a first-rate paper, putting into print many of the things John Cady had been saying. It also pointed me to the works of Bernard Fall and the newly published book by George Kahin and John Lewis, *The United States in Vietnam* (1967), sources that immensely helped to fill out my knowledge of the war.

Although the University of Kentucky (UK), where I moved in the summer of 1969, seemed by comparison an oasis of quietude, my education continued there. To be sure, the war remained a major part of the campus dialogue. There was some student participation in local and national antiwar protests. Following President Nixon's "incursion" into Cambodia in the spring of 1970 and the killing of students at Kent State in Ohio and Jackson State in Mississippi, to the shock of many observers, our quiet university suddenly exploded. Steadily expanding demonstrations, including the burning of a World War I era building, the headquarters of the Reserve Officers' Training Corps (ROTC), brought to campus first the state police and then, incredibly, the Kentucky National Guard equipped with live ammunition. Following several tense days of military "occupation," including the tear gassing of student protesters, the university president, to spare further turmoil, closed the school and sent the students home before the end of the examination period.

The first class I taught on the war was at UK in the spring semester of 1973, a time when the United States and North Vietnam finally concluded and then began to implement a peace agreement providing for the return of US prisoners of war and the withdrawal of American combat troops by March 31. My preparation for teaching that class seems in retrospect to have been modest at best. I had finished my doctorate at the University of Virginia in 1965. My major field was what we then unabashedly called US diplomatic history. My dissertation dealt with the lend-lease program during World War II. I had a minor field in South Asia and several courses on East Asia, but I had no training whatever in Southeast Asia. Like most American universities at the time, the University of Virginia did not cover that area of the world at all. At the time of my graduation, I knew precious little about what was going on in Vietnam other than what I read in the newspapers or happened to see on television.

Between 1965 and 1973, my views on the war developed through several stages: from ignorance and acquiescence in 1965 to limited knowledge and rising skepticism to fuller understanding, outright opposition, and rising anger that our leaders stubbornly persisted in trying to salvage their credibility at huge cost to Americans and Vietnamese. By that time I was actively participating in antiwar protests. A southerner, moderate in my politics, influenced by the "realist" writings of Hans Morgenthau, I was never comfortable with the more radical rhetoric of some parts of the antiwar movement. I had never really been a hawk on the war, but by the late 1960s I had become what I once called a "flaming centrist." I was plainly a "dove."

During its last years, the war became for me a scholarly as well as a teaching interest. My research at that time still centered on World War II, but I was increasingly drawn to Vietnam. It was a case of the more I learned the more I wanted to know. As the end of the war approached,

I became intrigued with the idea of treating it as history, of giving it a beginning and an end and asking and trying to answer the sort of questions historians regularly address. In 1975 I wrote a pamphlet called "Vietnam: An American Ordeal" (an embarrassingly ethnocentric title!), which was published the following year by Forum Press for use in college classes. The excitement of that experience encouraged me to consider writing a book-length history. With a bit of pleading, I persuaded Robert A. Divine of the University of Texas to publish such a book in his America in Crisis series, at that time the best-selling series in our field. He felt it might be too early to write on that subject. With a full year's leave in 1975–76, I began serious work on what would become *America's Longest War*.

During the immediate postwar years, I taught courses on the war in several different semesters. My memory once again is short on what I did in the classes, although—strangely—I do have rather vivid mental pictures of the rooms in which they were taught. One incident stands out. In one of the classes, I had assigned Bernard Fall's *Street without Joy* to give the students some idea of what the First Indochina War was all about and how it related to the American war that would follow. During the discussion, one of the students asked, in all innocence, "What is napalm?" It suddenly struck me that already we were reaching a point where the youngest of our students were not bringing into the classroom any basic knowledge or memories of the war, however distorted.

During the 1980s a war that had been shoved under the rug after its conclusion again became a vital part of the national political conversation. The possibility of US military intervention, first in El Salvador, then in Nicaragua, provoked a sometimes heated debate in Congress and the country that often evoked references to Vietnam. In response to what they called the "Vietnam syndrome," the seeming reluctance of Americans to send troops abroad, conservatives produced a revisionist history that ennobled US intervention and claimed that the United States could have won in Vietnam if it had used its power wisely and decisively. At the same time, long silent Vietnam veterans began to express openly and sometimes quite vocally their anger at being asked to serve their country and then being spurned for taking part in a war the nation would prefer to forget. The tenth anniversary of the end of the war in 1985 brought forth extended media and public discussion as to its meaning and significance. Conferences were held nationwide to analyze the war from various perspectives. On college campuses, Vietnam

War courses proliferated and students whose parents had served in the war or gone to the streets to protest it flocked into the classrooms.

For a variety of reasons, my own teaching of Vietnam courses in the 1980s was limited. On several occasions, I did teach in the university's evening school program so-called television courses built around the PBS series *Vietnam: A Television History*, first shown in the fall of 1983. The thirteen-hour series was aired for classroom use on Kentucky Educational Television (KET). In addition I conducted four or five two-hour classroom sessions to discuss some assigned readings along with the television material. The television series was very well done, rich in wonderful film footage and full of revealing and often compelling interviews with Americans and North and South Vietnamese for all of whom the war was still very fresh in their memories and their emotions in some cases still quite raw. The material engaged a generation of students who were more and more ignorant of events that had occurred in their childhood. The television courses went very well and in their own way were quite rewarding.

The other thing I recall quite clearly from the courses I taught in the 1980s is the increasing use of classroom "visitors" to talk about their experiences in Vietnam. In 1984–85 I collaborated with colleagues from the UK library and KET to conduct more than fifty videotaped interviews, some running as long as several hours, with combat veterans, antiwar protesters, a conscientious objector who had served in a non-combat role, and an army nurse (an especially powerful interview), all of them Kentuckians. We later worked the interviews into a fifty-five-minute documentary shown on University of Kentucky Television on Veterans Day 1985 called *Vietnam Remembered: A Long Road Back*. The interviews and documentary provided rich material for classroom use and also introduced me to numerous Kentuckians who had exciting stories to tell. A number of these people visited my class. Through a Kentucky Association for Teachers of History conference held near Lexington in 1982, later written up by Fox Butterfield in the *New York Times Magazine*, I met Richard Pfeiffer, a Louisville businessman who also taught a course on the war at the University of Louisville. Richard was one of a handful of National Guardsmen to serve in Vietnam. He spoke to my classes several times, and, to the surprise of the students, who were expecting the stereotypical Vietnam vet à la Rambo, he appeared in a three-piece suit. Richard had served with a Guard unit that had been overrun by the North Vietnamese in 1969, making Bardstown,

Kentucky, according to some accounts, the US town that suffered the most deaths per capita in Vietnam. Other interesting visitors included a South Vietnamese refugee who had been a veterinarian in Vietnam and was working in Louisville, a Lexingtonian who for reasons of conscience had served three years in prison rather than be drafted into the military, Stanley Karnow, the award-winning journalist who wrote the companion book to the PBS documentary, and Dr. Thomas Miller of our local Veterans Administration hospital, a pioneer in research on post-traumatic stress disorder.

Teaching the war during these years brought some frustrations and rich rewards. The enrollments were large, and many of the students in my classes were eighteen- to twenty-year-old white males who seemed to be there mainly for the military action, for vicarious thrills, or to learn more about the US role in the war. They resisted the sort of coverage of the Vietnamese side that I thought absolutely essential. They complained that I did not do enough with battles. Some took one look at the syllabus and left, others hung on looking unhappy, and a few actually came to appreciate the complexity of war.

During the academic year 1993–94, I served as a visiting professor at the United States Military Academy, West Point, and the shift from academic to military/academic culture was fascinating. In academia I was middle of the road politically, slightly to the left of center, perhaps, but very much in the mainstream. Once I passed through the gates of West Point, my political orientation moved decidedly to the left. To be sure, most of the senior officers I worked with had done several tours in Vietnam and had different and often complex views on the war. Few I encountered bought into the simplistic notion that if the United States had just done this or that the war could have been won. Having been there, they knew better. The captains and majors who comprised the majority of the teaching faculty at the academy were another matter entirely. Born in the 1960s, they had graduated from West Point or other schools during the Reagan years. They were part of the new, post-Vietnam military, conservative in their politics, confident in US military power, and certain that Vietnam had been a self-inflicted aberration. They had all done graduate work at civilian universities, and many emerged with a marked hostility toward academia. Although I made close friends among this group, most of them, I suspect, regarded me as a lefty, a position I found rather mystifying—and not altogether unappealing.

My teaching experience at West Point, to my great surprise, was career changing. At UK I taught mainly large classes of fifty to a hundred students. The lecture mode was necessarily the norm. I invited and especially enjoyed answering questions, but there was no pretense of conducting discussion classes. At West Point I had to change. Classes were small, on the average around fifteen students. Cadets were expected to prepare on a daily basis and to engage actively in discussions. Participation was an important part of their grade. No one told me this before I got there, and I—foolishly—did not ask. Nor did I take into account the different teaching culture when I agreed to hold my classes in the early afternoon, the time I had found late-rising UK students most alert. The cadets, of course, rose early, went through a full morning of classes, ate a huge lunch, and were anything but alert at 1300 hours. When they got drowsy in class, they were instructed to stand. When most responded to my initial lectures by standing and I discovered what was going on, I knew I was in trouble. I struggled to change my style. I ended up working harder at teaching than I had for years. But I found the results very satisfying. When I returned home, I changed to smaller classes, mainly discussion, for the remainder of my teaching career.

By the mid-1990s my Vietnam War course was well set, and I followed, with generally small, periodic changes, a standard routine until my retirement in 2005. The course was organized around the themes, questions, and issues that were debated during the war and that historians have grappled with since its end. It explored the origins of the war by looking at the beginnings of the revolution in Vietnam in the broader context of Vietnamese history and culture. It examined the intricate, complex, and controversial relationship between communism and nationalism that so influenced the future course of events in Vietnam. It studied the military, political, and diplomatic dimensions of the First Indochina War, 1946–54, and looked at the causes and significance of America's involvement in that war. It analyzed how the First Indochina War evolved into the Second Indochina War. It explored in depth the dynamics of that war, and devoted extensive consideration to the two questions that have continued to perplex Americans: why did the United States make such a vast commitment of blood and treasure in an area so remote and seemingly so insignificant and why was the world's greatest power unable to impose its will on a seemingly backward third world country? The class did not focus on military operations. But I did

George C. Herring lecturing at West Point. (photo by Tim Collins, courtesy of the University of Kentucky Alumni Association)

give extensive consideration to the peculiar problems posed by fighting a limited war in a Cold War setting and to the formulation and implementation of strategy on each side. Still controversial issues such as the role of the US media and antiwar movement in the outcome of the war were considered in some depth. The personal experience of war was studied from the perspective of both Vietnamese and Americans. The course concluded with an examination of the continuing legacy of the war for both sides.

Throughout my career, I have tried to incorporate different sources and teaching methods in my classes on the Vietnam War. I have always used a survey history as a foundation for my class, often *America's Longest War*, but sometimes I also assigned William Duiker's *Sacred War: Nationalism and Revolution in a Divided Vietnam*, a history of the war from the Vietnamese perspective. Were I teaching now, I would certainly use Mark Bradley's excellent *Vietnam at War* to illustrate the "other side." Robert McMahon's anthology *Major Problems in the History of the Vietnam War* includes a fine selection of documents, which provide much grist for discussion. I supplement these readings with works of literature. I frequently paired Tim O'Brien's *The Things They Carried* with Bao Ninh's *The Sorrow of War*, both moving accounts of soldiers during and after the war. I also sometimes used Kentuckian Bobbie Ann Mason's *In Country* to explore the postwar experience.

I have acquired a rather large collection of political cartoons related to the war. For a local perspective, I used the splendid work of Hugh Haynie, cartoonist for the Louisville *Courier-Journal*. I also have cartoons dating from the early 1980s to the first decade of the twenty-first century, which connect Vietnam with contemporary crises in Central America, Somalia, the Balkans, Iraq, and Afghanistan. I find the cartoons an excellent device for helping students understand popular attitudes toward the war, how they changed, and how memories of Vietnam have continued to influence policy debates.

Audio and video materials make it possible to bring the Vietnam War to life in a way that cannot be done for earlier conflicts. Presidential tapes, many of which are easily accessible on the Internet, offer fascinating insights into the thinking of key policy makers as they debated America's actions in Vietnam. I frequently used music such as Barry Sadler's "The Ballad of the Green Berets" or Johnny Wright's "Hello Vietnam" to illustrate the Cold War consensus and early popular support for the conflict in Vietnam. For antiwar music, one of my personal favorites was Country Joe McDonald's "I-Feel-Like-I'm-Fixin'-to-Die Rag," whose tone ranges from whimsy to tragedy. The postwar mood, especially as it relates to veterans' issues is well exemplified by Bruce Springsteen's "Born in the USA" and Charlie Daniels's "Still in Saigon."

I have also used clips from documentaries and feature films to bring the war to life. *Vietnam: A Television History* includes wonderful footage ranging from the colonial period and the French War to American intervention and the Tet Offensive. A 1994 episode from ABC's *Day One* series offers a superb account of the Battle of Ia Drang Valley, the first major encounter between US and North Vietnamese troops (and the subject of a short operational history that I wrote for the army's Combat Studies Institute). The film covers the history of the battle, complete with footage from the time and often quite moving commentary by surviving participants on both sides. I have also used some clips from Hollywood films, such as the famous opening scene from *Rambo: First Blood Part II* in which Sylvester Stallone's character, asked to return to Vietnam for a final mission, asks, "Sir? Do we get to win this time?"

In teaching the Vietnam War course, I sought to get across to the students several basic things. I attempted to acquaint them as best I could with Vietnam and the Vietnamese (North and South), which, after all, is what the war was all about. I tried to give some idea of that nation's rich history and cultural traditions, of its long and complicated relationship with its northern neighbor, China, of its people and their aspirations and how through the complex processes of history they came into conflict with each other. Above all I tried to show them as independent actors who had the capacity and will to shape their own destiny and were not simply pawns or victims of outside great powers. Throughout the course, I stressed how local circumstances had such an important and often decisive impact on the course of this war and especially on its outcome. I tried to get the students to look critically at the US intervention in Vietnam, to examine the reasons given by policy makers and how they held up under close scrutiny. To what extent was intervention the product of broad principles like containment, for example, and to what extent did it reflect more specific interests and the personalities of individual policy makers? I especially urged them to question the moral bases for US intervention in terms not only of the reasons given but also of the methods used, especially the heavy firepower that devastated both South and North Vietnam. In exploring the outcome of the war, I pushed them to consider not simply why *we* failed, the normal frame of reference for Americans, but also why the North Vietnamese and National Liberation Front succeeded, thereby getting away from simplistic, ethnocentric explanations built on this nation's historical illusions of omnipotence. I sought to get them to understand that a nation's power, no matter how great, will always have limits, a lesson we seem to have to relearn each generation. Through film, fiction, and oral history, I tried to give them a sense of what the war was like on the ground and especially how it was so very different in the different regions of South Vietnam and at different times over its long history. Finally, I attempted to show the enormous impact of war on individuals on both sides during and after the war.

My last Vietnam War classes at the University of Kentucky, in the fall 2002 and spring 2003 semesters, represented the best of what teaching the course had to offer. The fall '02 class was an undergraduate research seminar required of our majors that many, if not most, flat out dreaded. My department in its infinite wisdom had just segregated the top students into a special honors' seminar. I got what was left. Most of my students had waited until their last year to take the class. They seemed terrified of anything that even resembled research (beyond, perhaps, a quick scan of the Internet) and especially of writing. From the outset, the class was a struggle, so much so that early in the semester I came home one afternoon in a foul mood and announced to my wife that I was retiring at the end of the semester. She wisely dissuaded me from doing so, insisting that I should not go out on a low.

The class continued to be difficult until close to the end, but the results were far better than I ever expected. An honors student who enrolled in my class by mistake wrote a superb paper on Vietnamese women in the war that later won a prize in an undergraduate research competition. A paper on the National Liberation Front's use of booby traps was so rich in detail and interesting in its conclusions that it might have been published. The student-author instead went on to a career in the business side of baseball with the Tampa Bay Rays organization.

My last Vietnam War class at the University of Kentucky in the spring of 2003 was without question (as if to prove that my wife is always right) my best. The students were superb. They got into the material, engaged in discussions, and really grappled with the issues. That was the way to go out.

The last class I taught on the Vietnam War (at least to this point) proved to be a fitting—though totally unexpected—culminating experience. During the summer of 2009, I had the privilege of participating in an Alumni College program at Washington and Lee University in Lexington, Virginia. It was wonderful for me, of course, to be back in my home state, especially on that beautiful campus nestled between the Blue Ridge and Allegheny mountains. The course lasted only a week, but it was an intense, emotional, and enlightening five days for the students and faculty. The class was made up of about forty "students," all of them W&L alumni, most of them card-carrying members of the Vietnam generation. A high percentage of them had served in Vietnam or the military during that era. A number had also been actively involved in antiwar protests. Barry Machado, a diplomatic historian like myself and retired W&L professor, and I gave most of the lectures. Some other local faculty members gave guest lectures, as did Gen. Paul Gorman, a retired army officer who served in Vietnam, worked in the Pentagon during the war years, and was involved in writing the *Pentagon Papers*. During that week of often intense discussions, we relived the war. For some of those who had served, it was the first time they had really thought and talked about the war since they got out of it. Those who had fought in Vietnam and had quite fixed views on the war in several cases rethought their experiences and conclusions. The same happened with some of the protesters. All of us left the campus on Friday afternoon emotionally drained but enormously enriched by the experience. It seemed a good way after more than thirty-five years to conclude my teaching of the war.

I could not close this essay without mentioning the extremely important part played by graduate students in my teaching—and indeed my life—during my years at the University of Kentucky. From the 1970s on, I had a deeply committed cohort of graduate students, many from the region but increasingly also from different parts of the country. They were a first-rate group, like myself driven to learn more about the war and to share our knowledge with undergraduates and the public beyond academia. It was exciting and rewarding to help them find topics to work on. As they progressed through their studies, I found myself learning all kinds of new things. I immensely enjoyed sharing their excitement of discovery and helping them put their findings into prose. There was no greater thrill in teaching than to see them get over the numerous hurdles in our program, complete their degrees, prepare their research for publication, and, even in tight job markets, find employment. I still recall quite vividly one truly incredible week in which one of my recent PhDs got a contract from a prestigious university press to publish his dissertation and secured a teaching position. I continue to take enormous pride in the work of my former students.

The closest connections we form as teachers are with our students, and it was through a former graduate student in the fall of 2008 that I was made aware once again of the horrible toll taken by the Vietnam War on those who fought in it and were otherwise affected by it. Bob Topmiller, one of my doctoral students from the 1990s, as a young navy medic at the 1969 battle of Khe Sanh had witnessed horrific things. At UK he completed a fine dissertation on the Buddhist upheaval in I Corps in South Vietnam in early 1966, later published by the University Press of Kentucky. During and especially after his doctoral work, Bob traveled back to Vietnam numerous times to do research, to try to come to terms with the demons that still tortured him from his tour of duty there, and to help other victims of the war, most notably Vietnamese children affected by Agent Orange. Struggling to complete a book on the Veterans Administration's failure throughout US history to adequately address the problems of its clientele and still wrestling with major problems from post-traumatic stress disorder, Bob in September 2008 took his own life. For those of us who have been involved with the war in so many ways and for so long, it was yet another painful reminder that Vietnam truly is a war that never seems to go away.

PART TWO

Methods and Sources

Putting Students
in "Their Shoes"

A Decision-Making Approach
to Teaching the Vietnam War

KEVIN O'REILLY

America's experience in the Vietnam War was a result of a series of decisions made within specific historical contexts. Many lessons can be learned by looking back and analyzing these decisions. Students, however, will learn most when making decisions for themselves, based on the information the decision makers had at the time, *before* they know what the decision makers actually did. In this sense we are moving students from hindsight to foresight, to the point where they are anticipating the various potential consequences of their actions. This "You Are There" approach engages students by making history come to life. Students, through this sort of experience, begin to understand the historical forces, perceptions, and human frailties involved in making life-or-death choices.

This chapter describes the decision-making approach to learning about the Vietnam War by focusing on two decisions made by President Lyndon Johnson and his advisers in 1965. The first decision, made in February, was to initiate a large-scale, sustained bombing campaign in North Vietnam. The second crucial decision, made in July, was to commit large numbers of American ground forces to fight in South Vietnam. These fascinating decisions, selected from among the many pivotal choices made before and after 1965 by American policy makers

41

about the Vietnam conflict, are ideal in illustrating the decision-making pedagogy.

The decision-making process described in the essay follows this sequence.

1. Students read the decision problem in a handout, along with information about the problem.
2. Students can ask questions about the problem.
3. Students decide.
4. Students receive and read the outcomes (what actually happened).
5. Students and teacher debrief the problem.

Decision I: Bombing

Students need a sound background on Vietnam and US policy in Vietnam up to 1965 before beginning this lesson. In my high school classes they have engaged in decision-making problems on, among other topics, whether to aid France in 1950, adhere to the 1954 Geneva Conference agreement, form the Southeast Asia Treaty Organization (SEATO), support Ngo Dinh Diem, send advisers to South Vietnam, support the overthrow of Diem, and respond to the Tonkin Gulf incident. They have also studied the Cold War and the decolonization period.

The lesson begins with handout 1, provided below, given as homework. Students are to answer the question at the end: "Will you approve a bombing campaign against North Vietnam?" Note that the information in handout 1 is the only information students receive. I make sure to clarify that this is a question only of whether the United States should bomb North Vietnam. The United States is already bombing in South Vietnam, a fact that confuses some students. They wonder why Americans would bomb the country they are trying to save. I explain that since the United States has intervened, via military advisers, in the fighting against National Liberation Front (NLF) forces (often referred to as the Viet Cong) in South Vietnam, the US military is already bombing in South Vietnam to support American soldiers. Hence, this question is limited to whether the United States will expand the bombing campaign to North Vietnam. Other than this one clarification, students are limited to the description on the handout. The danger in conveying information verbally is the tendency to give too many clues, tipping off the better options from the worse. To the extent possible, we want students to make decisions based only on the information that President Johnson had at the time. Students will have the opportunity to get more information by asking questions during the lesson.

Handout I
Should the US Bomb North Vietnam?

You are President Johnson in February 1965. There is a guerrilla war raging in South Vietnam in which National Liberation Front (NLF) forces (the "Viet Cong") are fighting against the South Vietnamese government. The NLF forces are backed by the Communist government of North Vietnam. The US supports the South Vietnamese government because Americans do not want to see Communism expand into South Vietnam. American advisers believe that if trends continue the way they are going now, the South Vietnamese government will be defeated and the Communists will control the whole country.

The US has about 23,300 military advisers in South Vietnam to help the South Vietnamese army fight the NLF. These are well-armed American soldiers who are supported by American air power and artillery, but whose primary mission is to train, advise, and assist South Vietnamese forces. However, recently NLF guerrillas have attacked two military bases, killing more than 30 Americans.

At this point the US has only bombed North Vietnam a few times, against only a handful of targets. Now you need to decide whether to begin a full-scale bombing campaign against North Vietnam. (As noted above, Americans are already bombing in South Vietnam to support US and South Vietnamese soldiers in combat.) The North Vietnamese are the main supporters of the NLF, providing them with equipment, training, and several thousand soldiers who are fighting in South Vietnam. So you have called a meeting to make a decision. Here are arguments by your advisers about whether to bomb North Vietnam:

1. Bombing won't cost a lot of American lives, will raise morale in the South Vietnamese government, might get North Vietnam to stop supplying and supporting the war in South Vietnam, and might help the US avoid getting into a larger ground war.
2. Limited bombing will encourage the North Vietnamese to negotiate.

3. The Joint Chiefs of Staff strongly favor all-out bombing, believing that the US should use all its power to inflict whatever damage Americans can on the enemy. The object of war is to defeat the enemy and then negotiate from a position of strength.

4. 60 percent of Americans favor bombing targets (factories, bridges) in North Vietnam.

5. A government study shows that strategic bombing (bombing factories, cities, and bases that you are not also attacking with ground forces) didn't work in World War II. The cost to the country doing the bombing was greater than the damage done, and bombing strengthened the will of the bombed country to fight.

6. Bombing could get the US more involved, increase South Vietnam's dependence on the US, bring China into the war, and turn world opinion against us. North Vietnam could just send down more troops into South Vietnam to counteract the bombing.

Will you approve a bombing campaign against North Vietnam?

At the beginning of the next class session, I have students pair up to discuss whether to bomb North Vietnam. The pairs are just discussing at this point; they do not have to agree on the better option. Next, students take a preliminary vote, and their votes are tallied on the board. The class as a whole then discusses the arguments for and against the two options, and students can ask questions to help them make a better decision. This sequence not only helps students understand a key decision in the Vietnam War, but it also helps them improve their ability to ask relevant and critical questions, one of the most important skills for doing well in the social studies classroom and for being an informed citizen.

Whenever a student asks a very good question, the whole class benefits, and students are more likely to make a better decision. In addition students benefit as critical thinkers by hearing examples of good questions. On the other hand, if students are struggling to think of good questions, the teacher can give them a menu of questions, such as the following, from which students will vote on the one question they most want to see answered:

1. How effective is the US Air Force? Can it hit the targets it chooses? Will the US lose many pilots and planes?
2. What does the US know about North Vietnam's will to continue fighting? Will NLF forces in South Vietnam surrender or compromise if the US bombs the North and hurts the North Vietnamese economy?
3. Are there many good targets in North Vietnam?
4. Will China or the Soviet Union get involved in the war if the US bombs North Vietnam?

The teacher reads the suggested answer to the top vote-getter. For example, if the most votes go to question 3, the teacher reads this suggested answer: "No. North Vietnam does not have a developed, modern economy and has few factories, oil tankers, or other easily identifiable targets. North Vietnam does have some railroads and bridges, but the supply of obvious targets will run out quickly."[1]

This exercise enables students to develop additional capabilities essential to making sound and informed decisions: the ability to see a problem from another point of view. In this conflict situation, we want students to consider the enemy's point of view. A direct way to facilitate the development of this skill is to tell students to imagine they are North Vietnamese leaders. They are to write out a specific action they would take in response to US bombing and what they would do if the United States chooses not to bomb. For example, in response to the bombing campaign, students might—as American military leaders did when they role-played the North Vietnamese in a war game in 1965—move high-priority bombing targets next to hospitals and schools. Or students, as the North Vietnamese, might try to acquire air defense weapons from the Soviet Union or China.

Next I put students back in pairs to discuss the problem once more and make their final decisions. I generally say something like "You have heard the arguments of your classmates about the various options, you have heard the answer to one or more questions, and you have considered the enemy's possible reaction to each of the options. Now you are going to make your final decision." Following the vote, students receive the outcomes (handout 2), which they read for homework and write three comments on the decisions President Johnson and his advisers actually made.

Handout 2
Outcomes of Bombing North Vietnam

President Johnson decided to approve bombing North Vietnam. The bombing campaign, called "Operation Rolling Thunder," was unsuccessful. President Johnson and his advisers did not adequately consider the viewpoint of the North Vietnamese regarding this decision to bomb North Vietnam. If they had, they would have seen that the North Vietnamese could counter all US bombing actions. The North Vietnamese managed to build an extensive air defense system, including surface-to-air missiles, which enabled them to shoot down many American planes.

In addition, the North Vietnamese dispersed possible targets, such as factories, so there was not much to bomb, and they put high value targets next to hospitals and schools, daring the United States to bomb them. (At that time bombs were not nearly as accurate as they are today, so bombing a target meant bombing a whole area.) Often, the bombs being dropped cost more than the targets being destroyed. Each plane shot down was more costly than dozens or even hundreds of targets bombed. The North Vietnamese also organized repair brigades. These groups could repair a bombed bridge within 48 hours in some cases.

The Institute for Defense Analysis issued a report in 1966 saying that US bombing of North Vietnam had no measurable effect on North Vietnam since there were few rewarding targets and since North Vietnam's will to fight seemed just as strong. The bombing did not affect the NLF in South Vietnam either, since the NLF got most of its supplies from their local areas. In 1967, a special military report stated that the cost to the US of the bombing campaign was ten times the value of the North Vietnamese targets that were destroyed.

The US dropped three times as many bombs on Vietnam as American planes dropped in all of World War II. Most of the bombs (about two-thirds) were dropped on South Vietnam. This extensive bombing caused significant environmental damage to the region.

Rebuilding a North Vietnamese bridge. (VA009042, Douglas Pike Photograph Collection, The Vietnam Center and Archive, Texas Tech University)

In the debriefing the class discusses what surprised them about these outcomes, what they think of President Johnson's decision making, what they think of their own decision making, and what they would have done differently now that they have learned about these outcomes. The teacher can ask which question, in retrospect, would have been most helpful. Were there questions not asked that would have been helpful in making a better decision? The teacher can also ask if taking the enemy's point of view helped in making a better decision.

To provide more structure, teachers can give students a model of decision-making skills, shown in handout 3. This model is meant to be a menu of possible skills to use rather than a step-by-step approach to decision making. Students look at the problem at hand and select the skills they think might be especially important to that case. Organizing it into the acronym "PAGE" is meant to serve as a mnemonic device to help students remember the skills.

Handout 3
PAGE Model for Analyzing Decision Making

P = *Problem*
— Identify any Underlying Problem
— Consider other Points of View
— What are my Assumptions? Emotions?

A = *Ask for Information (about)*
— Historical Context (History of this Issue; Context in the World)
— Reliability of Sources
— Historical Analogies

G = *Goals*
— What are my main Goals? Are they Realistic?
— Generate Options to help Achieve my Goals. Are they Morally Right?

E = *Effects*
— Predict Unintended Consequences
— Play out the Option. What could go wrong?

In this problem on whether to bomb, the analysis so far has empha-sized two skills: asking questions about the historical context and considering other points of view. Many other parts of PAGE could be discussed, such as "underlying problem" (Do students see the conflict as part of Communist expansion or a nationalist independence move-ment?) or "reliability of sources" (Who is making the arguments in handout 1 and how reliable are they?). In addition, a key element of decision making about the Vietnam War is whether the goals were realistic. Many historians have argued that President Johnson and his advisers never seriously discussed the goals of US involvement in Vietnam. Rather, they tried to avoid defeat and focused on tactics.

Decision 2: Ground Troops

In July 1965 President Johnson and his advisers met for two weeks to decide whether to send large numbers of American ground forces to South Vietnam. The United States had begun its bombing campaign against North Vietnam, which had increased the number of Americans stationed in South Vietnam since more soldiers were needed to guard the air bases from which the planes flew. This question about ground forces is not about such defensive troops, however. The troops in question would be ground forces used for offensive operations to defeat the NLF forces in South Vietnam.

Here, again, the decision-making approach to this problem ideally gives students only the information the president and his advisers had available to them at the time of the meetings (presented in handout 4). They read the handout for homework and decide tentatively what they will do. Since we want students to learn from the experience of making their own good and bad decisions, it is important to start the lesson by forcing each student to grapple with the problem individually. Too often students, especially adolescents, are swayed by the comments and reactions of the teacher or other students. The true strength of this exercise is to emphasize the contingent nature of making decisions with only limited information.

Handout 4
Should The US Send
Large Numbers of Combat Forces
to South Vietnam?

It is July, 1965. The US has about 23,300 troops in Vietnam to help the South Vietnamese army fight the Communists. South Vietnam is close to defeat and your military commander in Vietnam is calling for 100,000 combat troops. Polls repeatedly show that a majority of Americans support a stronger military role by the US in Vietnam. You've called a meeting to decide. Here are some arguments by your advisers on this important decision:

—If we don't stop the Communists in Vietnam it will be appeasement, just like giving in to the Nazis in the 1930s. If the Communists do win, other countries in Southeast Asia will fall like dominoes to Communism and China will be encouraged to try more expansion.

—In the Korean War, the US successfully stood up to Communist aggression by North Korea (backed by China and the Soviet Union) in its attempt to conquer South Korea. We can do it again in Vietnam.

—One adviser claims that Korea, where there was a clear invasion and more traditional battlefields, is not like Vietnam, where there is primarily guerrilla warfare. The terrain (geography) and political situation in Vietnam also make it fundamentally different than Korea.

—The French fought the Vietnamese for seven years with a large army and couldn't defeat them. We may not be able to defeat the NLF without unacceptable costs to our country.

—Two advisers feel that the present situation is different than the French situation in Vietnam. The French Army used defensive tactics that gave the initiative to the Communists. In addition, the war was unpopular in France, but it is popular in the US.

—One general estimates that it would take 500,000 US troops five years to win the war.

One adviser says, "The integrity of the US commitment is the principal pillar of peace throughout the world. If that commitment becomes unreliable, the communist world would draw conclusions that would lead to our ruin and almost certainly to a catastrophic war."

—Like the "loss" of China in 1949, the spread of Communism to South Vietnam would hurt the President's political standing.

—A senator who is a close adviser says that Vietnam has no strategic, economic, or tactical value, and we can never win there. Sending troops there would hurt us and help the Communists, since Vietnam is one of the worst spots in Asia to fight a war.

Will you approve sending large numbers of American combat troops into Vietnam?

After deciding individually as part of the homework, in class students pair up and discuss their decision. I then bring the class back together and tally the preliminary vote. As with the bombing problem, students make arguments for and against sending troops, and they can ask questions. Again, the teacher could have students vote on which question from this menu they would most like answered:

1. How popular is the South Vietnamese government with the South Vietnamese people?
2. What is the military situation in South Vietnam? How strong are the two sides?

3. What will the likely political effects be in the US of sending large numbers of troops to South Vietnam?
4. What does the public think about sending American troops to South Vietnam?

Question 1 is very interesting. The suggested answer in the teacher materials contains evidence from former NLF officers, interviews with returning American officers compiled in a study entitled "A Program for the Pacification and Long-Term Development of South Vietnam," known as PROVN, and a survey done with people in villages in South Vietnam for a TV broadcast. Students should evaluate the reliability of each of these sources, although all of them, as well as President Johnson's political advisers, agreed that the South Vietnamese government was unpopular.

In addition to focusing on making arguments and asking questions, the teacher can focus on other decision-making skills. According to Gary Klein, decision making is improved by doing a mental simulation of what might happen after a particular option is chosen. To develop this skill, Klein recommends a "premortem," trying to get students to do a postmortem analysis, but in advance of the actual decision. Students are instructed to pretend that their option was chosen and it turned out to be a disaster. They are to discuss what went wrong with this option. By playing out these options, students begin to anticipate some of the many possible unintended consequences. In this problem on whether to send large numbers of troops, either choice could lead to negative effects, so both choices should be discussed.

Using the PAGE analysis sheet (handout 3) raises some important points to discuss. The most prominent element of decision making on whether to send American troops is the use of analogies. Yuen Foong Khong's book *Analogies at War* catalogs the many analogies used by American leaders in their decision-making arguments. Indeed, the first four arguments in handout 4 are analogies or arguments against analogies. According to Khong, the most prominent analogy was to the Korean War. Students should ask how the cases are different whenever they identify an analogy. Interestingly, in the analogy to the French failure in Vietnam, National Security Adviser McGeorge Bundy and Secretary of State Dean Rusk argued that there were important differences between the French situation in 1954 and the American situation in 1965. Khong points out that their analysis was faulty. The two American advisers were comparing the French situation at the end of their war, when it was very unpopular, to the US situation at the beginning of its war. Had these advisers thought more carefully about their critique, they could have seen the French situation as a warning of what might be ahead for US involvement in Vietnam. Richard Neustadt and Ernest May, in their book *Thinking in Time* and a case study they used at Harvard University's Kennedy School of Government on Vietnam decision making, argue that decision makers need to use analogies for analysis, not for advocacy. The goal is to get the decision right, not to win arguments.

Just as in the bombing problem, students are paired to take their final vote after hearing the arguments, questions, and premortem analysis. After the vote students read the outcomes for homework (handout 5) and write three comments about what they think of President Johnson's decision to send large numbers of American troops into South Vietnam.

<hr>

Handout 5
Outcomes of Sending
Large Numbers of American Soldiers
to South Vietnam

President Johnson and his advisers met every day for a week and argued about the decision to send US combat troops to Vietnam. In the end, President Johnson decided to send in large numbers of US combat troops. This was a major turning point in the war; the US had escalated the situation from adviser to the South Vietnamese government to taking over the main combat role, and was now fighting the NLF and North Vietnamese forces directly. By January 1966 the US had 186,000 troops in Vietnam, and by 1968 more than 500,000. The war did not go well for the US.

—More than 50,000 Americans lost their lives and hundreds of thousands were wounded as a result of the war. More than a million Vietnamese died in the war. Millions were wounded, and millions more became refugees.

—The NLF used guerrilla fighters, so they blended in with civilians in villages. It was very difficult to fight the guerrillas without killing civilians. Naturally, US commanders used air power to help ground troops fight. It was, however, especially difficult to distinguish NLF forces and civilians from the cockpit of an airplane. A

Congressional report estimated that the US killed two civilians for every enemy killed in the fighting. Civilian deaths led to more NLF recruits (people started to hate the US and so joined the NLF) in an endless cycle of violence. The NLF used terrorist tactics to intimidate South Vietnamese civilians into supporting them. Nevertheless, due to civilian casualties, the US actually helped NLF recruitment of more guerrilla fighters.

—The North Vietnamese had an army of about 500,000 soldiers, of which only a few thousand were in South Vietnam in 1965. So, as the US raised the number of troops it committed to South Vietnam, the North Vietnamese countered it by sending more of their soldiers down to South Vietnam. The war simply escalated on both sides.

—Some American soldiers, frustrated by fighting against guerrillas and by losing fellow soldiers to booby traps and ambushes, started committing atrocities by killing civilians. The most well known atrocity is the My Lai Massacre. Lieutenant William Calley was convicted of a war crime for the massacre. It is unclear how many atrocities were committed, but the knowledge that some American soldiers were killing civilians hurt the reputation of the country and the army.

—The war led to racial tensions among American soldiers. Some African Americans felt they were enduring higher casualties than were white soldiers. Other African Americans questioned why they should fight for the US at all when they were deprived of rights at home. Leaders of the Student Nonviolent Coordinating Committee (SNCC) stated their opposition to the US role in Vietnam and declared their support for draft resisters. Stokely Carmichael said the draft was nothing more than "white people sending black people to make war on yellow people in order to defend the land they stole from red people." Blacks also demonstrated against, in the words of another SNCC protester, "the annihilation of Black men in the illegal racist war in Vietnam."

—The war also led to questions about social class. Some critics claimed that the war fell especially hard on poor Americans. The rich got college deferments and even if they did get drafted, they tended to receive desk jobs in the military. The poor were twice as likely to be drafted and twice as likely to see combat.

—Fighting in Vietnam, especially with hundreds of thousands of troops there, cost a great deal of money. President Johnson either had to raise taxes, cut spending on his Great Society programs, or deficit spend (spend more than the government takes in through taxes, borrowing the rest). President Johnson chose to deficit spend, which caused inflation. In addition, the war eventually led to cutbacks in Great Society programs—the war hurt domestic programs designed to help people in the US.

—As the war dragged on, public opinion turned against it, especially as casualties rose. Many Americans had trouble understanding why we were fighting in Vietnam and losing so many young Americans. By 1968 President Johnson's popularity was only about 40 percent.

—The war led to mass protests at home. Other people became angry at the protesters, wondering why people were not supporting their country in a time of war.

—The war split the country. It also split the Democratic Party into a peace wing and a continue-the-war wing. President Johnson decided not to run for reelection in 1968.

—The split within the Democratic Party helped the Republicans to win the presidency in 1968. The Republican, Richard Nixon, ran a campaign based on "Law and Order." The theme connected with many voters, who saw the Vietnam protests as a symptom that the country was falling into anarchy. Nixon supporters felt people should obey the law and respect those in the military who risked their lives. They were shocked to see protesters flying NLF rather than American flags. The protesters, meanwhile, felt they were being loyal Americans by questioning the government about an immoral war that was hurting their country.

—As the soldiers returned, they were generally ignored, and sometimes criticized. They were not welcomed home as heroes. The war was unpopular, so many people did not want to be reminded of it by parades and other ceremonies. The soldiers themselves suffered physical and psychological scars from the war. Many suffered from PTSD—Post Traumatic Stress Disorder. There was an increase in alcohol and drug abuse among Vietnam veterans. Unfortunately, there were not enough services for the returning veterans, so their psychological needs were not completely met.

—The war hurt the military itself. Some Americans associated the unpopular war with the military. Even some veterans were critical of the war, forming a group called the Vietnam Veterans against the War. Morale dropped in Vietnam. There were hundreds of cases of American troops shooting at their own officers, a practice called "fragging." In the 1970s, military leaders actually wanted to pull the army out of Vietnam because the war was hurting the military and the reputation of the military so much.

—As American soldiers took over much of the fighting, the South Vietnamese government and military became secondary in importance. It became more of America's war, rather than a war that the South Vietnamese needed to win for themselves. Some American soldiers were disgusted by the lack of effort by South Vietnamese soldiers.

—Many American leaders were upset by the tragedy in Vietnam. As a result, they were more hesitant to get involved in other conflict situations, experiencing what was referred to as the "Vietnam Syndrome."

The instructional focus of this chapter is on students making decisions before they find out what actually happened in history. By putting students in the role of President Johnson in 1965 and requiring them to make decisions before they know what he actually decided, they get a feel, through experience, for the difficulties involved in making those decisions. In a sense the choice to focus on the decisions of policy makers is itself a pedagogical decision, one teachers could discuss with students. As a result of this decision-making approach, students get a sense of historical empathy for President Johnson and a sense of humility in judging historical decision makers. The empathy comes from the recognition of their own frailties in making decisions. Over the years numerous students have recognized that the decisions confronting Johnson and his advisers were really difficult and felt they would not want to be president. When students later examine various elements of the war, such as those described in other chapters in this volume, they carry the knowledge that they also might have made decisions that led to often tragic results. Students benefit from watching portions of the film *Dear America: Letters Home from Vietnam*. Watching the film and hearing the letters of individual soldiers humanize the war, after the intellectual exercise of making decisions. In a sense students in this lesson are put in the White House to make decisions and then taken to rice paddies to see the effects of those decisions. It is sobering for many students. It is not as easy to judge historical actors as foolhardy when you have made some of the same foolish decisions yourself.

NOTES

Parts of this essay were previously published in Kevin O'Reilly, *The 1960s and the Vietnam War*, vol. 11 of *Decision Making in United States History* (Culver City, CA: Social Studies School Service, 2007); and my web simulation, *Escalation*, http://www.escalationsim.com. The handouts selected for this essay have been edited further for brevity. Activities and questions have also been simplified.

1. The full list of answers, as well as the handout itself, is available at *Escalation*, http://www.escalationsim.com.

KEY RESOURCES

Barrett, David. *Uncertain Warriors: Lyndon Johnson and His Vietnam Advisors.* Lawrence: University Press of Kansas, 1993.

Berman, Larry. *Planning a Tragedy: The Americanization of the War in Vietnam.* New York: W. W. Norton, 1982.

Kahin, George McTurnan. *Intervention: How America Became Involved in Vietnam.* New York: Alfred A. Knopf, 1986.

Klein, Gary. *Sources of Power: How People Make Decisions.* Cambridge, MA: MIT Press, 1998.

Logevall, Fredrik. *Choosing War: The Lost Chance for Peace and the Escalation of the War in Vietnam.* Berkeley: University of California Press, 1999.

Neustadt, Richard, and Ernest May. *Thinking in Time: The Uses of History for Decision-Makers.* New York: Free Press, 1986.

O'Reilly, Kevin. *The 1960s and the Vietnam War.* Vol. 11 of *Decision Making in United States History.* Culver City, CA: Social Studies School Service, 2007.

———. *Escalation.* web simulation, http://www.escalationsim.com.

Race, Jeffrey. *War Comes to Long An: Revolutionary Conflict in a Vietnamese Province.* Berkeley: University of California Press, 1971.

Tilford, Earl. *Crosswinds: The Air Force's Setup in Vietnam.* College Station: Texas A&M University Press, 1993.

VanDeMark, Brian. *Into the Quagmire: Lyndon Johnson and the Escalation of the Vietnam War.* New York: Oxford University Press, 1991.

Yuen Foong Khong. *Analogies at War: Korea, Munich, Dien Bien Phu, and the Vietnam Decisions of 1965.* Princeton, NJ: Princeton University Press, 1992.

Understanding the Vietnam Era through Music

HUGO A. KEESING

Over seventy-five years ago Sigmund Spaeth wrote that popular music "had become a most revealing index to American life." He went on to say, "[I]t will tell as much to future students of current civilization as any histories . . . of the time."[1] Even as music changed over the decades, its ability to capture the ethos of the times that produced it has remained.

What makes music a unique source for learning about the Vietnam War? Two qualities quickly come to mind: the music's immediacy and the fact that it was relatively unfiltered. Songs were often written, recorded, and released on 45 rpm records in a matter of days. Filtering done by radio stations and disc jockeys affected what records would be heard (and potentially become popular) but not what songs were released. Recorded songs are an unvarnished portrait of what Americans believed, or wanted others to believe, about the war.

The collection of more than 5,100 war-related recordings that this essay draws on represents the most comprehensive database ever assembled and has been more than two decades in the making. It goes far beyond the "popular" records—the less than 10 percent that were ever among the Top 100 singles on the Pop, Country or R&B charts. It also includes album tracks, as well as postwar formats such as audiocassettes, compact discs, and downloads. About half the songs appeared between 1962 and 1975, the period generally identified as the war years.

During the war years the prevailing perception was that folk music was antiwar and country was hawkish and patriotic. Pop mostly stayed away from taking a clear position on the war, and until 1970 African American musicians were mainly silent. After 1975, when the last US troops left Vietnam, no scholars kept track of war music. As a result, music written and performed by Vietnam veterans—an entirely new phenomenon with no World War II or Korean War precedents—was entirely overlooked. Vietnam's post-1975 music was also the first to address in rich detail a war's aftermath.

Studying the Vietnam War by means of music is a way to tap into a medium already popular with young people. Regardless of whether the source is a recording, a YouTube video, or an iTunes download, music can be accessed, stored, and consumed far more easily than written pages. Furthermore, research has shown that material set to music is better remembered than print only, leading to "stealth" learning.

While music alone cannot tell the story of America's involvement in Vietnam, it can be integrated into a Vietnam War curriculum in numerous ways. With songs opening the door, students might be tasked to compare and contrast commercial and "in-country" depictions of combat, to learn more about the roles of women in Vietnam, or to research whether peace marches and protest songs had any impact on hastening the war's end. Songs can also confront students with ethical issues such as the impact of "search and destroy" missions on civilian populations and a country's responsibilities vis-à-vis its veterans. The possibilities are endless, and teachers should establish the necessary context and then encourage students to create their own frameworks for using the music.

One way to integrate music into a Vietnam War curriculum is to place source material such as the three-hundred-plus tracks from *Next Stop Is Vietnam* on a school server that can be accessed in the library or dorms. That way students can listen by themselves and form their own opinions. It also permits class time to be used for discussion and evaluation. Another is for instructors to preselect songs or song segments, add appropriate context, and create focused podcasts that become the basis for student learning.

This essay groups songs that are especially useful for classroom discussions into ten topical areas: (1) Background on the War, (2) Going to War, (3) Teenage Soldiers, (4) Protesting the War, (5) Patriotic and Antiprotest Songs, (6) the Peace Movement, (7) In-Country Songs, (8) the War's Aftermath, (9) Depicting the Vietnamese Perspective, and

(10) Who Was Right? Their trajectory moves students from knowledge about Vietnam and the war to understanding the dynamics of the war and how it affected all those it touched to evaluating the war's impact. The discussion of each area highlights several songs whose lyrics and/or performance are appropriate launching pads for students to pursue the topic in more detail and in other media. While the essay focuses on a small number of songs, it also points teachers to several additional song titles and artists that relate to the discussed topic. Taken together, or individually, these songs provide starting points for broader and deeper musical and classroom explorations.

Background on the War

Understanding the Vietnam War can only begin with some basic knowledge of the country, its people, and America's intervention. Of the handful of songs that provide such background, the earliest is Ewan McColl's "Ballad of Ho Chi Minh." Written shortly after the French were defeated at Dien Bien Phu in 1954, the song presents Uncle Ho as the revolutionary hero of his country, the "father of the Indo-Chinese people." It tells of how he "trained a determined band . . . [to] drive invaders from the land." Just as Ho Chi Minh viewed the French as the enemy in the early 1950s, so he saw the Americans as the same a decade later.

One of the first songs to address the US military's presence in Vietnam is Phil Ochs's "Talking Vietnam" (1964). It foretells the US Army's transition from its advisory role to a combat role that was not made official until March 1965. As Ochs put it, we were "training a million Vietnamese to fight for the wrong government." Ochs would go on to be the most outspoken critic of the war with songs such as "I Ain't Marching Anymore," "White Boots Marching in a Yellow Land," and a dozen similar songs.

"The Dean Rusk Song" (circa 1967) provides a general overview of the 1965–67 period when, by all official reports, the United States was winning the hearts and minds of the South Vietnamese while defeating the Viet Cong and North Vietnamese Army with its superior equipment and logistics. It can be found on Bill Frederick's antiwar album "Hey! Hey . . . L.B.J!" Even more obscure in that it was not commercially available until 2010 is "The Battle Hymn of the Republic of Vietnam." Written and performed by an unknown Vietnam insider (circa 1967), it is one example of an in-country song that supported a claim of the anti-war movement, namely that news briefings on the war's progress coming out of Saigon were not to be believed.

These four songs, as well as others such as Tom Paxton's "Lyndon Johnson Told the Nation" (1965), presented the war as far more complex than a struggle between good and evil, a noble US attempt to stop the spread of communism from including the free people of South Vietnam. They stand in sharp contrast to Sgt. Barry Sadler's gung-ho "Ballad of the Green Berets," the United States' #1 single for all of 1966.

Other scene-setting songs include Staff Sgt. Bob Lay's "Marine's Ballad" (1965). It describes the arrival of the first combat troops near Da Nang, ready to "charge right through the enemy." Unlike World War II and Korea, however, there were few uniformed soldiers opposing the Marines and few objectives to take. Instead, the troops found themselves in the middle of an alien culture where it was difficult to distinguish between friend and foe. To maintain good relations with the South Vietnamese, all military personnel arriving in country were issued written rules of conduct. Jacqueline Sharpe based "Mind Your Manners, Boys" (1966) on a *New York Times* story about a Marine commander's order to his troops to observe those rules. Her lyrics, such as "If you gotta nab an old man . . . grab his arm or leg or neck, but not his beard," make clear that interactions with local Vietnamese could easily become strained.

Going to War

As in previous wars, thousands of American men and women went to Vietnam because they saw it as their duty to serve their country. Of the several hundred song titles that include the word *soldier*, some focus on the gulf between those fighting and those at home. Arlo Guthrie's "When a Soldier Makes It Home" (2007) puts it this way: "Back home they don't know too much / There's just no way to tell / I guess you had to be there." Most, however, deal with general issues such as being separated from loved ones and loneliness. It is the exceptions, those about real people, that can help students better understand the meaning of "going to war."

Ron Kovic was wounded and permanently paralyzed during his second tour of duty, but he came home alive. Tom Paxton's song "Born on the 4th of July" was released in 1977, a year after Kovic's

NINE RULES

FOR PERSONNEL OF US MILITARY ASSISTANCE COMMAND, VIETNAM

The Vietnamese have paid a heavy price in suffering for their long fight against the communists. We military men are in Vietnam now because their government has asked us to help its soldiers and people in winning their struggle. The Viet Cong will attempt to turn the Vietnamese people against you. You can defeat them at every turn by the strength, understanding, and generosity you display with the people. Here are nine simple rules:

DISTRIBUTION — 1 to each member of the United States Armed Forces in Vietnam

NINE RULES

1. Remember we are guests here: We make no demands and seek no special treatment.

2. Join with the people! Understand their life, use phrases from their language and honor their customs and laws.

3. Treat women with politeness and respect.

4. Make personal friends among the soldiers and common people.

5. Always give the Vietnamese the right of way.

6. Be alert to security and ready to react with your military skill.

7. Don't attract attention by loud, rude or unusual behavior.

8. Avoid separating yourself from the people by a display of wealth or privilege.

9. Above all else you are members of the U S Military Forces on a difficult mission, responsible for all your official and personal actions. Reflect honor upon yourself and the United States of America.

Wallet-sized card given to all inbound personnel.

autobiography became a best seller but twelve years before the release of the motion picture starring Tom Cruise. The album track tells how Vietnam changed Kovic from a gung-ho Marine to the protester who joined Vietnam Veterans against the War (VVAW). Danny Fernandez, honored as the first Mexican American soldier to be awarded the Congressional Medal of Honor for service in Vietnam, was killed in action. Eddie Harrison's tribute song (1966) was written eight months prior to Danny's posthumous award for "conspicuous gallantry and intrepidity at the risk of his life above and beyond the call of duty."

The thousands of women who served in-theater, whether as nurses, in military specialties, or as Red Cross volunteers, to name but a few, received scant attention during the war years. After the war they seemed to disappear altogether. It was not until the late 1980s that their service, too, was recognized and they were honored with a statue at the Vietnam Veterans Memorial in Washington, D.C. The eight nurses who died during the war are identified by name in John Black's the "Women on the Wall" (2003).

Country Joe McDonald's "The Girl Next Door (Combat Nurse)" could be the story of many of the more than five thousand army nurses who served at field hospitals. He wrote it for Lt. Lynda van Devanter, a surgical nurse who served in Vietnam in 1969–70. Her biography, *Home before Morning*, was one of the inspirations for the TV series *China Beach*. Van Devanter died in 2002 of causes she attributed to her exposure to Agent Orange. It is important for teachers to note that these four songs identify specific individuals who either lost their lives or had them inalterably changed by the war. They put faces on real people and bring home the personal tragedies of war. If students have relatives or acquaintances who served in Vietnam, or for that matter Iraq or Afghanistan, the stories these songs tell may make them more inclined to collect oral histories, or teachers can create activities that pair listening to these songs with the reading of oral histories that address the same topics. (See Andrew Darien's essay in this volume for more information about oral history collections.)

Teenage Soldiers

A theme that sets Vietnam War songs apart from those of previous wars is their emphasis on the soldiers' relative youth. One explanation is that the popular music of the time was aimed at a teenage audience. Another is that soldiers were younger—on average by several years—than during other twentieth-century wars. Whether the song was the Shirelles' "Soldier Boy . . . I'll Be True to You," a #1 hit in 1962, or Tommy Dee's "Goodbye High School—Hello Vietnam" mattered little. Their lyrics sought to connect singers with teenage listeners. It is instructive that the former did not mention Vietnam. In fact, very few songs did until 1965.

A related group of youth-oriented songs addressed the military draft. In the 1960s men were required by the Selective Service to register on their eighteenth birthday. From "Draft Time Blues" to "Drafted Minor," young listeners were reminded that as eighteen to twenty year olds they were old enough to kill but too young to drink or vote in most states.[2] Shortly after the voting age was lowered, "The Power 18" urged the newly enfranchised to use the ballot: "I'm gonna make sure I have a say before I put my damn life on the line." Voting became even more important after the draft "lottery," based solely on one's birthday, was instituted on December 1, 1969. It marked the end to most deferments, among them the II-S for college students.

After the draft was abolished in favor of an all-volunteer military force, songs about duty and service all but disappeared. Teachers might want to ask their students, "What conclusions can be drawn about the generation that came of age in the 1960s? Were they more or less patriotic than young people today? More or less naive?"

Protesting the War

The latter half of the 1960s brought a spate of war-related protest songs. "Political" music, such as "We Shall Overcome," had gained traction with the civil rights movement. Many of its singers, such as Joan Baez and Pete Seeger, quickly became fixtures at antiwar rallies. Links between the civil rights and antiwar movements are explicit in songs such as "Hell No, I Ain't Gonna Go" (1970), which was cowritten and recorded by Matt Jones. Jones was a member of the Student Nonviolent Coordinating Committee (SNCC) and its associated musical group, the Freedom Singers. In the song he says, "I ain't going to Vietnam / I got business in Harlem, Watts and Birmingham." Dr. William Truly Jr.'s "(The Two Wars Of) Old Black Joe" asks how in 1969 two black soldiers who died for their country could be denied burial in their hometown's all-white cemeteries.

A different style of protest song is best exemplified by Country Joe and the Fish's iconic "I-Feel-Like-I'm-Fixin'-to-Die Rag" with its catchphrase, "What are we fighting for? / Don't ask me I don't give a damn / Next stop is Vietnam" (1965). Up-tempo and filled with irony, it was well suited for mass rallies and venues such as Woodstock. A similar type of song, Phil Ochs's "The Draft Dodger Rag," with its theme of getting out of the draft for medical or other reasons, was aimed at high school and/or college age audiences. Still another subcategory pointed out inequities tied to race and socioeconomic class that allowed some young men, the "Fortunate Son[s]" (Creedence Clearwater Revival, #3, 1969), to avoid military service. The impact of these songs continues to be debated. Were the artists who recorded them unpatriotic and doing a disservice to their military counterparts? Or were the songs commenting on a conflict that few who were fighting it really understood?

More than thirty-five songs protest a single event, the May 1970 shooting of four students on the campus of Kent State University. The best known by far is "Ohio" by Crosby, Stills, Nash, and Young. It peaked at #14 that July. A special "Kent State mix" of the song is worth looking for because it includes excerpts of that day's newscasts. Students wanting to learn more about the four young people who died can start by listening to "Sandra, Allison, Jeffrey, and Bill," a record that describes something unique about each victim.

Initially confined to folk and pop music, protest songs cropped up in other genres as well following the January 1968 Tet Offensive. Although Tet represented a military defeat for the enemy, it caused US public opinion to tilt against the war. This made it easier for black artists and rhythm and blues/soul-oriented labels to release antiwar tracks. "War . . . what is it good for? Absolutely nothing" shouted Edwin Starr in the country's #1 hit in August 1970. In 1971 Marvin Gaye's best seller "What's Going On" went to #2 on the Pop charts and Freda Payne's "Bring the Boys Home" went to #3 on the R&B charts while selling over a million copies.

Another new phenomenon was protest from within the military. Several songs with antimilitary and antiwar sentiments were written and recorded by soldiers in uniform. One example is "Bring Our Brothers Home." The singers, collectively known as the Covered Wagon Musicians, were all active-duty soldiers at Mountain Home Air Force Base in Idaho. Protest from within the ranks was encouraged by folk singer Barbara Dane, who called for soldiers to "Join the GI Movement."

Patriotic and Antiprotest Songs

That the messages in protest music were being heard can be inferred from the backlash they created. As early as 1965 Barry McGuire's "Eve of Destruction," was widely banned for allegedly un-American lyrics. It is likely that this unilateral action by radio stations, including the military's American Forces Radio Network, which broadcast music in Vietnam, helped the song become America's #1 hit in September. "Eve of Destruction" also inspired the first "answer song," the Spokesmen's "Dawn of Correction."

To counter musical support for the protest movement, commercial songwriters had been writing patriotic songs since the mid-1960s. By the end of the decade many such songs were morphing into antiprotest songs. For example, Ernest Tubb went from "It's for God, and Country, and You Mom (That's Why I'm Fighting in Vietnam)" (1966) to "It's

America (Love It or Leave It)" (1970). Others, such as Merle Haggard's "Okie from Muskogee" (#41 Pop but #1 Country in 1969), gave voice to middle America's so-called silent majority, contrasting its values with those of "the hippies in San Francisco."

A great deal of musical anger was directed against the young men who refused to perform military service by avoiding the draft as conscientious objectors, evading it by burning their draft cards, or leaving the country. Draft card burners, especially, were targeted in antiprotest songs. The most (in)famous example is Victor Lundberg's "An Open Letter to My Teenage Son." It quoted a father telling his off-spring that if he burned his draft card he should burn his birth certificate, too, because "from that moment on I have no son." The song made the national Top 10 in December 1967. It is telling that the number of songs about draft card burners exceeds the number of those who were actually charged with the crime. Altogether, the Justice Department only brought charges against 50 young men, of whom 40 were convicted.[3] The total number of Americans who were accused of dodging the draft is around 210,000. Verlin Speeks's "The Red White & Blue" (1972) advised draft card burners that they should leave the country and run to Canada or Sweden, a step taken by about 30,000 young men.

The Peace Movement

Whether the peace movement had any impact on the war is a matter of opinion. After the first nationwide Moratorium Day on November 15, 1969, President Richard Nixon was famously quoted as saying, "As far as this kind of activity is concerned, we expect it, how-ever under no circumstances will I be affected whatever by it."[4] Nixon notwithstanding, music was integral to giving the peace movement a strong voice.

The song that would become the anthem for the peace movement had its genesis in a Montreal hotel room. John Lennon and his new wife, Yoko Ono, were on their "Bed-In for Peace" honeymoon when they and group of celebrities recorded "Give Peace a Chance." The song had already peaked on America's Pop charts in 1969 when Pete Seeger led demonstrators in singing its chorus at the Washington, D.C., Moratorium Day ceremonies. From that point until the war's end it was sure to be sung at every peace rally. The secondary title of Buffy Sainte-Marie's 1971 "Moratorium (Bring Our Brothers Home)" clarified the movement's overriding concern. Other songs calling for the troops' return included Skeeter Davis's "When You Gonna Bring Our Soldiers Home" (1970, B-side of a Country chart single) and Pete Seeger's "If You Love Your Uncle Sam (Bring Them Home)" (1965). Seeger's song was revived in 2003 with updated lyrics to reflect the fighting in Iraq and Afghanistan.

Country voices became more vocal when the call to bring the boys home was refocused on American prisoners of war (POWs). As early as 1971 "Prisoner of War" by Norma Jean Carpenter and Bobby Adams had expressed the hope that God would "bring all the prisoners home from North Vietnam." In 1973 some 1,350 Americans were listed as missing in action (MIA) or known to be POWs. President Nixon made the return of POWs the keystone of any peace accord. When the Paris Peace Accords were finally signed in 1973, 591 men were repatriated during Operation Homecoming. Their return is captured in Billy Holeman's "Prisoner of War (Welcome Back Home)."

In-Country Songs

News coming out of Vietnam was carefully controlled in much the same way as was the news that was shared with troops by way of the American Forces Vietnam Network (as noted in the film *Good Morning Vietnam*). Similarly AFVN had a "no play" list that included the previously mentioned "Eve of Destruction" and, allegedly, the Animals' "We Gotta Get Out of This Place" (1965). What couldn't be censored was the music soldiers wrote and performed outside of official channels. Fortunately a good bit of it was preserved thanks to the widespread availability of tape recorders.

Many such songs were written in "GI" talk, a highly specialized language requiring knowledge of terms, units, battles, geography, and more. Because it was often crude and lacked the political correctness of US-produced songs, GI talk captures a perspective missing from commercial records. Songs such as "Tchepone" and "Jolly Green" are about places, events, and experiences that were real to combat soldiers, nurses, and aviators but so far removed from life in the United States as to be incomprehensible to people at home. Listen, for example, to Lt. Hershel Gober's "Six Klicks" (1969), which describes the experience of "walkin' through Charlie's land." It makes clear that men who went out on daily patrols were in constant danger from booby traps, the jungle terrain, and the often unseen enemy. Bill Ellis, "the singing rifleman,"

Donut Dollie Emily Strange entertains troops of the Ninth Infantry Division at Tiger's Lair, Mekong Delta, circa 1969. (courtesy of Emily Strange)

described the tedium of being a combat infantryman on "Grunt" (1967). These four songs, taken together, paint a far more realistic picture of soldiering than most war films.

As for crude, few songs compare to "Napalm Sticks to Kids" (1972). One of its verses is "Flying low and looking mean / See that family by the stream / Drop some nape and hear 'em scream." According to the liner notes of the album, men attached to the First Air Cavalry wrote the lyrics, and "each person made a verse about an incident in which he had taken part."[5]

In-country songs performed or written by women are rare. One exception is "Incoming." Written by Emily Strange, an American Red Cross donut dollie with the Ninth Infantry Division and Mobile Riverine Force in Vietnam (1968–69), and Barbara Hager of the US Army Special Services, the song provides insight into what it was like to be a female in the field.

The War's Aftermath

Another new category of Vietnam War music was songs about its effects on those who fought and those who stayed at home. A few were written during the war but far more, many by Vietnam veterans, date from the 1980s forward. A recurring theme was a soldier returning home with a physical disability. An example is Bill Withers's "I Can't Write Left-Handed" (1973). The ready availability of various drugs in Vietnam also meant that many soldiers returned with drug dependencies. John Prine's "Sam Stone" (1971) is one example of this type of song.

It wasn't until after they were home, often for years, that some soldiers fell victim to a host of illnesses that would eventually be linked to their exposure to the chemical defoliant known as Agent Orange, so named for the colored stripe on the fifty-gallon barrel in which it was shipped. "The Agent Orange Song," with its line "They killed me in Vietnam and I didn't even know," is sung by Jim Walktendonk, one of thousands of vets affected by the herbicide. Both of Walktendonk's children were born with birth defects he attributes to his exposure to the chemical.

Another aftereffect that showed up after the men and women had returned home was post-traumatic stress disorder (PTSD). It could be triggered by a loud noise that had men believing they were "Still in Saigon" (Charlie Daniels Band, 1982) or leave them generally fearful and distrustful. In the song "Shell Shock PTSD," Vincent Gabriel, an "11 Bravo" infantryman, blames his divorce and losing his home on his second Vietnam tour, after which his "life came undone."

Vietnam also took a toll on the wives and families of service members. If servicemen returned home alive it was often as changed individuals. Such is the case in Arlene Harden's "Congratulations (You Sure Made a Man Out of Him)" (1971). Similarly themed songs about husbands who died include "I Should Be Proud" by Martha Reeves and the Vandellas (1970) and Steve Goodman's "The Ballad of Penny Evans" (1972).

For millions of Americans the Vietnam Veterans Memorial, "The Wall" and its more than fifty-eight thousand names of men and women who paid the ultimate price, symbolizes the war's aftermath. Even more so, however, "Every name's a father or a husband or a son / Or a daughter or a brother or a cousin to someone / Or a name might be a classmate or a friend you may recall" ("The Wall" by Michael McCann, 1997). What those names do not convey is the impact of those deaths on the children left behind, many of whom never got to know their fathers. Pat Garvey's "Sons and Daughters" (1990) tells their story.

Depicting a Vietnamese Perspective

A small number of recorded songs by American artists reflect the war through the eyes of the Vietnamese. Such songs provide insight into how the people whose freedom was purportedly being protected were impacted. This is especially true from 1954 to 1965 when American involvement was intended to support the government and peoples of South Vietnam.

Hershel Gober's "Picture of a Man" (1966) shows the conflict from the perspective of the brave Vietnamese man "who defends his home time and again." Barbara Dane's "Ballad of the Unknown Soldier" is about a member of the National Liberation Front (NLF), fighting both the South Vietnamese and US governments. In Vietnam vet Bill Homan's "Quang Tri City" (1973) a South Vietnamese survivor expresses only bitterness against those same forces: "I'm trying to free my people from all the planes that are killing all of my children and destroying all my fields." Gober's song was released as a single, initially around the time that fellow active duty soldier Barry Sadler's song popularized the Green Berets. An interesting question for students might be "What if Gober's, not Sadler's, song had become 1966's face of the war?

Songs also address the direct and indirect impact of the war on Vietnamese children. Yanah was inspired to record "The Girl in the Picture" by Nick Ut's photo of naked, nine-year-old Kim Phuc running for her life after a napalm attack. The photo won a Pulitzer Prize and angered President Nixon, who believed it to be a "fake." Thom Parrott's "Hole in the Ground" is based on a newspaper story about a Vietnamese boy who for some candy bars leads US soldiers to a tunnel where his father, a Viet Cong soldier, is hiding. When the boy goes back the next day the tunnel has been blown up and his father is dead.

When Saigon fell in 1975, a mass exodus from the now Communist-controlled country began. The most frequent escape route, by water, created a group of refugees sometimes called "Boat People." Some eventually made their way to the United States where they settled in communities such as those around "Galveston Bay." Bruce Springsteen's song is an apt postscript to the war and its lingering legacy of hate and distrust but also eventual reconciliation. Another song tracks a Vietnamese refugee family through the eyes of its daughter, born in Europe. "Hello Vietnam" is sung by Vietnamese Belgian singer Pham Quynh Anh, a nineteen year old who knows of Vietnam only through the stories of her refugee parents. Appropriately enough, it is the story of a young girl who longs to visit her ancestral homeland and be told about her color, her hair, and her little feet.

Although they fall outside the scope of this essay, there are numerous Vietnamese songs about what today is called the American War. They can be found among the compositions of Trinh Cong Son, dubbed the Bob Dylan of Vietnam by Joan Baez for his war-related songs, and on albums such as "Vietnam Will Win! Liberation Songs of the Vietnamese People Recorded in Vietnam" (Paredon Records, 1971). The latter includes an insert with song translations from Vietnamese to English.

Who Was Right?

In 1964, before the Vietnam conflict inspired broad protest, folk songs were already questioning the rightness of war. When Tom Paxton asked "What Did You Learn in School Today?," a little boy answers, "I learned that soldiers never die . . . and that war is not so bad / I learned of the great ones we have had." Meanwhile Bob Dylan wrote that America had always gone into battle "With God on Our Side." Nevertheless he concluded, "If God's on our side He'll stop the next war."

No group of songs (by last count at least fifty) better illustrates Americans' divergent views on the war than those dealing with army lieutenant William Calley and My Lai. Official records confirm that on March 16, 1968, some five hundred Vietnamese, mostly old men, women, and children, were killed by American troops at My Lai. As Calley stood trial for murder, the "Battle Hymn of Lt. Calley" by "C" Company featuring Terry Nelson (1971) pictured him as "a [heroic] soldier who never left his gun." In contrast, Thom Parrott's "Pinkville Helicopter" (1970)— Pinkville was the code name for a cluster of hamlets that included My Lai—painted Calley and his men as wanton killers. Parrott's song identified CW3 Hugh Thompson, a helicopter pilot who attempted to stop the killings, as the only hero. When a court-martial eventually convicted Calley of killing twenty-two civilians in the massacre, many questioned the guilty verdict and a cover story in *Time* magazine asked, "Who shares the guilt?" President Nixon eventually reduced Calley's life sentence, and he ended up serving only three years under house arrest.

Over the past thirty years veterans have written the vast majority of Vietnam War–related songs. It is they who continue to struggle with events and issues that are distant history to most Americans. It is important, therefore, to find musical examples that indicate "coming to terms with" or other signs of closure. Two songs that do so are by vets John Black and Michael J. Martin. Black's "Dr. Fall" (2003) concludes with" "We're okay / It's taken quite awhile to shake it all / But we did it, Dr. Fall." Relegating the war to history is Martin's recommendation. His "Time to Lay It Down [aka The Wall]" (1989), sung with Tim Holiday, is based on a note and simple gold wedding band left behind at the Vietnam Memorial. The note read, "I took this ring off a dead Viet Cong soldier. I've been carrying it for 18 years. It's time to lay it down. This boy is no longer my enemy." Martin's message to his fellow vets is simple: "A good grunt don't carry nothin' he don't need. It's time to lighten our load."[6]

The seventy-eight songs mentioned in this essay, written and recorded over a fifty-year period, are but the tip of the proverbial iceberg. They provide new, sometimes unique perspectives on the war that refuses to go away. They open the door for students to learn from the songs targeting youths, commercial songs from across the political spectrum, and songs written and performed by the soldiers who fought the war and look back on it as veterans. As always, teachers will want to think about what their larger goals and objectives are for their classes, but they should be confident that they now have access to some engaging primary sources that they can use to introduce topics, make comparisons with other sources, or cap discussions. Once they've made the larger pedagogical decisions, all that's left to do is hook up the speakers (or ask students to put on their headphones) and start listening.

Listed below in alphabetical order are the seventy-eight songs referenced in the text. Each is paired with an artist. In instances where more than one artist recorded the song, the most easily accessible version is noted. Many of the songs are on the boxed set *Next Stop Is Vietnam*, which includes song lyrics. The remainder can be found on the Internet, many as YouTube videos. A list of more than 4,900 Vietnam War–related tracks is at http://lasalle.edu/digital/Keesing/Vietnam_on_Record.pdf.

SONG AND ARTIST INFORMATION

"Agent Orange Song, The," Jim Walktendonk (Booneytunes Jukebox)
"Ballad of Ho Chi Minh," Ewan McColl (YouTube)
"Ballad of Penny Evans," Steve Goodman (YouTube)
"Ballad of the Green Berets," SSgt. Barry Sadler (*Next Stop Is Vietnam*)
"Ballad of the Unknown Soldier," Barbara Dane (YouTube)

"Battle Hymn of Lt. Calley," "C" Company (*Next Stop Is Vietnam*)

"Battle Hymn of the Republic of Vietnam," Unknown Artist (*Next Stop Is Vietnam*)

"Boat People," Dick Maloney (YouTube)

"Born on the 4th of July," Tom Paxton (*Next Stop Is Vietnam*)

"Bring Our Brothers Home," Covered Wagon Musicians (YouTube)

"Bring the Boys Home," Freda Payne (*Next Stop Is Vietnam*)

"Congratulations (You Sure Made a Man Out of Him)," Arlene Harden (*Next Stop Is Vietnam*)

"Conscientious Objector," Keith Everett (*Next Stop Is Vietnam*)

"Danny Fernandez," Eddie Harrison (*Next Stop Is Vietnam*)

"Dawn of Correction," The Spokesmen (*Next Stop Is Vietnam*)

"Dean Rusk Song, The," Bill Frederick (YouTube)

"Dr. Fall," John Black (*Next Stop Is Vietnam*)

"Draft Dodger Rag," Phil Ochs (*Next Stop Is Vietnam*)

"Draft Time Blues," The Midnight Sons (*Next Stop Is Vietnam*)

"Drafted Minor, A," Gary Laster (YouTube)

"Eve of Destruction," Barry McGuire (*Next Stop Is Vietnam*)

"Fortunate Son," Creedence Clearwater Revival (YouTube)

"Galveston Bay," Bruce Springsteen (*Next Stop Is Vietnam*)

"Girl in the Picture (Napalm Girl)," Yanah (*Next Stop Is Vietnam*)

"Girl Next Door (Combat Nurse)," Country Joe McDonald (*Next Stop Is Vietnam*)

"Give Peace a Chance," Plastic Ono Band (*Next Stop Is Vietnam*)

"Goodbye High School (Hello Viet Nam)," Tommy Dee (*Next Stop Is Vietnam*)

"Grunt," Bill Ellis (*Next Stop Is Vietnam*)

"Hell No, I Ain't Gonna Go," Matt Jones (*Next Stop Is Vietnam*)

"Hello Vietnam," Quyanh Pham Anh (YouTube)

"Hole in the Ground," Thom Parrott (YouTube)

"I Ain't Marching Anymore," Phil Ochs (*Next Stop Is Vietnam*)

"I Can't Write Left-Handed," Bill Withers (YouTube)

"I-Feel-Like-I'm-Fixin'-to-Die Rag," Country Joe & The Fish (*Next Stop Is Vietnam*)

"I Should Be Proud," Martha & the Vandellas (*Next Stop Is Vietnam*)

"If You Love Your Uncle Sam (Bring 'Em Home)," Pete Seeger (*Next Stop Is Vietnam*)

"Incoming," Emily Strange & Barb Hager (YouTube)

"It's America, Love It or Leave It," Ernest Tubb (*Next Stop Is Vietnam*)

"It's for God, and Country, and You Mom," Ernest Tubb (*Next Stop Is Vietnam*)

"Join the GI Movement," Barbara Dane (YouTube)

"Jolly Green," Bull Durham (*Next Stop Is Vietnam*)

"Lottery, The," Rochelle Rosenthal (YouTube)

"Lyndon Johnson Told the Nation," Tom Paxton (*Next Stop Is Vietnam*)

"Marine's Ballad," Staff Sgt. Bob Lay (*Next Stop Is Vietnam*)
"Mind Your Manners, Boys," Jacqueline Sharpe (*Next Stop Is Vietnam*)
"Moratorium (Bring Our Brothers Home)," Buffy Sainte-Marie (YouTube)
"Napalm Sticks to Kids," Covered Wagon Musicians (*Next Stop Is Vietnam*)
"Ohio (Kent State Mix)," Crosby, Stills, Nash & Young (YouTube)
"Okie from Muskogee," Merle Haggard (*Next Stop Is Vietnam*)
"Open Letter to My Teenage Son," Victor Lundberg (*Next Stop Is Vietnam*)
"Picture of a Man," Hershel Gober (YouTube)
"Pinkville Helicopter," Thom Parrott (*Next Stop Is Vietnam*)
"Power 18, The," Mustang (YouTube)
"Prisoner of War," Norma Jean Carpenter & Bobby Adams (*Next Stop Is Vietnam*)
"Prisoner of War (Welcome Back Home)," Billy Holeman (*Next Stop Is Vietnam*)
"Quang Tri City," Bill Homans (*Next Stop Is Vietnam*)
"Red, White & Blue, The," Verlin "Red" Speeks (*Next Stop Is Vietnam*)
"Sam Stone," John Prine (*Next Stop Is Vietnam*)
"Sandra Allison Jeffrey and Bill," Evoloution (YouTube)
"Shell-Shock PTSD," Blind Albert (*Next Stop Is Vietnam*)
"Six Klicks," Hershel Gober (*Next Stop Is Vietnam*)
"Soldier Boy," The Shirelles (*Next Stop Is Vietnam*)
"Sons and Daughters," Pat Garvey (*Next Stop Is Vietnam*)
"Still in Saigon," Charlie Daniels Band (*Next Stop Is Vietnam*)
"Talking Vietnam," Phil Ochs (*Next Stop Is Vietnam*)
"Tchepone," Toby Hughes (*Next Stop Is Vietnam*)
"Time to Lay It Down," Michael J. Martin & Tim Holiday (*Next Stop Is Vietnam*)
"(Two Wars of) Old Black Joe, The," Dr. William Truly Jr. (*Next Stop Is Vietnam*)
"Wall, The," Michael McCann (*Next Stop Is Vietnam*)
"War," Edwin Starr (*Next Stop Is Vietnam*)
"We Gotta Get Out of This Place," The Animals (YouTube)
"What Did You Learn in School Today," Tom Paxton (*Next Stop Is Vietnam*)
"What's Going On," Marvin Gaye (*Next Stop Is Vietnam*)
"When a Soldier Makes It Home," Arlo Guthrie (YouTube)
"When You Gonna Bring Our Soldiers Home," Skeeter Davis (YouTube)
"White Boots Marching in a Yellow Land," Phil Ochs (YouTube)
"With God on Our Side," Bob Dylan & Joan Baez (YouTube)
"Women on the Wall," John Black (*Next Stop Is Vietnam*)

NOTES

1. Sigmund Spaeth, *The Facts of Life in Popular Song* (New York: Whittlesay House, 1934).
2. The legal drinking age varied from state to state. During the Vietnam War, Americans could not vote in most states until they were twenty-one. The

federal voting age was reduced to eighteen by the Voting Rights Act Amendment on January 1, 1971.

3. Lawrence M. Baskir and William A. Strauss, *Chance and Circumstance: The Draft, the War and the Vietnam Generation* (New York: Alfred A. Knopf, 1978).

4. "1969 Year in Review: War Protests," http://www.upi.com/Audio/Year_in_Review/Events-of-1969/War-Protests/12303189849225-3/.

5. Liner notes, Covered Wagon Musicians, "We Say No to Your War!," Paradon 1015, 1972.

6. Liner notes, Michael J. Martin and Tim Holiday, "Time to Lay It Down," MJMusic, 1988.

KEY RESOURCES

Andresen, Lee. *Battle Notes . . . Music of the Vietnam War*. 2nd ed. Superior, WI: Savage Press, 2003.

Cleveland, Les. *Dark Laughter: War in Song and Popular Culture*. Westport, CT: Praeger, 1994.

Dane, Barbara, and Irwin Silber. *The Vietnam Songbook*. New York: The Guardian, 1969.

Fish, Lydia M. "Songs of Americans in the Vietnam War." http://faculty.buffalostate.edu/fishlm/folksongs/americansongs.htm.

Franklin, H. Bruce, ed. *The Vietnam War in American Stories, Songs, and Poems*. Boston: Bedford Books, 1996.

Keesing, Hugo A. *Next Stop Is Vietnam: The War on Record, 1961–2008*. Germany: Bear Family Records, 2010.

Lynskey, Dorian. *33 Revolutions per Minute: A History of Protest Songs, from Billie Holiday to Green Day*. New York: Ecco, 2011.

Perone, James. *Songs of the Vietnam Conflict*. Westport, CT: Greenwood Press, 2001.

Van Rijn, Guido. *President Johnson's Blues: African-American Blues and Gospel Songs on LBJ, Martin Luther King, Robert Kennedy, and Vietnam, 1963–1968*. Netherlands: Agram Blues Book, 2009.

———. *The Nixon and Ford Blues: African-American Blues and Gospel Songs on Vietnam, Watergate, Civil Rights, and Inflation, 1969–1976*. Netherlands: Agram Blues Book, 2011.

Whitburn, Joel. *Top Pop Singles: Billboard, 1955–2006*. Menomonee Falls, WI: Record Research, 2007.

Willman, Chris. *Rednecks & Bluenecks: The Politics of Country Music*. New York: The New Press, 2005.

"We Must Bear a Good Deal of Responsibility for It"

The White House Tapes and the War in Vietnam

MITCHELL B. LERNER

Americans seeking to understand (and teachers seeking to teach) a particular presidential administration or government policy rarely suffer from a shortage of primary materials from which to seek enlightenment. The sheer volume of documents produced by the American government can be overwhelming, especially if they are combined with materials from informal advisers or foreign officials who were relevant to policy making. Contemporary accounts of events by journalists and other insiders can provide additional insights, as can the spate of memoirs and oral histories that inevitably emerge from members of the administration. Yet, for just a few decades in the Cold War era, a window opened into presidential policy making unlike anything that had preceded it. Starting in 1940, American presidents began, secretly and sporadically, taping many of their phone conversations and meetings. These tapes remained largely inaccessible to the public for decades; indeed, until 1973 only a handful of people in the world even knew of their existence. Over the last few decades, however, the tapes have slowly been opened to public scrutiny, offering both a fascinating record of American history and a virtually unequaled teaching resource for those who cover modern American history in general, and the Vietnam War in particular.[1]

Although American presidents Franklin D. Roosevelt, Dwight Eisenhower, and Harry Truman each taped a small number of conversations, John F. Kennedy was the first to do so with regularity. In 1962 Kennedy ordered the Secret Service to install hidden recording devices throughout the White House and the Executive Mansion.[2] A number of hidden microphones were installed, including two in the drapes of the White House Cabinet Room and two in the Oval Office itself (one inside Kennedy's desk and the other in a coffee table on the other side of the room). The microphones were activated by the push of an easily accessible button; they then carried the conversations to a number of reel-to-reel tape recorders stationed in the basements of the White House and the Executive Mansion. Although JFK's motivation remains unclear, historians have generally assumed that he planned to use the tapes to assist with his memoirs and other postpresidential functions since he made no effort to listen to them or have them transcribed while he was in office. Regardless of the reason, Kennedy used the system frequently until his assassination, eventually producing almost three hundred hours of recorded conversations.

When Lyndon Johnson inherited the presidency in November 1963, the taping system became both more elaborate and more extensively used.[3] Johnson seemed to have two general motives: first, to maintain a record of the political deals that he made in the course of his duties; and, second, to assist with his presidential memoirs after he left the White House. His system carried conversations from numerous hidden microphones to machines that recorded them by cutting grooves in plastic discs called dictabelts. The system was first installed on LBJ's Oval Office phone line. When he wanted a conversation recorded, Johnson signaled one of his secretaries who pressed a switch at her desk to activate the system. Soon Johnson installed recording devices on the phones in the Old Executive Office Building, the White House master bedroom, and even the LBJ Ranch in Texas, where he frequently vacationed. In 1968 he also began taping Cabinet Room meetings, likely with an eye toward establishing a record of his peace efforts in Vietnam. This system relied on a standard reel-to-reel recording machine and eight tiny microphones hidden underneath the Cabinet Room table, which Johnson could activate with the touch of a button. Other dictabelt machines were installed in the White House Situation Room, and in the

White House Communications Center. The Johnson tapes are quite extensive, totaling over 9,400 telephone conversations that comprise almost 650 hours.

Johnson had the system removed just before he left office, with the exception of the components at the LBJ Ranch. Within a few years, however, his successor would install his own.[4] Richard Nixon was informed of Johnson's taping practices by FBI director J. Edgar Hoover even before he was sworn into office (his chief of staff later discovered the remnants of one of the systems in a closet in his White House office).[5] Initially, Nixon was uninterested in taping, but in 1971 he reversed his position, especially after Johnson informed him that tapes had been extremely helpful to him in writing his memoirs.[6] Like his predecessors, Nixon seems to have viewed the tapes as a way to preserve a record of behind-the-scenes deals, as well as a means of providing him with details that he could use to defend his record and write his memoirs; for Nixon, whose distrust of the bureaucracy was such that he rarely communicated details to others and tried to keep attendance at meetings limited to as few people as possible, such a record promised to be particularly helpful. Accordingly, Bob Haldeman, Nixon's chief of staff, and one of his aides, Alexander Butterfield, directed the Secret Service's installation of a new recording system in early 1971. Unlike previous models, the one they selected was voice-activated since, Haldeman noted, Nixon was "far too inept with machinery" to operate a manual system.[7] Butterfield also ordered the agents overseeing the job to maintain no paperwork about the installation and to tell no one of its existence.[8] They installed numerous recording stations, including ones in the Oval Office, the Cabinet Room, the Executive Office Building office and sitting room, various White House telephones, and the presidential retreat at Camp David, Maryland. In the end the Nixon system produced approximately 3,700 hours of tapes from February 1971 to July 1973, when the taping was stopped just a few days after Butterfield admitted to its existence before the Senate Watergate Committee.[9] The system itself was removed in 1974, after Nixon's resignation.

Even after Butterfield's revelation, it was decades before the bulk of the tapes were made available to researchers. Prior to the passage of the Presidential Records Act of 1978, presidents had a great deal of latitude in determining what was their personal property, and each White House occupant considered the tapes to fit into this category, and thus not subject to federal regulation. Butterfield's admission, however, sparked pressure for them to be released to the public. The John F. Kennedy Library soon formed a screening committee to consider whether and how to disseminate the tapes, which were still under the legal control of the Kennedy family estate. In 1976 the family followed the committee's recommendations and deeded them to the government, and the library staff began organizing and archiving them under the direction of the National Archives and Records Administration (NARA).

The Johnson tapes followed a similar pattern. LBJ's tapes remained untouched until a week after his death in January 1973, when one of his longest-serving aides deeded the Johnson Library control of a collection of recordings and transcripts, with the qualification that Johnson wanted them to remain sealed for fifty years after his death.[10] The library staff began slowly organizing and cataloging the tapes. However, the declassification process was sped along by Congress, which, in the wake of the controversial movie *JFK*, required in 1992 that all records maintained by the federal government relevant to the assassination be opened to public and congressional scrutiny. By 2009 the phone conversations had been entirely released, except for a small number of conversations excised for security or other legal reasons. The meeting tapes began to emerge in 2011.

The release of the Nixon tapes was more controversial. Butterfield's revelation sparked a series of subpoenas from the House Judiciary Committee and the Watergate special prosecutor. Nixon, claiming executive privilege, rejected the requests until a unanimous Supreme Court decision in 1974 forced him to release almost forty hours of tapes, the contents of which incriminated him in the Watergate cover-up and helped drive him from the presidency. After his resignation, Congress passed the Presidential Recordings and Materials Preservation Act, placing his tapes under the control of NARA and ordering the opening to the public of all materials related to the abuse of presidential powers "at the earliest release date."[11] Nixon and his estate continued to fight for control, however, and the tapes remained locked away, essentially in limbo with a few exceptions, mostly related to Watergate.[12] In 1996 an agreement was finally reached allowing NARA to release all tapes related to "abuses of governmental powers," and beginning the process of opening the rest of the tapes, except for those that met certain limited criteria for exemption. Currently almost twenty-five hundred hours of tapes have been declassified and released.

Despite their many obvious benefits, the tapes do have their short-comings in the classroom. Teachers do not have to be reminded, although students may have to be, that they reveal just one part of a larger and more complicated decision-making puzzle. They also need to be re-minded that presidents can, to some extent, manipulate this media. Kennedy and Johnson could choose which conversations to tape and which to ignore (although evidence suggests that they often left the machines running without realizing it). The presidents also knew they were being taped, but other participants did not. Students listening to the tapes can rarely detect sarcasm; they do not know if the speaker may simply be thinking out loud or even saying something for the benefit of someone else in the room; and they do not usually know what went on before the conversation that may be impacting the decision-making process.

Even when there is no conscious manipulation, the nature of the medium invites problems. The systems had constant problems with volume, often leaving one side of a conversation inaudible; they also sometimes picked up interference from nearby phone lines and other devices. Meeting room tapes are usually harder to understand than phone tapes, since meetings often involved many different voices, sometimes all talking at once, and more background noise. Casual references and nicknames used between friends often leave the listener befuddled; anyone trying to eavesdrop on LBJ's discussions about the 1965 Dominican Crisis would meet "J.B.," "Colonel C.," "Columbo," "The Bang-Bangs," and the "Baseball Players" (so nicknamed because their politics were "in left field"). Inadvertent background noise, such as that coming from the ticking clock that Nixon kept on his desk or the loud air conditioning in the White House Cabinet Room, along with many other complicating factors make some conversations nearly impossible to decipher. Some of the resulting problems have been amusing, albeit unimportant, such as when Johnson's secretary transcribed her boss's lament that he had to meet "A pack of them bastards," rather than correctly as "the Pakistani Ambassador," or when an early version of a Nixon transcript incorrectly had him calling Judge John Sirica "A god-damned wop," rather than praising him as the kind of "judge I want." In other cases, though, the difficulty in understanding specific words and phrases have led to more significant problems of historical interpretation. The Cuban Missile Crisis tapes in particular have generated fierce disputes. Did Kennedy say, at an

October 27, 1962, meeting, that the Soviets would not pull the missiles out of Cuba until they got some "compensation" or some "conversation"? Did Secretary of Defense Robert McNamara suggest "we call off these air strikes tonight" or "we call up these air squadrons tonight"? Vietnam tapes have offered similar problems. In a July 1965 conversation between LBJ and former president Eisenhower, Johnson lamented that escalating the war would cost the United States many allies; Eisenhower's response has been reported as both "We would still have the Australians. And our own convictions" and "We would still have the Australians and the Koreans," two very different sentiments.[13] Despite these problems, however, the tapes remain a vital historical resource, one that can enhance both the classroom and the historical record of the Vietnam War.

Teachers looking to integrate this resource into their Vietnam curricula might begin with the tapes from the Kennedy White House, especially those from late 1963 when the administration began to reconsider its future in Vietnam. Perhaps the most heated debate among scholars regarding this period centers on the question of the strength of Kennedy's commitment, as many of his defenders have insisted that he planned to remove almost all American forces from Vietnam after the 1964 presidential election.[14] Kennedy, in this depiction, recognized the potential trouble that lay ahead and would never have been dragged into the morass that entrapped his successor. On the surface there appears to be some merit to this argument. In October 1963 the president accepted a proposal by McNamara to remove one thousand American troops at the end of 1963, which the defense secretary envisioned as the first step toward a total withdrawal; "We need a way to get out of Vietnam," he told Kennedy in a critical meeting on October 2, "This is a way of doing it."[15]

And yet the tapes suggest that the reality is more complicated than it first appears. Kennedy's October 1963 decision was made at a time of guarded optimism, when McNamara and other officials thought the United States could begin removing its troops because of perceived improvements in the South Vietnamese armed forces. Yet, when Lyndon Johnson made his fateful decision to escalate, conditions on the ground no longer justified such optimism. Would Kennedy still have withdrawn American troops in 1965, as he had planned, knowing that it might have led to an American defeat? The tapes, including this conversation with General Maxwell Taylor in October 1963, suggest that he was less committed to the withdrawal plan than his defenders suggest.

> TAYLOR: I will just say this: that we talked to 174 officers, Vietnamese and U.S., and in the case of the U.S. [officers], I always asked the question, "When can you finish this job in the sense that you will reduce this insurgency to little more than sporadic incidents." Inevitably, except for the Delta, they would say, "[19]64 would be ample time." I realize that's not necessarily . . . I assume there's no major new factors entering [*unclear*]. I realize that—
> PRESIDENT KENNEDY: Well, let's say it anyway. Then [19]65, if it doesn't work out, we'll get a new date . . .[16]

The president expressed similar sentiments at a meeting that same evening, noting he had concerns about publically committing to the withdrawal of a thousand men since the war might turn bad; "My only reservation about it," he admitted "is that it commits us to a kind of . . . if the war doesn't continue to go well, it'll look like we were overly optimistic, and I don't—I'm not sure we—I'd like to know what benefit we get out at this time, announcing a thousand."[17] Other conversations convey the same idea; even McNamara acknowledged that he supported the plan on the assumption that even if the military campaign had not proven victorious by late 1965, "we believe we can train the Vietnamese to take over the essential functions."[18] What was left unanswered was whether the plan would still be implemented if that belief proved unfounded. The tapes thus certainly show that Kennedy wanted an American withdrawal, but they seem skeptical of the assertion that he was willing to accept an American defeat in order to obtain it. Teachers trying to convey the way American presidents were dragged down a disastrous path toward war even while they hoped to avoid it need only to play a few of the tapes from early October 1963 to make this point clearly.

Another critical element of the war from the Kennedy period was the 1963 coup against South Vietnamese president Ngo Dinh Diem. Diem's ouster (and murder) by South Vietnamese military leaders was a critical moment in the war, most historians agree, as it opened the door to governmental instability and factionalism, which helped persuade American officials to escalate the US role in order to prevent a complete collapse. Publicly, the White House denied any involvement in the coup (although few officials denied that they were pleased by the removal of the obstinate Diem). Still, no classroom discussion about America's role in this vital event would be complete without JFK's taped comments from November 4, 1963, in which he admits, "I feel that we must bear a good deal of responsibility for it [the coup], beginning with our cable of early August in which we suggested the coup. In my judgment that wire was badly drafted, it should never have been sent on a Saturday. I should not have given my consent to it without a roundtable conference at which McNamara and Taylor could have presented their views."[19] Numerous tapes prior to this lament demonstrate why he felt some responsibility, as a number of conversations from August 26–29 in particular reveal that many administration officials were aware of an impending plot and generally favored it.[20] Kennedy, the tapes reveal, was hesitant to endorse the coup, but his ambiguous feelings and the administration's internal division on the question generated mixed signals, which the Vietnamese plotters took as a green light to proceed. And anyone listening to JFK acknowledge some responsibility cannot help but be struck by the genuine sense of regret that seems to run throughout the president's powerful commentary.

Interestingly, the Diem coup also clearly reveals some of the limitations of the tapes, as numerous conversations after the event are highly misleading when considered in isolation. Perhaps the most famous such tape is from February 1, 1966, when Johnson unloaded his frustration about Vietnam to Senator Eugene McCarthy: "But they started with me on Diem, you remember? . . . [That] he was corrupt and he ought to be killed. So we killed him. We all got together and got a goddamn bunch of thugs and we went in and assassinated him."[21] Richard Nixon would make a similar claim five years later, exploding to Reverend Billy Graham that Kennedy had "started the damn thing! He killed Diem."[22] Such comments attracted much attention from the general public and the American media, as they seemingly offered proof of American complicity in arranging the murder of a foreign head of state, one who was at least a nominal ally. And yet those looking at the documentary evidence recognize that these were merely emotional laments that did not reflect reality. The record is clear; the Kennedy administration itself had not killed Diem. Students listening only to these conversations and not integrating the larger record, in this case as with so many others, will thus emerge with an incomplete and misleading picture.

Other issues from the Kennedy years have attracted less notice but still offer good classroom materials. For example, the tapes offer an interesting glimpse into the administration's views of the media coverage of the war, with most officials lamenting what they saw as biased and unfairly negative assessments. "The Vietnamese government loathes them [American reporters] equally," General Earle Wheeler informed JFK in a February 1962 conversation. "And this is based upon the feeling that they write only the bad and not the good about what goes on in Vietnam, and as they say, there is much good to be reported, and I would agree with this."[23] This concern with the media was so extreme that the White House, another conversation revealed, was willing to "discipline" soldiers who gave reporters descriptions of battles that deviated from the official line.[24] Other tapes reveal the bellicosity of some of JFK's military advisers, who often pushed him to take a stronger stand in Vietnam in much the same way they did against the missiles in Cuba. "The Vietcong are not bleeding in this war," Wheeler told the president. "The South Vietnamese are bleeding . . . in other words, they are suffering sizable losses, but the losses suffered by the Vietcong are negligible. . . . [The United States needs to] let the blood that we feel needs to be let in order to make Ho Chi Minh recognize that he can't fight this war for free."[25] Both of these issues, press freedom and the civilian/military relationship during wartime, offer the potential to arouse passionate discussion within the classroom.

Although the Kennedy tapes offer many valuable tools for teaching the early years of the war, those from the Johnson years have attracted the most public attention and offer some of the best teaching materials overall. Perhaps the most interesting material from the Johnson tapes relates to the question of motivation. The early historical literature (and general contemporary memory) holds that an overconfident LBJ escalated American involvement convinced that victory was inevitable, secure in his belief that, although some short-term resistance was to be expected, the massive power of the United States would soon overwhelm a backward and somewhat primitive enemy. This portrayal, however, hardly squares with the Lyndon Johnson who spoke with National Security Advisor McGeorge Bundy on March 2, 1964.

BUNDY: What is your own internal thinking on this, Mr. President: that we've just got to stick on this middle course as long as there's any possible hope and—

> JOHNSON: I just can't believe that we can't take 15,000 advisors and 200,000 people and maintain the status quo for six months. I just believe we can do that, if we do it right. Now, I don't know enough about it to know.
>
> BUNDY: God knows I don't. The only thing that scares me is that the government would up and quit on us or that there would be a coup and we'd get invited out.
>
> JOHNSON: There may be another coup.
>
> BUNDY: Yeah.
>
> JOHNSON: But I don't know what we can do if there is. I guess that we just. . . . What alternatives do we have then? We're not going to send our troops in there—are we?

The sense that Johnson went into the war with his eyes open to the difficulties it would present is a common refrain throughout these conversations. At about the same time that he was bemoaning the situation to Bundy, LBJ solicited the views of newspaper titan John Knight. "I think long range over there, the odds are certainly against us," Knight acknowledged. "Yes," Johnson replied, "there is no question about that."[26] Three months later LBJ spoke with Senator Richard Russell.

> RUSSELL: It's the damned worst mess I ever saw, and I don't like to brag, I never have been right many times in my life, but I knew we were going to get into this sort of mess when we went in there. And I don't see how we're going to ever get out without fighting a major war with the Chinese and all of them down there in those rice paddies and jungles. I just don't see it. I just don't know what to do.
>
> JOHNSON: Well, that's the way I've been feeling for six months.
>
> RUSSELL: It appears that our position is deteriorating, and it looks like the more we try to do for them, the less they are willing to do for themselves. It's just a sad situation. . . . It's a hell of . . . a hell of a situation, it's a mess. And it's going to get worse . . .
>
> JOHNSON: How important is it to us?
>
> RUSSELL: It isn't important a damn bit.
>
> JOHNSON: [*sighs*]

Teachers playing such tapes can expect a riveted audience, as listeners can sense the frustration and dismay in the voice of the president as

Lyndon Johnson's recordings offer a wealth of information for teachers. (courtesy of the Lyndon B. Johnson Library)

he laments his position. They can also expect another question that inevitably arises: if Johnson believed that the war would be so arduous and yet was not very important to the United States, why did he choose to escalate? Numerous explanations have been advanced in the historical literature, including LBJ's belief in traditional Cold War doctrines, which demanded the containment of communism; his instinctive need to appear strong and manly in the face of a challenge; and his conviction that the region, if not Vietnam itself, was critical to perpetuating the American capitalist world system. Snippets related to all of these explanations can be found in the tapes (reflecting, most likely, the fact that all of them to some extent were relevant to his decision). Still, the factor that one hears most clearly is the president's desire to maintain his political influence at home in order to pass his ambitious program of domestic reform. Johnson was determined not to suffer the fate of Harry Truman, whose legislative success was crippled by Republican allegations that he had been less than steadfast in his defense of China against the communists. He could, LBJ noted, "run and let the dominoes start falling over. And God Almighty, what they said about us leaving China would be just warming up compared to what they'd say now. I see Nixon's raising hell about it today. And [Sen. Barry] Goldwater too."[27] Two years later he unloaded on Senator McCarthy: "What they [war critics] really think is we oughtn't be there and we ought to get out. Well, I know we oughtn't be there, but I can't get out. I just can't be the architect of surrender. . . . I'm willing to do damn near anything. If I told you what I was willing to do, I wouldn't have any program. [Senate minority leader Everett] Dirksen wouldn't give me a dollar to operate the war. I just can't operate in a glass bowl with all these things."[28]

More specific aspects of the Vietnam conflict that might prove fruitful in the classroom also run through the Johnson tapes. For years historians debated the events that occurred on August 2 and 4, 1964, at the Gulf of Tonkin, where alleged attacks on American destroyers provided a pretext for Johnson's escalation of the war. Although the scholarly consensus is now clear that the August 4 attacks did not occur, there is still debate over whether Johnson knew the truth yet still used the incident to rush through Congress a long-planned declaration of war, or if there was genuine uncertainty within the administration regarding the reported attacks of that day. Students who find it difficult to believe that confusion could exist about something as simple as whether or not an attack took place should listen to Admiral U. S. Grant

Sharp, commander of the Pacific Fleet, talk by phone with General David Burchinal of the air force on August 4.

BURCHINAL: How many were engaged? Do you know?

SHARP: Let's see. There must have been a total of six engaged, I think. Not sure on that yet.

BURCHINAL: Any aircraft?

SHARP: You mean enemy?

BURCHINAL: Yeah.

SHARP: No, I don't. . . . Wait a minute, now. I'm not so sure about this number of engaged.

BURCHINAL: Right.

SHARP: We'd have to check it out here.

BURCHINAL: OK.

SHARP: It may not be that high. No, no report on. . . . We did have a report on bogeys [enemy aircraft] at one time, but we haven't any confirmation of that . . .

BURCHINAL: Are they still exchanging fire?

SHARP: I've been so busy doing other things I haven't looked at the last—whether they're still shooting each other or not. . . . I can't . . . I don't see that they have. Here's another one now I just got, let me see. [*Reading report and summarizing*] Well, the Maddox says she's evaded about ten torpedoes. [*Chuckles*] Two, two craft are sunk. No casualties to us and they got some ADs and A-Ds on the scene. But they're having trouble with illumination. The Turner Joy, or one of the two, was given star shell illumination for the planes. As far as we can tell there are only three [North Vietnamese] boats, but that doesn't count up to that many torpedoes, I don't think. Sounds to me like there are more boats than just three."[29]

While the sense of genuine confusion about the details of the Gulf of Tonkin Incident is obvious, the tapes also leave little doubt that subsequent claims by the Johnson administration that the destroyers were conducting routine patrols, rather than operating as part of a covert operation against the North, were disingenuous. The day after the August 2 attack, LBJ and McNamara spoke about how to brief Congress. The tapes record McNamara admitting that US actions had helped spur the attack: "I think I should also, or we should also at that time, Mr. President, explain this Op Plan 34-A, these covert operations. There's no question but what that had bearing on, and on Friday night, as you probably know, we had four . . . boats from Vietnam manned by Vietnamese or other nationals, attack two islands. And we expended, oh, a thousand rounds of ammunition of one kind or another against them. We probably shot up a radar station and a few other miscellaneous buildings. And following twenty-four hours after that, with this destroyer in that same area, undoubtedly led them to connect the two events."[30]

Other interesting aspects related to the decision to escalate in late 1964 and early 1965 are easily found in the tapes. A series of conversations between Johnson and McNamara on August 4, 1964, reveal the two men engaged in a long dialogue about the best way for the United States to seize control of the war.

> PRESIDENT JOHNSON: What I was thinking about when I was eating breakfast, but I couldn't talk it—I was thinking that it looks to me like the weakness of our position is that we respond only to an action and we don't have any of our own. But when they, when they move on us, and they shoot at us, I think we not only ought to shoot at them, but almost simultaneously pull one of these things that you've, you've been doing—
> SECRETARY MCNAMARA: Right.
> PRESIDENT JOHNSON:—on one of their bridges or something.[31]

Other tapes have Johnson regularly calling to seek the advice of top officials who were familiar with foreign policy, including Dwight Eisenhower, chairman of the Senate Foreign Relations Committee J. William Fulbright, and longtime friend and mentor Senator Richard Russell.[32] From most of these tapes there emerges a clear sense that Johnson felt trapped, unwilling to risk political impotence and Cold War defeat by withdrawing but recognizing that the United States stood on the brink of disaster. His desperation is tangible, powerful, and riveting in the classroom; "I don't know, Dick," he complained to Russell. "The great trouble I'm under, a man can fight if he can see daylight down the road somewhere, but there ain't no daylight in Vietnam. There's not a bit."[33]

The despondency found in Johnson's tapes, and the uncertainty found in Kennedy's, are matched by the sense of calm machination that generally emerges from the Nixon tapes. Historians have long debated the "Decent Interval" thesis,[34] which alleges that, despite Nixon's promise to attain a "peace with honor," the president actually wrapped his plans regarding the American commitment in Vietnam around his reelection campaign. In this interpretation, a scheming Nixon removed just enough troops to imply that his policy of "Vietnamization" was working while leaving just enough troops to stave off defeat until after the 1972 election, a defeat that he knew was imminent and which he regarded as fairly inconsequential for American foreign policy. Although many Nixon supporters have rejected these claims, the tapes offer a fairly strong rebuttal, suggesting clearly that thousands of Americans died fighting a war whose primary function seemed to be serving the political interests of the White House.

Many such tapes exist. Students will likely be stunned to hear the callous discussions between Nixon and his chief foreign policy adviser, Henry Kissinger, in which Vietnam's impact on the 1972 election is the clear focus. Kissinger was frank with his boss in March 1971, when Nixon began hypothesizing about a possible peace treaty. "Well, we've got to get enough time to get out. We have to make sure that they don't knock the whole place over. . . . We can't have it knocked over brutally, to put it brutally, before the election." "That's right," Nixon responded. Even more blatant was a conversation between the two men on August 3, 1972.

> NIXON: I look at the tide of history out there, South Vietnam probably is never going to survive anyway, I'm just being perfectly candid. . . . There's got to be, if we can get certain guarantees so that they aren't. . . . We also have to realize Henry, that winning an election is terribly important. It's terribly important this year, but can we have a viable foreign policy if a year from now or two years from now, North Vietnam gobbles up South Vietnam? That's the real question.
>
> KISSINGER: If a year or two years from now North Vietnam gobbles up South Vietnam, we can have a viable foreign policy if it looks as if it's the result of South Vietnamese incompetence. If we now sell out in such a way, say that in a three-to-four month period, we have pushed [South Vietnamese] President Thieu over the brink, we ourselves, I think there is going to be, even the Chinese won't like that. I mean, they'll pay verbal, verbally they'll like it—

NIXON: But it'll worry them.

KISSINGER: But it will worry everybody. And domestically, in the long run, it won't help us all that much because our opponents will say we should've done it three years ago.

NIXON: I know.

KISSINGER: So we've got to find some formula that holds the thing together a year or two, after which—after a year, Mr. President, Vietnam will be a backwater. If we settle it, say, this October, by January '74, no one will give a damn.

Other fascinating elements of the Nixon years emerge from the tapes. The administration's hostility toward the antiwar movement is a common refrain. Even the most cynical students may be shocked by Nixon's efforts to infiltrate the protest movement; as he tells Haldeman, "We've got to have a couple of long hairs. Can I suggest that's one mistake we may be making? Do we have three of four guys—hire long-haired, dirty looking bastards, you know. . . . Have somebody, have some people that have our confidence, I mean, get some long-haired bearded guys and let them move among them. I think they could be terrifically advantageous to us." Haldeman responds, "We have." The president's sense of paranoia also resonates through many of the discussions, as Nixon presents himself as beleaguered on all sides, fighting against an elitist conspiracy that had never accepted him and opposed him at every turn. "Of course, we're fighting a very tough battle here, you know, everybody wants to pull out," he lamented to Reverend Billy Graham in 1971. "But I have to go against the tide. I got to do the right thing."[35] Nor will listeners miss the clear willingness of his administration to go to almost any lengths to advance its goals; in one conversation from June 1971, Nixon, Haldeman, and Kissinger discuss the possibility of blackmailing Lyndon Johnson by suggesting to him that they had materials allegedly proving that he used his 1968 bombing halt for political purposes.[36]

The administration's proclivity to link the war in Vietnam to the larger Cold War is also on clear display in an October 16, 1972, conversation between Nixon and Kissinger, as the president celebrates his decision to order increased bombing raids in May, just before a Moscow summit meeting, despite concerns from some sources that it might antagonize the Russians: "[I]f you thought that meeting at the dacha was tough, you should have seen what it would have been otherwise.

We would have been scorned."[37] And the tapes about the Pentagon Papers, a massive collection of Defense Department documents related to the escalation of the war that were leaked to the press in 1971, offer a number of shocking conversations, as Nixon seems determined to exact vengeance on the person who leaked them to the press. "Now goddamn it, [*pounding desk*] somebody's got to go to jail on that," he stormed. "Somebody's got to go to jail for it. That's all there is to it."[38]

Overall, then, the White House tapes simply offer a resource without parallel for those teaching American history. Their historical contributions are extraordinary, going well beyond the Vietnam War. They offer insights into other foreign policy events, including the Cuban Missile Crisis, the Dominican intervention, and the emergence of détente. They help us to explore the fundamental beliefs of policy makers about a variety of issues that framed their worldviews. And above all else, they can transport listeners through time and place, taking them back the Oval Office or the Cabinet Room at the very moment that decisions were being made whose impact would be monumental. A history teacher simply cannot ask for more.

NOTES

A smaller version of this essay first appeared in the Organization of American Historians' *Magazine of History* 24, no. 4 (October 2010): 19–24. It is reprinted here with the kind permission of the editors. The author would like to thank Robert Johnson and Marc Selverstone for their assistance in the preparation of this version.

1. Teachers interested in integrating the presidential tapes into the classroom should start with the excellent website run by the University of Virginia's Miller Center for Public Affairs, www.whitehousetapes.org. This well-designed site offers links to hundreds of the most important conversations and provides streaming video of the scrolling text to accompany the audio segments. The Miller Center page also offers relevant background information, a special page of classroom activities and relevant syllabi, electronic copies of the president's daily diaries, and much more. Useful links can also be found at various presidential libraries, especially the Lyndon B. Johnson Library, http://www.lbjlib.utexas.edu/johnson/archives.hom/Dictabelt.hom/content.asp; and the Richard Nixon Library, www.nixonlibrary.gov/virtuallibrary/tapeexcerpts/index.php. Other websites offer more narrow selections but still touch on Vietnam. The largest collection of Nixon tapes is actually at http://nixontapes.org/, an excellent site that also offers extensive background material and analysis.

2. For a good general description of the Kennedy tapes, see the overview at the web page of the Miller Center for Public Affairs at the University of Virginia, http://whitehousetapes.net/info/kennedy-tapes-overview (accessed July 27, 2011). Other good sources include Philip Zelikow and Ernest May, preface to *The Presidential Recordings: John F. Kennedy—The Great Crises*, vols. 1–3 (New York: W. W. Norton, 2001); and Max Holland, *The Kennedy Assassination Tapes* (New York: Knopf, 2004).

3. For a good general description of the Johnson tapes, see especially the introduction to *Presidential Recordings of Lyndon B. Johnson, Digital Edition*, http://presidentialrecordings.rotunda.upress.virginia.edu/essays (accessed July 27, 2011); Michael Beschloss, *Taking Charge* (New York: Simon and Schuster, 1998); Michael Beschloss, *Reaching for Glory* (New York: Simon and Schuster, 2002); and *The Presidential Recordings: Lyndon B. Johnson*, various editors, vols. 1–8 (New York: W. W. Norton, 2005–11).

4. Two good sources on the Nixon tapes are H. R. Haldeman, "The Nixon White House Tapes: The Decision to Record Presidential Conversations," *Prologue* 20, no. 2 (Summer 1988): 12–16; and Stanley Kutler, *Abuse of Power* (New York: Touchstone, 1998).

5. Haldeman, "The Nixon White House Tapes," 81.

6. Richard Nixon, *RN: The Memoirs of Richard Nixon* (New York: Grosset and Dunlap 1978), 500–501.

7. Haldeman, "The Nixon White House Tapes," 84.

8. Louis Sims, "Secret Service Participation in Tapings," December 6, 1973, Richard Nixon Presidential Library, RG 87, Records of the US Secret Service, Installation and Maintenance of the White House Sound Recording System and Tapes, CO-1-23206–WH Taping System, box 1 of 5, http://whitehousetapes.net /louis-sims-secret-service-participation-tapings-6-december-1973 (accessed July 21, 2011).

9. Due to the voice-activated nature of the Nixon system, however, many of these hours consist of meaningless sounds that inadvertently triggered the system, making the high number of total hours taped somewhat deceptive.

10. Lyndon B. Johnson Library, *Recordings of Telephone Conversations, White House Series: Introduction*, October 11, 1996, http://www.lbjlib.utexas.edu /johnson/archives.hom/dictabelt.hom/dictaintro.asp (accessed July 27, 2011); *Austin-American Statesman*, February 12, 2001, http://www.statesman.com/news /local/longtime-lbj-aide-mildred-stegall-finally-tells-her-1250137.html (accessed July 24, 2011).

11. Presidential Recordings and Materials Preservation Act, sec. 104, http://www.archives.gov/about/laws/nara.html#2111-note (accessed July 27, 2011).

12. The Watergate trial tapes were released to the public in 1980, for example, with more Watergate materials following in 1991.

13. LBJ Library, Recording of Telephone Conversation between Lyndon B. Johnson and Dwight D. Eisenhower, July 2, 1965, 11:02 AM, Citation #8303, Recordings of Telephone Conversations–White House Series, Recordings of Conversations and Meetings file.

14. See especially Howard Jones, *Death of a Generation* (New York: Oxford University Press, 2004); John Newman, *JFK and Vietnam: Deception, Intrigue, and the Struggle for Power* (New York: Warner Books, 1992); and James K. Galbraith, "Exit Strategy," *Boston Review*, October–November 2003.

15. (Morning) conversation among Kennedy, McNamara, Taylor et al., October 2, 1963, http://whitehousetapes.net/clip/john-kennedy-robert-mcnamara-maxwell-taylor-et-al-1000-troop-withdrawal-south-vietnam (accessed July 27, 2011).

16. Marc Selverstone, "It's a Date: Kennedy and the Timetable for a Vietnam Troop Withdrawal," *Diplomatic History*, June 2010, 485–86.

17. Kennedy, McNamara, Taylor et al., October 2, 1963 (evening) conversation, http://web1.millercenter.org/dci/1963_1002_withdrawal_aftrn.html (accessed July 27, 2011).

18. Kennedy, McNamara, Taylor et al., October 2, 1963 (morning) conversation, http://whitehousetapes.net/clip/john-kennedy-robert-mcnamara-maxwell-taylor-et-al-1000-troop-withdrawal-south-vietnam (accessed July 27, 2011).

19. John Kennedy, November 4, 1963, http://whitehousetapes.net/clip/john-kennedy-john-kennedy-jr-caroline-kennedy-jfks-memoir-dictation-assassination-diem (accessed July 27, 2011).

20. "Kennedy Considered Supporting Coup in South Vietnam," August 1963, *National Security Archive Electronic Briefing Book No. 302*, December 2009, http://www.gwu.edu/~nsarchiv/NSAEBB/NSAEBB302/index.htm (accessed July 27, 2011).

21. Lyndon Johnson and Eugene McCarthy, February 1, 1966, http://web1.millercenter.org/dci/1966_0201_critics.htm (accessed July 27, 2011).

22. Richard Nixon and Billy Graham, April 7, 1971, http://web1.millercenter.org/dci/1971_0407_graham.html (accessed July 27, 2011).

23. John Kennedy and Earle Wheeler, February 2, 1963, http://web1.millercenter.org/dci/1963_0202_general.htm (accessed July 27, 2011).

24. "Status Report on Vietnam," January 8, 1963, John Kennedy et al., http://web1.millercenter.org/dci/1963_0108_status.htm (accessed July 27, 2011).

25. John Kennedy and Earle Wheeler, February 1, 1963, http://www.jfklibrary.org/About-Us/News-and-Press/Press-Releases/Kennedy-Library-Opens-15-More-Hours-of-JFK-Recordings-Tapes-Offer-Insights-on-Vietnam-and-US-Relatio.aspx (accessed July 27, 2011).

26. Lyndon Johnson and John Knight, February 3, 1964, http://web1.millercenter.org/dci/1964_0203_vietnam.html (accessed July 27, 2011).

27. Lyndon Johnson and John Knight, February 3, 1964, http://web1 .millercenter.org/dci/1964_0203_vietnam.html (accessed July 27, 2011).

28. Lyndon Johnson and Eugene McCarthy, February 1, 1966, http://web1 .millercenter.org/dci/1966_0201_critics.htm (accessed July 27, 2011).

29. Admiral U. S. Grant Sharp Jr. and General David Burchinal, August 4, 1964, http://web1.millercenter.org/dci/1964_0804_burchinal.html (accessed July 27, 2011).

30. Lyndon Johnson and Robert McNamara, August 3, 1964, 10:30 AM, http://www.gwu.edu/~nsarchiv/NSAEBB/NSAEBB132/tapes.htm (accessed July 27, 2011).

31. Lyndon Johnson and Robert McNamara, August 4, 1964, 9:43 AM, http://www.gwu.edu/~nsarchiv/NSAEBB/NSAEBB132/tapes.htm (accessed July 27, 2011).

32. For representative Eisenhower conversations, see http://whitehouse tapes.net/exhibit/exceptional-alliance-johnson-eisenhower-and-vietnam-war; for Fulbright, see http://web1.millercenter.org/dci/1963_1202_hopeless.html; for Russell, see http://whitehousetapes.net/clips/1964_0527_benmilam /index.htm, and http://web1.millercenter.org/dci/1965_0306_aint_no_ daylight.html (all last accessed July 27, 2011).

33. Lyndon Johnson and Richard Russell, March 6, 1965, http://web1 .millercenter.org/dci/1965_0306_aint_no_daylight.html (accessed July 27, 2011).

34. The best summary of the decent interval thesis can be found in Jeffrey Kimball, *The Vietnam War Files: Uncovering the Secret History of Nixon-era Strategy* (Lawrence: University Press of Kansas, 2004), and Ken Hughes, *Fatal Politics*, in *Diplomatic History*, June 2010. Hughes has placed many of these transcripts online as part of his web-based documentary miniseries, *Fatal Politics*, which can be found at http://fatalpolitics.blogspot.com.

35. Richard Nixon and Billy Graham, April 7, 1971, http://web1.millercenter .org/dci/1971_0407_graham.html (accessed July 27, 2011).

36. Richard Nixon, Henry Kissinger, John Erlichman, Bob Haldeman, June 17, 1971, 5:15 pm, http://whitehousetapes.net/exhibit/first-domino-nixon-and-pentagon-papers (accessed July 27, 2011).

37. Richard Nixon and Henry Kissinger, October 16, 1972, http://web1 .millercenter.org/dci/1972_1016_linebacker.html (accessed July 27, 2011).

38. Richard Nixon and Bob Haldeman, June 15, 1971, 9:56 AM, http:// whitehousetapes.net/exhibit/first-domino-nixon-and-pentagon-papers (accessed July 27, 2011).

KEY RESOURCES

American Radio Works, http://americanradioworks.publicradio.org/features /prestapes/.

Beschloss, Michael. *Taking Charge.* New York: Simon and Schuster, 1998.

C-Span Radio, http://www.c-span.org/Series/American-Political-Archive .aspx.

Haldeman, H. R. "The Nixon White House Tapes: The Decision to Record Presidential Conversations." *Prologue* 20, no. 2 (Summer 1988): 12–16.

Holland, Max. *The Kennedy Assassination Tapes.* New York: Knopf, 2004.

Lyndon B. Johnson Library, http://www.lbjlib.utexas.edu/johnson/archives .hom/Dictabelt.hom/content.asp.

Kutler, Stanley. *Abuse of Power.* New York: Touchstone, 1998.

May, Ernest, and Philip Zelikow. *The Kennedy Tapes.* Boston: Belknap, 1998.

Miller Center for Public Affairs, University of Virginia, www.whitehousetapes .org.

Nixontapes.org, http://nixontapes.org/.

Prados, John. *The White House Tapes.* New York: New Press, 2003.

The Presidential Recordings: Lyndon B. Johnson, vols. 1–8, various editors. New York: W. W. Norton, 2005–11.

Richard Nixon Library, http://www.nixonlibrary.gov/virtuallibrary/tape excerpts/index.php.

Movies and
the Vietnam War

SCOTT LADERMAN

Whether we like it or not (and, I suspect, most of us do not), movies are how many of our students first encounter the Vietnam War. In fact, it is often the only way they have encountered it. They may have been touched by the depictions of heroism and sacrifice in Mel Gibson's *We Were Soldiers*. They may have been thrilled by the exploits of Rambo, arguably America's most famous Vietnam veteran, in a late-night cable TV marathon. Or they may have laughed at *Tropic Thunder*, the Ben Stiller send-up of the entire Vietnam War genre. Yet few students appreciate how influential these and other films may have been in shaping their understandings of the war's history. Sure, movies can be entertaining. They can be funny, terrifying, or sad. But they are significant for reasons beyond their entertainment value. Movies offer not merely a couple of hours of escape. They can, in fact, help us to understand the profound effects of the Vietnam War on American politics, culture, and society.

Movies, in other words, can be used by educators as primary sources. And as "screen" documents, they have the added benefit of being materials with which our screen-obsessed students are likely to engage. They can, in addition, be useful for their ability to illustrate rich ideas in a short period of time. It is hardly necessary to show most films in their entirety. On the contrary, many of them are best appreciated in an abbreviated form. I more often use a three-minute clip here or a ten-minute clip there than I do a full feature-length film. Such snippets can be deeply insightful in conveying how Americans came to understand colonial Vietnam, the revolutionary struggle, and the legacies of that struggle for Americans and Vietnamese.[1] And with Hollywood's long history of screening Vietnam—far longer, in fact, than most Americans realize—there is a wealth of such primary documents available to the educator.

Most of the films seen by our students are films that were made after the war officially ended in 1975. The Vietnam War with which they are generally familiar is the Vietnam War of Oliver Stone, Mel Gibson, and Sylvester Stallone. These are important films, and they can tell us a great deal about Americans' efforts to come to terms with the nation's experience in Southeast Asia. But these are, strictly speaking, postwar movies. The insights they provide are in most instances limited to the postwar era. Fortunately for us, Hollywood actually has a deep history of placing "Vietnam"—the war as well as the country—on the American silver screen. From 1929 through 1948, when the Vietnamese revolution first appeared in a Hollywood motion picture (*Rogues' Regiment*, a fascinating anti-Nazi production starring Dick Powell and Vincent Price), filmmakers set over half a dozen movies in that Southeast Asian nation. In the 1950s there were a handful of others, from *A Yank in Indo-China* in 1952 to *Five Gates to Hell* in 1959. The decade that followed, a ten-year period in which the US military commitment grew from hundreds of "advisers" in the early months of the Kennedy administration to over half a million troops by 1969, witnessed the creation of several more. From John Ireland's understated performance in *Brushfire* (1962) and Marlon Brando's diplomatic turn in *The Ugly American* (1963) to Burt Reynolds's appearance in *Operation C.I.A.* (1965) and John Wayne's critically derided but commercially successful *The Green Berets* (1968), the years of the American War were marked by a greater proliferation of Hollywood pictures than has often been appreciated by scholars. Individually, most of these pre-1975 films might be considered somewhat forgettable. Collectively, however, they provide an enlightening portrait of America's descent into war. Hollywood traced the evolution in America's understanding of that country—from a sleepy colonial backwater to a major battleground—in ways that can be richly illuminating to our students.

Historians such as Mark Philip Bradley and Seth Jacobs have demonstrated how, in the decades before the US military escalation in the 1960s, the decisions made in Washington relied on Americans' often problematical perceptions of Vietnamese.[2] Among the conclusions drawn by Americans in the first half of the twentieth century was that

the Vietnamese were a childlike people unprepared for the grave responsibility of self-government. This was a notion reinforced in countless
cultural productions, from novels and travel writing to reportage.
Hollywood also contributed to this view. From the primitive simpletons
of *Where East Is East* (1929) to the mixed-bloods wishing only that they
were white in *Lady of the Tropics* (1939), American films during the
French colonial era explicitly cast the Vietnamese people in a manner
that subscribed to fluid hierarchies of race. To convey this idea to
students, educators can show them two brief clips from *Red Dust* (1932).
Starring Clark Gable and Jean Harlow, *Red Dust* is probably the most
popular and critically appreciated Vietnam-related film of the decades
preceding World War II. In 2006, in fact, it was selected for the prestigious National Film Registry of the Library of Congress. The film centers
on a gruff rubber plantation owner (Gable) in colonial Cochin China
who has an affair with the wife (Mary Astor) of his newly arrived
engineer. Vietnamese serve as little more than an exotic backdrop to the
main story. This is typical of early Hollywood pictures set in Southeast
Asia. Yet how the Vietnamese were represented still matters, for their
portrayal offered subtle cues to the mostly white audiences of the 1930s
about the nature and inherent capabilities of the Vietnamese people.

One could begin by showing the first two and a half minutes of the
film. Gable in this scene is inspecting his rubber trees and growing
increasingly infuriated by the decision of one of his trusted employees
to tap them early. His anger is only further heightened by his half-
dressed Vietnamese workers, who are sitting around idly rather than
earnestly working the plantation lands. "Look at those slugs!" he fumes
to a colleague. Gable then proceeds to yell at the Vietnamese workers
while throwing water at them, pushing them around, and threatening
them with a shovel—anything to get them back to work. At that moment
a dust storm arrives and sends the Vietnamese scurrying for cover
rather than securing the roof of a nearby building. Gable must physically
pull the workers out of their shelter in order to obtain their assistance.
The scene is significant because it suggests the laziness and frightful
innocence of the Vietnamese, at least as perceived by Hollywood. But
it can be valuable, too, in that it invites a discussion about what were
potentially subtle forms of resistance employed by Vietnamese laborers
during the French colonial era. Should we assume that Vietnamese
workers were merely the lazy "slugs" portrayed in *Red Dust*, for instance? Or might their refusal to overly exert themselves have been a

means of resisting the exploitative impositions of the colonial labor system? On a plantation in which positions of importance were held by whites and Vietnamese were inevitably relegated to manual labor, what incentives did the native population have to work harder? And why labor for the furtherance of French colonialism?

The other scene one could show—the arrival at the plantation of Gary Willis (Gene Raymond) and his wife Barbara (Astor)—reinforces and builds on some of the ideas suggested by the opening sequence. Entering the plantation's main house, the Willises are assisted by a Vietnamese servant, Hoy (Willie Fung), whose every utterance suggests imbecility. Hoy speaks in broken English, laughs absurdly when showing the young couple where to bathe, and repeats himself when describing their quarters. He appears, in other words, to possess the intellect of an adolescent. The scene is thus important in its suggestion that Vietnamese are not only lazy but imbecilic. Released at a time when Vietnamese nationalists were heightening their agitation against French colonialism, this depiction suggested that such people could not possibly be entrusted with independence.

If *Red Dust* and a number of like-minded films hinted at the necessity of the French *mission civilisatrice* in the years preceding World War II, Hollywood took a decidedly anticommunist turn in the late 1940s and 1950s. Like policy makers in Washington, filmmakers increasingly situated the Vietnamese revolutionary struggle within the context of the unfolding Cold War. The Vietnamese revolutionaries, viewed through this lens, were not anticolonial nationalists seeking Vietnamese independence. On the contrary, their aspirations were decidedly anti-nationalist: they were communist stooges of Moscow and Beijing intent on gradually taking over the world. A couple of commercially available films from the 1950s nicely illustrate this idea. Depending on how much time one wishes to devote to the issue, an instructor can show either a ninety-second clip from *China Gate* (1957) or *The Quiet American* (1958) in its entirety. Both were made after the French agreed to withdraw from Vietnam in the 1954 Geneva Accords, so neither is strictly contemporaneous. But both nevertheless serve as valuable primary documents of Cold War culture.

China Gate cuts straight to the chase. Made by celebrated filmmaker Sam Fuller, it was the first Hollywood film to acknowledge the Vietnamese leader Ho Chi Minh. It does so in a newsreel-style opening that, unusually for a Hollywood picture, features actual footage of the

French–Viet Minh war, including the human suffering it caused. But, according to *China Gate*, the blame rests solely with one party. The narrator is unequivocal in celebrating French colonialism and damning the revolutionary struggle. For Fuller—despite his later claims to the contrary—the war in *China Gate* was an uncomplicated story of French heroism and Communist tyranny.[3] Indeed, the narrator begins by dedicating "[t]his motion picture . . . to France." "More than three hundred years ago," he continues,

> French missionaries were sent to Indochina to teach love of God and love of fellow man. Gradually French influence took shape in the Vietnamese land. Despite many hardships, they advanced their way of living and the thriving nation became the rice bowl of Asia. Vast riches were developed under French guidance until 1941 when Japanese troops moved in and made the rice bowl red with blood of the defenders. In 1945, when the Japanese surrender was announced, a Moscow-trained Indochinese revolutionist who called himself Ho Chi Minh began the drive to make his home country another target for Chinese Communists. Headquartered in the north, he called the new party Viet Minh. With the end of the Korean War, France was left alone to hold the hottest front in the world and became the barrier between Communism and the rape of Asia. Members of the Foreign Legion, imported from North Africa, fought valiantly under the French flag, but the ammunition pipeline from Moscow could not be found. Bombs and shells made in Russia were stocked in secret tunnels along the mountain range of the China Gate. This arsenal was winning the war for the Communists. Bombs and shells stocked underground smashed village after village. But still fighting for their life, one hundred miles from the China Gate, is the dying village of Son Toy, the last holdout in the north. Her supplies have been ambushed, her ammunition depleted, but she fights as she starves. Her only chance of survival is the American food airdrop from the south.

The political story *China Gate* tells is simple: France is not an imperial aggressor but a beneficent defender against the "rape of Asia." Ho Chi Minh is serving not the Vietnamese people but inhumane Chinese Communists. The United States is assisting the starving but valiant fighters who have survived the Communists' relentless smashing of their villages. All of this is, historically speaking, ridiculously simplistic or wrong. But—and here one can see its value in the classroom—it is a quick and contemporaneous illustration of the Cold War ideology of the 1950s with respect to the war in Vietnam.

The Quiet American reveals its ideological orientation more slowly. Based on the 1955 novel of the same name by the British author Graham Greene, *The Quiet American* completely inverts the critical orientation of Greene's original work of fiction. Whereas Greene wrote a story that took issue with American involvement in Vietnam, the film's director, Academy Award winner Joseph Mankiewicz, worked with US counterinsurgency specialist Edward Lansdale to craft a story that instead celebrated that involvement. The basic plot of the film is centered on the struggle between two westerners in Vietnam—a middle-aged British journalist, Thomas Fowler (Michael Redgrave), and an unnamed young American (Audie Murphy)—for the love and affection of a local Vietnamese woman played by the Italian actress Giorgia Moll. There are several ways that the film can be used in the classroom.

First, *The Quiet American* cinematically illustrates the American desire in the 1950s for a "third force" in Vietnamese politics that would serve the interests of the United States. This was an important consideration in the context of the Cold War. If the first two forces were those of communism and French colonialism, this third force would be anticommunist and anticolonialist and thus, the film assumes, both popular in Vietnam and inherently friendly to Washington. The film in fact makes subtly apparent the identity of the man presumed to be Vietnam's natural third-force leader: Ngo Dinh Diem, who served as president of the Republic of Vietnam (RVN) from 1955 to 1963. Mankiewicz dedicated the film to Diem as the RVN's "chosen President," and he had the "American" at one point noting to Fowler that, in an obvious reference to Washington's so-called miracle man, there was a "very prominent Vietnamese living in exile in New Jersey" who, "if all goes well, if Vietnam becomes an independent republic . . . will be its leader." The film thus invites discussion about the American vision for a third force in Vietnam, the creation of the RVN, the authoritarian rule of Ngo Dinh Diem, and the growing American frustration with Diem's resistance to advice emanating from Washington. It also invites discussion about how the United States, at the time the film was set, saw itself as somehow transcending the legacy of French colonialism while at the same time opposing the Viet Minh, the most popular force for Vietnamese nationalism during the long war with France. How, we might ask, did

Washington move from an alliance with the Vietnamese revolutionaries during World War II to a confrontation with them in the years that followed? What accounts for this transformation?

The Quiet American is similarly effective in demonstrating not only how filmmakers sometimes create motion pictures in order to communicate certain political messages but also the extent to which Hollywood is capable of rewriting history. This is a lesson for students that transcends *The Quiet American* or the Vietnam War. The most obvious manifestation of this phenomenon in Mankiewicz's film is the representation of a real-life Saigon bombing that, according to the motion picture, was responsible for the deaths of "at least fifty" innocent civilians. As the film approaches its end, viewers learn that the Viet Minh was responsible for this moral outrage, an act of terrorism that firmly pulled Fowler into the communist conspiracy that proved his ultimate undoing. But, as Mankiewicz very well knew—the evidence is found in correspondence the director exchanged with CIA agent Edward Lansdale—it was in fact a third-force ally of the United States, General Trinh Minh The, who almost certainly orchestrated the bloody January 1952 event.[4] Wishing, however, to create an anticommunist film that would transform a novel critical of the American role in Vietnam into a motion picture that spoke admiringly of that American involvement, Mankiewicz flipped reality on its head, showing the Viet Minh to have been responsible for the atrocities after all.

Finally, as a fascinating and instructive tangent, educators can point to how *The Quiet American* has continued to generate political controversy. In particular, the film was remade by Philip Noyce in 2001 as a more faithful adaptation of Greene's original novel. This meant assigning responsibility for the 1952 Saigon bombing to the United States, not the Viet Minh. Such an attribution of guilt implicitly made Washington a sponsor of terrorism, however, and this was a notion deemed verboten in the wake of the September 11, 2001, attacks. Miramax thus sought to kill the film before it was ever commercially released. The company ultimately backtracked, but in this way *The Quiet American* got swept up not only in the politics of the Cold War but in the politics of the so-called war on terror as well.[5]

Most students associate the Vietnam War with the 1960s, when the United States undertook a direct combat role in Southeast Asia. Of the several films made about American involvement in Vietnam during that decade, none was more popular—and probably none is more effective as

John Wayne in *The Green Berets*.

a teaching tool—than *The Green Berets* (1968), the John Wayne picture made with White House cooperation. An unabashed prowar polemic released as much of the public was turning against the war, *The Green Berets* was enthusiastically embraced by fans of Wayne and the militarist views he represented. Wayne plays a colonel in the US Army Special Forces who is sent to Vietnam to, first, secure a mountain camp and, second, kidnap a revolutionary general. Despite the Vietnam setting, it is in fact a fairly typical Wayne-style cowboys and Indians story, only in this movie the cowboys are American military personnel and the Indians are Vietnamese insurgents. Overall it provides rich material for the classroom, though it is hardly necessary that the film be shown in its entirety. A couple of clips will suffice.

Particularly instructive is the press conference and public presentation that opens the movie. Here, in a ten-minute segment (though one interrupted by a brief display of John Wayne's military chops), is a distillation of some of the hawks' principal arguments and complaints. Those in the audience, both filmic and actual, learn that the Vietnamese insurgency is in no way indigenous; it is part of a global conspiracy to achieve "communist domination of the world." What is happening in Vietnam is not really even a war; it is a communist-perpetrated bloodbath. As such, "they need us . . . and they want us," a military doctor (Raymond St. Jacques) informs the audience. As for those whom the United States is said to be defending, the Saigon-based government, which at that time was widely regarded as corrupt and authoritarian, is portrayed as a fledgling democracy on the road to constitutional rule.

Viewers also see that the press is as intensely hostile to US foreign policy as it is demonstrably ignorant and unrepresentative of public opinion.

While the film was released in 1968 before the Nixon administration entered office, the public audience in this opening clip from *The Green Berets* is very much representative of what Richard Nixon would soon come to call the "silent majority," those millions of Americans who, Nixon claimed, believed in the justness of US policy but, unlike members of the antiwar movement, were not taking to the streets to demonstrate their views. Audience member and housewife "Gladys Cooper," for instance, is shocked to learn the truths revealed by the film's moral authorities and finds it "strange that we've never read of this in the newspapers." There is a reason. Journalists oppose the war without ever having actually witnessed it, Wayne scoffs, implying that their views are inherently suspect. To rectify this experiential lack, an especially annoying reporter, George Beckworth (David Janssen), decides to accompany Wayne's troops to Vietnam. Not surprisingly, Beckworth then undergoes a metamorphosis, becoming a staunch believer in America's mission. To illustrate why, instructors can play a brief clip that lends support to what has been called the "bloodbath theory." The bloodbath theory posited that American intervention was a moral imperative because it prevented widespread Communist massacres of a generally defenseless civilian population.

The idea was made explicit by Wayne in a letter he wrote to Lyndon Johnson's press secretary, Bill Moyers, in planning for his film in 1966. "We want to bring out that if we abandon these people, there will be a blood bath of over two million souls," Wayne explained to the White House.[6] He accomplished this feat in a scene in which Beckworth accompanies Wayne and some other military personnel to a village of indigenous Vietnamese who had accepted aid from the Americans. What the special forces discover is horrifying. Bodies are strewn everywhere. Buildings are on fire. A note hanging above a corpse warns the Green Berets to go away (*di di*). Even a little girl for whom Beckworth had earlier developed an innocent fondness is dead; she was dragged into the jungle and slaughtered—and perhaps raped—by "five Viet Cong soldiers," a survivor tells one of the Americans. The insurgents' inhumanity was beyond comprehension. "It's pretty hard to talk to anyone about this country 'til they've come over here and seen it," Wayne says to a speechless Beckworth. "The last village that I visited, they didn't kill the chief," he continues. "They tied him to a tree, brought his teenage daughters out in front of him, and disemboweled them. Then forty of them abused his wife. And then they took a steel rod and broke every bone in her body. Somewhere during the process she died." *The Green Berets* represented an unambiguous argument in favor of continued American intervention. As such it offers an illustration of how some Americans responded to the developing political divisions in the United States: not with introspection but with aggression. Wayne, as a right-wing patriot who thought that Washington must always project an image of strength, was worried about the country's growing war weariness. *The Green Berets* was his response.

John Wayne's picture is also notable for being the last major fictional film Hollywood made about the war before its official end in 1975. (Peter Davis's Oscar-winning documentary *Hearts and Minds* appeared in 1974.) The war had simply become too controversial. The industry would eventually return to it, though it would do so in a way that, more often than not, reimaged the US experience in ways that bore little relation to historical reality. The first big wave of postwar films began in 1978. In that year Hollywood released *Go Tell the Spartans*, *Coming Home*, and *The Deer Hunter*, the last of which won the Academy Award for Best Picture. *Apocalypse Now*—an adaptation of Joseph Conrad's *Heart of Darkness* set in the jungles of Southeast Asia—would make its appearance shortly afterward in 1979. This was merely a warm-up for the 1980s, which witnessed a slew of motion pictures, many of them cartoonish prisoner of war (POW) films but others that aspired to more artistic accomplishment.

Among these is *The Killing Fields* (1984), a film that is most effective when shown in its entirety. It works well in the classroom for several reasons, the most obvious of which is that it is an extremely gripping and powerful story. The acting is excellent, the cinematography is spectacular, and the narrative is emotionally wrenching throughout. It is a movie that pulls students in. But the film is an excellent classroom tool for other reasons, too. It spans much of the 1970s, bridging the last years of the American war and the first years of the postwar era. And, significantly, it does so through the lens of Cambodia, reminding students that what we call the Vietnam War was not just a war fought in Vietnam. By focusing on the Khmer Rouge genocide, students can begin to appreciate that the war did not end with the US withdrawal in 1975. Its legacies have continued to haunt Southeast Asia for decades. Unlike most other Vietnam War films, moreover, in *The Killing Fields* those on the receiving end of America's military might—in this case, the people of Cambodia—are not simply a backdrop to the larger action involving the American protagonists. They are front and center as developed characters in the film. Through the figure of Dith Pran, in particular, students learn to see the peoples of Southeast Asia as not merely abstractions in the calculus of US global power. They are, in fact, regular and real human beings. There are, to be sure, a number of short-comings with the film.[7] Still, it is an excellent means of getting students to ponder several important questions. How did the war in Cambodia relate to the war in Vietnam? What was probably the most significant legacy of the American war in Cambodia? How might US actions have contributed to the Khmer Rouge genocide? What was the US response to the genocide? And—this is a question that the film does not directly address but is definitely worth exploring—how did Washington respond to the Vietnamese invasion of Cambodia, which drove the Khmer Rouge out of Phnom Penh?

Of the various films made after 1975 that are set in Vietnam, I usually show brief clips from two. They are films that could not appear to be more different. *Rambo: First Blood Part II* (1985) was a ridiculously improbable but wildly successful action flick starring Sylvester Stallone. *Platoon* (1986), a recipient of the Oscar for best picture, was the first in director Oliver Stone's trilogy of Vietnam War movies.[8] They are two of the best-known films related to the Vietnam War. Students will likely be familiar with both of them. But one of the movies they probably will have considered a mindless shoot-em-up intended to appeal to the same demographic that is fond of superhero comic books and violent video games. The other has been widely touted as a realistic portrayal of the war, and there is little reason to believe that students will have viewed it any differently. As such, *Platoon* is, pedagogically speaking, arguably the more dangerous of the two.

The purpose of this essay is not to offer a detailed critique of *Platoon* and *Rambo*. Educators can turn to a number of published studies that have already done so.[9] Rather, I want to suggest that if one of the princi-pal cultural trends of the decades following 1975 was to essentially rescript the memory of the war as a uniquely *American* (rather than Vietnamese) tragedy, then both of these films can be useful in this regard. *Platoon* ends with Chris (Charlie Sheen) bizarrely asserting in a narrative voice-over that "we did not fight the enemy. We fought ourselves. And the enemy was in us." It would be difficult to more explicitly articulate the view that Americans were the war's ultimate victims, in essence erasing the Vietnamese from the war's popular narrative, but one need not screen the entire film to capture that closing impression. Instructors could show only the first couple of minutes, a scene in which Chris arrives for his service in Vietnam. From the body bags and anguished faces of those young American men finally going home to the haunting music (Samuel Barber's *Adagio for Strings*) playing in the background, there is little doubt that Stone intended to present the conflict in painful and tragic terms. His is no celebration of the war.

Nor, directly, is Stallone's *Rambo*, though like *Platoon* it is remarkably Americacentric. *Rambo* allowed Americans to move past the troubled memories of the Vietnam War by kicking some postwar Vietnamese ass. The movie is, from beginning to end, a lionization of American masculinity; indeed, it can be used as exhibit A in what feminist scholar Susan Jeffords called the "remasculinization of America."[10] If, as President Nixon claimed, the United States was left looking like a "pitiful, helpless giant" in the wake of its experience in Southeast Asia, *Rambo*, tapping into the militarist fantasies of the Reagan era, allowed the country to once again assert its strength and imperial authority. Rambo (the character) viewed the war as ultimately a betrayal of the American men sent to fight it, and he sees much the same in the efforts of government bureaucrats to cover up the existence of Americans still imprisoned in Vietnam. In this way the film is a wonderful illustration of the politics of the Reagan era, a period in which the White House tried to rewrite the history of the war as a "noble cause" betrayed by the antiwar movement, the mass media, and civilians in Washington, while at the same time feeding the POW/MIA (missing in action) myth that in considerable part prevented the normalization of postwar US–Vietnamese relations.

As with *Platoon*, one could show only a brief clip from *Rambo*. There is an eight-minute sequence that begins shortly after the forty-one-minute mark that starts with Rambo running—an emaciated American POW in tow—through a paddy field to meet a reconnaissance unit and ends with him hanging nearly naked in a pool of pig feces while being brutalized by a Vietnamese. It is a powerful sequence for several reasons. We see a duplicitous Washington bureaucrat preventing America's warriors from completing their mission—just as, according to the Reagan administration, happened during the war itself. We see evidence of Vietnamese inhumanity, thus associating atrocious behavior in

Sylvester Stallone as Rambo in *Rambo: First Blood Part II.*

Vietnam with Vietnamese rather than Americans. We see the Soviet Union pulling the strings of its Vietnamese puppets, reinforcing the notion that the war was really about the global spread of communism after all. And we see a story that revolves around still-captured Americans, a myth that in many ways stood at the heart of postwar American political culture. *Rambo* allowed the United States to essentially refight the Vietnam War, though this time, as an uncharacteristically clothed Stallone powerfully framed his betrayal at the beginning of the film, America's fighting men would "get to win."

Good teaching of course requires much more than showing films. The motion pictures of the Vietnam War can be extremely useful in the classroom, but they are best used in complementing other forms of instruction, not replacing them. With that in mind, the American experience in Vietnam offers a particularly rich subject for filmic pedagogy, as the country engendered a long record of Hollywood filmmaking—much longer, in fact, than most historians realize. From the early racist representations in *Red Dust* to the postwar fantasies expressed so well in *Rambo*, there are dozens of possibilities for classroom employment. The challenge for instructors, in fact, will be how to limit the use of filmic examples, not how to find pictures that might potentially be helpful. The preceding examples should be viewed merely as potential starting points.

NOTES

1. This essay focuses on English-language films made primarily for an American audience. While there can be tremendous value in drawing on Vietnamese-language motion pictures (as well as French-language productions), most of these have not been subtitled or made widely available and thus remain inaccessible to the majority of American students. For an excellent analysis of a number of Vietnamese films, see Mark Philip Bradley, "Contests of Memory: Remembering and Forgetting War in the Contemporary Vietnamese Cinema," in Hue-Tam Ho Tai, ed., *The Country of Memory: Remaking the Past in Late Socialist Vietnam* (Berkeley: University of California Press, 2001), 196–226.

2. Mark Philip Bradley, *Imagining Vietnam and America: The Making of Post-colonial Vietnam, 1919–1950* (Chapel Hill: University of North Carolina Press, 2000); Seth Jacobs, *America's Miracle Man in Vietnam: Ngo Dinh Diem, Religion, Race, and U.S. Intervention in Southeast Asia* (Durham, NC: Duke University Press, 2004).

3. On Fuller's misremembrance of what his film actually claimed, see Scott Laderman, "Hollywood's Vietnam, 1929–1964: Scripting Intervention, Spotlighting Injustice," *Pacific Historical Review* 78:4 (November 2009): 590–93.

4. For more on the bombing, see Laderman, "Hollywood's Vietnam," 595–96.

5. The travails of the Noyce version of *The Quiet American* are related in Scott Laderman, "Spotlight Essay/Film: *The Quiet American*," in Sara E. Quay and Amy M. Damico, eds., *September 11 in Popular Culture: A Guide* (Santa Barbara, CA: Greenwood, 2010), 197–99.

6. Lawrence H. Suid, *Guts and Glory: The Making of the American Military Image in Film*, rev. ed. (Lexington: University Press of Kentucky, 2002), 248.

7. See, for example, Scott Laderman, "Burying Culpability: *The Killing Fields* (1984), U.S. Foreign Policy, and the Political Limits of Filmmaking in Reagan-Era America," *Historical Journal of Film, Radio, and Television* 30:2 (June 2010): 203–20.

8. The other films in Stone's trilogy are *Born on the Fourth of July* (1989) and *Heaven and Earth* (1993).

9. See, for example, Edwin A. Martini, *Invisible Enemies: The American War on Vietnam, 1975–2000* (Amherst: University of Massachusetts Press, 2007), 116–61.

10. Susan Jeffords, *The Remasculinization of America: Gender and the Vietnam War* (Bloomington: Indiana University Press, 1989).

KEY RESOURCES

Adair, Gilbert. *Hollywood's Vietnam: From "The Green Berets" to "Full Metal Jacket."* London: Heinemann, 1989.

Anderegg, Michael, ed. *Inventing Vietnam: The War in Film and Television.* Philadelphia: Temple University Press, 1991.

Auster, Albert, and Leonard Quart. *How the War Was Remembered: Hollywood and Vietnam.* New York: Praeger, 1988.

Bradley, Mark Philip. "Contests of Memory: Remembering and Forgetting War in the Contemporary Vietnamese Cinema." In Hue-Tam Ho Tai, ed., *The Country of Memory: Remaking the Past in Late Socialist Vietnam.* Berkeley: University of California Press, 2001.

Chong, Sylvia Shin Huey. *The Oriental Obscene: Violence and Racial Fantasies in the Vietnam Era.* Durham, NC: Duke University Press, 2012.

Devine, Jeremy M. *Vietnam at 24 Frames a Second: A Critical and Thematic Analysis of over 400 Films about the Vietnam War.* Austin: University of Texas Press, 1995.

Dittmar, Linda, and Gene Michaud, eds. *From Hanoi to Hollywood: The Vietnam War in American Film.* New Brunswick, NJ: Rutgers University Press, 1990.

Laderman, Scott. "Hollywood's Vietnam, 1929–1964: Scripting Intervention, Spotlighting Injustice." *Pacific Historical Review* 78:4 (November 2009): 578–607.

Lanning, Michael Lee. *Vietnam at the Movies.* New York: Ballantine Books, 1994.

Malo, Jean-Jacques, and Tony Williams. *Vietnam War Films: More Than 600 Feature, Made-for-TV, Pilot, and Short Movies, 1939–1992, from the United States, Vietnam, France, Belgium, Australia, Hong Kong, South Africa, Great Britain, and Other Countries.* 2 vols. Jefferson, NC: McFarland, 2012.

Muse, Eben J. *The Land of Nam: The Vietnam War in American Film.* Lanham, MD: Scarecrow Press, 1995.

Smith, Julian. *Looking Away: Hollywood and Vietnam.* New York: Scribner, 1975.

Taylor, Mark P. *The Vietnam War in History, Literature, and Film.* Tuscaloosa: University of Alabama Press, 2003.

The Books We Carry

Teaching the Vietnam War through Literature

MAUREEN RYAN

The unnamed narrator-protagonist of Ward Just's 1984 novel *The American Blues* is struggling to complete his history of the Vietnam War. Like Just, the narrator was a journalist in Vietnam earlier in the war, and he is "obsessed" with America's long misadventure in Southeast Asia. It is April 1975, and the television coverage of the looming, dramatic fall of Saigon summons the narrator's memories of his time in-country. He watches as a journalist interviews an American diplomat about the end of the war. "Looking back on it is something we'll do for a very long time," the diplomat opines. "It'll become an industry. There are so many of us who've been here."

More than twenty-five years after Just's novel and thirty-five and counting after the fall of Saigon, popular and scholarly preoccupation with America's war in Vietnam remains "an industry" in the United States. Newly declassified documents, conferences and symposia, memoirs by important participants, and revisionist histories have appeared in a steady and unabating stream since the 1980s. Yet the controversies and questions linger as well: why we went, whether we should have, why we lost, how the experience affected American domestic and foreign policy for the next quarter century, why it is the war that does not go away.

The Vietnam War "industry" remains so relevant and vexing because the war—its duration, its costs in human lives and dollars, its unsettled conclusion—continues to profoundly affect Americans and American society in the new century. Inextricable, as it was, from other 1960s and 1970s social phenomena such as the civil rights and women's movements, the war, its aftermath, and the domestic war *against* the war fundamentally transformed American life. These are matters that cannot be addressed solely by means of official documents and histories. These are matters for fiction, film, memoirs, photographs, and paintings—the cultural artifacts inspired (and being inspired still) by the trauma and resonant power of the Vietnam War. Arguably, it is through literature that Americans and the Vietnamese—veterans of the war and the movement against the war, survivors, descendants, and bystanders ("There are so many of us who've been here")—have most successfully and forcefully documented the Vietnam War and its lingering influence in the postwar years.

It is an astonishingly large and diverse body of work, this assemblage of fiction, poetry, drama, comic books, and graphic novels about the Vietnam War. LaSalle University's special collection Imaginative Representations of the Vietnam War currently includes some eighteen thousand short stories, plays, filmscripts, works of graphic art, paintings, videos, TV productions, and sound recordings, including nine thousand novels and books of poetry—what LaSalle calls "fictive writing." For a teacher introducing a post-Vietnam generation to the broad, dramatic implications of the war for all aspects of American society in the late twentieth and twenty-first centuries, literature can personalize the war and engage students in ways that journalism, history, political commentary, and facts and figures never will. The challenge, given the huge and growing concatenation of literary interpretations of the war, is to identify aesthetically satisfying, thematically relevant texts and to devise techniques and strategies for deploying them as instructional resources in lessons about the war.

In *Walking Point*, one of the first (1988) scholarly examinations of the then nascent subject "American Narratives of Vietnam," Thomas Myers calls the first wave of American veteran-authors (Tim O'Brien, Philip Caputo, Michael Herr, Ward Just, and others) literary point men, "author(s) and caretaker(s) of a credible collective memory" just as, in combat, the point man—the soldier who leads the unit through dangerous territory—is the "eyes, ears and brain for the soldiers who depend on his intuition, his powers of observation, and his creative decisions." In this essay I propose to be a scholarly "point man," guiding the teacher whose expertise might lie outside the fields of literary fire through the dense, tangled, but rich jungle of literature about the Vietnam War.

It is commonly accepted that for a decade or more after the end of the Vietnam War (i.e., America's 1973 peace treaty and the North Vietnamese rout of the attenuated southern forces in spring 1975), Americans retrenched into a collective "national amnesia" about the unprecedented military defeat. But during this period, the so-called first-wave authors produced numerous narrative accounts of the war. These included powerful memoirs such as Ron Kovic's *Born on the Fourth of July* (1976), Philip Caputo's *A Rumor of War* and Michael Herr's *Dispatches* (both 1977), as well as now canonical novels such as John M. Del Vecchio's *The 13th Valley* (1982), Larry Heinemann's *Close Quarters* (1977) and *Paco's Story* (1986), and Tim O'Brien's *Going After Cacciato* (1978). These "literary point men" were combat (or journalist) veterans writing from direct, firsthand experience of the war. And the early scholarly assessments of the new genre of Vietnam War literature invariably tacitly accepted the still common privileging of autobiographical testimony from its participants.

By the mid-1980s, the war and its aftermath had inspired a more diverse cadre of authors and today a more expansive definition of Vietnam War literature embraces the voices of women, antiwar activists, Vietnamese refugees, the children of veterans, former prisoners of war, and others. This more accurate and inclusive definition underscores Michael Herr's well-known assertion at the conclusion of *Dispatches*: "Vietnam Vietnam Vietnam, we've all been there."

The Cold War

The teacher who seeks a literary introduction to a broad analysis of American foreign policy, American imperialism/exceptionalism, and Cold War era politics might turn to British novelist Graham Greene's canonical *The Quiet American* (1955), perhaps the first (and most prescient) novel about America's involvement in Vietnam. The interplay between the narrator, apolitical English journalist Thomas Fowler, and the naive, idealistic American government representative Alden Pyle—set against a love triangle involving the two men and a Vietnamese woman—suggests complex themes of patriotism, betrayal, and American arrogance in foreign affairs.

An interesting corollary (or alternative) to Greene's pre–Vietnam War narrative is Ward Just's 1999 novel *A Dangerous Friend*, set in Vietnam in 1965. Like *The Quiet American*, the action takes place early in the war. But Just's novel was written long after the event. It features another well-meaning but ingenuous American whose motives for going to Vietnam are at once honorable and lethal. Adding the French involvement in Vietnam to Greene's subjects, Just similarly explores the complexities of Vietnam and US involvement there to offer a nuanced story that explores the misleading simplicity of explanations for the war that end with "fear of communism" or "the domino theory."

Either of these narratives would introduce students to the political dimensions of America's sojourn in Vietnam, with an emphasis on the myriad, sometimes murky motivations for well-meaning but ill-informed nonmilitary operatives to involve themselves in initiatives that are inevitably more subtle and complicated than the characters recognize.

The Traditional Combat Novel and Memoir

Despite the broad range of literary material that is now considered "Vietnam War literature," texts that capture the drama and horrors of the combat experience are among the best-known narratives about the war, and scholarly commentary that examines Vietnam literature within the tradition of the war narrative is common. Teachers and scholars often consider Vietnam War texts as representatives of a tradition in American literature that includes Stephen Crane's 1895 Civil War novel *The Red Badge of Courage*; John Dos Passos's 1921 novel *Three Soldiers*, about World War I; and Norman Mailer's 1948 World War II epic, *The Naked and the Dead*. These traditional, realistic, coming-of-age novels present one or more young, untested male protagonists proving their manhood in the primitive, horrific environment of the battlefield. The canon of Vietnam War literature includes a large number of ambitious novels that offer that war's variation on the collective fictional story of the so-called melting plot platoon. And overtly autobiographical factual accounts of the combat experience in Vietnam make the memoir or autobiography a compelling complementary genre.

Fictional narratives set in Vietnam during the American war, such as James Webb's *Fields of Fire* (1978), Larry Heinemann's *Close Quarters* (1977), Winston Groom's *Better Times Than These* (1978), John M. Del

Vecchio's *The 13th Valley* (1982), Tim O'Brien's short story collection *The Things They Carried* (1990), Susan Fromberg Schaeffer's *Buffalo Afternoon* (1989), Donald Pfarrer's *The Fearless Man* (2004), Dennis Johnson's *Tree of Smoke* (2007), and Karl Marlantes's *Matterhorn* (2011), generally echo the traditional war novel's thematic preoccupation with the trial by fire of the young, untested male protagonist(s). Memoirs such as *A Rumor of War* and *Born on the Fourth of July* narrow the novel's focus to the personal, unique experience of the author. Most offer variations on some common themes: only those who actually experience combat can truly understand its horrors and exhilarations; in the Vietnam War, officers, rear-guard military personnel, and politicians and Pentagon officials are incompetent, ignorant about the realities of life on the fields of fire, or cynical, craven exemplars of a society that doomed the United States to lose the war by forcing its combatants to fight "with one hand tied behind their backs." These novels and memoirs often explore the increasingly fractious interracial relationships among the soldiers, along with the unassailable fraternal bonds and camaraderie of men struggling to stay, and keep each other, alive. They also highlight the frustrations of conducting war in unfamiliar jungle conditions against an enemy that lacked America's technological superiority but was fighting on its own terrain. To generalize, while few of the veteran-authored combat novels repudiate the Vietnam War as unnecessary and inhumane (as many Vietnam texts and assessments do), they do acknowledge the complexity and uniqueness of the Vietnam experience.

The Return Home: Combat Veterans after the War

The most compelling literary responses to the Vietnam War include narratives (novels and short stories, memoirs, oral histories), poetry, and plays—often but not necessarily written by veterans of the war—that present the challenges of the veteran's readjustment to civilian and American life after his Vietnam experience. Surely the most encouraging contrast between America's wars in Iraq and Afghanistan and the Vietnam War is that we seem to have learned not to blame the warrior for the war. As the Vietnam War (and its costs and casualties) escalated, the increasing unpopularity of the war was demonstrated in home-front hostility against the returning veteran. First-wave literary texts and films invariably present the veteran as a peacetime misfit, mercurial, possibly drug addicted, and generally misunderstood and feared by a society that wants to forget about the Vietnam War (think Rambo in *First Blood*). In later texts the vet, suffering from post-traumatic stress disorder, continues to struggle with personal relationships and everyday life, but he is more pitiable than malevolent or crazy. Most aftermath novels include characters' flashbacks, or interpolated chapters, that revisit the battlefield—in other words, these texts introduce students to both the in-country and the postwar dimensions of the veteran's experience.

Caputo's *Indian Country* (1987) presents a familiar type: the decent veteran whose postwar life is chaotic because of his suppressed (and undeserved) guilt over a friend's death in combat. Chris Starkmann's difficult relationship with his pacifist minister-father (a rare middle-aged antiwar character) and his long-suffering wife frame his long post-war journey toward healing and reconciliation. Other texts present the particular challenges of life as an African American veteran of the war: Wallace Terry's *Bloods: An Oral History of the Vietnam War by Black Veterans* (1984) and Albert French's 1997 memoir *Patches of Fire*.

Wounded Vets

The postwar adjustment of most literary veterans is complicated by emotional and physical wounds. Larry Heinemann's eponymous character in *Paco's Story* (1986), one of the best Vietnam narratives, suffers from both. The spare, lyrical novel, narrated by the ghosts of Paco's dead comrades, is too graphic for young readers, but it allows consideration of the unspoken horrors of the war for its combatants, as well as analysis of its highly literary technique.

Larry Brown's elegant *Dirty Work* (1989) presents two vets whose lives intersect twenty years after the war. One, African American Braiden Chaney, is a limbless torso who desires only death; the other, Walter James, suffered a severe head injury in Vietnam. In their shared hospital room they discuss the war, race, fathers, women, and their sad fate as "leftover guys" in postwar America.

Born on the Fourth of July (like *Indian Country*) turns on Kovic's repressed responsibility for the death of a fellow grunt in Vietnam. Paraplegic Kovic's account of his shabby treatment by the Veterans Administration and difficult postwar adjustment is readable and (because of the Oliver Stone movie based on it) well known. It is not particularly insightful or well written. Multiple amputee Lewis Puller

Jr.'s "long road home," which he partially chronicles in the Pulitzer Prize–winning 1991 memoir *Fortunate Son,* meandered through alcoholism, professional success, clinical depression, and divorce before ending with his 1994 suicide.

Combat nurse Lynda Van Devanter offers a different perspective on the war in her autobiographical *Home Before Morning: The True Story of an Army Nurse in Vietnam* (1983). After an emotionally wrenching year as a surgical nurse in Vietnam, Van Devanter returns home to endure the same lingering emotional trauma and civilian indifference that the combat veterans recount—as well as the health care system's dismissal of her professional skills. Her memoir is the first of many autobiographies, novels, and oral histories by and about women who served in Vietnam as nurses and Red Cross workers. Because of Van Devanter's candor about her postwar struggles, it remains one of the best. Keith Walker's *A Piece of My Heart* (1985), a collection of oral histories by women who served in Vietnam, offers more compact alternatives to Van Devanter's memoir.

Lanford Wilson's 1978 play *Fifth of July,* part of his trilogy about the Missouri Talley family, features Kenneth Talley Jr., a gay paraplegic Vietnam veteran, and his colorful family. In addition to its genre, and its relatively sympathetic presentation of a homosexual character, it varies from other aftermath texts due to its semicomic tone and sensibility. The Tony-winning *Sticks and Bones* (1971) is the second play in David Rabe's Vietnam trilogy. Blind combat veteran David returns to his family and home in a dark, satiric turn on the pre–Vietnam era television situation comedy *The Adventures of Ozzie and Harriet,* which represents the perfect suburban American family and the romanticized, nostalgic ideal of a post–World War II, stable American society.

The Home Front

Numerous texts focus on American society during the war years and in its long aftermath, a home front eight thousand miles away from the fields of fire but dramatically affected by the war, its expense in money and lives, and its unprecedented unpopularity at home. The stories of the lingering wounds of the survivors and caretakers— much like texts that address emotionally and physically damaged veterans—yield important discussions about trauma, memory, and the lingering, painful effects of the war on American society.

In her 1984 novel *Machine Dreams,* Jayne Anne Phillips focuses on the family of a soldier missing and presumed dead in Vietnam. Two years after Billy Hampson's disappearance in Vietnam, his sister Danner has not recovered from her loss. *Machine Dreams* is one of many novels that present the tragic repercussions of the war for the families and friends who stayed behind, watching and waiting for their soldiers' return, and those who have to pick up the pieces when their loved one comes home emotionally or physically scarred. In *The Waiting Room* (1989), Mary Morris tells the story of another sister, Zoe Coleman, who has to overcome her sense of complicity in her brother's Vietnam-induced emotional devastation.

Eighteen-year-old Samantha Hughes, the protagonist of Bobbie Ann Mason's *In Country* (1985), has grown up without the father who was killed in Vietnam before her birth and with the postwar struggles of her uncle, Emmett, a damaged veteran of the war. Sam's coming-of-age journey in the summer after her small-town Kentucky high school graduation, as she contemplates her own opportunities, are set against her—and the country's—preoccupation with the lost war a decade after its end. *In Country* is brief and easy to read—yet the integral Vietnam War material (the lasting legacy of a combatant's death, the emotional and physical wounds of war for the combat survivor, the veterans' resentment at civilians' inability to understand their travails yet their dismissal of anyone—like Sam—who tries) can be discussed in the broader context of the female bildungsroman, southern literature, noted minimalist Mason's literary technique, and America in the mid-1980s. The novel is both accessible and complex, therefore ideal as a classroom text for non-English majors and courses.

The American War

America's Vietnam War was, for the Vietnamese, the American War. As a people accustomed to foreign occupation, the Vietnamese have not remained preoccupied with that war as Americans have, but the Vietnamese literature inspired by the American War is an important accompaniment to the American literary responses.

Like *Dispatches* and Tim O'Brien's fiction, combat veteran Bao Ninh's autobiographical novel *The Sorrow of War: A Novel of North Vietnam* (1994) illustrates combat's traumatic bequest for the combatant through an experimental, fragmented style that captures the chaos and ambiguity of the Vietnam War. The novel is the story of Kien, a former North Vietnamese soldier who, in 1975, writes to exorcise the demons of his ten long years of war. *The Sorrow of War* emphasizes the horrific legacy of combat for soldiers, as well as the tragic lives of millions of Vietnamese civilians who were inevitably damaged by the long war. Novels that present the experiences of America's enemies in the war, such as *The Sorrow of War* and Duong Thu Huong's *Novel without a Name* (1991), offer protagonists who are similar to American combat veteran protagonists in their disillusionment with war.

The Vietnamese diaspora—the story of the million and more Vietnamese and their American-born descendants who fled the war-torn country for a new life in America—is among the least-known but most compelling aftereffects of the Vietnam War. In *Monkey Bridge* (1997), Lan Cao (who emigrated from Vietnam to the United States as a teenager) presents another coming-of-age narrative, textured by protagonist Mai's attempts to assimilate into American society as her dependent mother and her mother's insistent silence about the family's tortured past pull her toward family, history, and Vietnam. As a(nother) novel about a college-bound young woman determined to discover her family's secrets, *Monkey Bridge* is a compelling companion to Mason's *In Country*.

Lê thi diem thúy's *The Gangster We Are All Looking For* (2003) and Dao Strom's *Grass Roof, Tin Roof* (2003) are brief, readable novels that similarly present the unique challenges of Vietnamese-born, American-raised characters as they guide their immigrant parents through life in a confusing new land. Kien Nguyen's memoir *The Unwanted* (2001) offers a variant on the story of the child of Vietnam who flees to the United States (along with hundreds of thousands of others who left Vietnam for financial or political reasons in the decades after the end of the war). As a *bui doi* (a "child of dust," mixed race, Vietnamese and American), Nguyen is ostracized in his home country, and his harrowing "memoir of childhood" concentrates on the years before he leaves Vietnam in 1984.

Robert Olen Butler's Pulitzer Prize–winning story collection *A Good Scent from a Strange Mountain* (1992) is sui generis, since it presents the stories and voices of Vietnamese emigrants to Louisiana written by an American veteran of the war. These poignant stories of the real victims of the war challenge Americans' provincial perception of the war by showing that it was, for the majority of those who engaged in it directly, daily, and often disastrously, an American War. Although Olen Butler's stories—like O'Brien's *The Things They Carried* and Susan O'Neill's *Don't Mean Nothing* (2001), about combat nurses in country—are integrally connected, any can be taught independently or in small groups.

The novels and memoirs by Vietnamese natives who experienced the war present the perspective of our southern Vietnamese allies and northern opponents in the war. The texts by and about the Vietnamese who fled Vietnam to become refugees in America after the war (and their children born in the United States) might open up important discussions about the always vexed issue of immigration.

The Protest Movement

Courses on America in the Vietnam era might venture further than combat, the aftermath for veterans and their families, or the Vietnamese diaspora. The protest movement, which remains perhaps the most controversial aspect of the war and its era, and its crazy cousin, the counterculture, are the subjects of many autobiographical and fictional narratives. The memoirs—such as Bill Ayers's *Fugitive Days* (2001) and Tom Hayden's *Reunion* (1988)—are generally interesting more for historical than literary reasons. The quality of the novels (e.g., Jay Cantor, *Great Neck* [2003]; Neil Gordon, *The Company You Keep* [2003]; Sigrid Nunez, *The Last of Her Kind* [2006]; Marge Piercy, *Vida* [1979]; and Dana Spiotta, *Eat the Document* [2006]) varies as well. I frequently teach Philip Roth's *American Pastoral* (1997). Although it is more about the decline of American society after World War II (particularly in the 1960s) than about the war, it is the most sophisticated, nuanced (if conservative) fictional account of the vertiginous 1960s in America—and, of course, it exposes students to one of America's most important contemporary novelists.

Poetry and Anthologies

While narrative is the dominant form in Vietnam War literature, many courses in nonliterary subjects may not have the time to devote to the full-length novel or memoir. Short stories are a viable alternative, and, in addition to collections of short stories such as those by O'Brien, O'Neill, Olen Butler, and Gologorsky, and oral history compilations (Mark Baker, *Nam*; Wallace Terry, *Bloods*; Keith Walker, *A*

Piece of My Heart), several anthologies do offer broad coverage and brief selections on varied aspects of the war.

Wayne Karlin, Le Minh Khue, and Truong Vu's *The Other Side of Heaven* (1995) includes fiction (both short stories and excerpts from novels such as *Paco's Story* and *The Sorrow of War*) from both American and Vietnamese writers. Stewart O'Nan's *The Vietnam Reader* (1998) is a comprehensive, inexpensive collection of American fiction and non-fiction about the war. It includes excerpts from the best-known novels and memoirs, as well as poems, song lyrics, oral history pieces, and background on films, as well as a map, timeline, and glossary. Older (but still in print) collections include *The Vietnam War in American Stories, Songs, and Poems* (H. Bruce Franklin, 1995) and *Vietnam Anthology: American War Literature* (Nancy Anisfield, 1987). Vietnam veteran, poet, and memoirist W. D. Ehrhart's edited collections of poetry about the war, *Carrying the Darkness: The Poetry of the Vietnam War* (1985) and *Unaccustomed Mercy: Soldier-Poets of the Vietnam War* (1989), are often used in courses. Philip Mahony's *From Both Sides Now: The Poetry of the Vietnam War and Its Aftermath* (1998) includes poetry by Vietnamese writers, as well as the best-known American poets.

Pedagogy

Obviously, how a teacher selects texts and incorporates them into a course depends on the subject matter and scope of the course, the time that can be devoted to the literature of the Vietnam War, and the students' interests and abilities. While teachers must make course and source decisions based on their knowledge of the subject, their time limitations, and their student population, some general comments about pedagogical decisions might help them make their choices. What follows are a few suggestions for how teachers can use the different genres of Vietnam War writing to engage students in their own college or secondary classrooms.

Teaching the Combat Novel or Memoir

The best straightforward combat narratives (those by Webb, Groom, Heinemann, and Caputo) can complement and personalize the more academic or "objective" presentation of the war in a history or political science class. These works often highlight the participants' ambivalent and evolving attitudes toward combat in general and the Vietnam War in particular. I ask students to compare and contrast the different accounts, focusing on what they suggest (individually and together) about American society's conflicted and changing attitudes about the war as it dragged on.

A teacher can also combine one of the American combat novels with a novel (such as *The Sorrow of War* or Duong Thu Huong's *Novel without a Name*) that presents the Vietnamese experience of the war. A course with more limited time for combat literature would be well served to excerpt chapters or stories from Tim O'Brien's oft-taught *The Things They Carried* (1990); a pairing of the title story and "How to Tell a True War Story" (a story/essay that problematizes the genre and purpose of "war stories"), for instance, makes for a compelling class period or two. Other brief, readable stories from *The Things They Carried* explore the moral aftereffects of war ("The Ghost Soldiers") and the unlikely immersion of a high school girl into the deepest jungle of Vietnam ("Sweetheart of the Song Tra Bong"). From the same collection, "Notes" and "Spin" can introduce a discussion of how the ambiguities of the war and innovations in storytelling in the late twentieth century propelled authors like O'Brien (and Herr in *Dispatches* and Stephen Wright in *Meditations in Green* [1983]) to engage the war in metaliterary, self-consciously experimental prose. Almost any one of the twenty-two discrete sections or stories of O'Brien's collection offers a compelling entry into the complexities of the war and the often experimental literature it evoked.

A teaching unit focused on the combat experience might pair one of the "melting pot platoon" novels (I generally teach *Fields of Fire*, which is pro-war but not simplistically so) with a memoir (Caputo's is more complex than Kovic's) in order to examine questions about authenticity, memory, and the generic conventions of fiction and autobiography. Given controversies about apparent memoirs that are exposed as fictional or fictionalized (e.g., James Frey's *A Million Little Pieces*), analysis of an autobiographical text, or a novel-memoir pairing, would allow discussion of the ubiquitous "you had to be there" theme, as well as inquiry about readers' assumptions about authenticity.

Another fruitful pedagogical use of the Vietnam combat novel or memoir is to pair it with a narrative from another war. Although most combat novels are by veterans of the combat experience, Stephen Crane wrote his great Civil War novel *The Red Badge of Courage* before he ever saw battle. Students could be asked to consider what *Fields of Fire* or *Born on the Fourth of July* suggests about the combatant's claim on the experience and whether someone who has never been under fire can understand and appreciate the combat experience. Comparisons and contrasts between Stephen Crane's novel (or Hemingway's *A Farewell to Arms* or Norman Mailer's *The Naked and the Dead*) and a Vietnam combat narrative can show the essential commonalities and important differences between wars of different eras.

In his memoir of his year as a marine second lieutenant early in the war, *A Rumor of War*, Philip Caputo writes that "it had been an experience as fascinating as it was repulsive, as exhilarating as it was sad, as tender as it was cruel." Students could be asked to consider whether Caputo's apprehension of his war experience evolves as the memoir unfolds and what his story suggests about American society's conflicted and changing (as the war dragged on) attitude about the war. Pairing Caputo's memoir with, for instance, Anthony Swofford's 2003 Gulf War memoir *Jarhead* (which presents a brief war with a clear victory and more boredom than frightening action), again, challenges students to expand their understanding of the Vietnam War.

Another approach to the postwar experience that succeeds in the classroom is to use the usually brief oral history selections (Mark Baker, *Nam*; Wallace Terry, *Bloods*; Keith Walker, *A Piece of My Heart*) to introduce students to personal accounts of the war. Students can then be assigned to record their own oral histories from interviews with family members who fought in or remember the Vietnam War, or with veterans of the more recent wars in Iraq and Afghanistan. For more ideas about how to prepare students for the oral history component of such an enterprise, teachers should read Andrew Darien's essay in this volume.

Teaching the Home Front and the Aftermath

A course unit that combines literature about the veterans' return home and families affected by the war might include "Speaking of Courage" (from *The Things They Carried*), about a vet trying to come to terms with his in-country experience or Bobbie Ann Mason's "Big Bertha Stories" (1985, widely anthologized). O'Brien's "On the Rainy River" (from *The Things They Carried*) is a compelling account of his decision about whether to go to Vietnam or to evade the draft; it works well with James Fallows's easily available 1975 essay "What Did

You Do in the Class War, Daddy?" Both invite spirited discussions about guilt and responsibility and would segue well into a consideration of America's recent wars and the all-volunteer military. I often use Mason's 1985 novel *In Country* to explore the effects of the war on veterans and their families. In it the character Sam Hughes tries to understand a war that claimed the life of her father, a man she never knew. The novel is a classic coming-of-age story, one that can be used to discuss the students' own experiences journeying from adolescence into adulthood. It also facilitates a discussion about the female experience of war.

Philip Roth's *American Pastoral*—a more ambitious novel with a broader scope—would introduce sophisticated readers to a complex consideration of the implications of the war for American society in the second half of the twentieth century. Roth's account of the successful Jewish businessman Swede Levov and his sixties-era daughter turned bomber, who "transports him out of the longed-for American pastoral and into everything that is its antithesis and its enemy, into the fury, the violence, and the desperation of the counterpastoral—into the indigenous American berserk," fosters discussions of the American dream, the "generation gap," the often painful disagreements about the Vietnam War within families, and the many ways in which the war spread beyond the jungles of Vietnam to dining room tables throughout America.

Teachers who want to talk about the still controversial antiwar movement—and later perceptions of the protesters—have many other options. Historian and activist Todd Gitlin (in *The Sixties: Years of Hope, Days of Rage*) complains that the 1960s has often been reduced to caricature. Similarly, historian H. Bruce Franklin (in his 2000 book *Vietnam and Other American Fantasies*) decries the simplification, demonization, and denial of the antiwar movement, which he calls the "movement we are supposed to forget." Students themselves may have developed strong opinions about antiwar demonstrators as a result of the way they have been depicted in movies, on television, or in media coverage (or, more compellingly, noncoverage) of opponents of the conflicts in Iraq and Afghanistan. Using the Vietnam War can allow students to contextualize current political disputes and connect a historical event to one that has more immediate bearing on their daily lives. Teachers can look to David Steigerwald's essay in this volume for more historical context and teaching ideas for this subject.

The postcombat, aftermath experience can be brought more up to date with a consideration of Ben Fountain's 2012 Iraq War novel *Billy Lynn's Long Halftime Walk* and Stephen Wright's similarly satiric *Meditations in Green* or Tim O'Brien's *Going After Cacciato*. Like Joseph Heller's World War II novel *Catch-22* (1961), these texts examine the comic absurdity of the combat (or, in Fountain's book, war era home front) experience for the combatant.

Creative Writing

Vietnam War texts that reflect in technique the commonplace assumption that the war—like the mercurial enemy—was opaque and chaotic offer the student of creative writing interesting, complex material for attention to the techniques of imaginative writing. Influenced by postmodernism and New Journalism, novels such as Stephen Wright's *Meditations in Green*, O'Brien's *Going After Cacciato*, *The Things They Carried*, and *In the Lake of the Woods*, and Herr's *Dispatches* reward pedagogical attention that foregrounds the authors' methods and techniques. The obvious selection here (as well as for thematic consideration of journalists' experience of the war) is *Dispatches*. Its fragmented structure and experimental style are audacious, clearly evocative of its author's experience of the ambiguities and absurdities of the war. *Dispatches* is, Herr states, "a book about the writing of a book."

The massive size of the "library" of literary interpretations of the Vietnam War and its corollary subjects, while daunting, allows for a variety of approaches and the exploration of countless subtopics. This essay highlights a small percentage of readings and classroom ideas that have worked well in my classes. They should provide a useful starting point for teachers who want to use literature as a way to engage students in the complex history of the Vietnam War and its aftermath.

KEY RESOURCES

Greene, Graham. *The Quiet American*. Text and Criticism edited by John Clark Pratt. New York: Penguin Books, 1996.
Jason, Philip K., ed. *Fourteen Landing Zones: Approaches to Vietnam War Literature*. Iowa City: University of Iowa Press, 1991.

Jeffords, Susan. *The Remasculinization of America: Gender and the Vietnam War.* Bloomington: Indiana University Press, 1989.

Myers, Thomas. *Walking Point: American Narratives of Vietnam.* New York: Oxford University Press, 1988.

O'Nan, Stewart, ed. *The Vietnam Reader: The Definitive Collection of American Fiction and Non-fiction on the War.* New York: Anchor Books, 1998.

Ryan, Maureen. *The Other Side of Grief: The Home Front and the Aftermath in American Narratives of the Vietnam War.* Amherst: University of Massachusetts Press, 2008.

———. "The Vietnam War and Literature." In *America and the Vietnam War: Re-examining the Culture and History of a Generation,* edited by Andrew Wiest, Mary Kathryn Barbier, and Glenn Robins. New York: Routledge, 2010.

Searle, William J. *Search and Clear: Critical Responses to Selected Literature and Films of the Vietnam War.* Bowling Green: Bowling Green State University Popular Press, 1988.

Teaching the Vietnam War in the Internet Age

Libraries, Websites, and Information Literacy

RICHARD HUME WERKING and

BRIAN C. ETHERIDGE

Introduction: Going Beyond "the Log"

In December 1871, Congressman James A. Garfield addressed his fellow Williams College alumni during a banquet at Delmonico's in New York City. "I am not willing," Garfield offered in praise of the college's president, "that this discussion should close without mention of the value of a true teacher. Give me a log hut, with only a simple bench, Mark Hopkins on one end and I on the other, and you may have all the buildings, apparatus, and libraries without him." The popular and briefer version of the future president's statement captures an even more sylvan image: "The ideal college is Mark Hopkins on one end of a log and a student on the other." Hopkins's biographer, Frederick Rudolph, notes that over time Garfield's remarks "came to be looked upon by many as the most satisfactory definition of what an American college ought to be."[1]

In at least one respect, things haven't changed much since 1871: an effective teacher is still as invaluable to student learning in the twenty-first century as he or she was in the nineteenth. What has changed, however, is the context in which the teacher-student relationship is situated.

Whether James Garfield could justifiably dismiss the educational context (buildings, apparatus, libraries) surrounding the relationship with his teacher even in the nineteenth century is certainly debatable. But no reasonable person today would claim that the resources available to teachers and students are inconsequential to their relationship.

The decades since 1871 have witnessed the emergence of an information-rich environment that would have been difficult, if not impossible, for Garfield and his contemporaries to imagine. Recognizing the challenges posed by such an environment, teachers and scholars in the twentieth century were quick to point out the essential role that specialized institutions and individuals played in making modern scholarship and teaching possible. In an engaging piece titled "Thoughts on the Fun and Purpose of Being an American Historian," noted historian William Appleman Williams made clear that he saw the academic library as the laboratory of the historian and history student. He emphasized how much fun and substance there was to be found in doing history and observed that he always sent "undergraduates as well as graduate students off into the bowels of the library to read other people's mail." Comparing learning history with learning chemistry, he quoted a chemistry major in his senior foreign policy seminar, who told him, "I never knew that I could do history like I could do silicon crystals. You got me into something new; you put a new window in my head. There's no formula for this one. I get to write my own equations. And, man, that is fun." Williams's emphasis here on "doing history" with primary sources is in line with a point made by Lynn D. Lampert, an academic librarian with BA and MA degrees in history: "[T]he key to training students to critically understand historical research methods is to incorporate primary resource materials into their typically overindulgent diet of secondary source research."[2]

Consequently, we hope this essay proves useful not only in informing and shaping lectures and classroom assignments on the Vietnam War but also in encouraging and empowering instructors and students to move "beyond the log" and indulge in the virtues and challenges of research. Such assignments might range from students undertaking a version of the traditional research paper to simply finding and critiquing one or two contemporary magazine or newspaper articles, or locating and using published book reviews in their own reviews of a particular book. In our experiences both as students and as teachers, we have found that much valuable learning occurs outside the classroom, as students conduct and reflect on their research. Nor are we alone in this belief; a survey of teaching conducted by the Society for Historians of American Foreign Relations (SHAFR) showed that four out of five courses taught by the respondents required research in materials beyond those specified by the instructor.[3]

For these reasons, and others that will be developed below, we have eschewed a categorical approach. We might have concentrated on listing and perhaps describing the "most important" print and digital works on the Vietnam War. But that conflict continues to be a complex and at times controversial subject, and there is an enormous wealth of material available to teachers and students. So, although it is part of our aim to point teachers to material that would likely enhance their own knowledge and lectures, classroom discussions, and students' reading assignments, we wanted to do more—to empower teachers (and thereby their students) to engage with a broader range of materials by framing ways for them to navigate the information byways more confidently. We also encourage the use of "information literacy" as a way to engage students in *doing* history, helping them to confront directly historians' interpretations, controversies, and evidence. What we teachers do in the classroom is of central importance, but what students are learning to do outside the classroom is also important.

The rest of this essay is designed to meet the various needs of teachers based on the extent of coverage given to the Vietnam War in the classes they teach. The next section highlights what we consider to be some of the most useful websites for this subject. It is followed by an example of how to incorporate a range of sources from several sites into one classroom presentation or student assignment on the Tet Offensive. Next are brief sections on some challenges related to the Internet, a discussion of information literacy that will help teachers encourage their students to think critically about primary and secondary sources on the war, and the creation of "LibGuides." Finally, we provide a sample research guide that could serve as a model for teacher-librarian collaboration.

Websites and Assignments

As the essays in this volume indicate, there is a plethora of Vietnam-related materials available on the Internet. This situation presents teachers with both opportunities and obstacles. The opportunity is that we can be reasonably certain that the types of resources we want to enhance our teaching about the Vietnam wars are available to us and our students, most often free of charge. We have easy access to videos, documents, music, art, maps, and interviews that we can use to make history seem more urgent and alive to our students. The obstacles to finding and using these amazing resources are significant, however. The enormous number of sites, their relative instability, and their often questionable contents should make us reluctant to simply "google" a key term or browse YouTube for the most watched relevant video. As we argue throughout this essay, the best option for teachers in this situation is to work with their campus's information specialists—librarians— well in advance of the time when they will need the resources, but, as instructors ourselves, we realize that this is not always possible. With that in mind, we suggest the following Internet sites and assignments. Together, they provide teachers with resources to increase their own knowledge of the Vietnam wars, as well as ideas for how to teach the subject—lesson plans, assignments, and in-class activities.

As with most topics in the history of the United States since the ratification of the Constitution, teachers can consult the National Archives and Records Administration (NARA) website for primary sources and teaching materials. When constructing their lessons and units on the Vietnam War, they should consider giving special attention to NARA's "Teachers' Resources" pages. Here they can explore "DocsTeach," an online tool for teachers wishing to create their own primary source activities (http://www.archives.gov/education), but the section "Teaching with Documents: The War in Vietnam—A Story in Photographs" will likely be of most immediate value (http://www .archives.gov/education/lessons/vietnam-photos). Utilizing the NARA photograph analysis guides, this section features the close examination of thirteen photographs, group work, and an associated creative writing assignment, and it correlates clearly with National History Standards.

Additionally, NARA's pages for teachers on the presidential libraries, especially Truman's, Eisenhower's, and Kennedy's, are rich in online resources for students and teachers (some include lesson plans); most sites have an "Education" tab, and all the libraries are accessible via http://www.archives.gov/presidential-libraries/visit/. Other essays throughout this volume offer specific suggestions for how teachers can best utilize these libraries' resources.

An even more venerable federal agency, the Library of Congress, in 2000 established a "Veterans History Project" with this goal: "To collect, preserve and make accessible the firsthand remembrances of America's war veterans." In 2012 the project launched three installments of "Vietnam Experience: Looking Back" (http://www.loc.gov/vets/stories).

It is worth drawing special attention to the "Digital Classroom Initiative" presented by the University of Virginia's Miller Center's Presidential Recordings Program (http://whitehousetapes.net/content/classroom/index.php?n=Main.Vietnam). This site provides teachers with a carefully selected collection of key audio recordings, arranged by topic and helpfully annotated. One of the most important features of the site is that it includes transcripts of the recorded excerpts so that students can better follow the conversations, in addition to images and brief biographies of most of the people mentioned in the transcript and links to related primary sources and maps. For example, the site contains a recording of a short conversation President John F. Kennedy had with his advisers about the press coverage of the war, and visitors are directed to links for contemporaneous newspaper articles, Kennedy's daily diary, a David Halberstam *New York Times* article, and other connected materials. While the site offers a couple of Vietnam-related lesson plans and provides links to classroom activities from each recording's individual page, it will be most useful to teachers who want to create documents-based questions (DBQs) or want to add sound files to their classroom or assessment activities. (See Mitchell B. Lerner's essay in this volume for more information on using the White House tapes.)

Texas Tech University's well-known and highly regarded Vietnam Center and Archive has an especially rich site, particularly for teachers who want students to conduct a research assignment using primary sources. The site's extensive photo, oral history, and map collections are especially valuable, and the site is actively soliciting teacher contributions to its existing "Teachers' Resources" section (http://www.vietnam.ttu.edu).[4]

Many teachers will probably want to use documentary films to enhance their teaching of the Vietnam War, and most still find useful the Public Broadcasting Service's *American Experience* series *Vietnam: A Television History*. Originally produced in 1983, it was reedited and rebroadcast in 1997, and PBS has created a site to support those who want to use it in the classroom. Vietnam Online: An Online Companion to

"Vietnam: A Television History" contains detailed descriptions of the eleven episodes; a helpful "who's who" section with brief biographies of about forty figures from Cambodia, North and South Vietnam, and the United States; and a teachers' guide, along with suggestions for "active learning," at http://www.pbs.org/wgbh/amex/vietnam. The site's map section includes six maps of Vietnam from 1945 on, and it should be quite useful to teachers looking to explain the many transitions of the era. Another website rich in visual and audio resources is the Internet Archive, which provides links for hundreds of films, videos, audio files, and websites when "Vietnam War" is searched on the site's home page (http://archive.org).

A manageable number of key documents, along with other useful materials, may be found on a Vassar College site, The Wars for Vietnam, 1945-1975, located at http://vietnam.vassar.edu/index.html. Among other materials, the site contains the class materials for Robert Brigham's senior seminar on the Vietnam War. Its most significant contribution to teachers is offering Brigham's personal translation of key Vietnamese primary sources that he discovered as one of the first American scholars allowed to conduct research in Vietnam after the war.

The Pacifica Radio/UC Berkeley Social Activism Recording Project site holds a wealth of media material on anti–Vietnam War protests in the San Francisco Bay Area, http://www.lib.berkeley.edu/MRC/pacific aviet.html. Arranged in chronological order, with materials grouped in "the war" or "anti-war/political activism" categories, the materials range from links to transcripts of speeches to home-movie videos of protests, recordings of protest songs, photographs of key figures and events, and debates in the University of California, Berkeley, student newspaper. Teachers wishing to contextualize the antiwar movement, or to direct students to a specific site to do so, will want to consider using this resource.

Finally, teachers should know about Vanderbilt University's Television News Archive, which contains what the website describes as "the world's most extensive and complete archive of television news." Coverage begins in 1968, although much important pre–August 1968 footage is embedded in subsequent newscasts and is readily findable. The archive lends DVDs of news programs for a relatively modest fee; see http://tvnews.vanderbilt.edu/. According to the university's history bibliographer, Peter Brush, it "contains digital images and a searchable interface for all network newscasts since August 1968.

Students have used it to find famous images from the war. . . . Today many students underappreciate the importance of network television back in the pre-Internet period."[5] Even if teachers are not able to request specific film footage, they might want to query the database as a class activity, just to highlight how much Vietnam dominated news broadcasts in the late 1960s and early 1970s. Perhaps a comparison with the relatively scarce attention paid to the more recent conflicts in Iraq and Afghanistan could spark a meaningful conversation about the reasons for the differences in the depth and frequency of news coverage.

These are, of course, just a few of the many websites that college and secondary teachers can use to prepare for teaching about the Vietnam wars, to create effective assignments, to engage students in the classroom, or to have students conduct their own research on the wars. Most of the websites have special sections for educators, and engaged teachers will be able to devise any number of ways to use the materials contained on one or more of these sites.[6] Below we suggest one way to combine resources from several sites to help teach the Tet Offensive.

Teaching the Tet Offensive: An Example

The Internet hosts a wealth of resources on the Tet Offensive. Once students are familiar with the basic outlines of Tet and its aftermath, they can be directed to the Virtual Vietnam Archive at Texas Tech University, where they can find an extensive collection of oral histories. Searching the collection identifies several dozen oral histories that mention Tet, though sometimes only in passing. (Some of the accounts that discuss the Tet Offensive in detail include Jim Laible [item OH0144], Philip Watson [OH0165], Chad Spawr [OH0006], and Michael McGregor [OH0329]). Students can choose one account and summarize the subject's experiences. They should be aware that an oral history, like any other source, needs to be read critically (see, e.g., Andrew Darien's essay on oral history in this volume). They can also compare the subject's experiences to the description of the Tet Offensive that they find in a textbook such as George Herring's *America's Longest War* or Marilyn B. Young's *The Vietnam Wars*.[7]

Teachers can use Tet to analyze photographic images and think about them as historical sources. Tet was responsible for one of the most iconic photos of the war (and one of the most famous photos in modern American history), Eddie Adams's image of Nguyen Ngoc Loan executing an enemy guerrilla on the streets of Saigon (see Andrew Wiest's essay in this volume for more information about this image). The website of the Newseum includes two short clips of Adams talking about this photo and his other experiences as a journalist in Vietnam (http://www.newseum.org/warstories/interviews/mp3/journalists /bio.asp?ID=22). The clips are brief (about four minutes in total), so they can be played in class or students can listen to them on their own time. Students can use Adams's own ambivalence about the photograph—he says that "a lot of times pictures do lie"—to discuss the advantages and disadvantages of drawing conclusions from a single image. Teachers might ask students to find other iconic images related to the Vietnam War, such as the ones depicting the victims at Kent State University, Kim Phuc after being hit with napalm, or Thich Quang Duc's self-immolation. Students can analyze the content of the photograph, but they can also do some research to find out about the context of the image, the photographer's thoughts about the photo, and even in some cases the reflections of the subject.[8]

Adams's photo and other sources, both online and in print, can also be employed to explore Tet's role in shaping American public opinion about the war. Students can watch Walter Cronkite's famous broadcast from Vietnam shortly after the Tet Offensive or read an excerpt from Cronkite's report. They can also read some secondary materials on Tet. Any basic textbook on the war will have considerable coverage of the Tet Offensive, but students looking for even greater analysis can consult Donald Oberdorfer's *Tet!* or Peter Braestrup's *Big Story*.[9] Using these varied sources, students should be able to write a paper or engage in a classroom debate about Tet and its consequences.

The Internet's Challenges

Because the amount of information available on the Internet continues to increase exponentially, and therefore the kind of information available to teachers and students about the Vietnam War will change with time, we wanted to discuss some fundamental issues associated with research on the web, so that teachers and students can feel confident extending their reach beyond the limited number of websites discussed here. Although the web has made readily available a great deal of reputable and reliable information, we know all too well that it has also provided the same easy accessibility to information that is considerably less reputable or reliable, especially on controversial subjects such as the Vietnam War. As a result, teachers and librarians need to spend considerable time steering students toward worthwhile sources, including good websites. More than we used to do with print resources, we need to help students understand the importance of using several criteria—the most important among them being questions of authority, objectivity, accuracy, currency, and coverage—in evaluating websites.[10]

Regarding coverage, our students are often surprised to learn about this aspect of the web's limitations. In their eyes, the Internet appears to reach everywhere. But of course it does not. After all, the great majority of contemporary news (via newsmagazines, journals of opinion, and newspapers), as well as scholarly books, journal articles, and various finding tools, are not found free and in their entirety on the Internet.[11] Even when available in digital form, they are often part of proprietary databases. Academic, school, and public libraries have paid to provide these resources, sometimes using web-supplied content, at other times continuing to rely on the paper format.

Another challenge presented by the web is the fragility of many URLs (uniform resource locaters) and the inability or unwillingness to maintain websites and keep them reasonably up to date. A related concern is that the contents of sites may change with shifts in the policies of the parent organization, whether that entity is a university, a publisher, or something else. Perhaps in the future, professional associations such as SHAFR or the Organization of American Historians (OAH) might collaborate with publishers, universities, research libraries, and other entities to help preserve the most important portions of recorded knowledge residing in this still fragile medium. In the meantime, the Internet Archive is attempting to preserve websites as well as other kinds of electronic media (http://archive.org).

There is also the problem that the "point-and-click" retrieval method for identifying and obtaining electronic publications, for all its enhanced opportunities, necessarily distances us from the original tangible format. For the uninitiated researcher, this situation makes it more difficult to distinguish one kind of source from another. It is a phenomenon we have begun to notice among our students, and it does not appear to have received much attention. Simply stated, many students have become unable to distinguish between newspapers and magazines. As "digital natives" they are used to retrieving information at their computer or, increasingly, via a mobile device. In such a context, differences in provenance among format types that were established in a fixed, print-on-paper world have become, for some of our students, blurred and in some cases indistinguishable. All of this "stuff" comes from the same place—the electronic screen.

Finally, and perhaps most difficult to tackle conceptually, is that even if we assume that the online sources are reputable, functioning, and accurately understood, the sheer plenitude of available resources often is an impediment to students successfully completing assignments. This is most obvious in students' research projects; put bluntly, they frequently have no idea where to begin. Many times they turn first to a search engine such as Google, and once they do so with a widely encompassing term like *Vietnam War*, they are immediately overwhelmed with websites of varying degrees of reputability and functionality. The amount of controversial and conflicting information available on any subject, but especially on issues like the Vietnam War, can intimidate even the most intrepid students.

Information Literacy as Discovering, Obtaining, Evaluating, and Using Information

As the amount of information available has steadily increased, and indeed exploded after the advent of the web in the mid-1990s, it has become more important than ever to provide assistance to both teachers and students in identifying, accessing, and utilizing relevant material. And so we thought it prudent to follow the lead of others and turn to the first professionals to address this issue in a systematic fashion—namely, librarians.

While some of the issues associated with accessing reliable information on the Internet are unique to the digital medium itself, the challenges associated with identifying, accessing, and using relevant material in an information-saturated environment are not unprecedented. Because of their historic role in housing and managing ever-growing stores of information, as well as in providing expertise in accessing the collections under their care, librarians wrestle with the best ways to conceptualize, implement, and teach a systematic approach to working in a world that seems overwhelmed with information. Indeed, they were doing so well before the personal computer and the web became commonplace, at a time when the problem was more likely to be a scarcity of information than an overabundance.

During the 1970s the instruction work of academic librarians in the classroom really took off and became a significant part of reference librarians' responsibilities. It was commonplace to see librarians in the classroom with students discussing resources and search strategies. By the late 1980s and early 1990s, the term "information literacy" began to be used by academic librarians and library associations (especially the Association of College and Research Libraries [ACRL]), and subsequently by regional accrediting organizations and grant-funding agencies. It is an umbrella term with a broader reach than "library/ bibliographic instruction." It seeks to describe the objective of teaching students how to identify, obtain, evaluate, and use information, effectively and responsibly, in the context of their academic work. Or, in the words of the ACRL's standards for higher education: "locate, evaluate, and use effectively the needed information."[12] One prominent regional accrediting body identifies information literacy as a set of skills that "relate to a student's competency in acquiring and processing information in the search for understanding."[13]

It is understandable that since the mid-1990s the popularity of information literacy as a concept has coincided with the information revolution caused by the proliferation of the Internet. This revolution has fundamentally altered our relationship with information; no longer are institutions, libraries, and teachers able to claim any exclusive dominion over knowledge. As a result, the leveling of the relationship between teacher and student brought about by this transformation has accelerated the demands of some teaching experts that teachers should be "guides by the side" instead of "sages on the stage" (in a common and simplistic phrase of the day, as if this were a dichotomy). In particular, experts have realized that while the incredible amount of material available on the Internet undeniably offers new kinds of opportunities for student engagement, the unmediated access of students to this information also presents new challenges to effective instruction.

For teachers of history, however, these problems present opportunities for developing the kinds of skills that we value in our discipline.

The competencies of information literacy identified by the ACRL dovetail nicely with the skills deemed necessary to think historically. According to the ACRL, an information-literate student can accomplish the following.

1. Define the need for information (in historical terms, define the subject)
2. Access needed information effectively (find sources)
3. Evaluate information and its sources critically (interrogate sources for bias, authorship, and intended audience)
4. Use information to accomplish a purpose (write a paper or project)[14]

In a happy coincidence, we can help our students work on their historical skills at the same time that we encourage the development of their literacy in finding and using information. An excellent resource to assist us is Esther Grassian's website Teach Information Literacy and Critical Thinking, including sections on topic selection, topic narrowing and broadening, finding and selecting websites, and various self-assessment exercises, at https://sites.google.com/site/teachinfolit.

LibGuides

In addition to integrating information literacy into our work with students, we urge teachers to encourage their students to take advantage of available expertise in navigating the web. As part of their efforts to help develop the library research skills of students, academic librarians for many years have prepared bibliographies and other guides to library-based resources pertinent to students' academic work. The best of these, in the hands of skilled librarians and prepared via librarian-faculty collaboration, have always been more than lists of the "best" sources or finding tools such as periodical indexes or subject encyclopedias. Not only did they often address simple forms of search strategy, but they were conceived as pathways for leading students into scholarly conversations and disputes, and often into the primary sources that formed the basis for scholars' interpretations and the resulting dialogue. Intended as a "toolkit" for students, these have served as very useful complements to the librarians' in-class presentations and individual research assistance.

In recent years digital technology has enabled and encouraged newer forms of these research guides, resource-rich information platforms that are likely to be especially appealing to students. One popular application is the "LibGuide," a web-based software package developed and marketed by Springshare; it permits individuals (usually librarians) to create "portals to high-quality research information" that are much more robust than the print-on-paper "pathfinders" and "research guides" of earlier decades.[15]

One especially resource-rich LibGuide for teaching the Vietnam War has been developed by Denise Karimkhani, director of learning resources at the University of Mary Hardin–Baylor in Belton, Texas (http://libguides.umhb.edu/histinquiry). She provides an abundance of information about finding books (including recommended "best" titles), articles, and high-quality websites, and she identifies key players and other subject terms. Her site contains a section entitled "War and Popular Culture," which includes films (commercial and documentaries) and music, and one entitled "Coming Home" on American veterans. Included are links to websites of questionable authoritativeness, so that they can be analyzed for their reliability. (See, e.g., a site of the Vietnam Helicopter Flight Crew Network, at www.vhfcn.org/stat.htm, which is linked from the LibGuide.) Her guide's many features include an extensive "New Books and AV" listing and some video clips, as well as a detailed "Vietnam Veterans Oral History" assignment in which students interview Vietnam veterans in the local community. In another assignment, "Clio's Court," student teams have to convince the Goddess of History of the "truth" of what occurred "in a significant, but disputed, historical event"; the instructor stands in for Clio.[16]

There are many other LibGuides on teaching the Vietnam War; they suggest additional possibilities for how teachers and librarians might design one to fit local preferences and circumstances. Among those that look especially interesting and useful are Eric Kidwell's at Huntingdon College, which includes links to other valuable sites, such as *Life* magazine's photo archive and Tim O'Brien's home page, at http://libguides .huntingdon.edu/content.php?pid=60570&sid=465657; Michael Unsworth's very extensive site at Michigan State University, which provides links to other sites with varying perspectives, such as those of the Vietnam Helicopter Pilots Network, and the Vietnam Veterans against the War, at http://libguides.lib.msu.edu/content.php?pid= 211618&search_terms=vietnam; and Gyorgy Toth's site at the University of Iowa, which covers the 1960s and includes syllabi for various courses on the 1960s at Iowa in the Departments of History, English, and American Studies, at http://guides.lib.uiowa.edu/content.php?pid= 183947&sid=1546509&search_terms=vietnam.[17]

A Sample Research Guide for Students— with an Introduction for Teachers

Before our students embark on a project by simply "googling" a subject, we should encourage them to use traditional outlets for expertise. As scholars are aware, academic literatures index themselves via citations in notes and bibliographies. As part of their research, students should exploit that custom, of course. But they should also be ranging farther afield, using not only Google and other search engines but also the tools that the discipline, publishers, and libraries intentionally provide for such purposes. In the process they will be conducting research in a more intelligent, effective, and efficient manner.

We offer below a sample research guide of the sort we would distribute to students in a class on the Vietnam War, a toolkit that is a product of faculty-librarian collaboration. Teachers and librarians would need to customize such a guide, depending on the resources at hand and the teacher's course objectives. Many college and university libraries do not own some of the electronic collections that are available, such as *Readers' Guide Retrospective*, *New York Times Historical File*, or *JSTOR*.

Librarians often encourage students to use subject encyclopedias. Not only can someone beginning a research project obtain basic (and reliable) factual information quickly, but the short introductory articles will often provide a small bibliography, a list of references, or explicit suggestions for further reading. Hence the research guide encourages the student to begin there, with background sources. After that it's a matter of identifying interesting topic areas that can suggest a topic to be pursued.[18] To be sure, there are many other places where students and other researchers can dive into the literature and data on various subjects to begin their quest; good subject encyclopedias provide one avenue that we have found works well.[19]

In addition to stressing sources for background information, the research guide places considerable emphasis on prompting student encounters with contemporary news magazines and newspapers (and thereby with their images, as well as text), journals of opinion, and television news broadcasts. In our age of information saturation, some-times reaching flood level, students often fail to appreciate the importance of these information outlets to populations in an era before the web, cable television, talk radio, and social media. Such encounters are especially important for students to see firsthand the information the American public was receiving about the wars in Vietnam, in formats from an increasingly bygone era.

Research Guide for the United States and the Wars in Vietnam, 1945–1975

Introduction

This research guide is intended to acquaint you with, or remind you of, some tools and other resources for conducting research. In addition, the librarians at our campus library will be of great assistance in helping you identify and obtain the most pertinent materials (books, articles, documents, etc.).

In a few days our class will meet with one of the librarians, which will be an opportunity for you to pose questions you have about your research.

Background Sources

Use these reference books to find overviews, basic information, and citations to some important books about your topic. Also a good source of ideas for paper topics. Some are available electronically as well as in print.

Tucker, Spencer, ed. *Encyclopedia of the Vietnam War: A Political, Social, and Military History.* Santa Barbara, CA: 2011. 4 volumes. Start with this one. Note the variety of vantage points, here and in the other reference books cited below, from which to view the wars in Vietnam— and those at home in the United States.

Anderson, David. *The Columbia Guide to the Vietnam War.* New York: 2002.

Farber, David R., and Beth L. Bailey. *The Columbia Guide to America in the 1960s.* New York: 2001.

Holsinger, M. Paul, ed. *War and American Popular Culture: A Historical Encyclopedia.* Westport, Conn.: 1999. Chapter 12, "The War in Vietnam," 357–428.

Jason, Philip K. *The Vietnam War in Literature: An Annotated Bibliography.* Pasadena, CA: 1992.
Moise, Edwin. *Historical Dictionary of the Vietnam War.* Lanham, MD: 2001.
Schwartz, Richard A. *Cold War Culture: Media and the Arts, 1945–1990.* New York: 1998.
Willbanks, James H. *Vietnam War Almanac.* New York: 2009.

Subject Bibliographies

Use them to identify in-depth books and articles about your topic.

Beisner, Robert L., ed. *American Foreign Relations since 1600: A Guide to the Literature.* Santa
   Barbara, CA: 2003. 2 volumes. An excellent compilation of annotated listings, provided by
   some of the leading historians in the field. Kept up to date by an electronic version.
Peake, Louis A. *The United States in the Vietnam War, 1954–1975: A Selected, Annotated
   Bibliography of English-Language Sources.* New York: 2008.

Books

The best tool for identifying additional books on your topic, and locating those
you have identified, is the library's catalog. This is true also for audiovisual materials,
such as documentaries produced for television and commercial films on DVD.
   Some tips on using a library catalog:

- Locate books you have already identified by searching under author or title.
- See in the bibliographic record what subject headings are used for books you
  have identified that are especially relevant for your topic, and use that subject
  heading, as well as key words, to search for additional titles.
- When searching by subject or key words, consider arranging your search results
  by publication date, with the most recent titles appearing at the top of the list if
  they do not automatically display that way. Discriminating in this fashion could be
  important if you are facing an especially long list.

Popular News Magazines and Journals of Opinion

These articles, and also the photographs in the magazines, provide very important
windows into a multitude of subjects in many historical periods. They are often
used by historians as primary sources upon which to build an understanding of
what was happening and what people were thinking at the time.
   To find them use either the *Readers' Guide to Periodical Literature* (a print
index that has been published for more than 100 years) or its electronic version,
Readers' Guide Retrospective.[20]

142

Newspapers

Like news magazines and journals of opinion, newspapers provide essential windows into the past, often in greater detail and generally closer in time to events because of their daily publication schedule.

The *New York Times* is available on microfilm, and also electronically through the New York Times Historical File. The print *New York Times Index* is not only virtually indispensable for finding articles on microfilm; it is also quite useful in conjunction with the electronic version of the newspaper, and even may serve simply as a stand-alone chronicler of events. Also familiarize yourself with the *Lexis-Nexis* database as a guide to newspaper articles.

Television News

The college belongs to a consortium that subscribes to the Vanderbilt Television News Archive, a repository of television network news broadcasts. Although extensive coverage does not begin until August 1968, the Archive does include some especially important footage from earlier years. See http://tvnews.vanderbilt.edu/.

Scholarly Journal Articles

These are written by historians, political scientists, and other scholars for their colleagues and published as contributions to knowledge in the field. Examples of important scholarly journals for our subject include *Diplomatic History*, *The Journal of American History*, and *The Journal of Military History*.

To identify pertinent articles, use indexes such as *America: History & Life*, *Historical Abstracts*, and *Academic Search Premier*. Sample each of these and see which you find most helpful. In addition, familiarize yourself with *JSTOR*, a database containing the back issues of some major journals. The subject bibliographies noted above also contain references to some of the most important scholarly articles.

U.S. Government Documents

The first two titles below are available in both print and electronic versions.

Foreign Relations of the United States is the official record of the history of U.S. foreign relations since 1861. Several volumes per year.

Public Papers of the Presidents of the United States includes the President's speeches, press conferences, proclamations, etc. One volume per year.

The Pentagon Papers: The Defense Department History of United States Decision-Making on Vietnam (Senator Gravel edition, Boston 1971–72, 5 volumes), and Gareth Porter, ed., *Vietnam: A History in Documents* (New York, 1981).

Presidential Libraries

Also provided by the U.S. Government are the various Presidential libraries. These contain materials, print and electronic, from the administrations of the presidents from Herbert Hoover through George W. Bush. For this course the Kennedy, Johnson, and Nixon libraries contain most, though by no means all, of the relevant material.

http://www.archives.gov/presidential-libraries/visit/.

Internet Sites

Consult this course's online management system for some especially good sites, taken from *Understanding and Teaching the Vietnam War* (Madison, WI, 2013).

Miscellaneous

For public opinion polls, see *The Gallup Poll*, first 5 volumes. Some data are also available online in the Roper Center's *Public Opinion Archives*, to which the library provides access.

The library owns a significant collection of DVDs dealing with the Vietnam Wars, both commercial films, like *Platoon*, and documentaries, such as PBS's *Two Days in October*. The latter juxtaposes a battle in Vietnam with a battle on the University of Wisconsin campus.

Concluding Thoughts

In addition to the resources cited above, the librarians for History, Political Science, English, and American Studies have posted on the library's website more extensive lists of sources—print, microform, or digital. Many of these are specialized collections such as: Declassified Documents, CIA Research Reports, National Security Council Documents, the Digital National Security Archive, etc.

Finally, in their books and articles, historians and other scholars provide an abundance of citations—to books, articles, official documents, minutes of meetings, films, recorded conversations, correspondence, etc.—that display the evidence upon which they base their arguments. Don't neglect these promising leads in your own research, as you seek to put together *your own* argument for how and why the past unfolded as it did.

Conclusion

In short there is an abundance of resources for teachers, many available on the web, and what is offered in these few pages obviously cannot begin to be comprehensive. (Indeed, today's professor and student conversing on a bench, or a log, might well have a laptop with them with which to consult and query the many conversations that are transpiring on topics of interest.) Rather, it is our hope that what is here will provide a useful introduction to some high-quality possibilities and that instructors will draw on their own imaginations and organizational skills to arrange productive encounters for their students by examining the websites identified here, browsing the web (including the teaching pages of the SHAFR website at www.shafr.org), assessing the quality and usefulness of websites and other research tools, and definitely tapping the expertise of their local librarians. If web links fail to connect, as often happens with this fragile medium when authors or webmasters modify an address, or when an institution drops a site, one can often track down the material by searching the web under the creator's name and some keywords, for example, "Grassian, teaching information literacy."

Whether instructors' collaborations with their librarians will employ a version of LibGuides or something else that prompts students to discover, obtain, evaluate, and use recorded knowledge, is relatively unimportant. What is important are successful learning experiences and helping our students, like Williams's chemistry major at Oregon State University, find both fun and substance in *"doing* history."

NOTES

The authors gratefully acknowledge the significant contributions of Esther Grassian, Distinguished Librarian, UCLA, who in addition to reading drafts of the essay helped gather contributions from other librarians; Dr. Michael Longrie, professor of English at the University of Wisconsin–Whitewater; Denise

Karimkhani, library director at Mary Hardin Baylor University in Texas; Matthew Masur, volume coeditor, for taking the lead authoring the sections on websites, assignments, and the Tet offensive; and helpful contributions from several other librarians in Annapolis and around the country. Of course, we alone are responsible for errors of either commission or omission. A final expression of appreciation goes to the editors of this volume for their flexibility, as we broadened our focus beyond websites and placed these within a wider discussion of libraries, student research, and information literacy.

1. Theodore Clarke Smith, *The Life and Letters of James Abram Garfield*, 2 vols. (New Haven, CT: Yale University Press, 1925), 2:812; Frederick Rudolph, *Mark Hopkins and the Log: Williams College, 1836–1872* (New Haven, CT: Yale University Press, 1956), vii.

2. *OAH Newsletter* [Organization of American Historians], February 13, 1985, 3, available at www.oah.org; Lynn D. Lampert, "Where Will They Find History? The Challenges of Information Literacy Instruction," American Historical Association (AHA), *Perspectives* Online, February 2006, http://www.historians.org/perspectives/issues/2006/0602/0602tea1.cfm. See also Steve Potts, "Using Primary Sources," in *The Vietnam War: Teaching Approaches and Resources*, ed. Marc Jason Gilbert (New York: Greenwood Press, 1991), 191–99, who notes, "One teacher has compared reading the survey texts to the combat experience: long stretches of boredom punctuated by occasional moments of action" (192); the teacher's students found primary sources to be much more interesting and worthwhile.

3. The figure was 79 percent, 255 such courses of the 323 taught by the survey's respondents. Richard Hume Werking and Dustin Walcher, "What We Teach and How We Teach It," *Passport*, December 2006, http://www.shafr.org/teaching/higher-education/teaching-articles. The survey was conducted by the SHAFR Teaching Committee. See also the American Historical Association's strong advocacy of student research in primary sources: "'Best Practices': Encouraging Research Excellence in Postsecondary History Education," AHA, *Perspectives* Online, October 2000, http://www.historians.org/Perspectives/Issues/2000/0010/0010aha1.cfm.

4. For a useful description, see Susanna Robbins, "Vietnam in First Person: The Virtual Vietnam Archive," *OAH Magazine of History*, 18 (October 2004): 64–65.

5. Peter Brush, e-mail messages to Richard Werking, June 8 and 10, 2011. Mr. Brush, a former Marine and Vietnam veteran, has authored articles on the Vietnam war. For details about the Archive, including a lengthy annotated bibliography, see http://tvnews.vanderbilt.edu.

6. See also Marc Jason Gilbert, "The Role of Critical Thinking in a Course on the Vietnam War," in *The Vietnam War: Teaching Approaches and Resources*,

ed. Marc Jason Gilbert (New York: Greenwood Press, 1991), 171–89. Still useful as well is Joe P. Dunn, *Teaching the Vietnam War: Resources and Assessments* (Los Angeles: California State University Los Angeles, Center for the Study of Armament and Disarmament, 1990); see especially his sample essays from a syllabus (88–90).

7. George C. Herring, *America's Longest War: The United States and Vietnam, 1950–1975*, 3rd. ed. (New York: McGraw-Hill, 1996); Marilyn Blatt Young, *The Vietnam Wars: 1945–1990* (New York: HarperCollins, 1991).

8. Denise Chong, *The Girl in the Picture: The Story of Kim Phuc, the Photograph, and the Vietnam War* (New York: Viking, 2000).

9. Donald Oberdorfer, *Tet* (New York: Da Capo Press, 1971); Peter Braestrup, *Big Story: How the American Press and Television Reported and Interpreted the Crisis of Tet 1968 in Vietnam and Washington* (Boulder, CO: Westview Press, 1977).

10. For good evaluative criteria for websites, supplied by some leading librarians in the field of information literacy, see Laura Cohen and Trudi Jacobson, "Evaluating Web Content," University of Albany, http://library .albany.edu/usered/eval/evalweb/; and the relevant portions of Esther Grassian's (UCLA) excellent umbrella site, Teach Information Literacy & Critical Thinking, https://sites.google.com/site/teachinfolit.

11. See "Everything Is On the Web?," in Joanna M. Burkhardt and Mary C. MacDonald, *Teaching Information Literacy: 50 Standards-Based Exercises for College Students*, 2nd ed. (Chicago: American Library Association, 2010), 89–91, including exercises for website evaluation. Their volume is a very good source for general information literacy assignments and ideas. See also Alex Wright, "Exploring a 'Deep Web' that Google Can't Grasp," *New York Times*, February 22, 2009.

12. ACRL, *Information Literacy Competency Standards for Higher Education* (2000), 2. http://www.ala.org/acrl/standards/informationliteracycompetency. The standards were endorsed by the American Association for Higher Education in 1999 and the Council of Independent Colleges in 2004.

13. Middle States Commission on Higher Education, *Characteristics of Excellence in Higher Education: Requirements of Affiliation and Standards for Accreditation* (Philadelphia, 2009), 42.

14. ACRL, *Information Literacy Competency Standards*, 2–3. For a much more in-depth treatment of information literacy, see Esther S. Grassian and Joan R. Kaplowitz, *Information Literacy Instruction: Theory and Practice*, 2nd ed. (New York: Neal-Schuman, 2009).

15. Springshare's "Introduction to LibGuides" for academic libraries may be found at http://www.springshare.com/libguides/academic. Other web-based tools, such as Drupal and the open-source Library à la Carte, are also

being used for similar purposes. Esther Grassian, e-mail message to Richard Werking, July 23, 2011. Moreover, it is worth emphasizing that alternatives and improvements to LibGuides will continue to be developed.

16. Denise Karimkhani, e-mail message to Richard Werking, June 13, 2011.

17. For these and additional Vietnam LibGuides, see "LibGuides Community" at http://libguides.com/community.php?m=s&it=0&search=vietnam +war.

18. As noted above, Esther Grassian provides helpful suggestions for teaching topic selection, topic narrowing, and topic broadening on her Teach Information Literacy and Critical Thinking site, https://sites.google.com/site /teachinfolit.

19. It might be a useful exercise to assign students to compare the treatments in such sources with those found in places such as Wikipedia.

20. Instructors should consider comparing the two versions if their library provides both; each has strengths and weaknesses. In addition, the library might make available online indexes that will provide citations to, and sometimes full-text articles for, contemporary magazines. However, their coverage of the 1960s and 1970s can be spotty at best. As with all these resources, we encourage teachers to become acquainted with them and use those that best meet their needs and those of their students.

KEY RESOURCES

Best of History websites, from EdTechTeacher. http://www.besthistorysites .net/USHistory_Vietnam.shtml.

Center for History and New Media, History Matters. http://historymatters .gmu.edu/.

Documents Relating to American Foreign Policy at Mt. Holyoke College. http://www.mtholyoke.edu/acad/intrel/vietnam.htm.

Dunn, Joe P. *Teaching the Vietnam War: Resources and Assessments*. Los Angeles: California State University Los Angeles, Center for the Study of Armament and Disarmament, 1990.

Gilbert, Marc Jason, ed. *The Vietnam War: Teaching Approaches and Resources*. New York: Greenwood Press, 1991.

McDougall, Walter. "Teaching the Vietnam War." Presentation at a Foreign Policy Research Institute conference. http://www.fpri.org/footnotes /063.200006.mcdougall.teachingvietnamwar.html.

Organization of American Historians, *OAH Magazine of History* 18 (October 2004). Most of this issue is given over to articles about teaching various aspects of the Vietnam War.

PBS. *Battlefield Vietnam*. http://www.pbs.org/battlefieldvietnam.

PBS. *Bill Moyers Journal*, videos of "LBJ's Path to War." http://www.pbs.org/moyers/journal/11202009/watch.html.

PBS. "Teacher's Guide" for its website Vietnam Passage: Journeys from War to Peace. http://www.pbs.org/vietnampassage/Teacher.

Schlene, Vicki J. *Teaching about Vietnam and the Vietnam War*. ERIC Document ED411175, 1996. http://www.ericdigests.org/1998-1/vietnam.htm.

Winsterstein, Stephen. "Teaching the Vietnam War: A Conference Report." *Footnotes* (newsletter of the Foreign Policy Research Institute), July 2000. http://www.fpri.org/footnotes/064.200007.winterstein.teachingvietnam.html.

Hearts, Minds, and Voices

The Vietnam War and Oral History

ANDREW DARIEN

The promise of oral history resides in the potency of voices from the past, and fewer collections of oral histories are more prodigious than those on the Vietnam War. Teachers and students can tap into audio, video, print, and the web to mine thousands of local, regional, national, and international oral histories of the Vietnam War. For nontraditional learners, reading, listening to, and conducting oral histories provides a unique pathway to the past. The personal dimensions of oral history appeal to students' emotional intelligence and sensitivity and can enrapture the most reluctant of learners. Students can download transcripts, read bound collections of interviews, listen to audio clips, and watch interviews with veterans, politicians, activists, civilians, and other "authentic" witnesses of the war. Many of these historical actors have made themselves personally available to secondary schools, colleges, and universities, allowing students to be the beneficiaries of face-to-face conversations with living history.

The rewards of oral history are plentiful, but instructors should be mindful of its methodological challenges. Historical actors, while invaluable resources, are not objective repositories of truth. Students who work with oral histories must grapple with voices from the past as products of time, setting, context, and speaker subjectivity. Voices need be respected but also framed in memory, perspective, and politics. Like other primary sources, oral histories should be subjected to verification, corroboration, and contextualization. Students who are to benefit from working with oral histories should consider which voices get privileged in the telling of this conflict and the ways in which those stories are connected to specific political narratives. The struggle for the hearts and minds of listeners can be as poignant as the conflict itself.

History instructors working with oral histories of the Vietnam War can produce meaningful learning experiences if they equip students with appropriate historical background and provide the tools for methodological scrutiny and analysis. Oral history will be of greater value to those students who critically analyze interviews rather than consuming them as a passive experience. In order to facilitate that process, instructors can teach students how to identify major interpretations of the Vietnam War and suggest how specific oral history resources might be evaluated in order to address them. The recommended assignments (available at the end of this essay) ask students to grapple with the complexities of listening to voices from the Vietnam War and furnish instructors with strategies for using oral history as a vehicle for student learning. This essay concludes with a best practices primer on conducting a Vietnam War oral history project with attention to legal, ethical, pedagogical, and methodological concerns.

Whose Minds? Historiography Driven Lesson Plans

When designing their activities, instructors should consider the skills and content knowledge they want students to possess at end of the project. One goal could be to impart knowledge of Vietnamese history and culture. Other instructors might focus on presidential politics or international diplomacy. Some teachers will find it useful to provide a comparative perspective on Vietnam and other American military ventures. Many will want to introduce students to the ravages of war and the plight of veterans. Still others could use this as an opportunity for students to grapple with the race and gender dimensions of warfare. Almost all will ask students to contemplate the difficult moral choices of war.

In defining the central questions of their projects, instructors will want to consider the major interpretations that have dominated American historiography of the Vietnam War: the United States as an immoral imperial power, the United States as a benevolent power hamstrung by internal strife or unfortunate miscalculations, and the United States as a misguided behemoth with honorable intentions.[1] Thinking about oral history in the context of these debates better equips students to make sense of them. Instructors working with oral history should use some class time to inform students of the broad contours of historiographic debate and the evidence that historians use in order to support these perspectives. Not all instructors will have the same time frame within which to work. Some may need to schedule a Vietnam War oral history project that is limited to a few days, while others will have the luxury of an entire semester. Whatever the time constraints, instructors should begin with an assessment of what students know and believe about the Vietnam War and create assignments that inform, enhance, and challenge these preconceptions.

Whose Voices? Oral History Sources and Analysis

Collections of oral histories offer students varied stories about the purpose, execution, and meaning of the Vietnam War. The defining ethos of many of these collections is as divided as the historiography itself. The voices in these collections do not merely speak for themselves but support or challenge the major interpretations of the war. What is often invisible to the instructor and student is the way in which the theses embedded in these collections is a product of interviewee selection, questions asked, interviewee relationship to the author, and interview setting.

Students should speculate about interviewer and interviewee motives when reading a transcript or listening to an oral history. In order to ensure that students do not uncritically consume the interviews, instructors should ask them to consider the factors that might influence the subjectivity of the speaker. It is worth noting if the speaker is a politician, veteran, journalist, or antiwar activist. Likewise, it matters whether or not the speaker is American, Vietnamese, Russian, or Chinese. Even then, not all "American veterans" or "Vietnamese civilians" speak with one voice. It also matters when and where the interview was conducted. A military debriefing immediately following a firefight is quite a different setting than a journalist's interview several weeks later or a historian's questioning many years down the road. The point of the exercise is not to equate motives with fabrications, propaganda, or even bias but rather to start a conversation about perspective, subjectivity, and agenda.[2]

No single book can capture the entire breadth of voices on the Vietnam War, but Christian G. Appy's *Patriots: The Vietnam War Remembered from All Sides*, comes close. *Patriots* offers a kaleidoscope of perspectives from American and Vietnamese soldiers, diplomats, and citizens of all political persuasions. Appy uses the ideal of patriotism as an organizing principle and illustrates how Vietnamese and American soldiers, protesters, and civilians all believed that they were acting in the best interest of their nation. Instructors who use this collection will have ample opportunity to get their students to reconsider what it means to be a patriot, and the multiple ways in which historical actors defined *patriotism*. Instructors who choose only one collection of interviews to scrutinize would do well to consider the comprehensive and edifying *Patriots*.

Other oral history compilations tend to be more focused in their outlook or subject matter. Kim Willenson's *The Bad War: An Oral History of the Vietnam War* is the collection most representative of the "honorable yet misguided" view. Willenson, an editor for *Newsweek* surveyed a dizzying array of interviews with well-known American political figures such as J. William Fulbright, Clark Clifford, Eugene McCarthy, George Ball, John McCain, and Walter Rostow. Her collection provides access to Vietnamese leaders such as Tran Van Don and Nguyen Van Canh. While the collection primarily includes well-known political figures and journalists, there are some perspectives from ordinary veterans. The theme of the collection, suggested by the title, is the confusion, misinformation, brutality, and ultimate futility of the war. While American policy makers such as Clark Clifford and Walter Rostow believed that the United States possessed the responsibility and power to stop the spread of communism, Willenson contends, they were deluded by their misapplied "political science" and a "failed military strategy."[3] Hers is a damning portrait of the war in Vietnam.

Also in the honorable yet misguided camp is Robert Mann's *Grand Delusion: America's Descent into Vietnam*, which provides an excellent starting point for those interested in the machinations of American presidential administrations.[4] Mann's account, which weaves oral sources with traditional written accounts, focuses on administrations from Truman to Nixon but also teases out the voices of the lesser-known congressional figures who shaped foreign policy. These interviews illustrate how politicians deluded themselves about the nature of the communist threat and the degree to which Vietnam represented a vital interest.

Presidential libraries offer a treasure trove of online oral histories for students interested in sampling interviews on their own. An excellent place to start is the website of the Johnson Library. In addition to audio clips from Johnson interviews and speeches, students can access full-text interview transcripts with the American architects of the Vietnam War, including George Ball, McGeorge Bundy, Clark Clifford, Walter Rostow, Dean Rusk, and Cyrus Vance.[5] Likewise, the Kennedy Library's online site hosts a wealth of interviews with key political figures such as Dean Acheson, Robert Amory, Charles Baldwin, McGeorge Bundy, Harlan Cleveland, and Peter Edelmen and journalists such as Walter Cronkite and John Alsop.[6] The Nixon Archives will be especially appealing to students who want to listen to and *view* some of these political figures. The Nixon site hosts high-quality video interviews with major American political players such as Charles Colson, Jon Huntsman Sr., David Gergen, George McGovern, Dick Cheney, Charles Rangel, and George P. Shultz.[7]

Video interviews provide a particularly useful opportunity for students to consider factors such as voice inflection, facial cues, and body language. When transcripts are available, instructors can design a lesson in which the class is divided into thirds. Students are asked to read, listen to, and view the same interviews and then report to the class about what they learned from and observed in them. Even when the words are the same, reading, listening, and viewing can elicit different responses. Most instructors are familiar with the famous Nixon-Kennedy presidential debate, in which Nixon was rated poorly by television viewers but favorably by radio listeners. The 1960 debate and Kennedy's ultimate victory have been portrayed as a triumph of style over substance, but one could suggest that viewers identified something substantive in Nixon's body language or facial expressions that provided a clue about his character. With dozens of video interviews on the Nixon website, students could mine his staff for similar clues.

Top-down political history needs to be complemented with the experience of ordinary veterans, but these subjects ought to be held to the same scrutiny. Soldiers, marines, seamen, airmen, and other military men and women can provide direct accounts of the fighting, but instructors must remind students of the partiality of their vantage points. Veterans might not, for example, tell us much about the geopolitical dimensions of the war or the larger overarching forces that shaped their combat. In some cases, the trauma of war wreaks havoc with memory. In other cases, soldiers may accentuate their roles in a particular conflict or frame the narrative in a way that defines them as more heroic. Even the most honest of veterans and politicians tell stories that unwittingly borrow ideas and perspectives from private conversations and public media.

It is also worth considering when the interview was conducted, and how time may have influenced interviewees' perspectives. News reports, films, and other public narratives get folded into veterans' memories in ways of which they might be unaware.[8] As a novelist and Vietnam War veteran, Tim O'Brien notes, "In any war story, but especially a true one, it is difficult to separate what happened from what seemed to happen. What seems to happen becomes its own happening and has to be told that way."[9] The challenge for the instructor and student of history is to identify the ways in which the individual narrative of biography meets the collective narrative of history.[10]

Students who feel disillusioned with the American wars in Iraq and Afghanistan will relate to interviews with veterans who impart the futility of the war and its incongruence with American ideals. Richard Stacewicz's *Winter Soldiers: An Oral History of Vietnam Veterans against the War* offers the perspectives of those veterans who were not merely disillusioned with the war but also with the gap between America's principles and its geopolitical performance. These soldiers became active antiwar protesters who sought to change the course of American foreign and domestic policy as part of their duty as "citizen-soldiers."[11] A similar collection is Gerald R. Gioglio's *Days of Decision*, which focuses on interviews with conscientious objectors in the military during the Vietnam War. Like Stacewicz, Gioglio highlights his subjects as heroic for their resistance to the war and their willingness to run against the grain of the traditional American view of patriotism.[12] Another collection of interviews based exclusively on conscientious objectors is James W. Tollefson's *The Strength Not to Fight*. Tollefson concedes in his introduction that, due to time and memory, his subjects may have mistaken their chronology. He notes that some may have exaggerated or even lied, and that he has eliminated the most obviously misleading of these. Instructors will find this collection especially geared toward pedagogy. After Tollefson describes the situation of his subjects, he poses a number of questions to readers about choices that they might make under similar circumstances. There are ample opportunities for role-playing, counterfactual history, and discussion.[13]

Instructors working with students from blue-collar backgrounds will want to explore Christian G. Appy's *Working-Class War: American Combat Soldiers and Vietnam*. Appy interviewed more than one hundred veterans, mostly from Massachusetts, and determined that 80 percent of them were working class, the "children of waitresses, factory workers, truck drivers, secretaries, firefighters, carpenters, custodians, police officers, salespeople, clerks, mechanics, miners and farm workers."[14] Using the words of veterans, Appy paints an apocalyptic picture of the Americans fighting in Vietnam in which soldiers had a poor sense of mission, fought in unfavorable terrain, and encountered dissension and brutality. A complement to *Working-Class War* is Terry Wallace's *Bloods: An Oral History of the Vietnam War*, which chronicles the experience of African Americans and the terse racial dynamics that likewise divided the troops.[15]

An apt counterpoint to *Bloods* and *Working-Class War* is Eric M. Bergerud's *Red Thunder, Tropic Lightning: The World of a Combat Division in Vietnam*.[16] Bergerud debunks the myth of American soldiers and marines as disillusioned, cynical, drugged out, and malicious. *Red Thunder, Tropic Lightning* tracks the Twenty-fifth Infantry Division, whose members, he claims, are representative of all American troops who served admirably despite the challenges of the Vietnamese environment. Likewise, Otto Lehrack's *No Shining Armor: The Marines at War in Vietnam: An Oral History* proffers a more heroic view of American marines with little of the dissension or lack of mission in Appy's account.[17] It would be interesting for students to read excerpts from each of these accounts and try to make sense of the contradictions.

Vietnam was not merely an American or Vietnamese war but a seminal event in world history. For those instructors looking to pull students outside of American provincialism, Xiaobing Li's *Voices from the Vietnam War: Stories from American, Asian, and Russian Veterans* offers personal accounts of veterans representing multiple political beliefs and perspectives. Li, a Chinese native and former soldier in the People's Liberation Army, spent seven years gathering hundreds of accounts from multiple sources. Students will learn a good deal about Russian and Chinese roles in the war, particularly their geopolitical relationships and ideological foundations for soldiers' service.[18] Li's voices help to impress on the reader the international dimensions of this conflict in general, and flesh out the Vietnamese one in particular. His book is part of a larger attempt to identify the transnational dimensions of the conflict such as how and why Vietnam became a factor in European colonialism and how western currents of liberalism, nationalism, and socialism influenced Vietnam's response.[19]

Whose Hearts? Planning an Oral History Project

The gap between students and historical figures can be bridged by reading transcripts, listening to oral histories, and watching videos, but the act of interviewing brings them even closer. Students who conduct oral histories document the historical record while forging personal bonds with their subjects. This gives them an inordinate amount of power and responsibility. Living sources can provide rich historical narratives, but instructors must remind students to contemplate war roles, geographic origins, and political allegiances. Students who have sifted through the aforementioned interviews will be amply prepared. Many of the same principles for interpreting oral history apply to conducting interviews. Students will need to consider the challenges that come with the subjectivity of their interviewees. Likewise, students should consider not only the "authentic" American veteran but also the perspectives of groups such as Vietnamese refugees, antiwar protesters, political activists, and ordinary citizens.

Instructors should employ the "backward design" model in putting together an oral history project.[20] "Thinking backward" means starting from the final goals and objectives as the guidepost for the project, and only then creating assignments and assessments that bring the students toward those ends. While it may be tempting to speak directly with the grizzled veteran who lives down the block, it is more important that the instructor considers what it is that he or she would like the students to derive from the experience. In what ways will this accentuate, complicate, or challenge students' understanding of the Vietnam War? Which aspects of the war do instructors want students to learn more about? Does one want students to learn about the politics of the war, the nature of the fighting, Vietnamese culture, or the tradition of protest? Once those questions have been answered, instructors can think about interviewees who would be most informed and capable to speak about the issues of concern. The essential questions are shared with students so that they know which aspects of the Vietnam War their interviews should explore.

When the instructor has compiled a list of appropriate contacts, the next step is to focus on logistics and communication. Ideally, the instructor will be the primary point of contact with potential interviewees. While there is great value in having students take responsibility for correspondence, a college professor or secondary instructor is more likely to command the respect and attention of an interviewee. The instructor also has a valuable role to play in mediating the concerns of both interviewee and student. In many cases the school's institutional review board will need to vet the interview, and that, too, should be negotiated by the instructor. It is also the instructor's responsibility to inform potential subjects of the purpose, procedure, and potential uses of the interview. Interviewees should know why the project is being conducted, the manner in which it will be recorded, and how their words will be used. Interviewees will want to know who will be present at the interview and who will have access to the audio, transcript, or video at the end of the process. Instructors should be clear about whether this is a mere educational exercise or whether the subjects' words will be distributed through radio, television, or the web. Legal permission must be granted for the interview in what is referred to as either "consent" or "deed" form. The form should be very clear about who owns the interview and what rights of distribution come with ownership. Interviewers must ensure that their subjects understand the extent of their rights to the interview and request that those rights, as well as those putting restrictions on access, are yielded to a repository or other party.[21] The form should be signed before the interview.

The location of the interview can influence its quality. One of the primary aims in determining a location is the comfort level of the interviewee. In this case some consideration should be given to the interviewer as well, since he or she is relatively inexperienced and likely to be much younger that the interviewee. On the one hand, interviewees are most likely to be comfortable in their own homes. On the other hand, housing the interview at a school or university has the advantage of welcoming the interviewee into one's academic community, and it is often the place where the recording equipment is located. One should also be sensitive to the physical condition of the interviewee and his or her ability to travel. The ideal setting will be in a quiet and comfortable area free of outside intrusions and accessible to recording equipment.

There is often an inverse relationship between the quality of the recording equipment and the ease of scheduling the interview. A television studio may house high-tech equipment, but it is neither mobile nor conducive to easy scheduling. Another challenge with video is that the equipment can intimidate both interviewer and interviewee. Video does, however, offer a dimension unavailable in audio. A general principle is to use the highest quality equipment that does not significantly interfere with the ability to conduct the interview and to make that equipment as unobtrusive as possible.

Successful interviews will be a product of students' individual skills and their level of preparation. Students who are naturally endowed with emotional intelligence, communication skills, and sensitivity will thrive in an interview setting. Students should begin with knowledge of their subjects, becoming well informed about the overarching history of the Vietnam War, and the particulars of the historical experience of their interviewees. Students should also have self-knowledge. They should be introspective about their own personal, political, and philosophical proclivities, and they should try to check them at the door before the interview. Students whose families have a record of military service or political activism may bring strong preconceptions to the interview. In many ways their informed perspectives can be a resource in building question lists and considering the historical significance of the interview. The challenge is to move beyond fixed ideas about the war's significance and create opportunities for interviewees to flesh out the historical record.

The most valuable tool for the interviewer is the biographical information form. The bio form identifies very basic information about the interviewee such as birth date, geographic residences, occupations, family history, and military service dates, locations, and roles. It can also include, when relevant, information such as race, religion, and political affiliation. Instructors and students should be clear that interviewees are only required to complete those sections of the form with which they are comfortable. The bio form will save the student a good deal of time in not having to ask basic informational questions of the interviewee and instead moving on to substantive and qualitative inquiries. It also makes for a more informed question list and enables the interviewer to identify areas of research in order to arrive more prepared.

There are a number of useful guidelines for crafting an effective question list. Students should be allowed to take ownership of the interview, but it is the instructor's role to ensure that questions are appropriate, accessible, and logical. At the top of the question list should be a proper introduction that includes the names of interviewer, interviewee, and oral history project, as well as the date and location of the recording. The goal of the first question should be to put the interviewee at ease. Most oral historians recommend a "softball" question for opening inquiries. This would entail a target that the interviewee can easily hit out of the park. Since most questions will track the chronology of the subject's life, beginning with childhood, an apt first question would be "Tell me like what it was like to grow up in [interviewee's hometown]." The rest of the questions should be divided into thematic categories. For example, an interview with a Vietnam veteran could be divided into the following categories: early life and hometown, family, coming of age, entering the military, war experiences, civilian life, and political and historical perspectives.

Students should come armed with a mixture of targeted and open-ended questions. Targeted questions enable the questioner to focus on specific information, whereas open-ended questions allow the interviewee to ruminate more broadly in an area of his or her interest. Too many targeted questions feel like an interrogation and provide the interviewee with insufficient latitude to offer his or her own perspective. Too many open-ended questions provide the interviewer with less control and can result in a rudderless, unstructured interview. Interviewers should also guard against "loaded questions" or those embedded with controversial assumptions. For example, if interviewing an antiwar activist, a loaded question might be "Why do you think the Chicago Police Department was so intent on using excessive force against protesters outside the 1968 Democratic Convention?" This assumes that the interviewee agrees that the force was excessive, and that the police department had been intent on using it. While this may very well have been the case, a more apt question would be "Why do you think the Chicago Police Department used force against the protesters outside the 1968 Democratic Convention?" Finally, a sound question list should have a wrap-up question that enables the interviewee to put his or her final stamp on the history. One technique is to have subjects speculate on the future of their history: "Fifty years from now when historians are listening to this interview, what would you want them to most remember about the Vietnam War?"

All parties need to be aware of time parameters. Students may have limited time in the recording studio or classroom. Audio and video recording time will be limited. Interviewees may only be available for a certain period of time. The interviewer should work within these constraints by crafting an extensive list of prioritized questions that can be adjusted as the interview unfolds. One never knows how extensive a subject's answers will be. There will also be unanticipated follow-up questions when new and rich tangents are explored. The interviewer should have a visible timepiece placed somewhere in the interview room. If an assistant is operating the recording equipment, it will be his or her responsibility to indicate remaining time. This can be done by preprinting time cards that can be unobtrusively flashed at the participants.

First-time interviewers will benefit from the advice often given to novice teachers: "embrace the silence." When one's question is met with silence, it is natural to feel uncomfortable, as if one has failed in not properly framing the inquiry. The impulse is to fill the gap by quickly rearticulating the question or providing an answer. What is most likely is that the inquiry simply requires a bit of reflection. More often than not, a response will be forthcoming. Ten seconds can feel like an eternity in an interviewer, but it is an appropriate period of time to wait for a response. This is a useful opportunity to think about the body language and facial expressions of both one's interviewee and oneself. The more attuned student can sense when one is formulating an answer versus simply not understanding the question. Likewise, one can communicate openness and encouragement to the interviewer by unfolding arms, making eye contact, and smiling. These are apt general practices for the entire interview.

The power dynamics between a relatively young student and an adult interviewee, not to mention a historical individual, can be quite daunting. There can be a beneficial component to this gap in which the interviewee takes on a paternal or maternal role with the student; however, this could undermine the student's authority and turn the conversation into a monologue. Students need to guard against rehearsed stories or canned answers that interviewees have recited multiple times throughout their lives. Many subjects will go on automatic pilot and carry the entire interview after the first question. Disrupting that narrative requires gentle intervention with follow-up inquiries that take the interview down unexplored paths. Ideally, this will be a shared enterprise, in which students can pursue their historical lines of inquiry while interviewees have ample space to flesh out the historical record.[22] Students should also guard against off-the-record remarks, as these do not exist in oral history. Oral history is about documenting the historical record. If there is something an interviewee wants to mention off the record, he or she should be encouraged to frame it in a way that it can be on the record, or simply not say it at all.

Finally, students may wonder whether or not they should ask potentially uncomfortable or embarrassing questions. This remains something of a judgment call, but a good rule of thumb is to ask the question if it has historical validity and does not put the interviewee in a compromising position. One approach is to use a quote from a third-party source to address a controversial question. This allows the interviewer to triangulate by remaining neutral while offering the interviewee an opportunity to respond to a legitimate inquiry. For example, rather than asking a veteran directly about the untruths of the Johnson administration that led to American involvement, one could read an excerpt from the Pentagon Papers that describe this process.

Once the interview has been completed and the subject thanked for his or her time, the process of preservation, transcription, and analysis begins. All interviews should have at least two copies, ideally one physical and one "in the clouds." It is a polite gesture to produce a copy of the interview for the interviewee in the form of a CD or DVD. All copies of the recording should include the same identifying information listed earlier. Instructors will also want to consider where the interviews will be housed. Institutions with their own archives or libraries are ideal settings.

Students should be responsible for transcribing their own interviews. Many will be surprised to learn how arduous this process can be, requiring as much as eight hours of transcription for each hour of interview. The transcriptions are useful for any future researchers wishing to access the interview and explore its contents, but they are also vital for students to review and share their work. Transcriptions are essentially verbatim text reproductions of audio or video interviews. There are varying schools of thought about the format of such transcriptions, and there is no one accepted standard. All transcriptions should clearly identify each of the speakers and contain the aforementioned identifying information.

Class time will not likely allow for a full screening of all interviews. A more economical option is for students to select short audio or video clips that they deem representative of their particular interviews. The transcripts can be reviewed much more efficiently. The transcriptions should be made available to all students so that they can review the work of their peers and begin to make sense of the larger project. Ideally, this will be shared on a widely accessible web-based learning system.

This is the time to return to the essential questions defined at the beginning of the project and collectively evaluate the historical relevance of the interviews. The final assignment should require students to integrate the historiography, background readings and lectures, interviews, and oral history methodology. Students should be asked to determine whether or not these interviews validated, challenged, or shed new light on the historiography that they read in preparation for the project. They should reflect on the quality of the interviews, the subjectivity and biases of the speakers, and what new understanding about the Vietnam War, if any, was born out of the project. There ought to be some analysis of the questions left unanswered and the direction in which one might go for further research.

Assessing oral histories and assigning grades is complicated by the fact that students' dispositions and temperaments are part of the equation. In evaluating the interview in particular, one wants to be sensitive to students who may have been well prepared but are otherwise introverted, anxious, or socially uncomfortable. One approach is to relieve the anxiety by simply not grading the interviews. Another strategy is to provide clear expectations and communicate them to the students *before* the interview. Students will feel as if they are being evaluated according to an objective standard rather than the instructor's assessment of their personalities. The two broad sets of criteria for interview evaluation are the quality of the preparation and facilitation of the interview, with the former being the more significant of the two. A student who receives high marks for preparation will have completed the biographical information and deed forms, read extensively on the background of the Vietnam War and integrated those materials in the question list, tailored the interview to the particulars of his or her interviewee, provided a mix of open-ended and targeted questions, avoided loaded questions, and offered effective opening and closing inquiries. The secondary set of criteria related to the performance include making eye contact, providing reassurance to the interviewee, asking appropriate follow-up questions rather than sticking to a script, being aware of time parameters, picking up on body language and facial cues, and navigating through challenging or uncomfortable interview moments.

The final assignment that integrates this material should constitute a substantive portion of the students' grades. This is the moment for students to demonstrate how their interviews intersect with the literature on the Vietnam War, the major schools of historiographic thought, and the essential questions of the project. Students should be expected to connect the voices of their historical figures with the primary documents and secondary sources that they have read for the class. They ought not be required to include every interview in their assignment, but they should include a breadth of perspectives that reflect the scope and diversity of the project. The most effective papers will be those that grapple with questions of subjectivity, bias, and methodology. They will identify the value of oral history, but also its limitations. The best students will use their hearts and minds to dissect the factual, philosophical, political, and emotional dimensions of these historic voices.

NOTES

1. Paul Vincent Budra and Michael Zeitlin, *Soldier Talk: The Vietnam War in Oral Narrative* (Bloomington: Indiana University Press), 144; Marc Jason Gilbert, *The Vietnam War: Teaching Approaches and Resources* (New York: Greenwood Press, 1991), 9.

2. See Gilbert, *The Vietnam War*, 163; and Patrick Hagopian, "Voices from Vietnam Veterans: Oral Histories in the Classroom," *Journal of American History* 87 (2000), no. 2: 593–601.

3. Kim Willenson, *The Bad War: An Oral History of the Vietnam War* (New York: New American Library, 1987).

4. Robert Mann, *A Grand Delusion: America's Descent into Vietnam* (New York: Basic Books, 2001).

5. "Oral History Collection," Lyndon Baines Johnson Library and Museum, Division of the National Archives and Records Administration, accessed August 1, 2011, http://www.lbjlib.utexas.edu/johnson/archives.hom/biopage.asp.

6. "Oral History Collection," John F. Kennedy Presidential Library and Museum, accessed August 1, 2011, http://www.jfklibrary.org/Search

.aspx?nav=Rpp:50,Nrc:id-14 | id-3 | id-2-dynrank-disabled,N:16-25-4294965211&id=2.

7. Unfortunately, some of the most compelling interviews, such as those with Daniel Ellsberg and G. Gordon Liddy, are inaccessible and remain "under review." See "Oral Histories," Nixon Archives, accessed August 1, 2011, http://nixon.archives.gov/forresearchers/find/histories.php.

8. Fred H. Allison, "Remembering a Vietnam Firefight: Changing Perspectives over Time," *Oral History Review* 31, no. 2 (2004): 66–83.

9. Tim O'Brien, *The Things They Carried: A Work of Fiction* (Boston: Houghton Mifflin, 1990), 71.

10. Budra and Zeitlin, *Soldier Talk*, 5.

11. Richard Stacewicz, *Winter Soldiers: An Oral History of Vietnam Veterans against the War* (Chicago: Haymarket Books, 2008), 5.

12. Gerald R. Gioglio, *Days of Decision: An Oral History of Conscientious Objectors in the Military during the Vietnam War* (Trenton, NJ: Broken Rifle Press, 1989).

13. James W. Tollefson, *The Strength Not to Fight: An Oral History of Conscientious Objectors of the Vietnam War* (Boston: Little, Brown, 1993).

14. Christian G. Appy, *Working-Class War: American Combat Soldiers and Vietnam* (Chapel Hill: University of North Carolina Press, 1993), 6–7.

15. Terry Wallace, *Bloods: An Oral History of the Vietnam War* (New York: Random House, 1984).

16. Eric M. Bergerud, *Red Thunder, Tropic Lightning: The World of a Combat Division in Vietnam* (Boulder, CO: Westview Press, 1993).

17. Otto Lehrack, *No Shining Armor: The Marines in War at Vietnam: An Oral History* (Lawrence: University Press of Kansas, 1992).

18. Xiaobing Li, *Voices from the Vietnam War: Stories from American, Asian, and Russian Veterans* (Lexington: University of Kentucky Press, 2010).

19. See Gilbert, *The Vietnam War*, 6. Some other useful oral history collections that bridge the Asian American divide are Carina A. Rosario, *A Different Battle: Stories of Asian Pacific American Veterans* (Seattle: University of Washington Press, 1999); Steven Debonis, *Children of the Enemy: Oral Histories of Vietnamese Amerasians and Their Mothers* (Jefferson, NC: McFarland, 1994); Joanna C. Scott, *Indochina's Refugees: Oral Histories from Laos, Cambodia, and Vietnam* (Jefferson, NC: McFarland, 1989); and Cecil B. Currey, *Long Binh Jail: An Oral History of Vietnam's Most Notorious Prison* (Washington, DC: Brassey's, 1999).

20. Grant Wiggins and Jay McTigh, *Understanding by Design* (Alexandria, VA: Association for Supervision and Curriculum Development, 2005).

21. "Best Principles and Practices," Oral History Association, accessed October 23, 2011, http://www.oralhistory.org/do-oral-history/principles-and-practices/.

22. Michael Frisch, *A Shared Authority: Essays on the Craft and Meaning of Oral and Public History* (Albany: State University of New York Press, 1990).

KEY RESOURCES

Appy, Christian G. *Patriots: The Vietnam War Remembered from All Sides*. New York: Penguin, 2004.

Audra, Paul Vincent, and Michael Zeitlin. *Soldier Talk: The Vietnam War in Oral Narrative*. Bloomington: Indiana University Press, 2004.

Bergerud, Eric M. *Red Thunder, Tropic Lightning: The World of a Combat Division in Vietnam*. Boulder: Westview Press, 1993.

Frisch, Michael. *A Shared Authority: Essays on the Craft and Meaning of Oral and Public History*. Albany: State University of New York Press, 1990.

Gioglio, Gerald R. *Days of Decision: An Oral History of Conscientious Objectors in the Military during the Vietnam War*. Chicago: Broken Rifle Press, 1989.

John F. Kennedy Presidential Library and Museum. "Oral History Collection." http://www.jfklibrary.org/Search.aspx?nav=Rpp:50,Nrc:id-14 | id-3 | id-2-dynrank-disabled,N:16-25-4294965211&id=2.

Li, Xiaobing. *Voices from the Vietnam War: Stories from American, Asian, and Russian Veterans*. Lexington: University Press of Kentucky, 2010.

Lyndon Baines Johnson Library and Museum, Division of National Archives and Records Administration. "Oral History Collection." http://www.lbjlib .utexas.edu/johnson/archives.hom/biopage.asp.

Oral History Association. "Best Principles and Practices." http://www.oral history.org/do-oral-history/principles-and-practices/.

Stacewicz, Richard. *Winter Soldiers: An Oral History of Vietnam Veterans against the War*. Chicago: Haymarket Books, 2008.

Tollefson, James W. *The Strength Not to Fight: An Oral History of Conscientious Objectors of the Vietnam War*. Boston: Little, Brown, 1993.

"Veterans History Project." http://www.loc.gov/vets.

Wallace, Terry. *Bloods: An Oral History of the Vietnam War*. New York: Random House, 1984.

Willenson, Kim. *The Bad War: An Oral History of the Vietnam War*. New York: New American Library, 1987.

PART THREE

Understanding and Teaching Specific Content

Nationalism, Communism, and the Vietnam War

MATTHEW MASUR

Two narratives or frameworks tend to dominate historical teaching of the Vietnam War. In the "nationalist" narrative, the struggle in Vietnam pitted local nationalists against traditional French colonialism and its successor, American neo-imperialism. In the "Cold War" narrative, the United States, guided by the dictates of containment, gradually and incrementally intervened in Vietnam to stem the spread of communism. The nationalist and Cold War narratives are not mutually exclusive. In fact a full understanding of the wars in Vietnam requires teachers and students to understand how nationalism and communism became linked in Vietnam and how the United States reacted to this phenomenon.

The implied dichotomy between nationalism and communism parallels a common discussion about the ideology of Ho Chi Minh, the most famous figure in modern Vietnamese history.[1] For much of Ho's life, and in much of the historiography about the Vietnam War, observers have wondered whether Ho Chi Minh was primarily a nationalist or a communist. This question plagued American officials as they contemplated the appropriate policy toward Vietnam in the 1940s, 1950s, and 1960s. What students may not know is that Ho Chi Minh's communist allies were similarly uncertain about his true motivations and guiding principles. Moreover, supporters and critics of the war, both while it was being fought and in the decades since, often used Ho's political ideology to support their arguments. Thus, teachers can use the rise of Ho Chi Minh and America's response to his popularity to show that nationalism *and* communism, decolonization *and* the Cold War, were all part of the Vietnam War.

Using Ho Chi Minh to establish an overarching narrative about the war and to illustrate the ambiguities within this larger story can be advantageous for teachers and students alike. It capitalizes on the fact that many students are at least vaguely familiar with Ho Chi Minh as an important historical figure. Focusing on a famous individual can humanize and bring to life a topic that students might otherwise find dry or bland. This is particularly true because decolonization and Cold War anticommunism are topics that do not always resonate with students in the twenty-first century. Moreover, Ho Chi Minh has been a regular subject in the historiography on the Vietnam War, so there is ample source material for teachers to draw on. At the same time, assessments of Ho can be quite varied, and no historical consensus has emerged on the man and his life. This ambiguity will force students to wrestle with the evidence and come to their own conclusions about Ho Chi Minh and, more broadly, the Vietnam War.

Ho Chi Minh spent the better part of sixty years working for national independence and social revolution in Vietnam. He was born in Nghe An province in 1890 and spent his early years in Hue, where he met important Vietnamese nationalists like Phan Boi Chau and developed a strong sense of Vietnamese patriotism. Around the age of twenty, Ho Chi Minh took a job on a steamship and left Vietnam. He traveled widely, including extended stops in France, the United States, and England. Around the end of World War I he returned to France to promote left-wing political causes.

Ho's political activities in the aftermath of World War I provide a good avenue for exploring his anticolonialism and developing Marxist attitudes. Ho was in Paris in 1919 during the Versailles Conference as delegates from around the world met to hammer out a series of international agreements. He seized the opportunity to petition the conference for greater political rights for the Vietnamese people (although he did not explicitly demand Vietnamese independence).[2] The Russian Revolution had a similar influence on Ho Chi Minh and other anticolonial figures. Ho's exposure to Leninism, particularly Lenin's "Theses on National and Colonial Questions," inspired him to side with a radical socialist faction and join the Communist Third International. Moreover, Ho and his Vietnamese compatriots were not alone in demanding greater rights and autonomy. While in Paris Ho had close contact with Korean and Chinese activists who also demanded more equitable treatment and greater national autonomy. World War I and the Russian

Revolution had provided a spark not just for Ho Chi Minh but for subjugated people everywhere to demand reform.

Ho Chi Minh spent the next several decades pursuing the twin goals of national independence and social revolution for Vietnam. His travels brought him to Moscow and Guangzhou where he worked—and occasionally clashed—with the Comintern. In 1930 he ended up in Hong Kong, where he oversaw the creation of a unified Vietnamese communist party. Ho finally returned to Vietnam in 1941 during a period of international turmoil. France had fallen to Germany and allowed Germany's ally, Japan, to occupy Vietnam. Vietnamese nationalists quickly realized that the Japanese, rather than serving as Vietnam's liberators, had simply replaced one form of outside authority with another. In this chaotic environment Ho helped form the Viet Minh, a group of communist and noncommunist Vietnamese devoted to national independence. In announcing the Viet Minh's formation Ho abandoned the Marxist-Leninist language that he had used in some of his earlier public pronouncements. He couched his appeal in the language of patriotism rather than class conflict, calling on a diverse coalition of "[r]ich people, soldiers, workers, peasants, intellectuals, employees, traders, youth, and women" to join the struggle for national liberation.[3]

During World War II the Viet Minh and the United States worked together to fight the Japanese. The United States provided economic support for the Viet Minh, and the Viet Minh cooperated with American intelligence officers in northern Vietnam. When the war ended, the Viet Minh took the opportunity to seize power from the defeated Japanese before the French could reassert control. When Ho Chi Minh declared Vietnamese independence on September 2, 1945, several American intelligence officers stood nearby. Once again Ho's words gave little indication of the many years he had spent in international communist organizations. Rather than quoting Marx or Lenin he cited the American Declaration of Independence as he addressed the large crowd of cheering Vietnamese.

Students might be surprised to learn that Ho Chi Minh was a trusted American ally during World War II and that he expressed admiration for Thomas Jefferson's words. They should not conclude, however, that Ho had abandoned his earlier commitment to communism. Ho's activities during World War II show that he was a pragmatic leader who was willing to make compromises to reach his objectives. In this case he believed that national independence was a precondition—not a replacement—for Marxist social revolution in Vietnam. Ho's actions also reflected the political realities of the time. During World War II, international communist groups worked with capitalist democracies to defeat the Axis powers. Ho's willingness to work with Americans was not unlike Franklin Roosevelt's alliance with Josef Stalin or the Chinese Communists' willingness to join a united front with the Guomindang.

The circumstances that encouraged US–Viet Minh cooperation during World War II changed once the war was over. While many American officials continued to have doubts about colonialism, they grew more focused on opposing the spread of communism and maintaining good relations with America's allies, many of which had extensive overseas empires. When French efforts to preserve colonial authority in Vietnam led to a war with the Viet Minh in 1946, the United States initially tried to distance itself from the conflict. Over the next decade, however, American support for France increased. By the time the war ended in 1954, the United States was bankrolling the war effort and had come to see Vietnam as vital to American interests.

America's increasing involvement in Vietnam shows how Cold War concerns came to dominate American foreign policy after World War II.[4] By late 1945 and early 1946 the United States was growing increasingly suspicious of Soviet actions in Eastern Europe and the Middle East. At the same time, the Soviets believed that the United States was indifferent or even antagonistic toward Soviet security needs. In the next few years the United States took steps to "contain" the spread of communism through the Truman Doctrine, the Marshall Plan, and the North Atlantic Treaty Organization (NATO). Domestically, American politicians felt pressure to take a hard line toward the Soviet Union lest they be accused of being soft on communism.

The international and domestic climate influenced American policy toward Vietnam in a number of ways. Initially, American officials were much more concerned with events in Europe than those in far-off Southeast Asia. But keeping a good relationship with France (and, by extension, England) meant backing down on calls for self-determination in places like Vietnam. And the United States worried that the loss of Vietnam would contribute to political and economic instability in France, which would bolster left-wing French political parties and undermine America's position in Western Europe.

American officials were also worried about how a victory of the Viet Minh would affect the larger Asian economy. Once it became clear that the noncommunist Guomindang was unlikely to defeat the Chinese Communist Party in the Chinese civil war, Americans took steps to establish Japan as a reliable and economically stable noncommunist ally in the region. With China under communist control, Japanese economic growth was contingent on access to raw materials and markets in Southeast Asia. The establishment of a communist-oriented government in Vietnam would further isolate Japan and hinder its economic growth. Cornered and desperate, the United States feared that the Japanese would have no choice but to find common ground with its communist neighbors.

By the late 1940s American officials were growing increasingly concerned with events in Vietnam. The victory of the Chinese Communist Party in 1949 exacerbated fears that communism was on the march and gaining momentum in the Cold War. A year later Communist China and the Soviet Union extended official recognition to the Democratic Republic of Vietnam (DRV), the government formed by the Viet Minh at the end of World War II. If the Viet Minh defeated the French, Vietnam would be added to the list of territories that had been "lost" to communism. The United States responded by throwing its support behind the "Bao Dai solution," a French scheme to create a nominally independent Vietnamese government under the leadership of the former emperor. The United States believed that a native ruler could siphon support from the Viet Minh and deflect charges that the United States supported colonial rule. In early 1950, responding to Soviet and Chinese recognition of the DRV, the United States officially recognized the Bao Dai government and provided it with financial assistance to defeat the Viet Minh.

Neither the creation of the Bao Dai government nor American military aid changed the course of the war. In 1954 the Viet Minh surrounded and then overran a French military garrison at Dien Bien Phu. While the United States refused to intervene on France's behalf, it also refused to accept a total defeat in Vietnam. When France agreed to withdraw its forces from Vietnam the United States began taking steps to establish a viable noncommunist government in southern Vietnam. American support for a southern government would eventually evolve into a full-scale military intervention a decade later.

The United States intervened in Vietnam to contain communism and prevent it from spreading throughout Asia like a row of falling dominoes. But this Cold War narrative, while accurate, obscures the colonial background of the conflict. Vietnamese nationalists had been agitating against the French for most of the twentieth century. Many of the Vietnamese who fought against the French after World War II did so under the banner of nationalism, not Marxism-Leninism. By looking at Ho Chi Minh's life and experiences, students can see the nexus between nationalism and communism, and therefore the Cold War and anticolonial contexts for the Vietnam War.

In the Classroom

Exploring Ho Chi Minh, his background, and his political views makes sense for many classes that cover the Vietnam War. But before embarking on a discussion of Ho's ideology, students should be aware that he was not the first Vietnamese figure to address questions of social inequality and national independence. French colonial conquest in the nineteenth century had led to a period of soul-searching for Vietnamese intellectuals. What began as a debate over the proper strategies for ending French rule soon became a larger critique of the perceived failures of Vietnamese society and culture. These debates influenced Ho's own intellectual development, so students may want to know more about them. Teachers can find a concise and accessible overview in Mark Philip Bradley's *Vietnam at War*.[5] Many document readers and Internet sites include selections from the writings of Phan Boi Chau and Phan Chu Trinh, two of the leading early-twentieth-century Vietnamese nationalists. Students can use these excerpts to compare different responses to French colonialism and to contextualize later Vietnamese nationalists.

Once students have a better sense of the context, I ask them to think about Ho's political views. Many teachers, myself included, ask whether he was he a communist or a nationalist. This question can be used in many different classes that might address the Vietnam War. For classes on American history Ho Chi Minh's ideology was important because it contributed to the American decision to intervene in Vietnam. But this also makes sense for classes on world history. Ho Chi Minh was a figure of global importance, and the relationship between Marxism and nationalism is an important part of modern world history. Students can approach this question by analyzing Ho's writings and public statements, such as the founding statement of the Viet Minh

(1941), the Vietnamese Declaration of Independence (1945), and "The Path Which Led Me to Leninism," Ho's 1960 reflection on his earlier introduction to Lenin's writings. These pieces are well known and widely available in document readers and on the Internet.[6] They reflect Ho's attitudes at different points in his life and in the context of different historical developments. Finally, they are vivid examples of Ho's use of communist and nationalist rhetoric—sometimes in the same piece.

Ho Chi Minh announced the formation of the Viet Minh in 1941, shortly after France had fallen to Nazi Germany and allowed Japan to occupy Vietnam. In response Vietnamese communists joined with non-communist nationalists to fight for Vietnamese independence. Teachers might ask students to find evidence that the Viet Minh's rhetoric was more nationalist than communist. Students might notice that Ho invited Vietnamese of varying class backgrounds and occupations to join the movement, as long as they supported the call for national independence. He eschewed the class-based language that is commonly found in other communist documents, including the statement announcing the formation of the Indochinese Communist Party a decade earlier. Students might find other examples of Ho Chi Minh placing patriotism and national identity over class interest: his emphasis on "national salvation," his descriptions of Vietnamese history and shared suffering, and his allusion to national heroes.

Students can look at Ho's August 1945 Declaration of Independence in a similar fashion. His decision to quote the American Declaration of Independence is understandable in light of Viet Minh cooperation with the Allies during World War II. Students can also discuss whether this is evidence of Ho's weak commitment to communism or if it was simply a calculated effort to flatter American officials. Teachers can also ask students to discuss the effectiveness of this address. How does Ho Chi Minh make the case for Vietnamese independence? Is his argument persuasive? Why or why not?

In "The Path Which Led Me to Leninism," Ho Chi Minh describes the excitement of reading Lenin's writings on colonialism in 1920. This document gives students a lot to consider. They might start by thinking about the historical context that Ho is describing (although the recollection comes from 1960, he is referring to his experiences in 1920). Students may recognize that both World War I and the Russian Revolution exerted a deep influence on Ho's thinking. The war had created global instability and prompted a wave of anticolonial activity. The Russian Revolution suggested that Marxism could provide a political and economic alternative to the status quo.

Teachers using this source should consult Sophie Quinn-Judge's biography of Ho Chi Minh for a more detailed account of his early views. In it Quinn-Judge describes Ho's involvement with other communists during his stay in Paris in the early 1920s. The book also includes some of Ho's early writings, which capture his attitudes at the time rather than four decades after the fact. In one piece Ho attacks "the hydra of western capitalism" for "stretching its horrible tentacles towards all corners of the globe." He accuses the French of hypocritically talking about a "civilizing mission" while bringing "misery, ruin, and death" to their colonies. He criticizes the French Socialist Party for silence in the face of these policies and applauds the Communist International for taking up the colonial question.[7] Ho's language provides an early example of his belief that colonialism and communism were inseparable.

Teachers can also ask students why Ho Chi Minh was attracted to Leninism. Some students might emphasize his nationalistic motives. As Ho explains, he embraced Leninism because it offered a "path to liberation" for the Vietnamese people. But other students might pick up on another passage: when Ho describes Leninism as "the radiant sun illuminating our path to final victory, to socialism and communism," What are we to make of these comments? Are they contradictory?

While these documents can be read and discussed separately, they can also be studied together to provide a comparative perspective. For all of these documents, students can analyze the language and rhetoric that Ho Chi Minh employed. They can discuss which documents would be more likely to persuade ambivalent listeners and which would rally people already committed to the cause. They can explore the common themes that crop up in these documents and also look at the significant differences. Teachers might also want to remind students that they should look at the content of the document but also think about what is absent.

Many students might conclude from their reading that Ho Chi Minh was both a communist and a nationalist. Teachers should encourage them to dig deeper. Is the balance between communism and nationalism different in each document? Are there any fundamental incompatibilities between communism and nationalism? Why did some observers doubt his commitment to one ideology or the other? What are the dangers of reducing a complex individual to a label that itself carries a host of meanings? Teachers can also prompt students to think about the shortcomings of trying to judge Ho Chi Minh using three short documents. While these pieces offer insights into Ho's thinking, they are not the end of the story.

Courses focusing on America's involvement in Vietnam may also want to examine the influence of communism and nationalism in South Vietnam in the 1950s and 1960s. When Ngo Dinh Diem formed a government in South Vietnam after the Geneva Agreements of 1954 he incited opposition from Vietnamese who demanded political and economic reforms and called for national elections to reunify the country. Diem's opponents launched an insurgency against the government in the late 1950s and in 1960 formed the National Liberation Front (NLF). The NLF, like the Viet Minh before it, called for economic equality, social reforms, and national independence. It worked with the communist government of North Vietnam, but its membership included many noncommunists. The program of the NLF proved popular in South Vietnam and posed a threat to the southern government. In response, the United States increased its commitment to South Vietnam, supplying more economic and military aid and eventually introducing American combat troops and Americanizing the conflict.

Teachers who want to know more about the NLF and its role in the revolution in South Vietnam can consult recent scholarship by David Elliott and David Hunt.[8] Teachers can also use a variety of primary sources to help students understand the social conditions that contributed to the appeal of the NLF in South Vietnam. Michael H. Hunt's *A Vietnam War Reader* and Robert J. McMahon's *Major Problems in the History of the Vietnam War* include firsthand accounts of Vietnamese who joined the NLF and fought against the Americans.[9] These accounts are great teaching tools because they represent the experiences of a wide range of Vietnamese during different periods after World War II. Students can use these sources to once again explore the links between Vietnamese nationalism and Vietnamese communism. While some of the accounts seem more focused on national independence, others emphasize the economic conditions that plagued rural Vietnam from the 1940s to the 1960s. Astute students will also see that governmental

Tagged Viet Cong prisoners (tag reads The Tu Binh) ready to be shipped to rear areas after the fight of October 3–4, 1964, near Ca Mau, in which (SVN) government troops killed fifty-nine and captured eighty-six. (VA061447, George H. Kelling Collection, The Vietnam Center and Archive, Texas Tech University)

corruption and humiliation at the hands of landlords were also potent factors in supporting the Viet Minh and the NLF.

Teachers looking for longer and more detailed primary sources can assign memoirs of key figures in the NLF. One such option is Nguyen Thi Dinh's *No Other Road to Take*.[10] Dinh, a native of Ben Tre province in South Vietnam, had a long career as a Vietnamese revolutionary. She fought against the French, led an uprising against the Diem government, and helped form the NLF. Dinh's memoir is instructive because it provides a firsthand account of the reasons why a young person in southern Vietnam would join the revolution. Students might notice that Dinh was motivated by a combination of patriotism and anger over political corruption and economic exploitation. As with Ho, her attitudes suggest that nationalism and communism were both potent forces in twentieth-century Vietnam. Dinh's memoir also describes the deep dissatisfaction many South Vietnamese felt with the Diem regime after 1954. Finally, the memoir can be eye-opening for students who might not know the role that some women played in the Vietnam War.

Another memoir that is often used in classes on the Vietnam War is Truong Nhu Tang's *A Viet Cong Memoir*.[11] Tang was a high-ranking member of the NLF, which worked with the North Vietnamese to oppose the United States and the southern government in the 1960s. He eventually broke with the communists after the war ended in 1975 and was exiled to the United States. His memoir combines personal experiences with important developments in the Vietnam War from the 1940s until the 1970s, touching on the issues of communism and nationalism mentioned above.

A Viet Cong Memoir is commonly assigned in courses devoted to the Vietnam War, but it can be excerpted for classes that cover broader topics. The second chapter—just under nine pages—describes events in the aftermath of World War II, including the resumption of French control and Ho Chi Minh's efforts to negotiate with the French over the question of Vietnamese independence. Tang was present in Paris at the time, and he had an opportunity to meet Ho. This chapter is noteworthy for Tang's description of Ho, which emphasizes his charisma and charm. Tang emphasizes that it was Ho's personality, more than his identity as a nationalist, a communist, or something else, that earned Tang's loyalty.

Subsequent chapters describe Tang's involvement in the Viet Minh and his rise to prominence in the NLF. The final chapter, "Exile," offers a gripping account of his disenchantment after the war and his decision to escape from Vietnam in 1976. This, too, can be assigned for students and used as the basis for a discussion or paper assignment. Teachers can ask students whether events after the war affect our assessment of America's earlier decisions to intervene in Vietnam. Some students might conclude that Tang's account shows that the United States was correct to worry about the results of communist domination in Vietnam. They may argue that Tang's experiences show that Vietnamese communists disingenuously used nationalism and anticolonialism to disguise their true motives. Other students might suggest that the war, and therefore American intervention, contributed to political polarization and economic hardship that plagued Vietnam after unification. Others might argue that events in the 1970s do not change the circumstances as

Viet Cong captured by the South Vietnamese Army, 1961. (VA004407, Douglas Pike Photograph Collection, The Vietnam Center and Archive, Texas Tech University)

they existed in the 1950s. This sort of discussion is relevant not only to our understanding of the Vietnam War but also to the way students use history to craft arguments. While teachers might encourage students to consider how events in the 1970s are linked to earlier periods, they should also remind them not to fall victim to the logical fallacy of *post hoc ergo propter hoc*. In other words, if something happens after something else, the second event is not necessarily *caused* by the earlier event.

Teachers focusing on America's response to Ho Chi Minh and the Vietnamese revolution have a wealth of sources that they can use in their classes. One good starting point is the Pentagon Papers. Like the documents above, the Pentagon Papers is widely available in print and on the Internet.[12] Students may not be aware of the Pentagon Papers, so teachers can briefly explain the backstory. The Pentagon Papers refers to a classified Department of Defense report commissioned in 1967 to study the history of America's intervention in Vietnam. The report was completed in early 1969, and two years later Daniel Ellsberg, a government official involved in the project, leaked it to the press. The *New York Times* and the *Washington Post* published excerpts from the report after the US Supreme Court ruled that the Nixon's efforts to halt publication were unconstitutional. The publication of the Pentagon Papers revealed that American officials had long been pessimistic about the prospects for success in Vietnam but nevertheless continued to escalate American involvement. The study was also a boon to historians writing about Vietnam. They had access to a detailed and lengthy internal study before the war had even ended. Even today the Pentagon Papers is a key resource for people interested in understanding American policy in Vietnam.

The first volume of the Pentagon Papers has many sections that can be used effectively with students. One such section, "Ho Chi Minh: Asian Tito?," examines the possibility that Ho Chi Minh was like the post–World War II leader in Yugoslavia, who was a communist but did not enter the Soviet bloc. In doing so, it asks an intriguing counterfactual question: could the United States have worked with Ho Chi Minh in the late 1940s? This section is effective because it weighs the evidence and acknowledges both the repercussions of America's failure to understand Vietnam and the real obstacles to working with Ho Chi Minh after World War II.

Teachers can find a lot to work with in this part of the Pentagon Papers. The brief section comparing Ho Chi Minh to Tito is supplemented by several useful appendixes. One, about twenty-five pages long, includes examples of writers and officials ranging from Bernard Fall to William Fulbright who supported the "Asian Tito" hypothesis in the 1940s and after. The next appendix, also a little over twenty-five pages, is a detailed "political biography of Ho Chi Minh" and timeline of his life. The third appendix compiles about fifteen documents of communication between Ho Chi Minh and the United States in 1945 and 1946.

Teachers can use these materials in any number of ways. If time is limited, students can read the brief overview and summarize the main arguments. Students could then go a step further and assess the argument. Is it convincing? Why or why not? This could be done as a written assignment or in-class discussion. For classes with more time, students can use the supplemental materials to dig deeper into the topic. Students could demonstrate their reading comprehension by summarizing primary source documents. Or they could use the sources to construct an argument, either in favor of or against working with Ho Chi Minh. Teachers could also structure a debate around this question, asking the students to use the documents as evidence.

This section of the Pentagon Papers can be challenging for students who do not want to pass judgment on American officials. I have had many students who think the United States erred in opposing Ho Chi Minh after World War II. But they think American officials at the time could not have realized that Ho Chi Minh was more committed to national independence than communist revolution—that this only clear in hindsight. As this excerpt shows, there was ample evidence in the 1940s that Ho Chi Minh was at least as much a nationalist as a communist, and yet American officials ignored or downplayed this possibility.

Teachers should also remind the students that by the time the Pentagon Papers was written in the late 1960s many officials in the US government—from the Johnson administration, the Defense Department, and the State Department—had soured on the war. (Doubts about the war appeared much earlier but grew as the war continued.) Nevertheless, the fighting would continue for several more bloody years, leading to the deaths of millions of Vietnamese and Americans. In other words, American officials continued to pursue a flawed strategy in Vietnam not out of ignorance but in spite of grave and well-informed pessimism.

Students can think about what evidence suggests that Ho was a communist or a nationalist. But they should also ask why this question matters. Why did US policy makers and other Americans think it was important to identify Ho's political doctrine? Why did it matter to Vietnamese like Truong Nhu Tang? The answers to these questions might seem obvious to teachers who are well acquainted with the Cold War, through either their studies or their personal experiences. But most students have no firsthand recollection of living during the Cold War. They often find the fear of communism to be antiquated or even quaint. This is not surprising: the Soviet Union dissolved before they born, there are only a handful of communist countries left in the world, and even Communist China is seen more as an economic rival than a strategic threat to the United States. Therefore students may need some help getting into the mind-set of the historical actors from the past.

NOTES

1. Recent biographies of Ho Chi Minh include Pierre Brocheaux, *Ho Chi Minh: A Biography* (Cambridge: Cambridge University Press, 2007); William J. Duiker, *Ho Chi Minh: A Life* (New York: Hyperion, 2000); and Sophie Quinn-Judge, *Ho Chi Minh: The Missing Years* (Berkeley: University of California Press, 2003).

2. Quinn-Judge, *Ho Chi Minh*, 12.

3. This document is widely available in print and online. For example, see Fredrik Logevall, *The Origins of the Vietnam War* (Harlow, UK: Pearson Education Limited, 2001), 95–96. A shorter excerpt can be found in Michael H. Hunt, *A Vietnam War Reader: A Documentary History from American and Vietnamese Perspectives* (Chapel Hill: University of North Carolina Press, 2010), 12.

4. For a recent account of US policy toward Vietnam in the 1940s and 1950s, see Mark Atwood Lawrence, *Assuming the Burden: Europe and the American Commitment to War in Vietnam* (Berkeley: University of California Press, 2007). Also see Fredrik Logevall, *Embers of War: The Fall of an Empire and the Making of America's Vietnam* (New York: Random House, 2012).

5. Mark Philip Bradley, *Vietnam at War* (Oxford: Oxford University Press, 2009).

6. See, e.g., Hunt, *A Vietnam War Reader*.

7. Quinn-Judge, *Ho Chi Minh*, 32.

8. David W. P. Elliott, *The Vietnamese War: Revolution and Social Change in the Mekong Delta, 1930–1975* (Armonk, NY: M. E. Sharpe, 2002); David Hunt, *Vietnam's Southern Revolution: From Peasant Insurrection to Total War, 1959–1968* (Amherst: University of Massachusetts Press, 2009).

9. Hunt, *A Vietnam War Reader*; Robert J. McMahon, ed., *Major Problems in the History of the Vietnam War: Documents and Essays* (Boston: Cengage, 2008).

10. Nguyen Thi Dinh, *No Other Road to Take* (Ithaca, NY: Cornell University Southeast Asia Program, 1976). Dinh's memoir is also excerpted in Hunt, *A Vietnam War Reader*, 14–16.

11. Truong Nhu Tang, *A Viet Cong Memoir* (New York: Vintage Books, 1986). Tang's memoir is also excerpted in Hunt, *A Vietnam War Reader*, 17–19; and McMahon, *Major Problems in the History of the Vietnam War*, 285–88.

12. The full version of the Pentagon Papers is available at http://www.archives.gov/research/pentagon-papers/.

KEY RESOURCES

Bradley, Mark Philip. *Vietnam at War*. Oxford: Oxford University Press, 2009.
Bradley, Mark Philip, and Marilyn B. Young, eds. *Making Sense of the Vietnam*

Wars: Local, National, and Transnational Perspectives. Oxford: Oxford University Press, 2008.

Brocheaux, Pierre. *Ho Chi Minh: A Biography*. Cambridge: Cambridge University Press, 2007.

Duiker, William J. *Ho Chi Minh: A Life*. New York: Hyperion, 2001.

Elliott, David W. P. *The Vietnamese War: Revolution and Social Change in the Mekong Delta, 1930–1975*. Concise edition. Armonk, NY: M. E. Sharpe, 2002.

Goscha, Christopher E. "Courting Diplomatic Disaster? The Difficult Integration of Vietnam into the Internationalist Communist Movement (1945–1950)." *Journal of Vietnamese Studies* 1:1–2 (2006): 59–103.

Hunt, David. *Vietnam's Southern Revolution: From Peasant Insurrection to Total War, 1959–1968*. Amherst: University of Massachusetts Press, 2009.

Hunt, Michael H. *A Vietnam War Reader: A Documentary History from American and Vietnamese Perspectives*. Chapel Hill: University of North Carolina Press, 2010.

Lawrence, Mark Atwood. *Assuming the Burden: Europe and the American Commitment to War in Vietnam*. Berkeley: University of California Press, 2007.

Logevall, Fredrik. *Choosing War: The Lost Chance for Peace and the Escalation of the War in Vietnam*. Berkeley: University of California Press, 2001.

———. *Embers of War: The Fall of an Empire and the Making of America's Vietnam*. New York: Random House, 2012.

Prados, John. *Vietnam: The History of an Unwinnable War, 1945–1975*. Lawrence: University Press of Kansas, 2009.

Quinn-Judge, Sophie. *Ho Chi Minh: The Missing Years*. Berkeley: University of California Press, 2003.

From the French
to the Americans

KATHRYN C. STATLER

or most teachers and students, the story of American involvement in Vietnam begins in the 1960s, with a brief overview of earlier US actions there. Usually missing from this narrative is the French experience. France had consolidated control in Vietnam, Cambodia, and Laos by the 1880s and refused to relinquish its grasp as the post–World War II process of decolonization began. The Franco-Vietnamese conflict that ensued from 1946 to 1954 brought the United States into the fray and had important lessons for Americans arriving in Saigon in the 1960s, lessons that were, for the most part, ignored at the time, as they have been since.

This essay offers up some of those lessons (and ideas for associated lesson plans) while providing at least part of the answer to a major question in the historiography: why the United States intervened in Vietnam. It does so by highlighting how the Americans first aided the French war effort and then ultimately replaced France as the most important western power in South Vietnam in the mid-1950s. Moreover, many of the major American decisions made in Vietnam stemmed from how successive US administrations understood, or thought they understood, earlier French mistakes.

Teaching the transition from the French to the Americans in Vietnam can be tricky for a number of reasons. First, students want to get to the 1960s, where the "real action" is—the momentous Gulf of Tonkin Resolution, President Johnson's subsequent decisions to begin a sustained bombing campaign and send in ground troops, and the varied protests that made up the antiwar movement, to name a few. Second, it is just too easy to blame the French and ignore what their extensive experience in Vietnam might have to offer. A typical response by American policy makers at the time, when discussing French resistance to Vietnamese independence or the French military defeat at the remote garrison of Dien Bien Phu in North Vietnam, often goes something like "of course the French messed up in Vietnam. They're the French." Finally, although there is quite a bit of literature on the period before American intervention, a lot of it is in French.

The American experience in Vietnam, however, can only be understood within the context of the First Indochina War (also known as the Franco–Viet Minh War by westerners and the Resistance Struggle against Colonial France or French War by the Vietnamese) and its aftermath. The following pages outline exactly why this is so and offer some effective teaching practices to help students contextualize early American involvement in Vietnam. Therefore, the primary events discussed include a brief overview; the 1946–54 First Vietnam War, culminating in the battle of Dien Bien Phu (which always guarantees active student participation); and the transition from French to American leadership in Vietnam that began with the 1954 Geneva Conference. The chapter also discusses literature, documentaries, and films that highlight the French experience and its enduring influence on the Vietnamese and Americans. It concludes with sample assignments and suggestions for additional reading.

Background

When structuring lectures it is useful for teachers to provide a general overview of the long-term Vietnamese struggle to gain independence from foreign invaders. To the Vietnamese, the French were simply another enemy (as were the Americans) in a long line of adversaries, the most difficult being the Chinese, who dominated Vietnam off and on for centuries. Starting classes with a brief discussion of the Chinese invasion in 111 BCE, the Trung sisters' unsuccessful revolt against the Chinese in 39 CE, and Le Loi's successful one in 1426, gives students a sense of the developing process of Vietnamese ethnic and national identity and willingness to fight to the death to achieve independence. The 1858 French attack and subsequent 1862 treaty, which allowed France to gain its first toehold with three provinces in the south, three ports, and permission for Catholic missionaries to propagate their

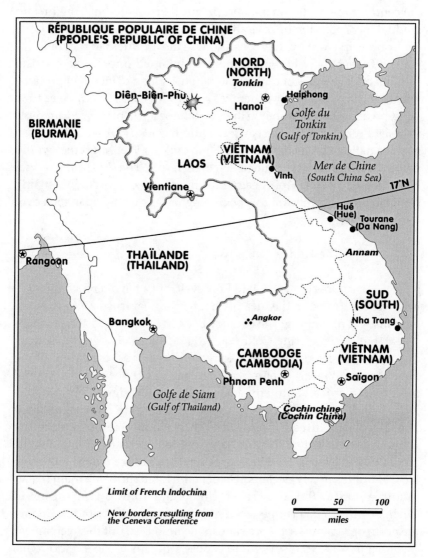

Southeast Asia after Geneva, 1954. (originally published in Kathryn C. Statler, *Replacing France: The Origins of American Intervention in Vietnam;* reproduced courtesy of the University Press of Kentucky)

faith, can be summarized quickly. Teachers should stress the artificial French division of Vietnam into the southern region of Cochin China, the central region of Annam, and the northern region of Tonkin, and gradual incorporation of Laos and Cambodia (see map). French formal control was in place by the 1880s and was most evident in the south.

The French colonial government maintained oppressive political rule and engaged in economic exploitation, leading to incipient protests, which, in turn, were immediately and ruthlessly crushed. Over time widespread resentment among the Vietnamese led to organized attempts to resist French rule in the early twentieth century. It would be Vietnamese nationalist leader Ho Chi Minh and his Viet Minh that would present the first serious challenge to French rule. The Viet Minh, or Viet Nam Doc Lap Minh Hoi (League for the Independence of Vietnam), began to play a significant role beginning in 1941 when Japan took over the entire country.

The First Vietnam War

President Franklin Roosevelt, not a fan of French colonialism, was interested in the idea of an international trusteeship for Vietnam instead of handing the country back to France after the Japanese defeat, but the escalating Cold War would eventually derail this idea.[1] The 1946–50 period encompasses the outbreak and escalation of the First Vietnam War. A preliminary agreement between French special representative Jean Sainteny and Ho Chi Minh, signed on March 6, 1946, was a last-ditch effort to avoid open warfare. The agreement stipulated that fifteen thousand French troops would replace the Chinese ones in Tonkin (China had liberated northern Vietnam at the end of World War II) for five years. In return France would recognize Ho Chi Minh's newly declared Democratic Republic of Vietnam (DRV) as a free state within the French Union and allow a referendum in Cochin China to determine whether it would reunite with the DRV in the north or remain a separate state in the union. To put the Vietnamese dilemma in context, it's useful to expose students to Ho's retort to his colleagues' criticism that the accords did not guarantee complete Vietnamese independence: "You fools, don't you realize what it means if the Chinese stay? Don't you remember your history? The last time the Chinese came, they stayed one thousand years. The French are foreigners. They are weak. Colonialism is dying. . . . [T]he white man is finished in

Asia. But if the Chinese stay now, they will never leave. As for me, I prefer to smell French shit for five years, rather than Chinese shit for the rest of my life."[2]

It would take eight, not five, years to get rid of the French, who were determined to cling to their empire. After the French shelled Haiphong Harbor in November 1946 over a customs dispute, which resulted in the deaths of thousands of Vietnamese, and the Viet Minh retaliated on December 18, war became almost impossible to avoid. It is at this point that the Cold War began heating up and the French started painting Ho as a communist agent in order to persuade the Americans that their cause was an anticommunist not a colonial one. Mark Atwood Lawrence's *Assuming the Burden* is very good on this time period, tracing the incremental American steps toward actively supporting the French against Ho that would culminate in full support by 1950.

In 1950 the Cold War collided with decolonization. The West was still reeling from the twin shocks of the Soviets exploding an atomic bomb and China "falling to communism" in 1949 when North Korea invaded South Korea in June 1950. Americans worried that communism would spread from country to country—a process that President Dwight D. Eisenhower later compared to a "row of dominoes." Meanwhile, a number of nations, after witnessing Philippine and Indian independence, begin clamoring for their own. It is within this context that Vietnam took on increasing global importance, and the Truman administration decided to support the French in Indochina with economic, military, and political support by committing fifteen million dollars to the war, sending advisers (the Military Assistance and Advisory Group), and recognizing the French puppet government led by Emperor Bao Dai.

When discussing these events, teachers should try to elicit from students the reasons why the Truman administration decided to reject Ho Chi Minh. Ideally students will mention the threat of world communism and the potential domestic backlash in the United States if another country "fell" to it.[3] Students might also recall the American interest in keeping France as a close ally and that by 1950 the American domestic scene had become one of fear and paranoia as Senator Joseph McCarthy's claims of communist spies in the federal government began to permeate the collective consciousness.

From 1950 to 1954 the war continued without a clear victory on either side. In discussing this period, it is worth pointing out rising French demoralization and protest at home as deaths and injuries increased due to Viet Minh guerrilla tactics. Military operations included Cao Bang in 1950 in which the Viet Minh bogged down an entire French army of six thousand men, with massive loss of equipment, and Operation Lorraine in 1952 in which thirty thousand French troops, tanks, and artillery were ambushed in the Red River delta. Successive French governments struggled to find a winning strategy as political opponents of the war and the public at home increasingly referred to events in Indochina as *la sale guerre*, the "dirty war."

The fighting in Vietnam culminated in 1954. In response to the incoming Eisenhower administration's admonition to fight to win in early 1953, French General Henri Navarre (the fifth commander of French forces in five years) came up with the so-called Navarre Plan, which called for a major military offensive. Navarre committed to a set piece battle to stop DRV support of the south through Laos, an additional ten battalions of French troops, and a substantial increase in troops from the Vietnam National Army (the forces of Bao Dai's State of Vietnam). In return the Eisenhower administration provided an additional $385 million in funds, and then another $400 million for 1954 alone. The decision to begin the *jaunissement* (yellowing) of the armed forces by relying on the Vietnamese to do their own fighting was a crucial one. Asking students if this strategy sounds familiar will probably prompt comments about later wars, such as those in Iraq and Afghanistan, but teachers should emphasize that in Vietnam the French tried this tactic first, followed much later by Richard Nixon's policy of Vietnamization, in which the South Vietnamese armed forces took on more duties and fighting as American troops were withdrawn. The result of this strategy was the fall of Dien Bien Phu on May 7, 1954, and the fall of Saigon on April 30, 1975.

There is a wealth of literature on Dien Bien Phu, but students will need to master a few basic facts to orient themselves. This was the set piece battle the French had been hoping for, and it was a complete disaster from the beginning. The French were convinced they had sufficiently fortified the garrison, but the Viet Minh, guided by military strategist Vo Nguyen Giap and with thousands of village helpers and Soviet and Chinese trucks and equipment, were able to move large artillery pieces into the surrounding hills. The supposedly impregnable strong points within Dien Bien Phu turned out to be imminently pregnable, evidenced by the Viet Minh March 13 attack. When the airstrip was destroyed two weeks later, the French had to use airdrops to resupply the base.

Once it became clear the French were failing, the sharpest Franco-Anglo-American disagreements occurred over whether and how the United States should intervene. One option was United Action, a multi-lateral effort that required both British and congressional approval, neither of which was forthcoming. In fact Congress was extremely reluctant to give Eisenhower broad authority in this situation, in contrast to the members of Congress in 1964, who overwhelmingly voted for the Gulf of Tonkin Resolution. The other interventionist option was uni-lateral American action in the form of Operation Vulture, a bombing raid. Historians disagree about the seriousness of American plans for military action, but certainly key players, including Secretary of State John Foster Dulles, Joint Chiefs of Staff chairman Admiral Arthur Radford, and Vice President Richard Nixon, pushed strongly in that direction.[4] Eisenhower ultimately chose not to intervene, Dien Bien Phu fell on May 7, and French recriminations against their perfidious ally continued long after the battle.

Bernard Fall's *Hell in a Very Small Place* is still a classic and captures French troops' desperation and the grim nature of the battle, which has often been compared to the trench warfare, rain, mud sucking at soldiers' boots, bodies piled up, lack of supplies, and disease of World War I. Teachers can use excerpts from the chapter 10, "Castor Dies," to help students understand and vicariously feel the frustration associated with successive loss of the strong points, sheer exhaustion of the men, superior Vietnamese tactics and weaponry, failure of the United States to come to French aid, internal French disagreements, and the last major Vietnamese offensive, which toppled the garrison. In terms of human costs, there were about 25,000 Viet Minh casualties and 10,000 deaths (mostly suffered during the initial human-wave attacks). For the French the cost included 1,500 initial deaths, 4,000 wounded, and 10,000 prisoners of war, over half of whom did not return.

Literary and visual aids are not numerous for this time period, but Graham Greene's novel *The Quiet American* has stood the test of time and can be contrasted with the original 1958 film (which had a clear pro-American agenda) and the 2002 remake (which is much closer to the novel's anti-American stance). Greene captures French desperation toward the end of the war and the American belief that they could do a better job saving Vietnam from communism. Teachers can highlight the presence of Trinh Minh The, the real-life leader of the dissident Cao Dai guerrilla group near the Cambodian border, who plays a small but important role in the novel. Trinh Minh The represents that most elusive of Vietnamese leaders, the third force that rejects communism and colonialism. The main character, Alden Pyle, is also worth exploring. In what ways is he the "quiet" American? He is quiet, he reads a lot, and of course he is really quiet once he is killed. But what does he represent? The scene in chapter 2, section 3, with two young soldiers from the Vietnamese National Army in a guard tower, is also a good teaching tool. During this scene Pyle proclaims that the Vietnamese people "don't want communism," and British journalist Thomas Fowler replies, "They want enough rice. . . . They don't want to be shot at. They want one day to be much the same as another. They don't want our white skins around telling them what they want." Fowler then goes on to dispel the domino theory: "I know the record. Siam goes. Malaya goes. Indonesia goes. What does 'go' mean?"

The 2002 film version of *The Quiet American* is also compelling and provides a great catalyst for classroom discussions about the central questions raised by this novel. Teachers can ask students what they think various Vietnamese leaders and people wanted for Vietnam. In answering this question, have students consider the character Phuong: is she a good representative of the Vietnamese people or not? Also, would she survive just fine if the two western powers, symbolized by Pyle and Fowler, stopped fighting over her? Finally, see if students pick up on the futility of the French war effort, as depicted in both the film and the novel. Who controls Vietnam?

Other sources include the first chapter of Le Ly Hayslip's memoir *When Heaven and Earth Changed Places* (1991), which captures a young Vietnamese peasant girl's experience with the French. Her depictions of French searches of Vietnamese villages help illuminate why the Viet Minh were so popular. The film *Indochine* (1992) also gives us the Vietnamese perspective. Catherine Deneuve stars as Eliane, representing France and its civilizing mission (as well as its brutality). The film explores the multifaceted nature of French colonialism: economic exploitation, education, culture, and violence. Students can debate whether the film is sympathetic to colonialism (a nostalgic look back at the glory days of French control?) and how the Vietnamese population is portrayed. For example, Camille, Catherine's adopted daughter, evolves as a helpless yet privileged child who needs tutelage to become a determined, capable nationalist. The last scenes, which depict how French prisons became breeding grounds for communist cells and the outcome of the Geneva Conference, provide an excellent visual aid to the end of the French presence in Vietnam. Another option, though harder to find, is *La 317ème Section* (1965), which provides interesting comparisons with later American combat: demonstrators on the mainland when soldiers return, the recognition that the French have "lost" the war, the nature of the battle the French face in Indochina, and the role of their "allies." Finally, episode 1, "Roots of a War," of the still superb 1983 PBS documentary *Vietnam: A Television History* is useful in capturing French confidence in engaging the Viet Minh at Dien Bien Phu, the battle itself, and views from both Vietnamese and French vets, as well as American officials. A more recent, and shorter, documentary is the 1999 *The Vietnam War: A Descent into Hell*, episode 1. Both are excellent classroom tools.

The Transition from French to American Control in Vietnam

The session of the Geneva Conference devoted to a political resolution of the conflict in Indochina began on May 8, 1954, the day after Dien Bien Phu fell. Key participants included French foreign minister Georges Bidault and later prime minister Pierre Mendès France, US undersecretary of state Walter Bedell Smith, UK foreign minister Anthony Eden, Soviet foreign minister Vyacheslav Molotov, Chinese foreign minister Zhou Enlai, Democratic Republic of Vietnam foreign minister Pham Van Dong, and representatives of Bao Dai's State of Vietnam. Most of the substantial negotiations took place between military representatives for the French and Viet Minh. Despite the clear momentum of the Viet Minh on the battlefield, the negotiators did eventually agree to the following: a cease-fire, temporary partition of the country at the seventeenth parallel pending nationwide elections in 1956, independence and neutrality of Cambodia and Laos, outlawing of any party entering into new military agreements, a regrouping of French forces south of and Viet Minh forces north of the seventeenth parallel, free movement of refugees, and the creation of the International Control Commission (ICC), headed by representatives from Canada, Poland, and India, to oversee the accords. These accords ended the war, but few were happy. Molotov and Zhou Enlai had pressured their DVR comrades to settle on less than ideal terms, fearing a wider war, and Bao Dai's State of Vietnam had been marginalized at the conference. The French believed the accords were about the best they could do, as did the British. The Americans had slowly distanced themselves from events, fearing an unacceptable agreement with the communists, and were determined to step up their own efforts in the global Cold War. The United States subsequently embraced a collective defense system similar to the North American Treaty Organization (NATO) for the East that included Vietnam under its umbrella—the South East Asia Treaty Organization (SEATO)—with the United States, United Kingdom, France, Australia, New Zealand, Thailand, the Philippines, and Pakistan as members. Perhaps most important, since the State of Vietnam negotiators were not invited to sign the accords and the Americans simply agreed not to interfere with them, a door remained ajar for future American involvement.

For the Americans, the way through this door would be Ngo Dinh Diem, prime minister under Bao Dai's government, which now administered the area below the seventeenth parallel. Diem continues to provoke controversy, both in Vietnam and in the scholarly community, over his viability as a capable alternative to Ho Chi Minh. A useful book in trying to assess Diem is CIA operative Edward Lansdale's memoir *In the Midst of Wars* (see especially 154–61). Lansdale describes Diem's remoteness from the Vietnamese people, his first impressions of Diem, Diem's family, and the problems associated with trying to conduct psychological warfare. After reading this excerpt with students, teachers can try to elicit from them Lansdale's purpose in Vietnam, his views on Diem, and the larger question of US interference in other countries' affairs.

After putting down various internal and external challenges to his power and consolidating political and military control, Diem held a national referendum in October 1955, pitting himself against the French-backed head of state, Bao Dai, and winning an impossible 98.2 percent of the vote and 605,000 votes from Saigon even though there were only 400,000 voters. Diem also refused to begin consultations with the north regarding the 1956 elections, arguing that since he had not signed the Geneva Accords he was not bound by them.

The fact that Diem was able to sabotage the 1956 elections was *the* crucial event that allowed the American presence to continue in Vietnam. With all immediate challenges overcome, Diem's regime became increasingly repressive, with no real economic growth, no distribution of land, and no legal political opposition. American leaders eventually split over whether to continue to support Diem while pushing for reform or to withdraw support. The first attempted military coup against him occurred in 1960, followed by a successful one backed by the Kennedy administration in November 1963.

An interesting aspect of Diem's character, and one that appealed to many Americans, was his embrace of a western religion—Catholicism. Seth Jacobs does an excellent job of illustrating this point in *America's Miracle Man in Vietnam: Ngo Dinh Diem, Religion, Race, and U.S. Intervention in Southeast Asia, 1950–1957*. James Carroll in *An American Requiem* also emphasizes the role American Catholics played in supporting Diem. Passages from *Deliver Us from Evil*, Catholic doctor Tom Dooley's well-known, not to mention sensationalized, account of the northern refugee exodus that took place after the Geneva Conference, can provoke interesting questions about the role of nonofficial actors, propaganda tactics, and refugee organizations. Wilson Miscamble's "Francis Cardinal Spellman and 'Spellman's War'" in *The Human Tradition in the Vietnam Era* provides a balanced account of Spellman's role in generating public support and money for Diem.

Following Geneva, both Diem and Eisenhower administration officials were determined to reduce the French presence in Vietnam. Diem's consolidation of power and refusal to begin consultations for the 1956 elections represented a major political setback for the French, compounded by the American decisions to take over military, economic, administrative, and cultural affairs previously directed by the French. American agencies also sought to replace the French language with English and French customs with American ones while rarely bothering to learn the Vietnamese language or its culture, politics, or history.

In pondering the Eisenhower administration's actions, teachers could ask students to think about the legacy left to newly elected president John F. Kennedy in 1961: the United States was pouring three hundred million dollars into Vietnam each year, US agencies were directing an extensive nation-building effort, a few thousand official Americans were living in Vietnam along with thousands more nonofficial ones, and there was no exit plan or end in sight.

Again, literary and visual aids for this time period are not numerous, but the first scenes of the films *Go Tell the Spartans* (1978) and *We Were Soldiers* (2002) remind students that the French were there before the

Americans and fared badly by underestimating the enemy. In *Go Tell the Spartans*, which focuses on the period directly before full-scale American involvement when Americans were still serving as "advisers," a number of references are made to previous French attempts to hold the imagined garrison of Muc Wa. Though dated, it still presents a powerful message about continuities between the Franco-Vietminh War and the American one and foreshadows later events. The film is based on Daniel Ford's 1967 prophetic novel *Incident at Muc Wa*. The film's title is taken from a quote by the Greek historian Herodotus about the battle of Thermopylae in 480 BCE, where three hundred Spartans died defending their ground: "When you find us lying here, go tell the Spartans we obeyed our orders." It can be compared not only to the 2007 action fantasy film *300*, which many students may have seen, but also to American soldiers' decisions to follow orders later in the Vietnam conflict. *We Were Soldiers*, adapted from the 1993 book by Harold Moore and Joseph Galloway, opens with French forces suffering defeat after being ambushed by Viet Minh troops at the end of the First Indochina War. Lieutenant General Harold G. Moore (played by Mel Gibson) is determined not to make the same mistakes the French did.

Novels that capture lingering French influence include Ward Just's *A Dangerous Friend* (1999), which looks at the period just before major American escalation. The main character, Sydney Parade, exhorts, "We're going to spend this war to death, deep-sea ports for ships and airfields for the biggest jets. And add to that the bridges and roads and so forth, and technical assistance for the government ministries so taxes can be collected and budgets balanced, little Vietnam will be the most modern country in Asia. It'll have the infrastructure, you see. It'll go from the Middle Ages to the twentieth century in five years. It'll look like California." Asking students to ponder this sort of zeal about nation building (and what the French have to say about it as symbolized by the character Claude Armand) can lead to interesting conversations about beliefs in American exceptionalism and intervention abroad. A more recent novel that incorporates the French experience is Tatjana Soli's *The Lotus Eaters* (2010). Although it is focuses on the actual American war effort, it has many examples of enduring French influence that can be culled as well, most visibly in the character of Annick and the point that every American arrives in Saigon with his or her copy of *The Quiet American*.

Sample Assignments

With respect to assignments, short-answer quizzes on assigned books and excerpts ensure actual reading. A longer assignment in the form of a policy paper has also proven effective in getting students to understand the French, Vietnamese, and American perspectives in the 1950s. I ask students to write a memorandum to the US secretary of state (writing as a midlevel Department of State official, CIA agent, or American ambassador to South Vietnam) about what to do regarding (1) whether the United States should provide military and economic aid to France in 1950, (2) whether the United States should intervene at Dien Bien Phu in 1954, or (3) whether the United States should try to support or sabotage the 1954 Geneva Accords. Of course, many other critical junctures can also be used as prompts. For college-level classes, teachers can require students to use the *Foreign Relations of the United States* volumes (online at the US Department of State's Office of the Historian (http://history.state.gov/historicaldocuments/pre-kennedy) to see how decision making occurred at the time. The most relevant volumes are numbers 288 (1950, vol. 6, *East Asia and the Pacific*); 322–23 (1952–54, vol. 13, *Indochina*, parts 1–2); 328 (1952–54, vol. 16, *The Geneva Conference*); 329 (1955–57, vol. 1, *Vietnam*); and 358 (1958–60, vol. 1, *Vietnam*).

A map quiz is critical (see map above), and students should memorize neighboring countries and capitals, the Gulf of Tonkin, the seventeenth parallel, Hanoi, Saigon, Hue, the Red and Mekong rivers, and Dien Bien Phu. Another excellent writing assignment asks students to take the position of either Vo Nguyen Giap, a French soldier, or Secretary of State John Foster Dulles and write a paragraph from their perspective on the Dien Bien Phu crisis. An additional short exercise is to have students create a graphic organizer to compare Ho Chi Minh, Bao Dai, and Ngo Dinh Diem, assessing strengths and weaknesses in leadership and character. A simple but effective way to start this process is to put up images of the three leaders, asking students to assess differences in bearing, dress, and interaction with the Vietnamese people. Having done this, either as individuals or in small groups, students will be ready to discuss these historical figures in detail.

Teacher-created study guides with key terms and questions have proven helpful in acclimating students to foreign terms and names.

When posing questions about French involvement, it is important to focus students' attention on how Vietnamese nationalism developed in response to French oppression. Be sure students understand what "French" Indochina entails. The most important question, and certainly the one that fascinates students the most, is who is Ho Chi Minh? Is he a nationalist or communist first and foremost? Could the United States have worked with him after World War II given American support of Ho Chi Minh and his Viet Minh forces during the war?

When discussing early American involvement, make sure students have a clear grasp of how the changing international context played a role in determining events in Vietnam. Why and how did President Harry Truman increase American involvement in Vietnam? Why and how did President Dwight D. Eisenhower do the same? Why did Eisenhower draw the line at US military intervention to relieve the siege of Dien Bien Phu? In asking students to draw some lessons from Dien Bien Phu, first and foremost consider the French overestimation of their own strength and underestimation of the enemy, something the Americans would also do from start to finish. Why did the battle of Dien Bien Phu occur? Was there any way the French could have avoided defeat? Why didn't the Americans intervene?[5] Given that Dien Bien Phu represented the first time in the post–World War II era that a colonial power was defeated on its own terms by its own subjects, what might this mean for other colonies? All of these questions provide numerous opportunities for students to draft short position papers or engage in structured in-class debates.

In discussing the transition from the French to the Americans, ask students to assess what the Geneva Accords actually accomplished. Was the Geneva Conference a missed opportunity for peace? Who won the First Vietnam War? Did the Americans simply follow in French footsteps and attempt to build a colony? Or were they successful in nation building after Geneva? Why or why not? Finally, what evidence can students point to demonstrating the scope of the American presence in South Vietnam by 1960? Did the Eisenhower administration deviate from or follow the Truman administration's policies in Vietnam? Did Kennedy follow Eisenhower's policies? A lot of scholarly attention has been devoted to what could have changed in Vietnam if JFK had lived. Perhaps the more important question is whether events in Vietnam would have turned out differently if Diem had lived. Would he have refused to allow a massive influx of American forces?

Conclusion

By the end of a unit (and certainly a class) on the Vietnam wars, students are usually amazed at the many similarities between the French and American efforts in Vietnam: increased reliance on Vietnamese forces as the military situation deteriorates; Dien Bien Phu, Muc Wa, and Ia Drang as excellent case studies of the dangers of underestimating the enemy; and the French and American attempt and failure to sway allies to their side while still trying to maintain complete control of the war effort. Other similarities include a French belief in the *mission civilisatrice* (civilizing mission) and American confidence in the benefits of modernization and nation building. The French and Americans were equally sure that they knew the best course of action in Vietnam, evidenced by their anger toward one another during Dien Bien Phu and the Geneva Conference, and Kennedy, Johnson, and Nixon's disgust with French president Charles de Gaulle's continued refusal to support the American war effort in the 1960s, which was retaliation in full measure for the American inability to learn from the French experience.

Certainly differences existed between French and American intervention in Vietnam. The Americans did not attack and acquire formal colonies. Rather, the Americans provided economic and military aid and sent advisers and CIA operatives. And, like Pyle, they may have had the best of intentions in doing so. From these humble beginnings, the United States would go on to establish firm control as the dominant western power in Vietnam by the time Kennedy came to office. And, as the rest of this book demonstrates, the United States would ultimately become even more involved than the French in terms of manpower wasted, money spent, lives lost, domestic and world credibility damaged, and physical and psychological destruction rendered. The four hundred thousand killed in the First Indochina War would be dwarfed by the numbers reached during the second one.

NOTES

1. Mark Philip Bradley's *Imagining Vietnam and America: The Making of Postcolonial Vietnam, 1919–1950* (Chapel Hill: University of North Carolina Press, 2000) focuses on the cultural gap between the Americans and Vietnamese and how broader American attitudes toward race (particularly American assumptions about the inferiority of the Vietnamese) would eventually lead the United

States to support the French. Stein Tønnesson makes the argument in *The Vietnamese Revolution of 1945: Roosevelt, Ho Chi Minh, and de Gaulle in a World at War* (London: Sage Publications, 1991) that FDR remained committed to an international trusteeship and that it was only when Harry Truman took over that this idea was doomed. David Marr, *Vietnam 1945: The Quest for Power* (Chapel Hill: University of North Carolina Press, 1995), provides a detailed account of how close Ho Chi Minh came to grabbing and holding power in 1945.

2. Pentagon Papers, Part I, Vietnam and the U.S., 1940–1950, Ho Chi Minh: Asian Tito? summary, p. 170, www.archives.gov/research/pentagon-papers/, accessed on February 10, 2013. This website provides the most complete version of the Pentagon Papers, which was released in 2011.

3. See Mark Lawrence, "Explaining the Early Decisions: The United States and the French War, 1945–1954," in *Making Sense of the Vietnam Wars: Local, National, and Transnational Perspectives*, ed. Mark Philip Bradley and Marilyn B. Young (Oxford: Oxford University Press, 2008), 29–34, for a brief but excellent overview of why the United States decided to actively support the French in 1950 and why the it did not intervene militarily in 1954.

4. Debate continues over how much support Radford promised visiting French general Paul Ely and whether Dulles offered French foreign minister Georges Bidault two tactical nuclear weapons for use at Dien Bien Phu during a subsequent mid-April meeting. The most recent argument that the offer occurred is in Ted Morgan's *Valley of Death: The Tragedy at Dien Bien Phu That Led America into the Vietnam War* (New York: Random House, 2010), 474–85. The preface of the book opens with a short but beautifully detailed description of how the battlefield looks today. See also, Fredrik Logevall, *Embers of War: The Fall of an Empire and the Making of America's Vietnam* (New York: Random House, 2012), 454–509.

5. To set up a student debate on the issue of American intervention, include excerpts from Chalmers Roberts, "The Day We Didn't Go to War," *Reporter*, September 14, 1954; and John Prados, "Assessing Dien Bien Phu," in *The First Vietnam War: Colonial Conflict and Cold War Crisis*, ed. Mark Lawrence and Fredrik Logevall (Cambridge, MA: Harvard University Press, 2007), 226–31. (Chalmers and Prados argue that Eisenhower wanted intervention.) To contrast this interpretation, include excerpts from Melanie Billings-Yun, *Decision against War: Eisenhower and Dien Bien Phu, 1954* (New York: Columbia University Press, 1988). Billings-Yun argues Eisenhower specifically set up impossible conditions for intervention—congressional and British approval and French agreement on faster independence for South Vietnam—to avoid armed conflict. See also George Herring and Richard Immerman, "Eisenhower, Dulles, and Dienbienphu: 'The Day We Didn't Go to War' Revisited," *Journal of American History* 71, 2 (1984): 343–44; David Anderson, *Trapped by Success: The Eisenhower Administration and Vietnam, 1953–1961* (New York: Columbia University Press, 1991), 25–39; and Kathryn Statler, *Replacing France: The Origins of American Intervention in Vietnam*

(Lexington: University Press of Kentucky, 2007), 86–95, for the view that Eisenhower was not a hawk on intervention but did not rule it out as an option. These excerpts can be contrasted later in the course as students debate Johnson's 1965 decisions and the uses of analogies. See John Burke and Fred Greenstein's *How Presidents Test Reality: Decisions in Vietnam, 1954 and 1965* (New York: Russell Sage Foundation, 1989). They compare Eisenhower's caution and formal advisory process with Johnson's less cautious and informal advisory system. Yuen Foong Khong, in *Analogies at War: Korea, Munich, Dien Bien Phu, and the Vietnam Decisions of 1965* (Princeton, NJ: Princeton University Press, 1992), promotes the idea that policy makers are not interested in learning from losers and tended to ignore the French experience in Vietnam, except when it came to the 1967–68 battle at Khe Sanh. Then American commander General William Westmoreland had French officers involved at Dien Bien Phu flown in to offer advice on the situation. See especially chapter 6. See also chapter 3 in Jeffrey Record, *Making War, Thinking History: Munich, Vietnam, and Presidential Uses of Force from Korea to Kosovo* (Annapolis, MD: Naval Institute Press, 2002), on Eisenhower's use of analogies in refraining from the use of force in 1954.

KEY RESOURCES

Anderson, David L. *Trapped by Success: The Eisenhower Administration and Vietnam, 1953–1961.* New York: Columbia University Press, 1991.

Brocheaux, Pierre, and Daniel Hémery. *Indochina: An Ambiguous Colonization, 1858–1954.* Berkeley: University of California Press, 2010.

Devillers, Philippe, and Jean Lacouture. *End of a War: Indochina, 1954.* New York: Praeger, 1969.

Dommen, Arthur. *The Indochinese Experience of the French and Americans: Nationalism and Communism in Cambodia, Laos, and Vietnam.* Bloomington: Indiana University Press, 2001.

Fall, Bernard. *Hell in a Very Small Place.* Philadelphia: Lippincott, 1967.

Gardner, Lloyd. *Approaching Vietnam: From World War II through Dienbienphu.* New York: Norton, 1988.

Lawrence, Mark Atwood. *Assuming the Burden: Europe and the American Commitment to War in Vietnam.* Berkeley: University of California Press, 2007.

Lee, Steven Hugh. *Outposts of Empire: Korea, Vietnam, and the Origins of the Cold War in Asia, 1949–1954.* Montreal: McGill-Queen's University Press, 1996.

Logevall, Fredrik. *Embers of War: The Fall of an Empire and the Making of America's Vietnam.* New York: Random House, 2012.

Prados, John. *The Sky Would Fall: Operation Vulture: The U.S. Bombing Mission in Indochina, 1954.* New York: Dial Press, 1983.

Statler, Kathryn C. *Replacing France: The Origins of American Intervention in Vietnam.* Lexington: University Press of Kentucky, 2007.

Teaching the Antiwar Movement

Confronting Popular Myths,
Teaching Complexity

DAVID STEIGERWALD

Although I have been teaching the history of the Vietnam War to college students for more than twenty years, I am always a little apprehensive about the things they carry into the classroom. However indifferent they seem, they are rarely blank slates.

Teaching the subject might be easier if they were. It is not what they don't know but what they think they know that worries me. Far more often than not, their knowledge of the subject is nothing more than bits of partial knowledge gleaned from equally ill-informed family and acquaintances and reinforced by some fragment of popular culture. Though much the same is generally true for many other subjects in American history—religion, slavery, the motives of "the founders," just to name a few—the Vietnam War has been a particularly fraught subject because of its central role in the conservative backlash that subsumed American public life with the ascent of Ronald Reagan in the 1980s. And while I think students in the twenty-first century are fairly well removed from those postwar ideological games, they come to the subject with baggage of their own, drawn from their experience as children of the war on terror. Whereas once students often brought with them myths about the "liberal sellout" of the military and the shabby treatment of Vietnam veterans, more recent students came of age amid a conflict that occasioned virtually no public controversy and that, moreover, demands an obligatory bow to American military personnel so clichéd that even clerks in Kuwait are celebrated as "heroes." These students instinctively trust the military, and it is far from self-evident to them that a democratic people has the obligation, as much as the right, to criticize war.

Still, a few myths have endured across the different student cohorts. Other than the one about all those prisoners of war still doing forced labor on Vietnamese potato farms,[1] the most common misapprehension concerns the treatment of vets at the hands of antiwar protesters. I'd like to have a dollar for every time a student has told me that he or she knows a guy who knows a guy who was spit on by protesters when he returned home from Vietnam. While it is possible that such a thing happened to a handful of men, it clearly was not anywhere near so common as is claimed, and it represents something of a collective false memory. Come to think of it, the spitting myth itself presents a teachable moment. How does it happen, we can ask our students, that such assumptions, unsupported by any independent body of evidence, become embedded not only in the minds of the general public but in the minds of people who actually have convinced themselves that they were so victimized?

One partial answer to this question is that the spitting myth connects to a broader misunderstanding that the antiwar movement was composed of pot-smoking, tie-dyed, anti-American hippies who heaped public scorn on soldiers. It is no surprise that both of these myths have come down in part through popular culture. *Rambo* popularized the spitting myth, which the sociologist Jerry Lembcke has argued originated in Nixon administration propaganda.[2] If students haven't seen that film, many have seen *Forrest Gump*, which distilled the mythology about the antiwar movement with such clarity that I continue to use it as a foil for explaining both what the movement was not and how media, time, and the right-wing shift in American politics distorted the history of the Vietnam War. *Gump* is, after all, a subtle but unimpeachably backlash film. There the southern white boy, an Adamic simpleton innocent of all things, meanders through the tumult of the Sixties and floats past, but is never besmirched by, the corruption of authority figures and the conceits of know-it-alls. Like the feather that lilts through the film as a metaphor for lives carried along by fate, Forrest finds himself swept up in an antiwar protest on the Washington Mall where he crosses paths with his boyhood soul mate, Jenny. Then in her hippie phase, Jenny has hooked up with the abusive leader of a student faction from Berkeley. All the tropes and cardboard cutouts of the backlash mythology are there: the Abbie Hoffman figure in his American flag shirt ("Right on, Man!"), the pompous student radical pronouncing against fascist America while beating his girlfriend, the black nationalists trying to steer the antiwar movement in their direction by playing on white liberal guilt. Political scientist Edward P. Morgan describes this portion of the film as "right out of a [conservative] attack on a sixties rogue gallery."[3]

Precisely because it promotes a politically charged mythology, I often use *Forrest Gump* as either a point of departure for or a conclusion to teaching the Vietnam era antiwar movement. As with all myths and stereotypes, *Gump* works from tiny kernels of truth that need to be recognized. Abbie Hoffman did wear an American flag shirt, though as far as I know never at an antiwar rally. It got him arrested when he wore it to a hearing of the House Un-American Activities Committee in October 1968, and it was censored out of a segment of the *Merv Griffin Show* a few months later; students are amazed to discover that it was once illegal to wear a facsimile of the flag. It is true that there were self-righteous misogynists among student radicals in the late 1960s, most famously within Weatherman. The relationship between the white Left and black nationalists was fraught with white guilt and a tendency among African American activists toward a "more radical than thou" rhetoric built on the primacy of racial grievance. But these were secondary tendencies that stood at the margins of the real movement and came to the fore, such as they did, only very late in the game, that is, after 1968. And at that point, the truly influential wings of the movement were finally having some effect in the most humdrum ways—through political lobbying.

Teaching the Vietnam era antiwar movement against these broad assumptions, accordingly, is an exercise in both debunking mythology and conveying the movement's complexity, and here I'll offer a few interrelated ways in which I conduct that exercise.

For undergraduates, my first aim is to demonstrate the diversity of groups, organizations, and motives within the movement. There was never one dominant organization. Many of the groups that participated in antiwar activism were organizations in name only that never asked for dues, never kept systematic membership records, and never had a system for choosing leaders. The people who flocked to antiwar activism, especially after 1965, hailed from a cross section of middle America.

While for the most part it is safe to call the bulk of participants "middle class," they ranged over the generations, occupied different sections of the mainstream political spectrum, represented the nation's religious diversity, and were urbanites and suburbanites. As Charles Chatfield, one of the preeminent scholars of American peace movements, has put it, while the "still-dominant image of the anti-war protest is that it was . . . confrontational, enlisted primarily youth, and operated mainly through mass demonstrations," in reality the movement "was composed of many groups at the national, regional, and local levels, with only loose connections among them."[4]

My second aim is to argue that Americans came to activism for different reasons, and most of those reasons were sound ones. The underlying social, political, and cultural changes in post–World War II American society pushed people into opposition in varying ways.

The mothers who organized Women Strike for Peace, for instance, first came together out of a shared dismay with the arms race and the security of the family; at the same time, these mostly northeastern, mostly well-off, mostly college-educated women were part of an embryonic second-wave feminism, which emerged fully after the publication of Betty Friedan's *Feminine Mystique* in 1963.

There were good moral and ethical reasons to oppose the war, some of which were deeply rooted in American religious and political traditions. It can come as a surprise to students—especially, I find, my conservative Christian students—to learn that one of the most important threads of outrage against the Vietnam War was sewn out of a long history of Christian pacifism. That many middle-aged clergy participated in protests—some of which were really quite confrontational— certainly doesn't jibe with the popular-culture images of antiwar activists, nor does the earnest conviction on the part of many younger participants that they were bearing Christian witness by resisting the draft.

At the same time, many others opposed the war for reasons grounded in hardheaded considerations of diplomacy and national interest. That there were sound criticisms of American policy based in the straightforward calculus of national interest—arguments that, to my mind, have been proved almost entirely correct—is an important antidote to popular myths and misunderstandings.

My third task, finally, is to make a case that the results of the antiwar movement were mixed and its success or failure still debatable. In its earliest phases, say, before 1966 or so, opposition to official policy was distinctly unpopular; to challenge Cold War orthodoxy was widely assumed to border on treason. As the futility of American policy in Vietnam continued, and the public at large began to sour on the enterprise, more and more people made their way to or showed sympathy for the movement; public protests grew into dramatic confrontations with authorities. Beyond a doubt, the movement had succeeded in hammering the issue of the war into the center of national life, and in so doing won millions of converts to its cause. But the spectacular nature of those high-profile protests made it easy for both the Johnson and, later, Nixon administrations to paint the antiwar movement as radical and well beyond the bounds of American opinion. Both of those presidents saw protesters as domestic enemies to be trampled rather than fellow citizens who deserved a hearing. And yet, quietly, the moderate wings of the movement persuaded more and more national leaders of the war's folly after 1969 and thereby constrained Richard Nixon's latitude. For reasons I'll outline by way of concluding, it is hard to argue, as some have, that the movement brought the war to an end. Still, the movement heightened the domestic political costs of waging war for political elites and to that extent kept the Cold War governing class from an even more catastrophic course.

The biggest problem with conveying the organizational diversity of the antiwar movement is that there was so much of it. Running down a list of all the groups that put up a masthead or chose a name would take half a class, and to no good end. The organizational proliferation partly came out of the variety of causes that preceded Vietnam; there were a dozen or more national antinuke groups by 1962 and a growing number of student organizations. In part, too, this organizational multiplicity reflected the tendency toward schism that always had been a major liability of left-wing politics in the United States. I see no profit in having students sort through the differences or remember a hundred acronyms. I have yet to have an undergraduate get excited over the doctrinal differences between the Revolutionary Youth Movement and the Progressive Labor Party, though for a month or two those differences took center stage as the student Left crashed after the 1968 Democratic National Convention in Chicago.

It seems reasonable, then, to focus on a few specific groups and one umbrella organization. My choice is based partly on their influence and partly on how I think they reflected the broader strains of postwar

America. In other words, I try to use these examples both to discuss the particulars of the antiwar movement and as windows onto the wider history in which the movement, as well as the war itself, was embedded.

I begin with the oldest group, the Fellowship of Reconciliation (FOR). Initially organized in opposition to American participation in World War I, FOR was the nation's leading pacifist organization and the institutional expression of Christian pacifism. Though it could only boast of twenty-three thousand members at its height near the end of the Vietnam War, FOR brought to the era's antiwar movement a long pedigree of left-wing activism and a weathered experience agitating on the margins of American political life. It also lent to the movement its main publication, *Liberation*, edited for many years by David Dellinger, and one of its senior statesmen, A. J. Muste.

The organization is useful because it links the Vietnam era movement with a dignified tradition and reminds us that the movement was not a whole-cloth creation of baby-boom college students. More important, FOR's Christian pacifism is unfamiliar to most of my students. Muste and his colleagues were not just opposed to the Vietnam War; they were opposed to war itself, to all wars, including World War II, the so-called good war.

Muste himself had been ordained in the conservative Dutch Reformed Church, about as close to old-school Calvinism as one can find in America. After an eye-opening experience ministering to New York City's poor immigrants, he opposed World War I, flirted with revolutionary violence in the late 1920s, and returned to pacifism after a spiritual "reconversion" in 1936. For Muste the Christian conscience required pacifism because the faith boiled down to the command to follow the example of "the gentle Jesus." Muste wrote a lot and over a long span of the twentieth century, so it is pretty simple to provide examples of his thinking. The journalist Nat Hentoff compiled a fair collection of Muste essays, the vast majority of which are pre-Vietnam and show, therefore, the maturity of Muste's pacifism. Some students, moreover, are moved by Muste's religious sincerity. The collection also demonstrates the overlap among antiwar sentiment, labor agitation, and civil rights activism. Muste believed that war erupted out of injustice and oppression, nationalism and militarism. His unwavering opposition to war is perhaps best revealed in the 1942 essay "War Is the Enemy," where he confronted the serious problem of pacifism in the face of nazism. Though surely nazism was a "monstrous evil," it was "a dangerous delusion" to think that the allied nations could wage war and not conjure up hatred or avoid the strong temptation to impose a victor's peace, as in fact they had done in World War I. Even the most necessary war, Muste believed, was counterproductive.[5]

Like Muste, many of the most passionate young opponents of the Vietnam War were acting on deeply held Christian convictions. Where mainstream America saw dangerous radicals defying authority, careful historians like Doug Rossinow and Michael P. Foley found young men and women bearing Christian witness against what they believed was an immoral war. This was particularly the case with Foley's Boston area resistance movement, which was centered in several local churches and nurtured by a handful of clergy. The religiously motivated students opted for individual displays of opposition rather than obscuring themselves in large protests. Bearing individual witness usually took the form of a public destruction of one's draft card, which was a federal crime and a symbol of the state's capricious power over the individual.[6]

The second organization I point to is the National Committee for a Sane Nuclear Policy (SANE). As the name implies, the group was organized out of a late 1950s spurt of protest against above-ground testing of atomic weapons, which studies were beginning to show had disseminated radioactive fallout into the atmosphere. From its inception, SANE was composed of well-placed "peace liberals" and "nuclear pacifists," as Charles DeBenedetti called them,[7] temperamentally moderate, middle aged, and institutionally rooted. In other words, SANE was very much mainstream America, except that it took issue with official policy. Even in doing that, the group was committed to presenting a respectable liberal face to the public. Its officials always took care to criticize the war rather than the US government and to blame both sides in equal measure. They were vigilant in keeping communists, suspected communists, or communist sympathizers out of the organization and unsuccessfully tried to impose that "exclusionism" on the rest of the movement. This organization demonstrates that the antiwar movement included members of the "establishment," that the war seemed a folly to well-informed and experienced people, and that politically moderate arguments against American policy were commonplace.

No one represented the establishment character of the organization better than Benjamin Spock, the renowned "baby doctor," who joined the group in 1962. It would have been hard to find a more apt representative of middle-class America. Spock's *Baby and Child Care* had become the veritable bible of middle-class child rearing, largely because of its calm reassurance to parents that natural affection and common sense should be their guides. A blue-blooded patrician in every respect, Spock was the surrogate family doctor of the baby-boom generation. He was "practically a great uncle to my children," fretted a South Carolina woman whose husband was serving in Vietnam and who was aghast at Spock's opposition to the war.[8]

Like SANE itself, Spock came to his wartime opposition from earlier antinuclear sentiment. Although he had been increasingly worried about the arms race in the late 1950s, he had been hesitant to voice public concern lest it compromise his public reputation. He never wanted to be seen as a radical. He also had faith in President John F. Kennedy, who had assured him personally that he would improve relations with the Soviet Union. When Kennedy announced his intention to resume nuclear testing in February 1962, Spock's dismay was mixed with a bit of personal pique, and he decided to take up a standing invitation to join SANE. He joined an antinuclear march on Easter weekend in Cleveland and could hardly have been more sheepish about it. He likened it to one of those nightmares "of being outside without any clothes on." He must have quickly become accustomed to the exposure, because in a matter of weeks, SANE published a full-page ad in the *New York Times* showing Spock standing behind a small child, his hands thrust in his pockets, with a legend that read "Doctor Spock Is Worried." The ad referred to the administration's testing decision, and in some of its republications (and it was widely republished), it included a small postcard addressed to the president and Mrs. Kennedy. It is an effective visual, fairly illustrative of SANE's moderate approach to its causes, and useful for students to see. There was nothing particularly confrontational about it, and the inclusion of the young child was intended to make the point that the organization's opposition to the arms race was rooted in a concern for the long-term future of humanity. Indeed, compared to the infamous "Daisy Ad" that the Johnson campaigned briefly aired during the 1964 presidential campaign, the "Doctor Spock Is Worried" ad looks positively tame.[9]

Composed as it was of mainstream liberals, SANE also helps me to get at a trickier issue. Vietnam was a liberals' war, not just because two of the three presidents who were responsible for militarizing American involvement were Democrats but because American Cold War policy was born out of the worldview of American liberalism, dedicated as that was to global free trade among nations with some form of western-style representative government. Not the least reason for SANE's moderation was that the group hesitated to oppose liberal politicians who otherwise shared the same values as its members. Yet as those political elites expanded the war effort, the "liberal pacifists" were forced to break ranks and reevaluate their liberalism.

In managing a moderate critique of the war, SANE arguably exercised more pointed influence among the American political elite than the other constituencies in the movement. It was exceedingly image conscious, so much so that it hired public-opinion consultants in the late sixties to help guide it on strategies of tone and temper. Its view was simply that, as longtime member Sandy Gottlieb once explained to a student radical, "in middle-class America, the neatly dressed, the well-groomed, and the restrained simply have greater acceptability" and, presumably, more influence.[10] As the student-led part of the movement careened toward increasing flamboyance and radical affect, SANE worked the corridors of Congress and gradually pulled enough liberal congressmen to its point of view that pressure began to build at the uppermost levels of government. This was especially true after 1968, when Richard Nixon's election, his penchant for escalated violence in Vietnam, and war-weariness in the general public made it easier for Democratic congressmen to move into the opposition.

The last distinct group I detail is Students for a Democratic Society (SDS), the main collection of radical students. No history of the antiwar movement can fail to give SDS a starring role. Founded in 1962 among college students disheartened with American society as a whole and specifically inspired by the activism of young African Americans in the civil rights movement, SDS took antiwar activism as its cause. From the very first major protest in April 1965 through the Kent State shootings of 1970 and beyond, these young radicals played a central role in the movement, and the group's fate was inextricably bound to the Vietnam War. It is possible to give SDS too much credit and attention, and doing so risks playing to that stereotype of the movement as youth dominated. But SDS did have its hand in every one of the benchmark events, from that first Easter march of 1965 through the Pentagon siege of 1967, the Chicago convention, and the Nixon era protests. So it is fairly simple to construct a narrative of the movement by focusing on SDS— and vice versa.

For me what is most intriguing about SDS is how the group reflected the state of young people at the time. Coming of age in the early 1960s, they were the first cohort of baby boomers; they had grown up amid the unprecedented affluence of postwar America and a popular culture that created severe tension between conformity and rebellion among "youth." It was fitting, maybe inevitable, that the politics of the Vietnam era would take on a youthful hue, given both the preponderance of "kids" in the population and the degree to which advertisers, radio, television, and the movies all aimed at the youth demographic. Nor was it surprising that college students would assume an important role; by 1968 there were roughly seven million of them, more than enough to constitute a political bloc of their own. Although the vast majority of them remained either apolitical or pro-war throughout the period, enough turned toward political activism to give the antiwar movement the feel of a student-led outburst. We can see that in the size of SDS. Born initially out of the efforts of a few dozen radicalized students in 1962, the group counted somewhere around one hundred thousand members at its height at the end of the decade, and perhaps as many as a million participated in the enormous student strikes of 1970, if only by cutting classes.

As members of a unique generation, SDS's founders advanced an appropriately distinctive critique of American society, on which they grafted their condemnation of the war. They created a "New Left." Reasonably well versed in traditional left-wing thought, Marxism included, they nonetheless rejected the old obsession with working-class revolution. Rather than grinding poverty, the essential problems of postwar America were conformity and alienation. As they made clear in their famous 1962 manifesto, the Port Huron Statement, SDS's founders believed that the bureaucratized hyperorganization of corporate capitalism had created the "remote-control" Cold War state. For them the nation's essential ills grew from a rigid status quo of interlocking structures of power that operated at a distant remove from average citizens, who had to either fall in line or live in an apathetic stupor. There was no better evidence of this state of affairs than the Cold War arms race, in which military bureaucrats connived with American corporations and conventional politicians to endanger the entire human race as they planned for nuclear war with the Soviet Union. What could be more antidemocratic, more antihuman, more irrational than a society set up so that a handful of men could push a button or two and destroy the earth?

The Port Huron Statement is a long and somewhat rambling manifesto—its structure alone spoke to the freshness and inexperience of those who wrote it—and so to use it in class requires some picking and choosing. I will have a class read the opening section, which runs through the comments on the students' place in American society. I always take a few minutes to have them read the famous opening line, not alone for its historical merit but also as a writing tip: "We are people of this generation, born of at least modest comfort, housed now in universities, looking uncomfortably to the world we inherit." I argue that it is the greatest introductory sentence in the history of English prose, with the exception of the opening line of the Declaration in Independence. Maybe I'm biased. But in a single sentence, Tom Hayden managed to capture the collective mood, stake out generational ground, and acknowledge that they were children of affluence who were "uncomfortable" rather than oppressed. It does everything, in short, I want my students to do in an introductory paragraph: set context, point to the general issues at hand, and identify actors.

The following section, "Values," explained the student radicals' discomfort with the rigidity of American life. "Students" not only described the deadened conformity of most of their peers but, more important, implied that young people would become the "vanguard" of political and social change and thus took up the historic role that older left-wing thought had assigned to the working class. The core of SDS's opposition to Cold War policy appeared in "The Individual in the Warfare State," where the authors noted, incredulously, how "a shell of moral callousness" made it possible for the citizenry to acquiesce in a world where "one simple miscalculation could incinerate mankind." Apathy, a creation of the bureaucratic society, had given the wizards of war leave to imperil all humanity.[11]

The Vietnam war seemed to bear out everything these students believed about the ills of American society. They insisted that the Vietnamese were engaged in a democratic movement to secure genuine independence from western colonialism and that American policy, impelled by the rigid orthodoxy of the Cold War, denied them that basic human right. Once American policy became primarily military, the United States engaged in killing people who merely sought a measure of control over their own lives. It was impossible to see how that modest goal somehow endangered America; no rational calculation of American interests could explain Johnson's decisions. Thus the war stemmed from a system that was running on its own illogic, pushing conventional politicians along against all common sense, let alone common decency. Horrendous enough in any case, the Johnson administration had to rely on the draft in order to quench Vietnamese aspirations, and in vastly expanding the draft, the administration had violated the most basic human right, the right to life itself. When antiwar students shouted the slogan "Not with My Life, You Don't," they applied the New Left's critique of the dehumanized society directly to their collective self-interest. It is hard to see a more direct and powerful intrusion of the state into individual rights than the compulsory demand that a young man prepare to die for a dubious cause.

It was a tidy analysis, one with the heft of considerable truth. Thankfully, there is an easy way to illustrate the New Left critique. At the 1965 Easter march, SDS leader Paul Potter used his prominent place in the speakers' lineup to deliver his "Name the System" speech. The name comes from Potter's reluctance to lay blame for the nation's injustices on capitalism; hoping to avoid sounding like an old-fashioned Marxist, he merely called on his listeners to "name that system. We must name it, describe it, analyze it, understand it and change it." Much has been made of this small part of the speech, because it bears on the growing internal divisions in the New Left. I largely ignore this element in it. I focus instead on the naive grandeur of Potter's address, which rested on his description of a system—by whatever name—that had escaped the control of those who claimed to hold the reins of power. It is a long and rambling speech and must be edited down to a manageable coherence, though too much editing eliminates Potter's refreshing spontaneity. In any case, because Potter insisted that the war marked the "dehumanization not only of Vietnamese people but of Americans as well," students can see the sympathy for the Vietnamese people and how the New Left connected its own alienation with all liberation movements, including the civil rights struggle at home. For my money, the most telling passages are those in which Potter described a system clearly beyond the control of otherwise decent, liberal men whose conceit was that they knew what they were doing. "The freedom to conduct the war," he argued, "depends on the construction of a system . . . that insulates the President and his advisors thoroughly and completely from the human consequences of the decisions they make. I do not believe that the President or Mr. Rusk or Mr. McNamara or even McGeorge Bundy are particularly evil men. If asked to throw napalm on the back of a ten-year-old child they would shrink in horror. But their decisions have led to mutilation and death of thousands and thousands of people."[12]

It is a dynamic commentary, and one, I have to confess, that moves me every time I work with it. Students can see the interconnections that the New Left made and how the war fit in the critique of the bureaucratized society. It doesn't take too much interpretive license, moreover, to take Potter as an example of how New Left activists believed that just taking a stand, putting oneself on the line, was an answer to the alienation and powerlessness that seemed a product of the times for many young people. From there I suggest that some in the New Left identified personally with the Vietnamese because they imagined their own psychic uneasiness with bureaucratic society to be akin to the Vietnamese struggle against American military power.

No one group ever dominated or managed to pull these varied strands into a coherent whole. Specific protests were typically local affairs, put together by offshoots of the national organizations. Many of the larger protests in Washington or New York were initiated by one group or another, which then issued invitations to others, and even then it required negotiations between the parties as to who would say what, when, and how. Still other episodes of protest, such as Stop the Draft Week in 1967, were simply calls for common action at a specified time announced with the expectation that local activists would respond.

Genuine umbrella groups developed only in a few important instances, and they were ungainly and, as it happened, temporary. The renowned (or infamous) Siege of the Pentagon in October 1967, for instance, was the handiwork of the National Mobilization to End the War in Vietnam (MOBE), a loose-knit coalition of prominent activists who hoped to coordinate the largest gathering possible beneath a very general strategy aimed at intensifying protest. A. J. Muste's protégé, David Dellinger, took the leading role, though he always insisted that he wasn't "the leader." Having concluded, as he told the audience in his keynote speech, that it was time to move from quiet protest and private disobedience to vigorous resistance, Dellinger cobbled together a coalition of over 150 different groups, which gathered at the Washington Mall for the event.

In short MOBE embodied the multiplicity of the antiwar movement, and to consider the Pentagon march not only offers the best specific example of that point, but it also offers an example of why the movement got its unruly reputation. Besides, it's a lot of fun to teach.

To begin with, Dellinger's efforts to the contrary failed to heal the breaches between the groups, and planners had to create essentially two events: one with the usual array of speakers criticizing American policy and occupying the Mall, the other intended for those who wanted something more dramatic, such as an assault on the Pentagon. In addition to the usual luminaries, including Spock, the poet Robert Lowell, the novelist Norman Mailer, and the legendary civil rights activist Bob Moses, Dellinger also invited "Yippie" founders Jerry Rubin and Abbie Hoffman to incorporate counterculture enthusiasm as an alternative to SANE's staid coats and ties, and that all but promised high jinks. The actual sit-in "siege" in the Pentagon's north parking lot included some of the era's most iconic moments: meditating protesters trying to "levitate" the building, young people putting flowers in the rifle barrels of the troops acting as military police, former Green Beret Gary Rader exhorting the soldiers to defy their commanders, and federal marshals clubbing protesters during a "charge" against the crowd. It's hard to resist noting how that unprovoked official violence stands against the myth of the radical movement. Just what would Forrest Gump do?

Supplementing the famous photographs of protesters loading rifles with daisies with texts depends mainly on how much time an instructor wants to devote to this single episode. Norman Mailer's *Armies of the Night* provides a full account in that peculiar Maileresque form of third-person autobiography. It is long and can be tedious, especially for those who aren't Mailer fans. Dellinger's *Liberation* dedicated its November 1967 number to the event, and an instructor can do better than Mailer by picking and choosing among the several descriptive essays. I occasionally use (and will cite in lecture if the piece itself is not assigned) George Dennison's "Talking with the Troops." Dennison focused his attention on the symbolism of the interplay between the troops and the protesters and read the affair as nothing less than a commentary on "the plight of individual life brimming against repressive force." He contrasted the vibrant young people, as playful as they were determined, radiating the youthful "energy of love," against the bewildered soldiers, coming toe-to-toe with people of their own age while exhibiting the "hangdog look of profound uncertainty in the conduct of life" and reduced, with a few exceptions, to "robot reaction." Against the "modest bravery" of those committed to "an extremely generous communal spirit" were arrayed the forces of order, "the very image of man at his worst," the power of which rested on "the masses of the Army . . . controlled by the nightmares of the relative few." It was fated, of course, that the uniformed robots would rout the happy, long-haired warriors. Still Dennison chalked the siege up in the victory column. The point, after all, was not to stop the war. "Our presence, our civil disobedience, *was* the message," he concluded.[13]

This is a telling piece of writing. It is, in my view, stunningly condescending, politically foolish, and apt testimony, therefore, to everything that was going wrong with the antiwar movement in its "revolutionary" phase. A deep reading can flesh out the overtones of early Cold War thinking about the social bases of totalitarianism and show that Dennison was all but saying that these young soldiers were the human material of nazism—indeed, he referred to the marshals' charge as a "fascistic assault." One needn't be so elaborate to see that he reduced the soldiers to plastic people. Bad enough on these grounds, Dennison presumed an absolute division of good and evil that was simply the mirror image of the establishment's dogmatic anticommunism. Most important, however, was the insistence that protest itself was revolutionary, regardless of whether it changed the objective structures of power. This was sheer self-delusion. And it exposed the central flaw in the New Left: because they were acting against the personal anxieties of alienation rather than objective oppression, the young radicals could convince themselves that protest alone was sufficient to address the fundamental problems of American society. Means, clearly, had become ends in themselves.

As this brief review of prominent groups suggests, there were many different reasons to oppose the Vietnam War, and I believe it is important to give those arguments a fair hearing. When I teach my Vietnam War course (as opposed to a general course on the Sixties), I spend a lot of time working through how policy was made (reading, among other possibilities, Robert McNamara's *In Retrospect*), and I let the antiwar arguments stand as critiques of that policy. I want my students to understand that American policy *was* deeply flawed and those who opposed it did so for sound reasons and far more often than not had the genuine best interests of the nation at heart. These are truths that get no telling in popular culture. Neither popular myth nor conservative revisionism bother to note that the opponents of war were the reasonable ones or broach the possibility that American policy was bankrupt from the start. The whole quarrel over whether we "lost" the war forgets to ask the basic question: What would we have "won," exactly, and at what grievous cost?

Indeed, the foolhardy perversity of American policy provided common ground for antiwar activists. Whatever their affiliation, they all routinely took issue with the main justification for the war: that North Vietnam had invaded the sovereign state of South Vietnam and was a tool of the international communist conspiracy bent on world domination. Virtually no one well informed about Vietnam accepted those official claims, and that included government officials who knew better but repeated them anyway. The conflict, opponents argued, was a civil war being waged by an indigenous movement to topple a regime that had little popular support and existed only because of US largess. Civil wars were won at the grass roots, and even if the United States had any business sticking its nose in another society's civil war, it was ridiculous to believe that Vietnamese popular support could be won through massive bombing, large-scale military operations, the routine killing of noncombatants, and the imposition of an oppressive regime.

Antiwar activists also debunked the "domino theory," that contrived attempt to claim that what happened in Vietnam was crucial to American national security. Opponents observed that even if the Vietnamese were communists, they were nationalists first and foremost and not pawns of either the Soviets or the Chinese. No crucial national security interests were at stake for the Americans. Quite the contrary: the longer the United States wasted blood and treasure in Vietnam in a war against an impoverished people, the more damage it did to its international reputation, the greater the toll on its relations with allies, and the stronger the Soviets became. Because the war could not be justified either as a defense of an ally against invasion or on national security grounds, it had to be reckoned as immoral.

Armed with sound arguments faithful to the facts, antiwar activists, especially the peace liberals, initially assumed that they would prevail through straightforward persuasion. But they discovered that Johnson administration officials had no intention of listening to them. Sweet reason stood no chance. Unable to lay out any convincing defense of the war, Johnson accused his opponents of communist leanings, ridiculed them, and constantly prevaricated. Having shown them that he refused to alter course, Johnson in effect pushed his critics into the streets. The escalation of the war, activists concluded, demanded the escalation of dissent.

Whatever else is said about the excesses of the antiwar movement—and any excesses were minor and short-lived—the true excesses were those of the American government: the waging of a war that took at least 2.5 million lives with no sound justification either on humanitarian or national security grounds, a war carried out in a high-handed, anti-democratic fashion that had critics accused of treason, harassed by national police agencies, and otherwise ignored. These were the excesses that compelled a baby doctor to denounce a president as a liar; that persuaded Martin Luther King Jr. to liken the war to mass murder even though in doing so he risked much of the political capital he had so laboriously built in leading the black liberation struggle; that goaded tens of thousands of young men to violate the law and risk prison in following their consciences and another fifty thousand to abandon their country and forfeit their citizenship in self-exile; that drove a young Quaker father, Norman Morrison, to commit self-immolation beneath the office window of the secretary of defense; and that pushed a million or so young people to participate in some measure of antiwar protest. That so many Americans from so many different walks of life, people of great good faith, took part in the antiwar movement really is testimony to how obviously the war threatened the nation's well-being. Somehow these historical realities haven't quite made the movies.

Precisely because so much of the movement was a response to Johnson's, and later Nixon's, refusal to engage in reasoned debate and rethinking, it is hard to measure its success. Obviously, the equivocal quality of any final assessment of the movement provides a good teaching opportunity, one in which students can weigh competing claims and evidence and come to their own conclusions.

There are activists—and historians—who claim that the movement stopped the war. Yet there is not much evidence that either the Johnson or the Nixon administration heeded its critics. It is true that Johnson offered several unilateral bombing halts in part as nods to his critics, but there were other motives involved in those decisions, including international public relations. If anything, the movement made both presidents—monumentally vain men both—dig in their heels. Nixon was particularly effective in parrying the movement in the court of public opinion. His policy of Vietnamization, the centerpiece of which was the gradual withdrawal of combat troops, siphoned public support away from the movement. Nixon did so, ironically, just as the movement's maturing organizational abilities allowed it to put together the largest protests, most notably the fall 1969 March against Death, when the second version of MOBE brought at least half a million people to Washington. Against that surge of protest, Nixon artfully appealed to "the Silent Majority," presumably that reservoir of average Americans who never made it on the news. Nixon assumed that the Silent Majority was entirely with him in his efforts to wind the war down and earn a "peace with honor," and he knew the average American reviled protesters.

This is simply to say, however, that there is not a direct causal connection between the movement and the end of the war. When is anything that simple? If we move beyond that, it is clear that the movement had important consequences. At the very least, the movement riveted the public's attention on a dubious war and thereby limited the military options for even the most aggressive policy makers. It was inconceivable that American troops would be sent into North Vietnam, and though he constantly flirted with those limits, even Nixon stopped short of a wholesale bombing of Hanoi proper. Nowhere were those limits better seen than in the public reaction to the Cambodian invasion of early 1970, which generated widespread editorial denunciations and huge protests on college campuses nationwide, which included, sadly, the state-sponsored murder of four students at Kent State University.

There is no discounting the gradual, cumulative political effect that the movement had within American liberalism. The patient cultivation of liberal congressmen, as well as the long-standing opposition of representatives like George McGovern, Wayne Morse, and Ernest Gruening, slowly pulled the Democratic Party away from its addiction to war. Members of SANE and other peace liberals supported Eugene McCarthy's primary challenge to Lyndon Johnson in 1968 and George McGovern's nomination in 1972. Obviously, those were two unsuccessful candidacies. But the blossoming of antiwar will among liberal congressmen after 1970 ushered in very important legislation, the War Powers Act, which did limit presidential latitude in war making and prevented Gerald Ford from reentering Vietnam in those fateful days of 1975 when the Communists overran the South. Of course, one might argue that it was fatal to the Democratic Party to have the antiwar wing rise to power within it. But while it is true that antiwar sentiment was a primary cause of the Democratic implosion at the 1968 Chicago convention, it was not the main reason for the collapse of the New Deal coalition.

I throw one final thought at my students, in the form of an open question. Is it possible, I wonder, that what we see as successful movement pressure limiting presidential war making was instead a reflection of the actual limits of American power? Is it possible that Johnson and Nixon recognized some "limits" not because of public pressure but because they knew that anything like a victory was unattainable?

We know that Lyndon Johnson, in his heart of hearts, understood from the first that escalated bombing and the introduction of ground troops would do nothing to stabilize South Vietnam and that the policy left in his lap was doomed to fail. In the last few years, I have used the early 1965 Johnson tapes to allow students to hear this from the horse's mouth, and when they hear the president confess to Robert McNamara or acknowledge to his mentor and oldest friend, Georgia senator Richard Russell, that there was no way to win under the circumstances, they are stunned. I once had a Reserve Officers' Training Corps (ROTC) student sitting in the fourth row of a lecture hall. It was spring term; he was to be commissioned within weeks and almost certainly was bound for Afghanistan. As he listened to Lyndon Johnson, he buried his head in his hands; when I shut off the tape, he raised his head, his face flushed red, and yelled, "Then why did he do it?" Richard Nixon, far less burdened with conscience, was nonetheless restrained less by domestic politics than by his realism, which ultimately warned him away from delusions of victory.

Is it possible, then, that what really limited American war making was not public pressure but the realities of national interest, international relations, and the inherent limits of power?

If the answer to this question is yes, then the American war in Vietnam deserves to be regarded as an obscene offense, since it sacrificed millions of lives to no good end. If the answer to the question is yes, then the antiwar movement, whatever its success or failure, must have been right, as even a simpleton like Forrest Gump could see.

NOTES

1. I was once asked, "Why are there those POW flags everywhere if there aren't any POWs still there?"

2. Jerry Lembcke, *The Spitting Image: Myth, Memory, and the Legacy of Vietnam* (New York: New York University Press, 1998).

3. Edward P. Morgan, *What Really Happened to the 1960s: How Mass Media Culture Failed American Democracy* (Lawrence: University of Kansas Press, 2010), 277.

4. Charles Chatfield, "Ironies of Protest: Interpreting the American Anti-Vietnam War Movement," in *Twentieth-Century Peace Movements: Successes and Failures*, ed. Guido Grunewald and Peter van den Dungen (Lewiston, NY: Edwin Mellen Press, 1995), 200, 199.

5. See Abraham J. Muste, "The World Task of Pacifism" and "War Is the Enemy," both in *The Essays of A. J. Muste*, ed. Nat Hentoff (Indianapolis: Bobbs-Merrill, 1967), 216 and 266, respectively.

6. Doug Rossinow, *The Politics of Authenticity: Liberalism, Christianity, and the New Left in America* (New York: Columbia University Press, 1998); Michael P. Foley, *Confronting the War Machine: Draft Resistance during the Vietnam War* (Chapel Hill: University of North Carolina Press, 2003).

7. Charles DeBenedetti, with Charles Chatfield, *An American Ordeal: The Antiwar Movement of the Vietnam Era* (Syracuse, NY: Syracuse University Press, 1990), 32.

8. Quoted in *Dear Dr. Spock: Letters about the Vietnam War to America's Favorite Baby Doctor*, ed. Michael S. Foley (New York: New York University Press, 2005), 24.

9. Benjamin Spock, quoted in Thomas Maier, *Dr. Spock, an American Life* (New York: Harcourt, Brace, 1998), 223. Any Google image search will call up various versions of the photo, which can then be put into a PowerPoint presentation. I use the version at the Bryn Mawr site: http://triptych.brynmawr.edu /cdm4/item_viewer.php?CISOROOT=/SC_Ephemera&CISOPTR=911. The "Daisy ad" may be found on YouTube, http://www.youtube.com/watch?v= dDTBnsqxZk.

10. Sandy Gottlieb, quoted in Milton S. Katz, *Ban the Bomb: A History of SANE, the Committee for a Sane Nuclear Policy, 1957–1985* (Westport, CT: Greenwood Press, 1986), 98.

11. The Port Huron Statement is widely available in its entirety online. See http://www.h-net.org/~hst306/documents/huron.html. It has also been published in a single edition; see Tom Hayden, *The Port Huron Statement: The Visionary Call of the 1960s Revolution* (New York: Thunder's Mouth Press, 2005).

12. There are many iterations of the speech available online. I appropriated these quotes from http://www.antiauthoritarian.net/sds_wuo/sds_ documents/paul_potter.html.

13. George Dennison, "Talking with the Troops," *Liberation* 12 (November 1967): 12–19.

KEY RESOURCES

Anderson, Terry H. *The Movement and the Sixties*. New York: Oxford University Press, 1995.

DeBenedetti, Charles, with Charles Chatfield. *An American Ordeal: The Antiwar Movement of the Vietnam Era*. Syracuse, NY: Syracuse University Press, 1990.

Dellinger, David. *From Yale to Jail: The Life Story of a Moral Dissenter*. New York: Pantheon, 1993.

Hayden, Tom. *Reunion: A Memoir*. New York: Random House, 1988.

Mailer, Norman. *Armies of the Night: History as the Novel, the Novel as History*. New York: New American Library, 1968.

Robinson, Jo Ann. *Abraham Went Out: A Biography of A. J. Muste*. Philadelphia: Temple University Press, 1981.

Rorabaugh, W. J. *Berkeley at War: The 1960s*. New York: Oxford University Press, 1989.

Varon, Jeremy. *Bringing the War Home: The Weather Underground, the Red Army Faction, and the Revolutionary Violence in the Sixties and Seventies*. Berkeley: University of California Press, 2004.

Woods, Randall B., ed. *Vietnam and the American Political Tradition: The Politics of Dissent*. New York: Cambridge University Press, 2003.

Zaroulis, Nancy, and Gerald Sullivan. *Who Spoke Up? American Protest against the War in Vietnam, 1963–1975*. New York: Rinehart and Winston, 1984.

The Vietnamese Sides
of the "American" War

TUAN HOANG

I have taught the Vietnam War classes a half dozen times at three universities.[1] In the final exam, I have always included a variation of the following question, whether as a regular essay or an extra-credit mini-essay: "In your opinion, which of the following years was the most significant in the long Vietnam conflict: 1950, 1954, 1963, 1965, 1968, 1973, 1975, or 1979? First, describe what happened. Second, place the year in the context of the entire conflict and explain why you consider it the most important one."

This question is meant to stimulate undergraduate thinking and argument, and it has prompted some of the best undergraduate exam essays I have graded. Equally interesting is the distribution of the years chosen by students. In my first class, students showed overwhelming preferences for 1965 and 1968. They were virtually neck-to-neck as the first choice of over 60 percent of the class, if memory serves. They were followed by 1950, 1963, 1954, 1973, and 1975. No one chose to write about 1979, the year of the Third Indochina War, typically covered in the last week of the course. Over time, however, these choices have changed a good deal. In the records of a more recent class 1979 remained at the bottom. But neither 1965 nor 1968 stood at the top, replaced by 1963. The year that saw the assassinations of Ngo Dinh Diem and John Kennedy raked in twenty essays in a class of nearly fifty students, or about 40 percent. Next was 1950, which saw eight essays. It was followed by 1965 (seven essays), 1954 (six), 1968 (four), and finally 1973 and 1975 (two each).

There are several possible reasons for these changes, including a greater amount of content on international involvement, which made 1950 more significant in the judgment of my students. But I believe the most important reason has to do with the fact that since that first class I have placed more and more emphasis on Vietnamese perspectives and experiences. For this reason, both 1965 and 1968—the most American-centric years among the choices offered—have declined significantly among the votes of my students. Similarly, the rise of 1963 to the top spot has much to do with an emphasis on Vietnamese developments. It is true that my students are exposed to Washington's strained relationship with Diem and the critical role of the United States in the coup against him. On the other hand, they learn a good deal about major Vietnamese-centered subjects. These subjects include the competition in nation building between the Democratic Republic of Vietnam (DRV) and the Republic of Vietnam (RVN); Diem's consolidation of power, Personalist vision, and political repression of communist and non-communist Vietnamese; the roots and rise of the National Liberation Front (NLF); and Buddhist nationalism behind the protests in Hue and Saigon during the summer of 1963. Again, the United States was never far from this story. But the main focus remained Vietnamese politics and society. "Although 1963 was not filled with just one big event or even a large military victory on the scale of Dien Bien Phu," one student wrote in favor of this particular year, "it instead consisted of mostly political changes and events that were interrelated and influenced more than one country or battlefield." One might quarrel with the student and suggest that 1963 did have "one big event" or two in Diem's and John Kennedy's assassinations. But one is hard-pressed to deny his contention that 1963 saw consequential "political changes and events" rather than a major military event such as Dien Bien Phu, Rolling Thunder, the introduction of US combat troops, the Tet Offensive, or the Ho Chi Minh Campaign.

Moreover, the shift in emphasis can be found in the main texts I have used for my course. In my first class, I used the fourth edition of George C. Herring's venerable *America's Longest War* (2001). This classic textbook provides a solidly chronological and thematically middle-of-the-road interpretation of the war. It concerns primarily the American perspective, but it also integrates materials from new research on the Vietnamese sides. It has not, however, been updated for over ten years. Besides, its title no longer stood once the war in Afghanistan replaced the Vietnam War as America's longest armed conflict. For the next class, I assigned Gerard J. DeGroot's arresting if underrated *A Noble Cause?* (2000). The book is meant as another synthesis of the war, and it has the additional virtue of individual chapters on South Vietnamese and communist soldiers. Its prose is breezy, it has many apt quotations from the war's participants, and it is generally a delight to read. Regrettably, it has never been updated. This prompted me to turn to Mark Philip Bradley's *Vietnam at War* (2009), which is based in part on Bradley's undergraduate teaching. It is the most Vietnamesecentric general textbook about the war since William J. Duiker's *Sacred War* (1995), which is perfectly appropriate for undergraduate reading but has not been updated either.[2]

The changes in my textbook adoption are suggestive of the broader scholarship about Vietnamese participants in the war. As late as the early 1990s there were hardly more than a handful of major memoirs by communist and noncommunist Vietnamese available in English, of which *A Vietcong Memoir* was easily the best known. Because of a general lack of research on the Vietnamese sides, textbooks necessarily and overwhelming focused on the United States at the expense of the RVN, DRV, and NLF. On the noncommunist side, popular accounts written by journalists—Stanley Karnow's *Vietnam* and Neil Sheehan's *A Bright, Shining Lie* were two best-selling examples—provided some of the best vignettes that instructors could appropriate for illustration in lectures about South Vietnam. Nonetheless, they came decidedly from a non-Vietnamese perspective and did not necessarily reflect those of the noncommunist South Vietnamese. On the communist side, students could watch clips of General Vo Nguyen Giap remembering the battles of Dien Bien Phu and the Tet Offensive from the PBS series *Vietnam: A Television History* or the Canadian series *Vietnam: The Ten Thousand Days War*. Giap's comments, however, were either short or repetitive in content. In short, accessible materials about the Vietnamese sides were lacking in quantity as well as quality.

Fortunately, this situation later underwent a significant change, primarily due to new scholarship on the Vietnamese sides. Among diplomatic and military historians, who form the traditional core of Vietnam War scholars, a number of young historians have conducted research in Vietnamese archives in addition to American ones. They overlap with an older generation of historians whose more recent publications range from new biographies of Giap and Ho Chi Minh to local histories of the NLF. There is also a new generation of historians of modern Vietnam whose training as Southeast Asianists naturally focuses on the Vietnamese sides when they write about the war. Further supplementing these two groups are the Europeanists, whose focus on late colonialism and the transition to independence carries strong implications for our understanding of subsequent American involvement. Enriching this scholarly pot are specialists on postwar Vietnam— political scientists, sociologists, and especially anthropologists—whose works invariably address the war in myriad ways. Since its appearance in 2006, the *Journal of Vietnamese Studies* has served as an informal home for research on Vietnamese involvement in and since the war. Beyond the academic halls, there has been a small but steady flow of memoirs and fiction (originals and translations) that present one or another of the Vietnamese points of view related to the conflict. A number of Vietnamese-language films on war-related themes have been shown in the United States and are available for classroom screening. There are also a number of oral histories by Vietnamese participants at the Vietnam Archives at Texas Tech University, which has made available through its website a large number of documents, photographs, and other materials related to all of the Vietnamese sides in the conflict. Finally, online media such as YouTube have made accessible audio and video clips, including many on the Vietnamese, that instructors could easily show in the classroom.

Given this relative profusion of materials, perhaps the most important decision instructors can make is how much of the Vietnamese perspective and experience they would like to incorporate into the content of their courses. Do they want to focus primarily on the United States but pay attention to a few aspects of the Vietnamese? Do they wish to give as much attention to the Vietnamese as they do to the Americans? Or do they aim to give equal value to American, Vietnamese, and international perspectives? To put it in a more quantitative way, do they want to devote less or more than 20 percent to reading materials on the Vietnamese? Or perhaps 30 or 40 percent, or even more? There are advantages to gain and sacrifices to make in these choices, and instructors will have to decide for themselves how much content about the Vietnamese is be sufficient for their classes. Below I will address some major thematic points and make suggestions on reading assignments that emphasize the Vietnamese perspectives. I will also focus on several particular readings that I have found to be very useful for student understandings of these perspectives.

Precolonial and Colonial Vietnam:
Relationships with China and the West

Advantages and sacrifices aside, I believe that instructors of any pedagogical and ideological persuasion should give students some ideas about the historical relationship between Vietnam and China. The most obvious reason for this recommendation is the complex relationship between the DRV and the People's Republic of China (PRC). It moved from close ideological comradeship and tremendous material support (on the part of China) during the 1950s and 1960s to growing fracture and warfare against each other in the 1970s, then to rapprochement since the late 1980s. An instructor may address this period in the context of the Sino-Soviet conflict, Sino-American rapprochement, and other developments. Nevertheless, students will gain a deeper perspective about this "war period" if they receive some background on the long-standing and complex relationship between Vietnam and its neighbor to the north.

There are several strong and undergraduate-friendly secondary sources that address this relationship, and instructors are encouraged to utilize one or more of them to give students a taste of precolonial Vietnam. One of the best choices is the first two chapters of D. R. SarDesai's general history of Vietnam, *Vietnam: Past and Present*. The first chapter provides a solid background on Vietnamese antiquity.[3] The materials would be new to most students, and some may be overwhelmed by the large amount of information about a largely foreign subject. But the chapters also highlight multifaceted Chinese influences, as well as invasions and occupations, and should be an excellent way to introduce students to placing the Vietnam War in the broader context of the country's history of conflict and nationalism. In the first chapter, students would learn that the Vietnamese began to form their identity early in antiquity, but it was a millennium of Chinese direct rule that led to influences as varied as the widespread use of the water buffalo and the plow for agricultural purposes, the field system and construction techniques against flooding, the introduction of Indian Buddhism, and the adoption of the Confucian classics as the basis for entrance into the dynastic bureaucracy. At the same time, this direct rule prompted a number of rebellions, some of which are listed in the readings. The most vivid example is the rebellion of the Trung sisters in the first century. The reading includes the following famous quatrain from one of the sisters.

> I swear, first, to avenge the nation;
> Second, to restore the [dynastic] Hungs' former position;
> Third, to have revenge for my husband;
> Fourth, to carry through to the end our common task.

Instructors may wish to have students analyze the quatrain, especially the multiplicity of aims and motives in the rebellion. They should highlight the fact that the rebellion was supported by the peasantry, as well as the nobility, and could use this to point out the significance of the peasantry throughout Vietnamese history, up to the contest to win the hearts and minds of the rural population during the Second Indochina War. The second chapter of the reading provides another illustration of the power of the peasantry through the example of the emperor Le Loi in the fifteenth century. Leader of a successful rebellion against a brief Chinese occupation, Le Loi was a landowner who rallied the peasantry to the cause of independence, engaged in guerrilla warfare, and founded the Le dynasty. The importance of the peasantry is further suggested by the fact that one of Le's successors actively invaded the southern neighboring kingdom Champa in order to gain land for the growing peasant population. Students may appreciate the complexity of the Vietnamese experience, which saw defensive warfare against China on the one hand and gradual expansion into contemporary southern Vietnam by military and political means on the other.

The second chapter of SarDesai's book also describes the emergence of a long partition of Vietnam that occurred in the sixteenth century, during which Le rulers were nominally in power. Instead, the real power rested with the Trinh family in the north and the Nguyen family in the south, and instructors may want to focus on this division to show students that national division during the Vietnam War was only the latest manifestation of the problem of unity for a country whose S-shaped geography does not yield easily to centralized political and military control. Attempts to unify the country resulted in civil warfare; aid from foreigners, including the Chinese and the French; the involvement of peasants; a famous victory of Vietnamese forces over China's Qing military in Hanoi (the so-called First Tet Offensive); and eventual unification under the Nguyen dynasty in the early nineteenth century. There is no question that all of this history looks very distant to the history of the Vietnam War, whose immediate causes were colonialism, nationalism, communism, and the Cold War. Nonetheless, students can benefit tremendously from a *longue durée* perspective on Vietnamese history.[4]

Two last points about Vietnamese *longue durée* are the absorption of outside influences and the tendency for Vietnamese to seek help abroad. The first point is well illustrated through the influences of Chinese civilization—such as agriculture, language, the arts, ruling ideology, and governmental structure—but also western ones such as the modern script that was widely adopted by the early twentieth century. The second point is underscored by Nguyen Anh, the lone survivor of the Nguyen family, who sought help from Siamese and Frenchmen in order to unify Vietnam and establish the Nguyen dynasty in the early nineteenth century. His example foreshadows Ho Chi Minh's search for ideas and assistance in Paris, and ultimately Moscow, in the 1920s and 1930s or Ngo Dinh Diem's quest for American aid while living in New Jersey in the early 1950s.

The Colonial Experience:
Modernization, Nationalism, and Communism

It is not uncommon that instructors of Vietnam War courses will gloss over the French threat and jump into discussing colonialism during the early part of a course. This is understandable for reasons of time. It is recommended, however, that they should at least note the shared experience between Vietnam and China of western domination, including military defeats such as those that occurred in the Sino-French War and the Tonkin Campaign. Students may appreciate learning, for instance, about Qing assistance (including the provision of soldiers) to help the Nguyen fight the French army in the latter conflict, a pattern displayed decades later in the PRC-DRV relationship. One useful reading is, again, chapter 7 of Brantly Womack's *China and Vietnam*, which is titled "The Brotherhood of Oppression."

There is, however, one somewhat atypical reading that I have found to be very helpful for student understanding of the colonial experience: the third chapter of William S. Logan's history of Hanoi.[5] The reading is atypical because it is somewhat beyond the common "oppression-resistance" trope, found in many narratives about the Vietnam War, which pays lip service to French colonialism. Entitled "Hanoi: Building a Capital for French Indochina," the reading is essentially a piece of urban history. It begins with a summary of the first years of colonial occupation and helpfully points out the colonial preoccupation with military matters that led to the fortification of existing edifices for security purposes. In particular, students may be delighted to encounter the early Hanoi Hilton, which was used to house Vietnamese rebels against the colonial regime. (Its Vietnamese name was Hoa Lo, literally, "Hell's hole.") Supported by a copious amount of illustrations, the chapter then focuses on the reconstruction of the old city as a modern and Parisian-inspired metropolitan center. The reconstruction involved, among other things, drainage of swamps and marshes and rice fields; enlargement of roads and the construction of boulevards; demolition or removal of pagodas and even entire neighborhoods; and the erection of parks, palaces, churches, government buildings, museums, and the opera house that in 1946 became the meeting site of the National Assembly of the Viet Minh–led DRV. Special attention is paid to the designs of the architect Ernest Hébrard and the construction efforts of Governor-General Paul Doumer, whose name graced the famous bridge that was built under his rule and became a bombing target for the Americans during the 1960s. Created, too, were new quarters and neighborhoods for the Europeans, which existed apart from those of the Vietnamese masses and the ethnic Chinese who engaged in commercial activities.

There is more to the Logan reading than an architectural and urban history of colonial Hanoi. Not all pagodas, for example, were removed or demolished, and there was a measure of sensitivity to cultural heritage on the part of the colonial rulers. This reflected the European intellectual climate at the time, especially the "dual-city" concept, under which Hébrard sought to build a new, Western-style municipality alongside the old native city. For their part, the Vietnamese felt much awe at the massive and remarkable scale of construction. It is true that they felt a lot of resentment toward the deliberate and racist separation of neighborhoods. But they were clearly impressed by the colonial achievement, and many of them seized on opportunities to move to quarters that allowed for more opportunities. One such location was the Bay Mau Quarter, which "became a chief location of the middle-class Vietnamese working for the colonial administration and private enterprises."[6] In my teaching experience, students often are awed by the changes made by the French in Hanoi. (It does not hurt to find some photos of Old Hanoi on the Internet and show them in class.) This reading helps them see that the relationship between the Vietnamese and French was more complex than is sometimes portrayed in a standard textbook. The Vietnamese wanted independence from colonialism. But the succession of military defeats and the draw of modernity, best symbolized by the reconstruction of Hanoi, pushed them toward finding new solutions for independence.

The darkest aspects of the Vietnamese experience of French colonialism are well described in the book *Colonialism Experienced* edited by Truong Buu Lam. It contains a very nice selection of twenty political documents that represent a variety of Vietnamese responses to colonial rule: oppositional and collaborationist, violent and nonviolent, reformist and revolutionary. The editor also contributes three lucidly written chapters about, respectively, colonial administration, Vietnamese perceptions, and the Vietnamese experience of French rule.[7] Any of these chapters—and one or more of the documents—would enhance student knowledge about the drive among Vietnamese to adapt and endorse new ideas and proposals toward independence. The first two documents in Lam's book come from Phan Boi Chau and Phan Chau Trinh, two prominent early leaders of the Vietnamese nationalist movement. True to the spirit of this volume, the chosen documents present an eloquent combination of anger at the horrible political and economic conditions, on the one hand, and promotion of nationalist sentiments and language on the other. Alternatively, instructors can also choose selections from two translations by Vinh Sinh: Phan Boi Chau's famous autobiography and Phan Chau Trinh's political writings. Each of these volumes also contains a detailed introduction by the translator, which explicates the life and work of the author in the political context of oppressive colonialism and emergent nationalism.[8]

Instructors who wish to focus on early communist developments may want to pay special attention to "Document 18" in *Colonialism Experienced*. This is an article written by Ho Chi Minh in the late 1920s, when Ho was working in southern China as an agent for the Comintern.[9] There are at least three reasons for the significance of this document for teaching purposes. First, it was entitled "The Communists Must Organize Themselves into a Single Party," and it called for a united front among peasants and workers to fight against colonialism. "The Communist Party," it reads, "is the avant-garde of the proletariat, and the peasantry is the leader of the proletariat, so the peasantry will overthrow the French imperialists, seize political power, and set up the dictatorship of peasants and workers in order to achieve a communist society."[10]

The call to arms was significant because the communists, at least those in Ho's vein, were deeply concerned with the question of the peasantry. This stood in contrast to major noncommunist, anticolonial movements, which focused squarely on urban people as the vanguard of the Vietnamese revolution. Elsewhere in the document, Ho refers to "workers and peasants who have had their consciousness raised." Second, the document showcases Ho's well-known skills in organization. Taking a page straight out of orthodox Leninist theory, Ho outlined three steps in the process of founding a communist party for all Vietnamese: creating a cell on the basis of a "unit of production"; expanding it into more cells; and organizing them into first a cell at the district level, then cells at the provincial, regional, and national levels. Last, the document highlights some of the tensions among the Vietnamese revolutionaries of different stripes. At one point, Ho demonized non-communist political movements as "parties of landowners, capitalists, intellectuals, petit bourgeois" and "either false revolutionaries or anti-revolutionaries." The stage was set, in theory if not yet in practice, for the civil dimension of the Vietnam conflict.

Those who wish to pursue these three points further should consult the next document in the same book. It was drafted as the "political theses of the Indochinese Communist Party" (ICP) and authored by Tran Phu, the first secretary general of the Comintern-approved organization that Ho helped to unite from several communist groups.[11] Three times longer than Ho's article, it placed the situation in Vietnam alongside developments in the world, including the appeal of the Soviet Union during the bleakness of the global economic depression. It offered an analysis of the conditions that would lead to a Vietnamese revolution and declared that capitalist and petit bourgeois Vietnamese would be ineffectual in leading it. An instructor can break down this analysis to explain to students how the concept of class struggle in Marxist orthodoxy became significant for a number of elite Vietnamese. In addition, the document reinforced Ho Chi Minh's point about the proletariat and peasantry and considered them the twin forces for the revolution to come, specifying that the "allies of the proletariat are the middle and poor peasants." At the same time, Tran Phu, a more orthodox Marxist than Ho, did not fail to stress the role of the workers as leaders and educators of the peasants. The document went on at length to attack the "bourgeois-democratic" revolution, which was advocated by "bourgeois intellectuals" and had failed to consider the lives of Vietnamese peasants in the revolutionary scheme.

The document ends with a fascinating section on the use of slogans for drawing mass support for the ICP-led revolution. They include "minimum slogans" such as "Reduce working hours" and "Cut taxes" at the early stage, then "transitional slogans" like "Establish councils to confiscate lands" and "Arm the workers and peasants" at a later stage. Instructors should seize on these slogans to generate discussion in the classroom. What did the slogans say about the conditions in colonial Vietnam from a revolutionary perspective? Why were some particular slogans employed at the start and why other slogans later? Much can be deduced from these seemingly simple slogans, especially on the communist strategy of appealing to immediate interests before educating the masses toward momentous revolutionary changes.

The August Revolution and the First Indochina War

Of course the ICP hardly dominated the nationalist movement because it only had about five thousand members in early 1945. In addition it faced competition from a plurality of Vietnamese noncommunist political activists prior to the August Revolution, which saw the communists take over political power in Hanoi and Ho Chi Minh deliver a declaration of independence. This political struggle among Vietnamese before the war period is demonstrated in two accessible articles. The first one comes from the French historian François Guillemot and suggests that the four Dai Viet (Great Viet) political parties were propagating a right-wing nationalist vision as a counter to the appeal of the communists among educated Vietnamese.[12] The second article, by the Vietnamese refugee historian Vu Ngu Chieu, details the limitations, as well as the accomplishments, of the short-lived Empire of Vietnam.[13] Instructors who want to highlight the noncommunist contribution to the revolution during the pivotal 1940s could do worse than introducing these readings to their students.

The August Revolution, too, has been studied from the Vietnamese perspective, especially in David G. Marr's book on the year 1945.[14] It is shown to have been a very messy affair, and full of contingencies and local initiatives rather than centralized directives. Supported by a wealth of archival and published materials, Marr's take largely confirms the conclusion of an older and handy article by the late émigré scholar Huynh Kim Khanh, which could be used as assigned reading on the subject.[15] Most other readings, however, tend to treat the revolution not separately but as one of a series of significant developments from 1945 to Dien Bien Phu and the Geneva Conference in 1954. This is where Mark Bradley's general history could be used for the classroom. The book is not without problems on the whole. Its view of the RVN, for instance, is conventional and does not take into consideration recent research about Ngo Dinh Diem and South Vietnam. Its emphasis on the Vietnamese leaves little room for any detailed discussion of US policies. But Bradley's chapter on the First Indochina War presents short but fine-grained consideration of the Vietnamese perspectives on top of a solid summary of events during the August Revolution and the colonial war.

It points out, for instance, the killings and assassinations among Vietnamese during and after the August Revolution, a result of earlier intra-Vietnamese competition and a foreshadowing of the greater violence to come during the Second Indochina War. The chapter describes the colonial war as having two distinctive stages, and instructors may want to point out that the Second Indochina War would have two stages as well. In my experience, this parallel helps students to begin thinking about the Vietnam War as a series of contingencies and changes rather than a single block of experiences. Similar to American involvement later, the French War saw shifts in momentum, strategy, and involvement of outsiders. This particular reading does well in explicating each stage of the French War and the transition from a colonial conflict during the first stage (1946–49) to an international one in the second (1950–54). It gives more space to the internationalization of the war, as is the case in other textbooks. But there is a significant amount of information about the struggles of Ho Chi Minh and the Viet Minh during the first stage. It notes, for instance, that the Viet Minh did not receive direct support from Stalin or Mao but was not completely isolated because it sought ties and support from other Southeast Asian countries that shared its anticolonial perspective. It also highlights the Viet Minh's application of the Maoist three-stage strategy throughout the war, and instructors should point out that this was another instance of the Vietnamese tradition of borrowing from the successes of the Chinese.

Bradley's textbook is better than most in highlighting the roles of the Vietnamese during the Cold War–fueled internationalization of the war starting in 1950. Succinctly described are developments on the Vietnamese noncommunist side, centering around the person of the former emperor Bao Dai as the titular leader of the State of Vietnam. There are more details about the Viet Minh side, including land reform and greater state control over intellectual thought and artistic production. In particular, the relationship between the Viet Minh and the Chinese communists receives a strong analysis peppered with interesting anecdotes and insights. As an overview of the second period of the French War, this reading stands head and shoulders above any other single reading that this author has encountered. Instructors interested in more details about the Viet Minh's shift from a nationalism- to a socialism-based structure should consult two essays from the political scientist Tuong Vu. One essay discusses the start of the Viet Minh's shift from broad coalitionist politics and the goal of national independence, which characterized the early DRV in 1945–46, to a more explicit desire to construct a socialist state with close internationalist ties to the Soviet Union and other communist countries.[16] Vu's second essay further reveals the long trajectory of the ICP's internationalist tendencies, including antagonism toward the United States long before Washington provided aid to the French military in 1950. The armed conflict "between the DRV and the United States in the 1960s," he contends, "was not unimaginable in 1945 as many have argued."[17] Based on archival research in Hanoi, Vu's essays are both informative and thought provoking about the ideological and political aspects of the Viet Minh experience during the First Indochina War.

While the Geneva Conference formally concluded the war, the battle of Dien Bien Phu has remained its best-known event. The victor of the battle, General Vo Nguyen Giap, has offered his recollections of the event in Vietnamese, and these have been translated, abbreviated, and published in Hanoi. Instructors might like to assign an excerpt of this memoir to their students.[18] Finally, research on the Geneva Conference has been dominated by internationalization. The diplomatic historian Pierre Asselin, however, has offered a more Vietnamese-oriented perspective about the Viet Minh's decision to sign the peace accords by delving into the volumes of party documents published since 1998.[19] Asselin shows that Chinese and Soviet pressure was only one factor among many, such as war-weariness on the part of the DRV, its desire for economic construction on a socialist model, and the expectation that it would win the national elections in two years. Whether it is used for lecture or classroom reading, this article would make a significant contribution to grasping an important Vietnamese perspective on the conference.

On the legacies of the war, it is once again Mark Bradley's textbook that shines. The last section of chapter 3 focuses on the problems of state building in the north that illustrated the broader problem of Vietnamese seeking answers to the question of modernization. The reading discusses the issues of land reform, agricultural cooperatives, and the relationship between the state and intellectuals. As with the three-stage strategy of guerrilla warfare, many of these practices derived from the Maoist model. Earlier in this chapter, Bradley points out some surface tension between Viet Minh leaders and their Chinese advisers, usually over the issue of Sino-Soviet relations. The tension eventually exploded into the Third Indochina War. For the most part, however, the Sino-Vietnamese relationship was strong during the 1950s and 1960s. An emphasis on this point would connect what occurred in the Vietnam conflict to what students learn about ancient Sino-Vietnamese relations from the SarDesai reading.

Divided Vietnam and the American War

The Second Indochina War is of course at the heart of all courses on the Vietnam War. How did the Vietnamese on each side experience the war? What had the greatest impact on the decision making of the Hanoi and Saigon leaderships? How did they counter the pressures exerted by their foreign allies? How did the NLF mobilize and overcome the challenges posed by Saigon and the United States? Indeed, why did the Vietnamese fight in the first place? These are some of the questions appropriate to consider when discussing Vietnamese perspectives on the war.

There are many readings that help instructors answer these questions—for a nonspecialist on the Vietnamese sides, probably too many. Most, after all, are quite specific in content and too specialized for general use. In the final analysis, this writer believes that chapter 5 of Neil L. Jamieson's now classic *Understanding Vietnam* remains one of the most useful readings for the classroom.[20] At over seventy pages, this chapter is not short. Instructors could also do without the simplistic "yin-yang" scheme that underlies this chapter and most of the remainder of the book. But there are several reasons to have it on the reading list. First, it covers the period 1955–70, which of course means the bulk of US involvement. (The next chapter discusses the last years of the war.) Second, it encompasses both of the northern and southern experiences. Third, it moves gracefully among historical research, literary analysis, and anecdotes drawn from personal experience and fieldwork (Jamieson is an anthropologist by training). Last, and perhaps best of all, it includes some of the best translations of Vietnamese poetry and prose (done by the author himself), which should be handy for analysis and classroom discussion. It carries many insights about Vietnamese politics and societies in the two regions, such as remarkable foresight about Ngo Dinh Diem and his nation-building vision almost a decade before archival research about Diem during the 2000s.

Instructors, indeed, are encouraged to begin the exposition of the Vietnamese perspectives on the war with Ngo Dinh Diem. Personalities played a large role in the competition for the hearts and minds of Vietnamese. While far more understanding of Diem's vision for postcolonial Vietnam than most scholars of his generation, Jamieson skillfully contrasts Diem's personality with that of Ho Chi Minh. He shows that the latter had a huge advantage in the competition for the affection and revolutionary support of Vietnamese. Instructors may seize on this contrast to expand student thinking about how leaders connect with the masses, and how these connections might explain the different resolutions to the turbulences in the north and the south. More particularly, they may want to compare Ho's deft dealings in the aftermath of the disastrous land reform on the one hand and Diem's heavy-handedness toward the renowned writer Nguyen Tuong Tam and other urban intellectuals on the other. (Tam's background is well conveyed in an earlier chapter of the book.) How did Ho's adoption of the informal salutation "Uncle" make him accessible to a society governed by intimate familial relationships? How did his willingness to appease the peasantry after the excesses of the land reform help and hinder the socialist cause advanced by Hanoi? Conversely, how did Diem's dealings with the anticommunist Tam reflect the lack of mass support for his regime? These are among the questions that could be pressed among students to generate debate and understanding.[21]

Jamieson's discussion of the Buddhists whose protests led to Diem's eventual demise is cursory. It is better on the rise of the NLF and, through extended literary translation, excellent on three main currents of thought: individualism and distrust of ideologies in urban South Vietnam (246–54), revolutionary fervor among the communist insurgents in the south (254–57), and collectivism and Marxist-Leninism in North Vietnam (257–84). Opportunities for analysis abound, and instructors should pick one or more translated passages from each section for discussion in the classroom. One example is the individual versus the collective. In passages from South Vietnamese writers, for instance, the first person appears often and war-related images of death and weaponry are personalized. In contrast, the collective "we" figures strongly in passages written by NLF members. Instructors should encourage students to find contrasting images and words in these two sections and ask what they might have suggested about different mind-sets among Vietnamese in the south during the 1950s and 1960s. But Jamieson's greatest service in chapter 5 may be the section on developments in the north. As he points out with another round of strong selections of prose and poetry, the desire for artistic freedom and dissatisfaction with state policies led a number of intellectuals, including the prominent poet and essayist Phan Khoi, speak out and publish protest literature in the second half of the 1950s. The Hanoi government, however, did not tolerate such protest and utilized an array of resources, especially other prominent writers, to attack the protesters and defend socialism as the goal of literary and cultural works in the DRV. Instructors could single out a particular passage from the poet Xuan Dieu (266), which reveals the outcome desired and expected by the North Vietnamese regime. Why were poets and writers referred to as "technicians"? Dedicated communist writers were described as "red" and "completely red"; who, then, were the ones with a "pinkish tinge"? Moreover, the state encouraged and enabled writers to seek solidarity with and learn from socialist internationalism. Students should be asked to look at pages 267–68 and 281–83 and dissect the passages on those pages. For example, the phrases "the Soviet homeland," "face looks at face," and "hand clasps hand" (268) point to a transnational imagination that extended beyond the Vietnamese nation, while "millions and millions of laboring people" suggests the fundamental commonality among Vietnamese and Russians. Or, on the poem about Walt Whitman starting on page 281, students could be called on to discuss the criticism of the old that hindered progress and the universalist and internationalist belief in the power of "the people." Given what they knew about the Vietnamese peasantry, how might this poem have reflected the enthusiasm for socialism and, consequently, an anti-capitalist, and ultimately anti-American, credo?

This credo was strongest in North Vietnam, but it was also essential to the strategy of the NLF in the south. On this subject, instructors may wish to introduce students to the document "Program of the National Liberation Front of South-Vietnam," which was helpfully translated by Robert Brigham and stored at the website of his Vietnam War course.[22] As was common in communist political documents at the time, the "Program" was a mix of anti-American propaganda, anti-Saigon propaganda, and appeals for a continuation of the socialist revolution in Vietnam. There are ten major headings in this document, and one useful exercise would have students sort out these three elements from it. A more challenging exercise is to focus on one heading at a time and determine which group(s) of southern Vietnamese it might appeal to the most—and which the least. Heading IV, for instance, would have drawn the interest of peasants and owners of small farms because it advocated reduction of land rent and redistribution of land. Heading VI would likely have found support among families with sons that were drafted into the South Vietnamese army, and the next heading would have appealed to ethnic minorities and educated women. As a political document, the "Program" was designed to gain as much support for the NLF as possible. The fact that the organization could survive and thrive until at least the Tet Offensive indicates that this document played a significant role in laying the ideological foundation of antiforeign nationalism mixed with a strong dose of socialism.[23]

As for the experience of noncommunist South Vietnamese, students can return to chapter 5 of Jamieson's book: a section called "The War, the Americans, and Vietnamese Society." Among other things, the author gives an array of cold numbers and statistics, which illustrate the influx of materials that accompanied the Americanization of the war. In the next sections, "Continuity and Change in Values in the South" and "Patterns in Chaos," he shifts gears to provide a combination of anecdotes, stories, and generalizations in anthropological fashion. Together these sections describe the South Vietnamese experience of the war perhaps better than any similar amount of pages in other books about the Vietnam War. They provide a vivid portrayal of the impact of the American presence in cities and countryside in material and social terms. But they also point out the complexity of the experience, which varied from one segment of South Vietnamese society to another but at times cut across the socioeconomic spectrum and even enemy lines.

Finally, for a North Vietnamese perspective on the war, this writer recommends the book *From Enemy to Friend* by Col. Bui Tin.[24] A long-time journalist and soldier of the People's Army of Vietnam (PAVN), which fought the French and the Americans, Tin defected to the West in the early 1990s and became a critic of the postwar regime. This book consists of a series of interviews conducted after the defection. It touches on some postwar subjects, including prisoners of war and soldiers missing in action (the POW-MIA issue), but the focus is on the war period. Given the nature of the interview format, there is a good deal of content along the lines of "hindsight" throughout the book. Nonetheless, it is well organized and easy to follow and should not take students a lot of time to read. It also covers a nice swath of military history, which should delight students with a disposition toward the genre. The author is frank in tone and alternates between praise and criticism of Hanoi's conduct during the war. For these reasons, this writer encourages instructors to assign students most of the book, if not all.

Some of Bui Tin's views were undoubtedly colored by his defection to the West near the end of the Cold War. He is not strong either when explaining the American experience. But this is not the main reason to read the book, whose value lies instead in Tin's description of North Vietnamese perceptions, tactics, and strategies. He does this by explaining and citing communist documents. Take, for instance, Hanoi's analysis of the first two major battles after Americanization (including the Battle of Ia Drang), which resulted in a "lesson learned" document that was widely disseminated. The document noted the "overwhelming firepower and technological superiority" of the United States, but also the disadvantage of having to announce "their presence ahead of time" by advance firepower before movement of ground troops. This practice took away "the elements of surprise and secrecy crucial to success in a military engagement."[25] This was the opposite of the strategy employed by communist soldiers, exemplified by another document that Tin cites in the book. According to General Nguyen Chi Thanh, the military commander in the south until his death in 1967, PAVN and NLF troops were to "keep your moves secret and unpredictable, giving special attention to creating diversions and dissimulation to throw off the enemy's calculations."[26] Along with General Vo Nguyen Giap's assessment of "search-and-destroy" (p. 23), these two documents could be utilized for a discussion about communist approach in combating the more materially powerful American and South Vietnamese enemy.

Another valuable resource from Bui Tin's book is his explanation of the Ho Chi Minh Trail (74–80). As is true of most subjects in the book, there are longer and more scholarly publications about the trail. Tin's take, however, is as arresting as it is succinct and should provide students a glimpse into Hanoi's fascinating mobilization of resources and the masses toward the war effort. Furthermore, it could be used in conjunction with video clips about the trail that can be found on YouTube or another media source. Last, some of the information given here reveals the extent of foreign aid to Hanoi, especially from the Soviet Union and China. It is a subject treated with more attention later in the book, which provides an opportunity to discuss the international aspects of the conflict from the North Vietnamese perspective. In particular, the relationship between Hanoi and Beijing is shown to have been very strong, especially on the battlefield. With some justice, Bui Tin insists in the book that Chinese troops were not involved on the battlefield. Nonetheless, Tin's recollections of the French War and Dien Bien Phu (96–99) illustrate the fact that Mao's China was intimately involved in the Indochinese theater long before the introduction of American troops to South Vietnam.[27]

NOTES

1. The following instructors of the Vietnam War have taught their courses from a Vietnamese perspective, and I wish to thank them for providing me with the syllabi of their courses: David Biggs, Robert Brigham, Diane Fox, Charles Keith, and Wynn Wilcox.

2. George C. Herring, *America's Longest War: The United States and Vietnam, 1950–1975*, 4th ed. (New York: McGraw-Hill, 2001); Gerard J. DeGroot, *A Noble Cause? America and the Vietnam War* (Harlow, Essex: Longman, 2000); Mark Philip Bradley, *Vietnam at War* (Oxford: Oxford University Press, 2009); William J. Duiker, *Sacred War: Nationalism and Revolution in a Divided Vietnam* (New York: McGraw-Hill, 1995). Another text that pays considerable attention to the Vietnamese side is William S. Turley, *The Second Indochina War: A Concise Political and Military History*, 2nd ed. (Lanham, MD: Rowman and Littlefield, 2009).

3. D. R. SarDesai, *Vietnam: Past and Present*, 4th ed. (Boulder, CO: Westview Press, 2005), chapters 1 and 2. Another suggestion is David G. Marr, *Vietnamese Anticolonialism, 1885–1925* (Berkeley and Los Angeles: University of California Press, 1971), chapter 1; it gives a concise and lucid description of precolonial

Vietnam, focusing also on the topic of Vietnamese ethnic and national identity. A third choice is Brantly Womack, *China and Vietnam: The Politics of Asymmetry* (Cambridge: Cambridge University Press, 2006), chapters 5, 6, and 7. These chapters are chronologically arranged and offer conceptually arresting discussions of the relationship from antiquity to 1950.

4. With time and desire, instructors might also like to highlight the growth of regionalism and the autonomous village in the period before the establishment of the Nguyen dynasty. These highlights, in turn, would prepare students to understand the challenges that communist and noncommunist revolutionaries later faced in winning over the rural masses. A recommended reading on this matter is Li Tana's short study of southern Vietnam under the Nguyen lords. Its fifth chapter describes "a new way of being Vietnamese" during this period in the south, including the state's patronage and promotion of Mahayana Buddhism. This development helped to make the south a fertile ground for eclectic religious movements subsequently, including the Hao Hao and the Cao Dai, which figured significantly before and during the First Indochina War. Li Tana, *Nguyễn Cochinchina: Southern Vietnam in the Seventeenth and Eighteenth Centuries* (Ithaca, NY: Cornell Southeast Asia Program Publications, 1998), chapter 5.

5. William S. Logan, *Hanoi: Biography of a City* (Seattle: University of Washington Press, 2000), 67–111.

6. Ibid., 108.

7. Truong Buu Lam, *Colonialism Experienced: Vietnamese Writings on Colonialism, 1900–1931* (Ann Arbor: University of Michigan Press, 2000).

8. Phan Boi Chau, *Overturned Chariot: The Autobiography of Phan Bội Châu*, trans. Vinh Sinh and Nicholas Wickenden (Honolulu: University of Hawai'i Press, 1999); Phan Châu Trinh, *Phan Châu Trinh and His Political Writings*, ed. and trans. Vinh Sinh (Ithaca, NY: Cornell Southeast Asia Program Publications, 2009).

9. "Document 18: *Do* [Red] Newsletter," in Lam, *Colonialism Experienced*, 275–79.

10. Ibid., 276.

11. "Document 19: Tran Phu (1904–31)," in Lam, *Colonialism Experienced*, 280–91.

12. François Guillemot, "Vietnamese Nationalist Revolutionaries and the Japanese Occupation: The Case of the Dai Viet Parties (1936–1946)," in *Imperial Japan and National Identities in Asia, 1895–1945*, ed. Li Narangoa and R. B. Cribb (London: Routledge, 2003), 221–48.

13. Vu Ngu Chieu, "The Other Side of the 1945 Vietnamese Revolution: The Empire of Viet-Nam (March–August 1945)," *Journal of Asian Studies* 45 (February 1986): 293–328.

14. David G. Marr, *Vietnam 1945: The Quest for Power* (Berkeley: University of California Press, 1997).

15. Huynh Kim Khanh, "The Vietnamese August Revolution Reinterpreted," *Journal of Asian Studies* 30 (August 1971): 761–88.

16. Tuong Vu, "'It's Time for the Indochinese Revolution to Show Its True Colours': The Radical Turn of Vietnamese Politics in 1948," *Journal of Southeast Asian Studies* 40 (October 2009): 519–42.

17. Tuong Vu, "From Cheering to Volunteering: Vietnamese Communists and the Coming of the Cold War, 1940–1951," in *Connecting Histories: Decolonization and the Cold War in Southeast Asia, 1945–1962*, ed. Christopher E. Goscha and Christian F. Ostermann (Washington, DC, and Stanford: Woodrow Wilson Center Press and Stanford University Press, 2009), 172–204. The quotation is on 174.

18. Vo Nguyen Giap, *Dien Bien Phu* (Hanoi: The Gioi, 2000).

19. Pierre Asselin, "Choosing Peace: Hanoi and the Geneva Agreement on Vietnam, 1954–1955," *Journal of Cold War Studies* 9:2 (Spring 2007): 95–126.

20. Neil L. Jamieson, *Understanding Vietnam* (Berkeley: University of California Press, 1993).

21. A benighted view of Diem's regime is found in Ronald B. Frankum Jr., "Vietnam during the Rule of Ngo Dinh Diem, 1954–63," in David L. Anderson and John Ernst, eds., *The War That Never Ends: New Perspectives on the Vietnam War* (Lexington: University of Kentucky Press, 2007), 121–42. A more sophisticated analysis of his nation-building project is Philip C. Catton, *Diem's Final Failure: Prelude to America's War in Vietnam* (Lawrence: University Press of Kansas, 2002), chapter 2.

22. Robert Brigham, trans., "Program of the National Liberation Front of South-Vietnam," http://vietnam.vassar.edu/overview/docnlf.html.

23. For a memoir by an NLF insider, Truong Nhu Tang, *A Vietcong Memoir: An Inside Account of the Vietnam War and Its Aftermath* (New York: Harcourt Brace Jovanovich, 1985), remains most accessible in content and availability.

24. Bui Tin, *From Enemy to Friend: A North Vietnamese Perspective on the War* (Annapolis, MD: Naval Institute Press, 2002).

25. Ibid., 16–17.

26. Ibid., 19–20.

27. There are many articles about Sino-Vietnamese relations during the Vietnam War. Perhaps the most accessible for classroom use is Xiaoming Zhang, "The Vietnam War, 1964–1969: A Chinese Perspective," *Journal of Military History* 60:4 (October 1996): 731–62.

KEY RESOURCES

Brocheux, Pierre, and Daniel Hémery. *Indochina: An Ambiguous Colonization, 1858–1954*. Berkeley: University of California Press, 2009.

Duiker, William. "In Search of Ho Chi Minh." In *A Companion to the Vietnam War*, edited by Marilyn B. Young and Robert Buzzanco, 19–36. Malden, MA: Blackwell, 2002.

Elliott, David W. P. *The Vietnamese War: Revolution and Social Change in the Mekong Delta, 1930–1975*, concise ed. Armonk, NY: M. E. Sharpe, 2007.

Frankum, Ronald B., Jr. "Vietnam during the Rule of Ngo Dinh Diem, 1954–63." In *The War That Never Ends: New Perspectives on the Vietnam War*, ed. David L. Anderson and John Ernst, 121–42. Lexington: University Press of Kentucky, 2007.

Lone, Stewart. "Remembering Life in Urban South Vietnam, circa 1965–1975." In *Daily Lives of Civilians in Wartime Asia: From the Taiping Rebellion to the Vietnam War*, ed. Stewart Lone, 219–46. Westport, CT: Greenwood Press, 2007.

Malarney, Shaun. "The Realities and Consequences of War in a Northern Vietnamese Commune." In *A Companion to the Vietnam War*, ed. Marilyn B. Young and Robert Buzzanco, 65–78. Malden, MA: Blackwell, 2002.

Phuong, Xuan, and Danièle Mazingarbe, *Ao Dai: My War, My Country, My Vietnam*. Great Neck, NY: EMQUAD International, 2004.

Taylor, Philip. *Fragments of the Present: Searching for Modernity in Vietnam's South*. Honolulu: University of Hawai'i Press, 2001.

Topmiller, Robert J. "Struggling for Peace: South Vietnamese Buddhist Women and Resistance to the Vietnam War." *Journal of Women's History* 17:3 (Fall 2005): 133–57.

Wright, Jackie Bong. *Autumn Cloud: From Vietnamese War Widow to American Activist*. Sterling, VA: Capital Books, 2001.

"America's Most Loyal Allies"

The Hmong and the War

CHIA YOUYEE VANG

The first time I taught a course on the Vietnam War it was to a class of two hundred students at the University of Wisconsin–Milwaukee. Similar to all first-day classes, I briefly introduced myself by highlighting my educational background, then my research and teaching interests before moving on to the syllabus. At a meeting with my teaching assistants the following week, one of them asked if it would be all right to tell students that I was Hmong. The teaching assistant shared that a couple of the students were wondering if I were Vietnamese since I was teaching about the Vietnam War. My initial reaction was that hundreds of other Americans teach about the Vietnam War and they are not Vietnamese, so what difference does my ethnicity make? I was certain that if I had been a person of any racial background but Asian, my ethnic identity would never be questioned. At the beginning of the next lecture, I decided to use their curiosity as a teaching moment by informing the class that I was indeed not Vietnamese. I told the students that the reason I was standing in front of them teaching about this war was an unintended consequence of the war itself. I further explained that in other classes about the Vietnam War, they might not get the chance to understand how a Hmong individual like me could end up in the United States. I reassured them that before the end of the semester they would be able to understand the impact of the war beyond the American and Vietnamese experiences.

World War II and the French War

Many students may not be aware of the role of Laos and the Hmong people in the Vietnam War. In fact they may be entirely unfamiliar with Laos, a small landlocked country that, like its neighbors Vietnam and Cambodia, fell under French control in the late nineteenth century. They are even less likely to have heard of the Hmong, an ethnic group that migrated from southern China to the mountainous northern region of Laos in the mid–nineteenth century. If students have heard of the Hmong it is more likely to have been in Clint Eastwood's film *Gran Torino* than any American history textbook. Despite its flaws in representing Hmong cultural practices, the film made Hmong people visible on the big screen, and thus requires people to ask, "Who are the Hmong and why are they in the United States?"[1]

Hmong settlement on Lao territory prior to French colonial rule was tolerated by the ethnic Lao elite, but their incursions into areas dominated by other indigenous groups generated tension.[2] This was exacerbated by French colonial rule, which drew Laos into the international political and military conflicts of the twentieth century. Ethnic minority groups could not remain neutral. They had to either collaborate with or resist these stronger foreign rulers and face tragic consequences.

During World War II, for example, a Hmong group under the leadership of Touby Lyfoung backed a French effort to reinstate colonial rule while his Hmong rival, Faydang Lo, collaborated with the Japanese, who had occupied the region. When France reestablished its authority at the end of the war, Touby Lyfoung was personally rewarded with an appointment as district governor (*chao muong*) for the Hmong of Xieng Khouang province.[3] Touby Lyfoung and his followers continued to support the French during the First Indochina War (1946–54), but the French defeat placed these native collaborators in a contentious position.

The 1954 Geneva Accords granted full independence to Laos, but the country quickly descended into civil conflict. Hmong who had once supported the French now backed the Royal Lao Government. Throughout the late 1950s, they worked with Royal Lao Government forces to fend off the communist Pathet Lao.[4] As the situation in Vietnam intensified, the United States backed the Lao government and provided it with military assistance. It sent military advisers to train the Royal Lao Army (RLA) and upgraded the Royal Lao Air Force.

By the time John F. Kennedy was elected US president in 1960, the future of Laos was tenuous. The Pathet Lao, backed by North Vietnam, threatened to take control of the government. In a meeting on the day before Kennedy's inauguration, outgoing President Dwight D. Eisenhower impressed on the president-elect the importance of Laos, saying that permitting Laos to fall would force the United States to "write off the whole area." Although some of Kennedy's advisers recommended direct military intervention, Kennedy supported the 1962 Geneva Accord reiterating Lao neutrality. The agreement established a coalition government under neutralist prime minister Souvanna Phouma in which the communist Pathet Lao shared power. This fragile coalition soon collapsed, however, and the factions resumed fighting.

Having failed to establish a pro-American Laos during the last half of the 1950s, American officials launched covert operations in the country beginning in 1961. American Central Intelligence Agency (CIA) operatives in Southeast Asia appealed to Vang Pao, an officer of Hmong ethnicity in the RLA, to collaborate with them. In return for direct US military and economic aid, Vang Pao enlisted thousands of Hmong men and boys to join the effort in what became known as the CIA's "secret army." This clandestine army grew from nine thousand in 1961 to forty thousand in 1969. Congress was eager to fund an army of Hmong irregulars because "they believed 'it was a much cheaper and better way to fight a war in Southeast Asia than to commit American troops.'"[5] The war efforts in Laos were "cheap" in part because, unlike in Vietnam, the vast majority of lives lost were not American. The war in Laos was operated from Thailand by CIA officers in collaboration with the US embassy in Laos. With no American ground combat troops, it was kept a secret from 1961 to 1969. As a Vietnam War veteran recalled, "During the Vietnam War, operations in Laos were a rumor, a legend. For us, the country was a bomb dump, a place to go when the weather was too bad for attacks over North Vietnam. Soon, however, word began to filter out to pilots in Vietnam and Thailand that there was 'another theater,' one where there was no higher echelon, no rank, and few rules. We heard about other pilots flying Cessna O-s and North American T-28s out of places with exotic names like Luang Prabang, Xieng Khouang, Pakse, and Long Tieng."[6] An unauthorized visit paid to Long Cheng by *Time* reporter and *Life* correspondent Timothy Allman and a French reporter exposed the top-secret operation in 1970.[7]

Distributing weapons. (Pat Landry, Box 1, CAT/Air America Archive, History of Aviation Collection, Special Collections Department, McDermott Library, the University of Texas at Dallas)

America's covert program had profound effects on Lao society. As Roger Warner describes it, "[Ambassador] Sullivan's biggest headache was controlling the secret U.S. air strikes. In the early months of 1965, navy jets had hit the wrong target three days in a row. In another incident a jet missed its target by twenty miles and bombed a village where Sullivan had been just the day before on a goodwill visit. He found it embarrassing to have to send some young USAID [US Agency for International Development] field guy in there to apologize and hand out money for the loss of innocent lives."[8] As if the "innocent lives" were no more than commodities, US representatives flippantly used their capital to ease the pain and suffering caused by American negligence. This behavior seemed to occur frequently. Warner further quotes a CIA case officer, who said, "They bombed a lot of friendly villages. We screamed a lot, and they promised it would never happen again; and then it would happen again the next week." The practice of providing financial compensation to families of soldiers killed in the line of duty is not unique to the Hmong experience with American officials in Laos. However, the practice had more egregious consequences there since financial compensation often served as a catalyst for the sacrifice of Hmong lives, which included not only combatants but also their families who lived near battle sites.

The enlistment of Hmong men and boys in the secret army remains a convoluted issue. On one hand, the outcome of American involvement with the Hmong in Laos and the larger Vietnam conflict contributed to the breakdown of agrarian society and destroyed the Hmong way of life. On the other hand, many Hmong individuals rose in the military ranks and obtained titles incommensurate with any other time in Hmong history. Unlike during French rule, when members of only a few families were appointed to provincial and village chief positions, Hmong associations with Americans facilitated a plethora of positions in the military, economic, and rural development arenas. Monthly salaries provided to registered soldiers served as an incentive for many who did not have any other way to earn a living. Because only a few Americans were present to oversee the operations in Laos, Hmong men also worked as mechanics, radio operators, and "backseaters" to support American pilots. Thirty-seven were even trained to become pilots, of which the most famous was Lue Lee, who flew T-28 aircraft. He flew more than five thousand sorties until he was shot down by antiaircraft fire on July 12, 1969. Some of the initial recruits from Xieng Khouang province who trained under American and Thai instructors during the early 1960s went on to achieve higher military rank when the United States stepped up its commitments in Southeast Asia.[9] Many young men enlisted due to the promise of rank and titles. Recruiters often elaborated opportunities to achieve higher status in society through the military. For some, promotions seemed to happen "overnight" during the height of American commitments from 1965 through 1969. However, for most Hmong soldiers the promises never materialized. Although it is not clear if leaders like Vang Pao truly understood the larger geopolitical situation, the offers by CIA agents were difficult to refuse. While US representatives in Laos during the 1950s and 1960s did not fully understand the history of ethnic minorities' relationships with lowland Lao society, they were successful in continuing the tradition of "divide and conquer" previously implemented by French colonial administrators. American military and civilian leaders made promises to Hmong representatives and supported their advancement in order to gain Hmong support. Military, economic development, and refugee relief agency staff worked hand in hand, using their material goods and financial backing to entice the "natives" in multiple ways.

While the clandestine army provided rank to some officers and monthly salaries to enlisted soldiers, USAID's village health program constructed clinics and hospitals in various locations throughout Laos. To divert the attention from the top-secret military base at Long Cheng, USAID established its refugee relief center at Sam Thong, approximately five kilometers north of Long Cheng. At Sam Thong, USAID constructed a hospital for displaced refugees, and the location became the showcase for visiting western dignitaries. Local women and men were recruited and trained as "nurses" to assist the few doctors.

The agency also supported the construction of village schools for Hmong children in and around Long Cheng and Sam Thong. Though minimal, many who became internally displaced during the war years had access to education not previously available to them. Salaried jobs for the native population also manifested themselves within the USAID bureaucracy. Few USAID staff members arrived in Laos with the necessary language skills to communicate with the local people. The vast majority relied on local representatives possessing some English language proficiency to serve as interpreters. In addition to medical aid workers, USAID employed a number of ethnic field assistants to help agency workers maneuver through the local system and to implement its refugee relief program.

Unfortunately for the Hmong, the opportunities that resulted from collaborating with Americans came at a high cost. While men and boys manned the front lines to protect their homes and families, as well as American interests, women's lives were turned upside down in most cases as well. The need to relocate whole villages to safer areas as the war dragged on brought about tremendous hardship. Hunger, disease, and indiscriminate bombings claimed thousands of lives that went uncounted as casualties of war. As the war progressed throughout the 1960s into the early 1970s, a large percentage of the Hmong population that was previously self-sufficient became dependent on US food drops, and USAID worked with the CIA and American embassy to provide food and supplies to some of the guerrilla fighters and their families. The CIA's airline, Air America, transported many Hmong from place to place.

Between fifteen and twenty thousand Hmong died in battles while an estimated forty thousand civilians lost their lives due to disease or hunger, as victims of firefights, or while trying to flee Laos in the post-1975 era. Those who successfully crossed the border into Thailand spent varied lengths of time in camps set up by the United Nations High Commissioner for Refugees (UNHCR). Most who left Laos in the immediate aftermath of the war thought they were seeking temporary refuge, and many hoped to return when the situation improved. That would not be the case for the thousands stranded in refugee camps who were eventually forced to make the decision to relocate to a host of countries that they had never heard of.

Postwar Impact

The Hmong alliance with the Americans during the war resulted in the vast majority resettling in the United States. In 2010 the US Census Bureau counted more than 260,000 people of Hmong ethnicity. France, Canada, and Australia each accepted a significantly smaller number of Hmong refugees, many of whom have subsequently reunited with family members in the United States. Initially dispersed throughout the United States, the Hmong faced extreme challenges acculturating into American society. Most arrived with little or no formal education and experienced difficulties maneuvering through the various systems and institutions. Their culture and its traditions frequently conflicted with US rules and regulations. Eventually the Hmong began to practice chain migration, resulting in the construction of new, large communities in several states. People often moved for economic and social support. In general they have worked hard to rebuild their lives in America. Many have pursued postsecondary education and work in various sectors. Others, in particular in California, Minnesota, and Wisconsin, have been inspired to become involved in the US political process. More than a dozen Hmong Americans have successfully sought elected offices at the local and state level. In comparison to their socioeconomic status nearly forty years ago, they have made tremendous gains; however, they remain one of the most impoverished Asian American groups.

Knowledge about the Hmong's role in the "secret war" in Laos has increased largely because of the Hmong presence in the United States. Though viewed by some as opportunists both during and after the war, many Hmong veterans living in the United States and Americans who worked with them in Laos have coordinated efforts to seek formal recognition for Hmong wartime sacrifices. Two such organizations are the Lao Veterans of America (LVA) and the Lao Hmong and American Coalition (LHAC). Efforts by the LVA resulted in a formal recognition ceremony in May 1997.[10] Held near the Vietnam War Memorial in

Lao Memorial at Arlington National Cemetery. (photo by author)

Washington, D.C., the event included congressional representatives, military officials, advocates, and Hmong community members. In addition to speeches acknowledging the Hmong contribution to American efforts in Laos, a roadside plaque was placed at Arlington National Cemetery to honor Hmong and Lao combat soldiers and their American advisers in Laos. Since then a memorial has been built in Sacramento, and the LHAC successfully led an effort to build a memorial in Sheboygan, Wisconsin. Many recognition ceremonies continue to take place annually in locations throughout the country where a large number of Hmong reside.

Lessons Learned from Teaching about the Hmong and the War

For a number of years I have taught a course on the Vietnam War in large lectures and small winter and summer sessions. Later I began offering the course online. In addition I teach a small course on Hmong history, culture, and contemporary life, and I spend a significant part of the class on the Vietnam War. Teaching the events in Laos as an integral part of the larger war effort in Vietnam has been instrumental in helping students understand the breadth and depth of US activities there. For the Vietnam War course, I use Robert J.

McMahon's *Major Problems in the History of the Vietnam War* as the main textbook because it contains a great deal of primary sources with essays exploring different viewpoints on the topics included.[11] Since it does not have a separate section on Laos, I include the covert operations in Laos in my lecture, and I have students watch the episode "Cambodia and Laos" from the PBS series *Vietnam: A Television History*. The film introduces students to CIA activities with Hmong in Laos, and it touches on the contradictory role that the late former general Vang Pao played. In addition I show clips from the film *No More Mountains*. Made in 1980, this documentary traces the challenges that Hmong refugees encountered as they became refugees in Thailand and their subsequent settlement in the United States. The strength of this film is that it examines the impact of Hmong involvement with the CIA and allows students to explore the social and cultural adjustment of Hmong in California and other parts of the world.[12] Due to time constraints, I show only about fifteen minutes of this hour-long film. If time permits, an instructor should show the film in its entirety, especially if many of the students had previously viewed *Gran Torino*, which should not serve as their only source of information on Hmong history and culture.

I have also incorporated oral histories from the volume *Wisconsin Vietnam War Stories* and its companion film into my lectures.[13] These sources are a great way to help students hear the voices of local people who served in the war. The book and the film include the experiences of US military personnel who served in Laos and a Hmong veteran of the secret army. In discussion sections and/or discussion forums when taught online, I pose questions that allow students to think about how Laos and Cambodia were pulled into the war. I encourage them to critically assess whether or not these neighboring countries could have avoided being drawn in. One exercise that instructors could conduct with students regarding *Wisconsin War Stories* is to have students watch the segment "Vietnam: Draw Down-Rescue," which is about seven minutes long. This video contains reflections of two American veterans and one Hmong veteran. Students can be asked to compare and contrast what the war in Laos meant to the Hmong veteran, Nhia Thong Lor,[14] and the American veterans, Robert Curry and Steven Schofield. The American veterans explain how they arrived in Laos and the complexity surrounding their identities. Each was given directions about how to behave and carry out his mission. Steven Schofield's public identity was as a public health adviser, but his real charge was to carry out rescue missions, whereas Robert Curry flew reconnaissance missions over North Vietnam. He was shot down while flying over Laos and rescued by a group of Hmong soldiers who were part of the Lao Special Guerrilla Units (SGU). Nhia Thong Lor, on the other hand, was a teenager who had seen his relatives become casualties of war. He was motivated to join the army to protect his people. Schofield had taken a photo of Lor while he served in Laos. Neither knew that years later Lor would live in the same US state as Schofield.

In addition to discussing films on the secret war in Laos, instructors may consider inviting local Hmong veterans to speak to their classes. The LVA and LHAC have chapters in a number of locations throughout the country. For background information, instructors should refer students to their respective websites.[15] The LVA website may be of particular interest to students because it contains photos and documents from the secret war years. Local Hmong community-based organizations are also a good resource for instructors who would like to find speakers, especially if the veterans themselves do not speak English. Community organizations can often provide interpreters. To find local Hmong community organizations, instructors should consult the Southeast Asia Resource and Action Center's (SEARAC) Directory of Southeast Asian Community Based Organizations.[16] From the SEARAC website, instructors can search for organizations throughout the United States. This is a helpful resource because instructors can search by ethnicity. If they are interested, they can search for Cambodian, Vietnamese, and Lao organizations in addition to Hmong. These community-based organizations can also provide opportunities for students to hear firsthand accounts of war experiences and stories of acculturation.

To encourage students to further explore the impact of war on Hmong refugees and immigrants in my Hmong history class, I assign a creative project. The assignment provides students with several ways to demonstrate their understanding of what happened to the Hmong and how they have made sense of their lives in the United States. Below is a description of the project.

The creative portion of your assignment can take different forms: a short story, a photo essay, a comic book, or a poem about the aftermath of the "Secret War in Laos" (Vietnam War) from the perspective of a Hmong immigrant/refugee. You are not required to do outside research for this assignment; however, your creation should reflect an understanding of the politics surrounding the aftermath of the war as well as a significant input of time, effort, and thought. Your creative project must be accompanied by an essay of at least four pages that explains: 1) the specific historical and political conversations in which your project intervenes about the aftermath of the war; 2) what your project contributes to those conversations; and 3) the process of creating this project. Your essay may reflect on any other element of the creative process or product, as long as it thoroughly addresses all three above topics and cites relevant books, articles, films, class lectures, and hand-outs from the course.[17]

For instructors who may wish to enhance their knowledge of Hmong experiences, I suggest several texts that examine the contentious military and political history of US involvement in Laos and the impact of the war on the Hmong. Timothy N. Castle's *At War in the Shadow of Vietnam: U.S. Military Aid to the Royal Lao Government* (1993) succinctly describes the increasing assistance provided to the Lao government and Vang Pao's army. *Shadow War: The CIA's Secret War in Laos* (1995) by Kenneth Conboy and James Morrison provides a comprehensive history of CIA activities in Laos. While the air evacuation of about twenty-five hundred Hmong from Long Cheng in May 1975 is in no way comparable to the evacuation in Saigon on April 30, it was a chaotic situation for those who witnessed it. Gayle L. Morrison's *Sky Is Falling: An Oral History of the CIA's Evacuation of the Hmong from Laos* (1999) offers reflections by Hmong and Americans on those few days that set in motion the flight of thousands. To learn more about what has happened to the Hmong who migrated to the United States following the Vietnam War, instructors should consult my book, *Hmong America: Reconstructing Community in Diaspora* (2010).

Summary

In states like California, Wisconsin, and Minnesota, many people have known, met, interacted with, or at least heard about the Hmong. Nationally and locally, Hmong frequently make the news, often negative news, in stroies about their culture and traditions. In one newspaper article after another, writers often reiterate the fact that the Hmong are a tribal group that served with Americans in Laos during the Vietnam War. Close scrutiny of their experiences in the US and in Laos only as backdrops of tragic incidents, such as the 2004 shootings in Wisconsin, are not effective spaces for learning.[18] These sporadic history lessons are often surface descriptions and contribute little to Americans' understanding of who the Hmong are and why they are in the United States.

Having taught a course on the Vietnam War for multiple years, it is evident that college students today have only a vague understanding of when and where the "Vietnam War" actually took place—in addition to sharing a broader misunderstanding among most US citizens regarding the war's goals and outcomes. While declassified information during the last two decades has made available a great deal of information on US activities in Laos, most Americans still misunderstand the nature of the events that unfolded there during the Vietnam War era, which explains why many students begin their college careers with little knowledge of groups such as the Hmong from Laos.

In hindsight US policies regarding Laos were never directed at Laos itself but always at the larger Cold War contest beyond it. It is fair to say that without the Cold War it is unlikely that the United States would have invested its vast power and resources in this remote Southeast Asian country. It should be noted that the Hmong were not the only ethnic minority group that became entangled in the Vietnam conflict. In the highlands of Laos and Vietnam, many ethnic minorities whose ancestors resided in these mountainous regions had historically been forced to take sides during wars, were they local struggles or conflicts imposed by foreign invaders. What is unique about Hmong experiences with the US military and humanitarian personnel from the early 1960s through the mid-1970s is that the contentious relationship impacted most of the estimated three hundred thousand Hmong in Laos at the time. Additionally, the transformations that began in the mountains of northeastern Laos and the legacy of this historical period have been sustained in the fabric of Hmong communities in the United States. The result of their more than three decades of advocacy work is several memorials symbolizing their sacrifices on behalf of American interests before they even set foot in the United States. While the secret war in Laos may have been conducted covertly, the memorials and many recognition ceremonies that take place annually across the United States serve as a reminder that secrets cannot be swept under the rug for long.

NOTES

1. Clint Eastwood, *Gran Torino* (Burbank, CA: Warner Brothers, 2008).

2. The Lao are the majority ethnic group in the Lao People's Democratic Republic (LPDR). This is the post-Vietnam War name of the country. However, it is commonly referred to as Laos. There are forty-nine recognized ethnic groups in Laos today. Lao is also the national language, and people from Laos are referred to as Lao or Laotians. The Hmong comprise one of the ethnic minority groups, but as people from Laos, they can also be referred to as Laotians.

3. Christian Culas and Jean Michaud, "A Contribution to the Study of Hmong (Miao) Migrations and History," in *Hmong/Miao in Asia*, ed. Nicholas Tapp, Jean Michaud, Christian Culas, and Gary Yia Lee (Chiangmai, Thailand: Silkworm Books, 2004), 79.

4. Keith Quincy, *Harvesting Pachay's Wheat: The Hmong and America's Secret War in Laos* (Spokane: Eastern Washington University Press, 2000), 135–38.

5. Leary Papers, "US Special Operations in Laos: 1955–1965," The CAT/ Air America Archive, The History of Aviation Collection, McDermott Library, University of Texas at Dallas, 1.

6. Ralph Wetterham, "The Ravens of Long Tieng," *Air & Space*, October–November 1998, 51–59.

7. "Laos: Deeper into the Other War," *Time*, March 9, 1970, http://www .time.com/time/magazine/article/0,9171,878776,00.html (accessed September 20, 2011).

8. Roger Warner, *Shooting at the Moon: The Story of America's Clandestine War in Laos* (South Royalton, VT: Steerforth Press, 1998), 157.

9. Lloyd "Pat" Landry Papers, History of Aviation Collection, McDermott Library, University of Texas at Dallas. Note that when Vang Pao was first contacted by CIA representatives in 1961, his rank was only that of a major. By the end of the Vietnam War, he had become a major general due specifically to his work with the CIA.

10. Although the organization names use the term *Lao*, the members and leaders of these two organizations are primarily Hmong.

11. Robert J. McMahon, *Major Problems in the History of the Vietnam War* (Boston and New York: Houghton Mifflin, 2008).

12. Judith Vecchione, Andre Libik, and Robert Montiegel, *No More Mountains: The Story of the Hmong* (Boston: WGHB Television, 1982).

13. See Sarah Larsen and Jennifer M. Miller, *Wisconsin Vietnam War Stories: Our Veterans Remember* (Madison: Wisconsin Historical Society Press, 2010); and Wisconsin Public Television, *Wisconsin Vietnam War Stories* (Madison: Wisconsin Public Television, 2010).

14. Nhia Thong Lor is now a naturalized American citizen.

15. Lao Veterans of America, http://www.laoveterans.com/ (accessed September 16, 2011); Lao Hmong US Memorial http://www.laohmongus memorial.com/ (accessed September 16, 2011).

16. See Southeast Asia Research and Action Center, http://www.searac .org/maa (accessed September 16, 2011).

17. This idea was shared with Dr. Jennifer Pierce by Dr. Pam Butler. Dr. Butler and I were classmates at the University of Minnesota and we both worked with Dr. Pierce. Dr. Pierce teaches a course on America in international perspectives. In her class she focuses a great deal on the Vietnam War era. In addition to traveling and conducting research in Laos and Vietnam together, we have shared resources and lessons learned from teaching the war.

18. In 2004 Hmong American hunter Chai Soua Vang killed six white hunters in northern Wisconsin during a hunting confrontation.

KEY RESOURCES

Castle, Timothy N. *At War in the Shadow of Vietnam: U.S. Military Aid to the Royal Lao Government, 1955–1975*. New York: Columbia University Press, 1993.

Chan, Sucheng. *Hmong Means Free: Life in Laos and in the United States*. Philadelphia: Temple University Press, 1994.

Conboy, Kenneth, and James Morrison. *Shadow War: The CIA's Secret War in Laos*. Boulder, CO: Paladin Press, 1995.

Dommen, Arthur J. *The Indochinese Experience of the French and the Americans: Nationalism and Communism in Cambodia, Laos, and Vietnam*. Bloomington: Indiana University Press, 2001.

Hamilton-Merritt, Jane. *Tragic Mountains: The Hmong, the Americans and the Secret War for Laos, 1942–1992*. Bloomington: Indiana University Press. 1999.

Hein, Jeremy. *Ethnic Origins: The Adaptation of Cambodian and Hmong Refugees in Four American Cities*. New York: Russell Sage Foundation, 2006.

McCoy, Alfred W. *The Politics of Heroin: CIA Complicity in the Global Drug Trade*. Chicago: Lawrence Hill Books, 2003.

Morrison, Gayle L. *Sky Is Flying: An Oral History of the CIA's Evacuation of the Hmong from Laos*. Jefferson, NC: McFarland and Company, 1999.

Quincy, Keith. *Harvesting Pachay's Wheat: The Hmong and America's Secret War in Laos*. Cheney: Eastern Washington University Press, 2000.

Tapp, Nicholas, Jean Michaud, Christian Culas, and Gary Yia Lee, eds. *Hmong/ Miao in Asia*. Chiang Mai: Silkworm Books, 2004.

Vang, Chia Youyee. *Hmong America: Reconstructing Community in Diaspora*. Urbana and Chicago: University of Illinois Press, 2010.

Warner, Roger. *Back Fire: The CIA's Secret War in Laos and Its Link to the War in Vietnam*. New York: Simon and Schuster, 1995.

Vietnamese Americans in the Context of the Vietnam War

KARÍN AGUILAR-SAN JUAN

In the decades since the end of the Vietnam War, the Vietnamese American community has claimed Little Saigon in Orange County, California, as its unofficial "capital." In other regions, such as San Jose, California; New Orleans, Louisiana; Houston, Texas; Falls Church, Virginia; and Dorchester, Massachusetts, relatively dense but smaller concentrations of Vietnamese exert their influence via radio stations, community development corporations, school districts, and environmental advocacy.[1] Although their political reputation is conservative, in fact their views span from right to left and everywhere in between. Consider for example, Viet Dinh, a key figure behind the USA Patriot Act, versus Tram Nguyen, an activist and author of *We Are All Suspects Now: Untold Stories from Immigrant Communities after 9/11*.[2] Rather than assuming that all Vietnamese are hard-core anticommunists, we should consider Thuy Vo Dang's argument that political stances are part of the "cultural work" that organizes, and disciplines, the Vietnamese American community.[3]

A plethora of organizations reflect many aspects of Vietnamese America, including artists and writers (Diasporic Vietnamese Artists Network, or DVAN), college and university students (Vietnamese Student Association), and community leaders and international policy advocates (National Congress of Vietnamese Americans). This list does not even include Vietnamese Americans who are organized under Asian American, feminist/queer, business, labor, religious, or other banners.[4] Clearly, any syllabus on Vietnamese Americans has plenty of material to cover.

Yet with the Vietnam War as the central frame for inquiry into Vietnamese Americans, an entire arsenal of ideas about war, displacement and migration, racism, and the global dynamics between the United States and Vietnam has already been mobilized. Without proper tools or critical perspectives, an overriding impulse among students and professors alike will be to shrink the complicated Vietnamese American experience into a simple tale of the "desperate turned successful refugee" and to embrace familiar narratives about the war and its aftermath.[5] Consequently, any lesson plan on Vietnamese Americans needs two tracks: one track for thinking about Vietnamese Americans and another for thinking about how the war frame predefines them, thus necessitating alternative frames that reveal and organize their experience in more accurate ways.

The growth of ethnic and Asian American studies—particularly of scholarship by and/or devoted to Vietnamese Americans—has reshaped and reorganized how many of us understand and teach about the era commonly referred to in the United States as "Vietnam." I situate my own teaching and research about Vietnamese Americans in an interdisciplinary Asian American studies context. Particularly because of the glaring absence of Vietnamese American perspectives in mainstream scholarship on the Vietnam War, the feelings, opinions, and perspectives of Vietnamese American students should neither be assumed nor dismissed. Since teaching about Vietnamese Americans in the context of the Vietnam War can be a complicated endeavor fraught with pedagogical and political minefields, I start out with a call for a critical approach that draws its cues from ethnic and Asian American studies, including Vietnamese American studies.[6]

Lessons from Ethnic and Asian American Studies

In Andrew Lam's short story "Show and Tell," an eighth-grade teacher in San Francisco named Mr. K invites the students to give what he calls "oral presentations."[7] The story is worth thinking about even if the lessons we want to create are for older high-school or university students, because the social and psychological dynamics can be similar despite the students' age. "Show and Tell" is told from the point of view of Bobby, a sensitive white boy with southern roots. Cao

Long Nguyen is the new student, introduced to the entire class by the well-meaning Mr. K as "Cao Long Nguyen—Refugee." Since Cao can't speak or understand English, Mr. K enlists Bobby to help Cao get through the lunch line during which the two become friends. Back in class, Billy—who in addition to being the son of a Vietnam vet also reigns as the class bully—shows off his father's army uniform and then delivers a crass litany of war stories, myths about the antiwar movement, and epithets about nasty "VCs." Without even trying, Billy brings Cao to tears. Suddenly, as if inspired by emotion, Cao jumps up and draws his own story on the board. Using hand gestures and facial expressions, he pleads with his new friend to help him, and Bobby ends up providing a spontaneous and heartfelt oral narrative. The story they tell together offers a condensed, teenaged version of an experience that in fact drives an entire field of grown-up inquiry: Vietnamese American studies. Lam's short story is a contribution to this new field.

"Show and Tell" is a useful teaching and learning device for several reasons. The story is told not from Cao's point of view but from Bobby's. Cao is marginalized in the class because he cannot speak English; worse, he is actually given a "refugee" label. If teachers learn only one thing from the story, it should be not to repeat Mr. K's mistake: treating the only Vietnamese person in the room as a unidimensional object whose whole life can be summed up in one label. Accidentally, Mr. K set Cao up for a miserable first day at school. Cao was forced to break his silence and speak out of turn because Billy's rendition of the Vietnam War effectively rendered Cao nonexistent: other than Cao's label, Billy has no useful tools for comprehending a Vietnamese person's life. Cao's spur-of-the-moment drawing, together with Bobby's intuitive narration, comprised a triage decision that a proper lesson plan on Vietnamese American history would have avoided.

What if Mr. K stepped up to the plate and rolled out a one- or two-week lesson plan on Vietnamese Americans? Since some non-Vietnamese students, like Billy, already know too many of the wrong things about the War and others, like Bobby, may be open-minded but clueless about Vietnamese people, Mr. K would do best to start by helping his students become aware of Cao's struggle to be heard, and then follow up with a few carefully selected readings and discussion topics on Vietnamese American history. On the way, Mr. K should remain mindful of the many ways in which Cao's story does and does not capture the reality of many Vietnamese Americans.

Tu-Uyen Nguyen's poem "Silence" serves as the basis for a well-thought-out lesson plan offered as part of a comprehensive high school curriculum on Vietnamese Americans developed by Vietnamese American scholars, teachers, and community advocates in Orange County, California.[8] In the poem a Vietnamese American girl makes it very clear that speaking up is

> not that easy . . . takes many dreams
> and remembering too
> takes my whole being
> takes also you
> so open your ears
> And listen . . .

Using this poem provides many potential ways for students to engage emotionally and personally with the material if they are not Vietnamese; more, the poem helps to diminish the ostracized feeling that Vietnamese Americans might struggle with if they cannot relate other aspects of the course to their lives. The homework assignments ask students to explore the meaning of silence in the poem and then create "identity collages" that invite "self-analysis and self-reflection." But if making art collages and facilitating student-centered self-talk is not up your alley, the bottom line is to develop a noncompetitive activity in which students feel encouraged to position themselves freely and honestly vis-à-vis the topic of silence and Vietnamese American history. Teachers should let go of right and wrong answers if they want all people to contribute to this reflective activity. All students should be empowered to understand themselves, "open their ears," and learn with and about others.

Mr. K's next step would be to lead students through an examination and discussion of how and why Vietnamese came to the United States, and what the experience of becoming Vietnamese American entails. Among the many excellent scholarly resources now available, two come immediately to mind for being relatively short and easy to read: anthropologist James Freeman's *Changing Identities: Vietnamese Americans, 1975–1995*, and artist/activist/literary critic Isabelle Thuy Pelaud's *This Is All I Choose to Tell: History and Hybridity in Vietnamese American Literature*.[9] Freeman's more conventional approach describes the refugee exodus from Vietnam and daily life in refugee camps, and ends with the efforts of Vietnamese Americans, including Amerasians, to express themselves and to become fully part of US society. Freeman's earlier monograph, *Hearts of Sorrow: Vietnamese-American Lives*, offers a sympathetic rendition of the massive losses forced by displacement and migration.[10] While Freeman's benevolent tone continues in *Changing Identities*, so, too, does his anthropological gaze: at times his descriptions of Vietnamese Americans bear a disturbing resemblance to a pet store clerk talking about the habits of strange fish and birds.

For that reason I favor Pelaud's book, which neither exoticizes nor glorifies the subject. Her writing is simple and straightforward, yet the way she leads us through Vietnamese American history and literature is theoretically complex and thought provoking. For example, she divides the book into two parts, "inclusion" and "interpretation." In the first part, she takes only fifteen pages to show Vietnamese Americans as conduits of a history that treats them variously as refugees, immigrants of color, and transnationals. Then she presents an overview of Vietnamese American literature, cast in terms of "hybridity," which provides a treasure trove of suggestions for additional reading, including novels, short stories, and poetry.

Selections from both of these books would allow students, Vietnamese and non-Vietnamese alike, to flesh out the answers to ten common questions.

1. Why did so many Vietnamese people leave Vietnam?
2. How many fled to the United States, or to France, Canada, and Australia?
3. What happened to the people who stayed behind?
4. How is a refugee different from an immigrant?
5. To what extent have Vietnamese kept their cultural identities?
6. What aspects of Vietnameseness have been lost and why?
7. How do Vietnamese Americans compare to other Americans with ancestors from other places?
8. Why do Vietnamese stay in places like Little Saigon?
9. How do Vietnamese Americans feel and think about the "Vietnam War"?
10. How do Vietnamese veterans feel and think about the "Vietnam War"?

These questions can be tweaked and served up in various combinations to form the basis for lectures, as well as many different chains of quick-response or exploration activities, creative assignments, oral presentations, group research projects, essay prompts, and student-led discussions. For example, using colored index cards attached to a clothesline with clothespins, the students can construct an old-fashioned timeline of the Vietnam War that incorporates students' family histories. Along with landmark events from official chronologies of the war, students can contribute one or two events that they have collected in a prior week, perhaps by interviewing friends or family members. Having the option of sharing those personal events with the rest of the class will increase students' overall investment in discussion and reflection.

Keeping in mind that no one wants to feel isolated and alone like Cao, teachers should develop assignments and activities like this time-line so that Vietnamese American students in particular have a dig-nified way to deal with silences and ruptures, to reflect on stories that have been handed down to them, and to acknowledge that they have many things to learn about their own history and the war from other people's points of view. Beware also that "expertise" and "authority" are relative concepts: knowledge derived from books does not always carry the same weight as knowledge born of firsthand experience; similarly, demonstrating one's familiarity with Vietnamese culture or language is not equivalent to growing up in a Vietnamese American community, even if many aspects of culture or language have been lost.

Reframing Vietnamese Americans

The heavy stamp of the Vietnam War and its deeply am-bivalent mark on the US national consciousness forces any systematic inquiry into the Vietnamese American experience to start by addressing the ten basic questions listed above. But as soon the answers to those ten come into view, a chain of much trickier ones immediately appears. Truly understanding the experience of Vietnamese Americans—without boiling everything down into a model minority success story that depends ultimately on the benevolence of the United States—demands close attention to the frames through which Vietnamese Americans are generally viewed.

Only recently have Vietnamese American memories found a place in the historiography of the Vietnam War. As former US allies, their stories, sadly, have been mostly forgotten or dismissed. Even in anthologies about the war, Vietnamese Americans are often ignored.[11] Yet the "good refugee" story is everywhere, tweaked and twisted to overemphasize individual hardship followed by triumph, ostensibly due to a wholehearted embrace of US capitalism and all of its underlying values. As Vietnamese American sociologist Yen Le Espiritu points out, this good refugee story "powerfully remakes the case" for the Vietnam War, and by extension, for all successive US military interventions.[12]

Espiritu makes a significant case against the good refugee story and for "critical refugee studies" that will provoke debate and discussion. A very fruitful use of her essay would be to invite students to read it carefully and develop their own positions on the matter. That is, they should see that Espiritu is not just stating information, but she is making an important argument that intervenes in current scholarly discourse. We should treat such arguments to careful analysis and also come to our own conclusions. First, have students search for scholarly and popular media depictions of Vietnamese Americans. In what ways do these depictions animate the "good refugee" theme? Then assign Espiritu's article with a set of prompts to guide reading and initiate in-class discussion, starting with a series of questions. What kinds of Vietnamese Americans do we encounter in history or literature, on campus, on the street, or at home? If there are so many kinds of Vietnamese people in the United States, why do we think they are all "refugees"? How does the good refugee motif help to make US intervention and imperialism a positive feature of history—and a necessary step for the future? Indeed, once we get a glimpse of what might lie behind the good refugee tale, we can see that real Vietnamese American stories pose immense, multifaceted challenges to preexisting narratives about the war and about what it means to "become American."[13]

War Memories and War Monuments

Perhaps the most fascinating Vietnamese American handling of the legacy of the Vietnam War takes a visual form in *Small Wars*, a book of art photographs by An-My Le.[14] A professor of photography at Bard College, Le came to the United States in 1975 as a refugee. Her book links three projects: "Viet Nam," "Small Wars," and "29 Palms." The first set of images depicts beautiful and sparse landscapes from her country of birth. The second set shows white American men engaged in reenactments of the Vietnam War set in North Carolina. Le appears in several of these pictures, posing as a Viet Cong. The third set focuses on actual combat exercises for the Iraq War at a US military training post in Southern California.

Le's book offers an imaginative counterpoint to stock notions of Vietnamese American memory in relation to the war. Clearly, she is not concerned about establishing an authentic identity for herself, whether Vietnamese or American.[15] Rather than pondering her own Vietnamese Americanness, this photographer has chosen refreshing new parameters that force us to reexamine what we think about the war, the era, and the people to whom the label "Vietnam" refers. Le is not using her photographs to make a speech about war. About her own work, she writes:

> I am not categorically against war. I was more interested in . . . the issues that envelop war—representations of war, landscape and terrain in war. . . . What [war] is meant to do is just horrible. But war can be beautiful. I think it's the idea of the sublime moments that are horrific but, at the same time, beautiful—moments of communion with the landscape and nature. And it's that beauty that I want to embrace in my work. I think that's why the work seems ambiguous.[16]

Thus, *Small Wars* reflects and expounds on representations of and memorials to the war. Not only does she provide a unique Vietnamese American perspective, but she also forces us to think about the relationships between cinematic ideas of "Vietnam" and physical re-creations of that war. In response, students can visit Vietnam War monuments and make their own photographs, drawings, or artistic rubbings (frottage). They can watch *Maya Lin: A Strong Clear Vision*, the documentary film about the Chinese American woman architect who designed the national Vietnam Veterans Memorial in Washington D.C.[17] The film invites a discussion about who is qualified to design a monument to war, and whether such monuments should celebrate or merely memorialize the dead.

In my book, *Little Saigons: Staying Vietnamese in America*, I discuss the towering statue of two soldiers and an eternal torch that the Vietnamese American community in Westminster, Orange County, California, put up for itself in 2003, and the fact that no other US Vietnam War monument even mentions the Vietnamese allies.[18] I also discuss two events, the protests in 1999 (which occurred after a Vietnamese American displayed a picture of Ho Chi Minh in his store) and the VAX

Vietnam War Memorial, Westminster, California. (photo by Larry McDonald, courtesy of Formosa Fountain and Engineering Co.)

controversy that followed it. The shortened title of *The Vietnamese Experience*, VAX was a short-lived MTV-style television show aimed at young Vietnamese Americans. The VAX controversy involved a 2004 episode that included a clip of *Saigon U.S.A.*, a documentary about the Hi-Tek protests that is worth classroom time.[19] Both events provide a rich agenda of questions about the politics of memorializing the war.

What does it mean for Vietnamese Americans to promote their own versions of the war? In what ways must we alter existing narratives of the war in order to make a space for their perspectives?

A very interesting issue to explore is whether or not all Vietnamese American places—even shopping centers like the Asian Garden Mall in Little Saigon, Orange County, California—might be misunderstood by non-Vietnamese as symbols of the Vietnam War because of the way many other Americans continue to see Vietnamese in the United States through a war lens. Even from within the Vietnamese community, among the exile generation for which time has essentially stopped because life in the United States has no more meaning, ethnic business districts can be more important for the way they anchor the past, freezing time, than for the commercial activities that go on there. How does history live on in the public spaces of the present? How do history and memory relate in the communities to which we belong?

Becoming American, Staying Vietnamese

Whereas An-My Le turns the idea of war into an astoundingly creative avenue of departure, other Vietnamese Americans artists and writers express frustration with always being associated with the war. "We refuse to perpetuate telling war stories," writes Danny Nguyen in a collection of works by Vietnamese American artists.[20] In the classroom, the problem is not how to erase the war from a conversation about Vietnamese Americans but rather how to help students relate existing war narratives to Vietnamese American history and literature. It is not only a matter of whether or not Vietnamese people hang onto their war memories—in the case of those born in the United States, they may have none of their own—but also to what extent dominant collective war memories are foisted on them.

Bao Phi is a second-generation Vietnamese American spoken word artist and poet from Minneapolis whose work has galvanized Vietnamese and Asian Americans on college and university campuses across the United States. His spoken-word CD *Refugeography* anthologizes live recordings of his campus performances; Phi's energetic interaction with his audience is especially exciting to hear.[21] Bring Phi to campus or invite students to listen to one or more of his recorded performances. His voice could prompt new spoken-word productions on themes ranging from racism to love, identity, and struggle.

In his subsequent print collection of poems, *Sông I Sing*, Phi takes more time to observe and describe the subtleties of a world ripped apart by racism and poverty and sewn back together with hope and solidarity.[22] Often he seethes with anger. Some readers, caught off guard, might fear and reject his words. For example, in "No Offense," Phi directs his ire toward the Delta Tau Delta fraternity at the University of Florida for throwing a "Mekong Delta" party where men dressed as US soldiers and women as Vietnamese prostitutes. Evidently, after apologizing, the frat held the same party a year later. "You wanted a Mekong Delta party," Phi writes:

> So party on
>
> as your frat house is bombarded
> the roof is on fire
> the roof is on fire
> you will dodge bullets on the dance floor
> your parents will be chained to sewing machines
> to make your uniforms and costumes
> your brothers will turn against you
> your sisters will become prostitutes
> you will starve
> you will get malaria
> you will not be able to get a job
> tanks will roll into your neighborhood
> your children will play with shell casings
> in crater-filled suburbs
>
> there will be nothing left
>
> there will be nothing left
>
> No offense.

Pelaud describes this poem as an "unapologetic reversal of history," adding that when Phi read it to an audience in Oakland, California, in 2004, "an older white woman . . . called Phi a racist."[23] This poem will definitely incite strong reactions. Invite students to pay close attention to the structure and language of the poem. How does the poem make you feel? How does your reaction differ from those of other people in the class? Is the poet's anger justified? If so, why? How does the poem switch from one point of view to another? When do we expect the "good refugee" to appear in the poem, and who shows up instead? Relating back to Espiritu's critical refugee studies statement, we should also ask in what ways the poem challenges the innocence of US aspirations for democracy and freedom around the world. By comparing Phi's work to that of older poets of color in whose footsteps he follows (e.g., Amiri Baraka, Jayne Cortez, Martin Espada, and Sandra Cisneros) and by contextualizing their writing in the context of international struggles for sovereignty and liberation, students may better appreciate Phi's harnessing of rage to build solidarity among Vietnamese Americans.[24]

Phi modulates anger into wisdom across many pages of this book. In a brilliant series of vignettes called "The Nguyens," he gives Vietnamese Americans stories and faces that many readers have never before heard about or seen.

> They sell cars in Orange County, they sell shoes in Queens,
> hustle from White Bear Lake to Frogtown, Minnesota,
> they drawl their way into your heart through Virginia and Texas,
> lost everything to Katrina
> fight for their lives every day in Boston
> bake mango cheesecakes in Oakland and San Francisco
> [. . .]
> They are one story for every Viet body, one song for every voice that
> sings or otherwise, every Vietnamese name is like a tattoo we all wear
> proud, a burst of color dug deep to dance
> across our skins.[25]

Nguyen, like Smith or Jones, is a common Vietnamese surname. But while we probably think of the "Smiths" as upper-middle-class, white, surburbanites with two children and a dog, the "Nguyens" carve out very unusual paths that challenge our assumptions about American success and assimilation. Vu Nguyen pumps iron in a gym and plots revenge against the racism of white men; Kaylee Nguyen delivers a blistering attack against Asian fusion cuisine; John Nguyen rails against war even as he trains as a soldier in Iraq; Dotty Nguyen pleads for reconnection to a mother who has kicked her out of the house for "being a commie"; and Quince Nguyen, "destined for futuresexy," impersonates the rock star Prince onstage during Vietnamese New Year.

With "The Nguyens," Phi creates a platform for a new conversation about Vietnamese Americans. Engage students in a response to these poem portraits. Ask them to form buzz groups in class, or require them to submit tumblr posts with related comments, links, or images before or after class. Do these seem like people you have met before, or people you would like to meet? Are these images positive or negative? What is lost or gained in this homage to ordinary, working-class Vietnamese people?

In the story "Show and Tell," the new Vietnamese kid Cao embodied the good refugee. His shy and nonverbal presence did not take up much space. But if one or more of the Nguyens showed up in class, it would probably be very hard for anyone to ignore them. For one thing, the Nguyens speak English; for another, they have strong personalities and well-developed opinions. If they felt dismissed or insulted, none of the Nguyens would fade into the wall or act like a docile or demure Asian immigrant stereotype. Poorly managed, they could become part of a horrible teaching nightmare. Conversely, if they felt respected and supported, surely the Nguyens would shine as students and might even agree to play leadership roles in class.

If we want to cultivate the minds of students like the Nguyens, we should move beyond teaching "about" Vietnamese Americans and instead strive to teach for, or even with, them. To include the Vietnamese American experience not only as a particular segment of a course about the Vietnam War but in the way we think about the war itself, we should ask:

1. What exactly do Vietnamese American students already know about the Vietnam War, and what do they still need to know?
2. How might their family stories and memories about the war affect their attitudes toward the course, or toward their non-Vietnamese teachers and classmates?
3. How do their non-Vietnamese classmates view them?
4. What kinds of blinders (racist, cultural, ideological, or other) need to be removed so that all students can benefit from the course?
5. What modes of teaching and learning might discourage or encourage students from participating in class discussions or activities? For example, if the professor uses Vietnamese words spoken with a North Vietnamese accent, what signals might be given to students whose families come from South Vietnam?

In fact, the idea of teaching *for and with* Vietnamese Americans, though it poses bigger pedagogical and political challenges than just teaching about them, is not terribly far-fetched. After all, a new

271

generation of Vietnamese American studies scholars—among them historians, literary critics, sociologists, and political scientists—are already out there, teaching, publishing, and influencing the world. The time has come to bring their insights into full view.

Going Beyond the Vietnamese Refugee

With the Vietnam War as primary backdrop for teaching and learning about Vietnamese Americans, a specific arsenal of ideas about history, memory, and identity has already been deployed. This essay makes the case that we should exercise caution and refrain from overusing the "desperate turned successful refugee" model when we teach about Vietnamese Americans. Some scholars argue that the refugee model has more to say about scholarly investments in the narratives of assimilation and the American Dream than it has to say about the actual complexity of Vietnamese American lives. Instead, our students will benefit from considering a wider range of categories for framing the Vietnamese American experience, including gender, sexuality, and class.

To press the matter even further, an accurate portrayal of Vietnamese people in the aftermath of the US war in Vietnam should not focus narrowly on Vietnamese Americans. After all, the majority of Vietnamese people remained in the country after the war; those people continue to play important roles in their national history as citizens and government leaders, and in the global economy as workers and businesspeople. How do those people memorialize the US war, and to what extent would the younger generations in Vietnam be interested in the same lessons we are creating for their peers here in the United States?

Finally, the dispersal of Vietnamese around the globe in the aftermath of the war has led to an emerging interest in "diaspora studies." A special issue of *Amerasia Journal* was devoted to the Vietnamese diaspora in 2003. Music, art, literature, and people travel across borders, in and out of Vietnam, making the lines of ethnicity, culture, and race even more difficult to discern. Yet according to Pelaud, the field of Vietnamese diaspora studies is still sparse; properly vetted, scholarly information is hard to find.[26] Still, upward of three million Vietnamese in Canada, Australia, France, and the rest of Europe constitute a large enough population to merit further study.

NOTES

1. See *A Village Called Versailles*, directed by Leo Chiang (New York: New Day Films, 2008), for the moving story of New Orleans' Vietnamese organizing against toxic dumping in the aftermath of Hurricane Katrina; and Eric Tang, "A Gulf Unites Us: The Vietnamese Americans of Black New Orleans East," *American Quarterly* 63, no. 1 (March 2011): 117–49, for an excellent analysis of cross-racial solidarity among Vietnamese and blacks in that context.

2. Tram Nguyen, *We Are All Suspects Now: Untold Stories from Immigrant Communities after 9/11* (Boston: Beacon Press, 2005).

3. Thuy Vo Dang, "The Cultural Work of Anticommunism in the San Diego Vietnamese American Community," *Amerasia Journal* 31, no. 2 (2005): 65–85.

4. See Gina Masequesmay, "Emergence of Queer Vietnamese America," *Amerasia Journal* 29, no. 1 (2003): 117–36; and Gina Masequesmay and Sean Metzger, *Embodying Asian/American Sexualities* (Lanham, MD: Lexington Books, 2009), for material on sexuality and lesbian/gay/bisexual/transgender Vietnamese Americans.

5. Yên Lê Espiritu, a Vietnamese American sociologist and also a key leader in the field of Asian American studies, has advanced the complete and critical statement about how we should understand and approach the "figure of the Vietnamese refugee" in US scholarship and popular discourse. See Yên Lê Espiritu, "Toward a Critical Refugee Study: The Vietnamese Refugee Subject in U.S. Scholarship," *Journal of Vietnamese Studies* 1, nos. 1–2 (February–August 2006): 410–33.

6. One of the major tenets of ethnic and Asian American studies is that racialized minority groups should speak for and represent themselves, rather than be spoken for by experts from dominant or majority groups. A related assumption is that everyone sees and understands the world from a particular vantage point, meaning that all of our perspectives are situated and invested, rather than universal or value free. Jean Yu-Wen Shen Wu's *Asian American Studies: A Reader* (New Brunswick, NJ: Rutgers University Press, 2009) provides an excellent point of departure for Asian American studies as a base of inquiry into Vietnamese American communities. Nevertheless, as Espiritu notes in "Toward a Critical Refugee Study," Asian American studies has had an "uneasy alliance" with Vietnamese American studies.

7. Andrew Lam, "Show and Tell," in *Watermark: Vietnamese American Poetry and Prose*, ed. Barbara Tran, Monique T. D. Truong, and Luu Truong Khoi (New York: Asian American Writers' Workshop, 1998).

8. The Orange County Asian and Pacific Islander Community Alliance (OCAPICA) 2001 resource is available at http://www.tolerance.org /magazine/number-25-spring-2004/vietnamese-americans-lessons-american-history, a project of the Southern Poverty Law Center (accessed June 28, 2012).

The poem "Silence" is available at http://www.tolerance.org/supplement /silence (accessed June 28, 2012).

9. James Freeman, *Changing Identities: Vietnamese Americans, 1975–1995* (Boston: Allyn and Bacon, 1996); Isabelle Thuy Pelaud, *This Is All I Choose to Tell: History and Hybridity in Vietnamese American Literature* (Philadelphia: Temple University Press, 2010).

10. James Freeman, *Hearts of Sorrow: Vietnamese-American Lives* (Palo Alto, CA: Stanford University Press, 1991).

11. For example, H. Bruce Franklin's *The Vietnam War in American Stories, Songs, and Poems* (Boston: Bedford, 1996) includes Asian American writers but no Vietnamese Americans. On the other hand, Christian Appy's *Patriots: The Vietnam War Remembered from All Sides* (New York: Viking, 2003) is a compendium of war reflections that includes a few Vietnamese American voices, and his introductory essay acknowledges their views in a meaningful way.

12. Espiritu, "Toward a Critical Refugee Study."

13. It has taken decades and many folds, or cycles, of history for Asian American studies scholars to contemplate fully and become one with the anti-communist/postwar/exilic perspectives of their Vietnamese American colleagues. After all, Asian American studies emerged as an educational extension of the Asian American social movement of the 1970s. Protests against the Vietnam War heightened political solidarities as Asian American activists saw their own faces in racist depictions of the wartime enemy. Asian Americanists have since found ways to talk about racism and US imperialism that acknowledges and treats as legitimate the distinct position and agency of Vietnamese refugees. As a result, Vietnamese American scholarship has inherited a many-sided lineage.

14. An-My Le, Richard B. Woodward, and Hilton Als, *Small Wars* (New York: Aperture, 2005).

15. I do not mean to dismiss art or literature that is concerned explicitly with identity. For example, Julie Thi Underhill's beautiful photographs of Vietnam, including her Cham relatives, represent an important and personal search for connection and self. Underhill is a member of DVAN.

16. An-My Le, http://blog.art21.org/2007/10/30/spotlight-on-protest-an-my-le/ (accessed June 30, 2012).

17. Freida Lee Mock et al., *Maya Lin: A Strong Clear Vision* (New York: Docurama, 2003).

18. Karin Aguilar-San Juan, *Little Saigons: Staying Vietnamese in America* (Minneapolis: University of Minnesota Press, 2009).

19. *Saigon, U.S.A.*, directed by Lindsey Jang and Robert C. Winn (Los Angeles: KOCE-TV, 2004), DVD.

20. Cited in Pelaud, *This Is All I Choose to Tell*, 59.

21. Bao Phi, *Refugeography* (Minneapolis: Bao Phi, 2005), audio CD.

22. Bao Phi, *Sông I Sing: Poems* (Minneapolis: Coffee House Press, 2011).
23. Pelaud, *This Is All I Choose to Tell*, 42.
24. For an important discussion of Afro-Asian solidarity in the context of the Vietnam War, see Vijay Prashad, *Everybody Was Kung Fu Fighting: Afro-Asian Connections and the Myth of Cultural Purity* (Boston: Beacon Press, 2001), chapter 5, "Kung Fusion."
25. Phi, *Sông I Sing*, 17.
26. Pelaud, *This Is All I Choose to Tell*, 141, n. 9.

KEY RESOURCES

Aguilar-San Juan, Karín. *Little Saigons: Staying Vietnamese in America*. Minneapolis: University of Minnesota Press, 2009.
Appy, Christian G. *Patriots: The Vietnam War Remembered from All Sides*. New York: Viking, 2003.
Freeman, James M. *Hearts of Sorrow: Vietnamese-American Lives*. Stanford, CA: Stanford University Press, 1989.
Le, An-My, Richard B. Woodward, and Hilton Als. *Small Wars*. New York: Aperture, 2005.
Mock, Freida Lee, et al. *Maya Lin: A Strong Clear Vision*. New York: Docurama, 2003.
Orange County Asian and Pacific Islander Community Alliance, *Vietnamese Americans: Lessons in American History, an Interdisciplinary Curriculum and Resource Guide*. Orange County, CA: Orange County Asian and Pacific Islander Community Alliance, 2001.
Phi, Bao. *Refugeography*. Minneapolis: Bao Phi, 2005. Audio CD.
———. *Sông I Sing: Poems*. Minneapolis: Coffee House Press, 2011.

The Tet Offensive in the Classroom

ANDREW WIEST

Teaching the Tet Offensive is always quite rewarding, in part due to Tet's unparalleled centrality to the outcome of the war and its role in the public perception of the Vietnam War era. For most who lived through that period, Tet and its aftermath remain etched in their memories—memories intimately intertwined with the societal tumult of 1968. The separate roiling streams that made up the 1960s all seemed to crash together in that fateful year. Tet shook the very foundations of the nation and felled a powerful president. A few months later Martin Luther King died at the hands of an assassin, and hundreds of cities went up in flames. In June, Robert F. Kennedy was assassinated following his victory in the California Democratic Primary. In August, riots raged through the streets of Chicago during the Democratic National Convention. To many observers America seemed to be slipping closer and closer to a state of anarchy or toward another Civil War. Tet was perhaps the most important part of, and cannot be separated from, the fateful year 1968. Thus, helping students understand Tet and its relevance to international and domestic contexts is essential for teachers of the Vietnam War.

Origins

By the end of 1967, the level of frustration was palpable in the Saigon headquarters of Military Assistance Command Vietnam (MACV). When the United States took over the fighting of the Vietnam War in 1965, Lieutenant General William Westmoreland had forecast

276

that the conflict would reach a favorable conclusion in only three years. His plan had been brutally simple. Utilizing lavish firepower support, ranging from artillery to helicopter gunships to massive B-52 bombers, American forces would pound North Vietnamese and Viet Cong (VC) military forces into submission, "bleeding them until Hanoi wakes up to the fact that they have bled their country to the point of national disaster for generations."[1] But communist forces had refused to play by Westmoreland's rules. Instead of standing and fighting, the Viet Cong and North Vietnamese had mainly avoided pitched battles, choosing instead to festoon the countryside with mines and booby traps and rely on ambushes and surprise attacks before slipping across the border to the safety of their base areas in Cambodia and Laos. As 1967 drew to a close Westmoreland saw that his strategy was pushing the communists to the breaking point, but he had little to show for his efforts except for a single, grim statistic—body count. By the end of 1967 the United States had lost 16,250 killed in Vietnam, while inflicting an estimated 143,000 battle deaths on enemy forces. Even though the communists fought on, Westmoreland believed that the end had to be in sight.

On the American home front, though, President Lyndon Johnson faced a singular problem. Although he regularly received positive reports on the war from MACV, public support for the war was slipping dramatically. When the Marines had splashed ashore at Da Nang in 1965, public support for the war had stood at 80 percent, but by the fall of 1967, support for the war had dipped to only 40 percent. Scapegoats for the sorry situation abounded, ranging from antidraft protests to the growth of the counterculture, but one cause stood out above all others. Westmoreland's military victories, his bleeding of enemy forces, had failed to resonate with the American public. There were no pins to move on maps to show the progress of US troops toward the enemy capital and assured victory. Vietnam was not a war about taking and holding territory; it was a war about attrition of the enemy's will to fight. In the view of MACV and the White House the war was being won, but that was something that the public could not or would not see.

In October 1967 an estimated one hundred thousand antiwar protesters descended on the National Mall in Washington, D.C., garnering national headlines with their serious messages and their attempt to levitate the Pentagon. Determined to retake ownership of the narrative of the war, the Johnson administration went on the offensive, blitzing the airwaves and talk shows with appearances by leading Cabinet and military figures, including Secretary of Defense Robert McNamara, who gave optimistic, even cheery, reports on the progress being made by US and South Vietnamese forces in the war. Most important was a visit to the home front by William Westmoreland, who, in November 1967, predicted, "We have reached an important point when the end begins to come into view. . . . The enemy's hopes are bankrupt."[2] His timing could not have been worse.

For their part, the Vietnamese communists were no less frustrated in 1967. They had hoped to unify Vietnam under their control long ago, but American intervention had changed everything. Propped up by over half a million American troops, South Vietnam was proving far more resilient than the North Vietnamese had expected. The Americans had done great damage not only to communist forces in the south but also to the nation and economy of the north through their ongoing bombing campaign, dubbed Operation Rolling Thunder. With more and more of its blood and strength directed south along the Ho Chi Minh Trail, the communists, too, had little to show for years of war other than a generation of young men killed in combat.

An argument brewed in the Politburo of the Democratic Republic of Vietnam. Proponents of a protracted war of attrition, including North Vietnam's famed military leader Vo Nguyen Giap, stood in favor of business as usual in the conflict in the south. Le Duan, secretary general of the Vietnam Worker's Party, argued that the strategy of attrition of American forces had failed and that North Vietnamese and Viet Cong forces should adopt a more aggressive strategy, but not a strategy aimed at defeating the mighty Americans. Their firepower was simply too great. Instead they favored a strategy aimed at what Le Duan and his supporters in the Politburo believed to be the enemy's weak points—the South Vietnamese military and wavering American support for the war on the US home front. In April 1967 the Thirteenth Plenum passed Resolution 13, ending the protracted war in the south in favor of an audacious plan aimed at seizing immediate victory—a plan that would become known as the Tet Offensive.[3]

A preparatory phase of the offensive began in the autumn of 1967, which involved attacks designed both to lure American forces away from the urban areas of South Vietnam and to mask a massive buildup of communist forces throughout the region. The offensive itself was timed to coincide with the onset of the Tet lunar new year in Vietnam, by far the nation's most important holiday and a traditional time of cease-fire. A force of over eighty-four thousand VC and North Vietnamese Army (NVA) fighters gathered in secrecy in tunnels, jungles, and base areas near South Vietnam's major urban areas. With the cities defended by the South Vietnamese as the Americans fought in the countryside, the communists planned to attack simultaneously across the country. Le Duan believed that the South Vietnamese military would crumble and the South Vietnamese people would rise up in support of the revolution, and that the collapse of the South Vietnamese state would convince the Americans of the hopelessness of their cause and bring about the end of the conflict.[4]

Tet as History

With American attention distracted by the ongoing siege by an estimated twenty thousand NVA troops of the US Marine base at Khe Sanh, at once a diversion to mask the coming of the Tet Offensive and part of the overall communist plan to expel the Americans from Vietnam, NVA and VC forces all over South Vietnam made ready for their coordinated attacks. In the early morning of January 30, 1968, the NVA and VC launched their offensive, with more than eighty thousand troops simultaneously attacking most of the major urban areas across the length and breadth of South Vietnam.

Much of the military storm understandably centered on Saigon, a city teeming with more than two million inhabitants that served as both South Vietnam's national capital and the nerve center of the US–South Vietnamese war effort. Thirty-five battalions struck six major targets across the city, including the Presidential Palace, the government radio station, the American embassy, and Tan Son Nhut Airbase. Instead of an organized attempt to overthrow Saigon, the communists hoped to paralyze government control of the city, cripple South Vietnamese military forces, and screen Saigon from interference from US troops—all of which would serve to spur the hoped for general uprising by the South Vietnamese people.

As part of the wider communist offensive in Saigon, nineteen men from the VC C-10 Sapper Battalion blew a hole into the wall surrounding the US embassy on Thong Nhat Boulevard and then opened fire in the embassy courtyard with automatic weapons and rockets. In a six-hour battle all of the VC fighters were killed or captured, without ever having penetrated the embassy proper. Having heard the gunfire and commotion, several members of the US media contingent in Saigon made their way to the embassy to cover the fighting, sending home alarming reports of the struggle for control over the seat of US authority in South Vietnam. In an attempt to quell the rumors of a communist takeover of the embassy, shortly after 9:00 a.m., General Westmoreland arrived to lead an impromptu tour with reporters to demonstrate that the embassy was firmly in US hands and that the communist plan for Tet had failed.

The backdrop for the tour, amid the rubble and scattered VC bodies, though, could not have been more disastrous for US policy in Vietnam. To millions of American citizens, the attack on the embassy, whether it failed or not, meant that there was no place in Vietnam that was safe— the enemy could and would attack anywhere. As news continued to pour in about Tet attacks all over South Vietnam, Westmoreland's confidence seemed more and more out of touch with reality. His predictions of an imminent communist collapse, made only two months prior, now seemed either badly misguided or outright fabrications. An enormous credibility gap ripped into the American body politic, a gap that would only widen as news of the Tet Offensive continued to hit the newspapers and airwaves of the American home front.

All across Saigon the VC had used surprise to make substantial initial gains, but it was met on all fronts with swift and powerful counterstrokes. The same was true throughout South Vietnam. The South Vietnamese population did not rise up in favor of the revolution; the South Vietnamese military did not crumble. With the failure of their wider revolutionary goals, VC and NVA forces stood vulnerable and exposed to massive US and South Vietnamese firepower. Normally, guerrilla forces survive by not standing and fighting. In Tet the guerrillas stood and fought, with predictable results. Across Saigon and throughout South Vietnam the VC fighters were slaughtered in the tens of thousands, tenaciously holding on to their meager gains.

Battles raged for days in several cities in South Vietnam, following the same general pattern. Fighting was especially grim in Quang Tri, Dalat, and My Tho, but once again much of the most severe fighting was reserved for Saigon. Even after the VC had been forced to abandon its most valuable targets, the Tet struggle lingered on in the rabbit warren of streets and alleys that make up the Cholon district, near to the Phy Tho racetrack. In desperation the remaining VC forces in the city fought to the end there, in part attempting to use the teeming

Viet Cong suspects captured during the Tet Offensive, February 1, 1968. (VA030787, Donald Jellema Collection, The Vietnam Center and Archive, Texas Tech University)

population of the area as cover. To achieve victory there, US and South Vietnamese forces had to evacuate the population, declare the area a free fire zone, and devastate many of the buildings with artillery fire and air strikes.

The Tet Offensive in Saigon had been a costly victory for US and South Vietnamese forces, but one that was quickly obscured in part by one of the most important media moments of the entire war. On February 1, near the An Quang Pagoda in Saigon, Vietnamese Marines brought a VC prisoner, clad in civilian clothing, to Brigadier General Nguyen Ngoc Loan, chief of South Vietnam's National Police. Loan placed a revolver to the prisoner's head and fired. The scene was captured by both Associated Press (AP) still photographer Eddie Adams and Vo Suu, a television cameraman for the NBC television network. The next day Adams's still photo appeared on the front pages of newspapers across the country, preempting the Johnson administration's attempt to put a positive spin on the events of the Tet Offensive.

Matters only worsened when Suu's footage appeared on the *Huntley-Brinkley Report* that evening.[5] Americans, already in shock over the suddenness of the Tet Offensive, were horrified by the brutal nature of Loan's actions, and more and more came to question their support for the war and America's ally South Vietnam.

The Tet Offensive reached its climax in the city of Hue, Vietnam's old imperial capital, located on the Perfume River. Understanding the powerful psychological value of the city, at the outset of Tet nearly eight thousand men of the NVA's Fourth and Sixth Regiments invaded Hue, seizing most of the walled Citadel and Imperial Palace to the north of the river, as well as much of the new city to the south. As the dire nature of the situation slowly dawned on US and South Vietnamese military leaders, reinforcements began to trickle into the stricken city, heralding an urban battle in which US Marines and South Vietnamese forces struggled from house to house and room to room to retake the city against dogged NVA resistance.

In a hellish inferno more reminiscent of Stalingrad in World War II than the jungle fighting most commonly associated with Vietnam, by February 9 the US Marines had cleared most of the city south of the river, while the struggle for the Citadel raged on. It was only when the South Vietnamese government assented to the use of heavy weaponry and air strikes in the Citadel that swift progress was made north of the river, destroying much of the historic city in the process. In the Citadel, the seat of Vietnamese emperors and kings, NVA defenders fought with fanaticism born of desperation, leading to hand-to-hand fighting for nearly every square foot of urban rubble. The fighting only came to an end on February 24, when South Vietnamese forces once again raised their flag above the Citadel. The struggle, though, had proven quite costly, with over 50 percent of the city destroyed and more than 100,000 homeless out of a population of 140,000. Tragically, as South Vietnamese rule returned to Hue, mass graves were discovered around the city. During their brief period of rule, communist forces had rounded up and killed more than three thousand civilians, leaving Americans and South Vietnamese alike to wonder what horrors might lay in store if South Vietnam ever fell to communist rule.

Coupled with the failure of the seventy-seven-day siege of Khe Sanh, the Tet Offensive stood as a military catastrophe for the North Vietnamese and VC. They had achieved none of their stated tactical goals, and had lost over fifty thousand dead out of a total force of eighty-four thousand—a staggering fatal casualty rate of nearly 60 percent. The South Vietnamese people had not risen up, and the South Vietnamese military had not collapsed, leading to the uncomfortable conclusion that South Vietnam was far stronger than most in the north had predicted. The VC had been devastated as a fighting force, and the remaining cadres had to retreat far into the countryside to rebuild almost from scratch. More and more North Vietnamese would have to make their way down the Ho Chi Minh Trail to make good the losses, a process that would last for months, if not years. The communists would fight on, but their defeat seemed comprehensive.

Amid the rubble of their failed offensive, though, there was hope. The American home front had been badly jolted by the shock of Tet, severely draining support for an already controversial war. Having toured the sites of the fighting in Saigon and after witnessing the waning moments of the battle for Hue, broadcaster Walter Cronkite returned to his CBS studio to prepare a special *Report from Vietnam*. The program aired on February 27 to an estimated audience of nine million. The "most trusted man in America" closed by stating:

> We have been too often disappointed by the optimism of the American leaders, both in Vietnam and Washington, to have faith any longer in the silver linings they find in the darkest clouds. . . . To say that we are closer to victory today is to believe, in the face of the evidence, the optimists who have been wrong in the past. . . . To say that we are mired in stalemate seems the only realistic, yet unsatisfactory, conclusion. . . . It is increasingly clear to this reporter that the only rational way out then will be to negotiate, not as victors, but as an honorable people who lived up to their pledge to defend democracy, and did the best they could.

After viewing the broadcast a despondent Lyndon Johnson turned to one of his aides and said, "If I've lost Cronkite, I've lost middle America."

Still confident that he had won a great military victory, but unable to come to grips with the volatile situation at home, Westmoreland made a secret request for more than two hundred thousand additional troops to press on to victory. When his request leaked to the public, it was another nail in the coffin of the credibility of the US government and military in the Vietnam War. If we had won such a great victory, why did we need more troops not less? Why was the troop request made in secret? What more did the government have to hide? Protests, which had already taken their toll on Johnson's psyche as early as 1967, sprung up across the nation as more and more people lost confidence in their leadership. The situation was so grave that two Democrats, Eugene McCarthy and Robert F. Kennedy, mounted powerful primary challenges to a sitting president of their own party—something almost unheard of in modern American history—challenges based on ending the Vietnam War. Amid the brewing storm, Johnson received the worst news of all. After studying Westmoreland's troop request in detail, Johnson's new secretary of defense, Clark Clifford, not only advised Johnson to reject the request but also informed the president that the United States should exit the conflict entirely.

With his war and his presidency unraveling around him, on March 31 Johnson delivered one of the most stunning televised speeches in American presidential history. First he informed the American people that the bombing of North Vietnam would cease and that the flow of reinforcements to Vietnam would end, as much as admitting that the war there had been lost. He closed his speech with a bombshell about which only he and his speech writer were aware.

> With America's sons in fields far away, with America's future under challenge right here at home . . . I do not believe that I should devote an hour or a day of my time to any personal partisan causes. . . . Accordingly, I shall not seek, and I will not accept, the nomination of my party for another term as your president.

The Tet Offensive, which had been such a crushing tactical defeat for the VC and North Vietnamese, was the signature moment that stood as the tipping point in the Vietnam War. What had once been a wildly popular war on the home front now became a political albatross—a war in need of a politically acceptable exit strategy instead of a war to be won. While it took the United States almost five more years to extricate itself from its Vietnam adventure, the Tet Offensive was certainly the beginning of the end of America's involvement in the Vietnam War.

Teaching Tet

Accessing and making sense of such an important series of events in the classroom can rightfully seem quite daunting. I have found that having students collect oral histories from participants helps to make the events of Tet and its era come to life. When discussing campaigns like Tet, though, sometimes finding veterans to interview who served in that particular narrow window of the war can be overwhelmingly difficult. But this is what makes Tet unique: in many ways everyone who lived through 1968 is a "veteran" of Tet and its attendant national fallout. Students can choose to interview their grandparents or the owner of a local business or the men and women at one of the meetings of the local Veterans of Foreign Wars chapter. Some will interview men who participated in the fighting, or who at least view the events of 1968 with the eyes of a soldier. Others will work with men and women who marched with protest signs on their college campuses in 1968. Some will speak with people for whom the loss of King was one of the formative moments of their lives.

Most, though, will interview people who have a much less direct connection to events—people who watched the discord and violence from afar on the nightly news, people who hardly consider themselves "veterans" but nonetheless represent the vast majority of the population at the time and have vivid memories to share. Considering the importance of the public reactions to Tet, almost anyone who was alive and old enough to remember 1968 is a potential interview subject. The results of such a class oral history project can provide a rich tapestry of viewpoints on one of the formative events in recent American history. Students will be able to compare competing versions and visions of the time—those of military men, housewives, college students, members of the civil rights movement, liberals, and conservatives. These histories will demonstrate the complexity of events and the difficulty of making hard and fast judgments concerning historical "certainties," and they will highlight the point that Tet's influence extended far beyond the battlefield. Additionally, in my experience, teaching Tet through the use of local oral history resources is very rewarding for both the interviewers and interviewees. The students learn much about the lives of people they often have known for years, while the interviewees have their past experiences validated by the process. Finally, the interviewing serves to collect valuable history before it is lost and forms contacts between the teaching unit, whether university, college, or high school, and the local community.[6]

The Tet Offensive had two very distinct faces—one of bloody victory as presented by the military and the Johnson administration, and another of doubt and near despair as presented by much of the American media.

The competing portrayals of Tet might seem mutually exclusive. In today's digitized world, though, students can access a vast array of documents to better come to grips with how the viewpoints of the time were reached and informed. While the same can be undertaken for very nearly every major event in the Vietnam War, Tet is one of the most fruitful subjects for such a classroom exercise. To access the military view of an event, students can visit the website of the Vietnam Virtual Archive at Texas Tech University, where they can easily locate military after action reports for most major battles. As one example I accessed the after-action report of Task Force X-Ray, commanded by the US Marine Corps, which engaged in much of the fighting to retake the city of Hue. The document (Record #226641) is located at http://www.viet nam.ttu.edu/virtualarchive/items.php?item=1201062076. The report gives a fascinating look at the day-to-day slog of the fighting to retake the city. It is strictly military and gives no flowery reports of battles won, but it is careful to point out that the struggle for Hue was *in fact* a major victory—a victory in which the Marines of Task Force X-Ray fought hard, killing 1,959 enemy combatants at a cost of 142 Marine dead. The victory was indeed heralded as a model of Marine/US Army/South Vietnamese cooperation.

Newspaper reports on the fighting in Vietnam are often a bit harder to find, since most have not been digitized or do not allow free access. Fortunately for teachers and their students, most public libraries and almost all academic libraries will provide access to the *New York Times* and a few other major newspapers' and magazines' archives online. Nonetheless, to access the reports and editorials students might have to go to the library and use microfilm copies, a useful experience in and of itself. A first interesting point for students is to discern whether there was a difference between national and local reporting on events. Were local papers more supportive of the military view than the majority of national news outlets? On the national level, though, the reporting of events was quite different than what students will have seen in after-action reports. A headline in *Life* on February 23, even as the Marines were closing in on victory in Hue, declared, "Wherever We Look, Something Is Wrong." In covering the battle for Hue, *Los Angeles Times* correspondent William Tuohy wrote that US Marines had been poorly supplied, that their chain of command had been confused, and that there had been little cooperation between the Marines and the South Vietnamese—a situation that was reported to be so bad that General Westmoreland himself was greatly dissatisfied.[7]

Eddie Adams's photo of Nguyen Ngoc Loan. (AP Images)

With two such different accounts of the same historical events to hand, instructors can organize a classroom debate, with one side representing the military and the other the media. Another option is to have students write a short paper or engage in a classroom discussion outlining how and why a singular event can be seen in such different ways by different audiences. Either way, accessing the documents allows students to come to grips with the controversies of the Vietnam War in an up-close and hands-on manner.

In rounding out my teaching on Tet, I often like to focus on the bigger story behind one of the signature moments of the war to demonstrate the complexities of the Vietnam War and its aftermath. After snapping his photograph of Nguyen Ngoc Loan executing the VC prisoner, Eddie Adams became famous, even winning a Pulitzer Prize. But, as time went on, the photographer began to question his most memorable work. Adams knew that just moments before the photograph was taken several of Nguyen Ngoc Loan's men had been gunned down by the VC. Adams also knew that Loan was a respected warrior taking part in a long and brutal civil war, a warrior who concentrated much of his energies on helping South Vietnamese poor. While he certainly did not condone the killing of the unarmed VC soldier, Adams was made very uneasy by the reaction to his photo—a photo that was only a single moment frozen in time. It was a photo that affected the judgment of many Americans on the nature of the war in Vietnam, but it was also a photo that provided no context for that judgment.

After the war was over, Nguyen Ngoc Loan, like so many supporters of the South Vietnamese government, fled to the United States to start his life anew. His moment of infamy, however, followed him to his new country. Trying to make it as a small businessman, the former general opened a pizzeria in northern Virginia. Initially things went well, but soon the identity of the restaurant's owner slipped out. Protesters flocked to the site; patrons refused to enter. The man in the photo was not welcome, and the restaurant had to close.

Watching events unfold from afar, Eddie Adams felt a deep pang of regret and was aghast at the effect of his famous photograph on the life of Nguyen Ngoc Loan. Adams made his feelings public in a *Time* magazine eulogy written after Loan's death in 1998.

> I won a Pulitzer Prize in 1969 for a photograph of one man shooting another. Two people died in that photograph: the recipient of the bullet and General Nguyen Ngoc Loan. The general killed the Viet Cong; I killed the general with my camera. Still photographs are the most powerful weapon in the world. People believe them, but photographs do lie, even without manipulation. They are only half-truths. What the photograph didn't say was, "What would you do if you were the general at that time and place on that hot day, and you caught the so-called bad guy after he blew away one, two or three American soldiers?" General Loan was what you would call a real warrior, admired by his troops. I'm not saying what he did was right, but you have to put yourself in his position. The photograph also doesn't say that the general devoted much of his time trying to get hospitals built in Vietnam for war casualties. This picture really messed up his life. He never blamed me. He told me if I hadn't taken the picture, someone else would have, but I've felt bad for him and his family for a long time. I had kept in contact with him; the last time we spoke was about six months ago, when he was very ill. I sent flowers when I heard that he had died and wrote, "I'm sorry. There are tears in my eyes."[8]

Utilizing Adams's photo in the classroom allows access to, and discussion of, a variety of important issues. Before discussing the after story of the photograph, ask the students to analyze what they see. Was it a brutal case of a military man executing a helpless civilian? Ask them for their immediate reactions to the photo—disgust, horror? Then ask them to discuss what the photograph might *not* show about the event. Who were both men? Why did one execute the other? It is important that the horror of the event never recede too far into the background, but a thorough analysis of the photo is a teaching moment that can lead to a discussion of one of the most vexing qualities of war—as a true moral quagmire. Was Loan only a brutal killer? Was he a man who was too intimately familiar with death and killing to discern the moral breach of his actions? Or was he simply a man forced to choose between bad and worse options?

Making sense of the most famous photograph of the Vietnam War and coming to terms with the complexities that it represents has implications beyond the study of a long ago war. In today's world of war reporting, unattributed images without an accompanying story increasingly stand on their own as glimpses into far-flung battlefields. Whether based on Twitter updates from the streets of the Arab Spring, YouTube footage of snipers firing on a crowd of civilians in Syria, or furtive photos of protesters on the media-starved streets of Tehran—our understanding of present and future conflicts will seemingly come to rely more and more on our ability to analyze the meaning of single images or short clips of film. Using the photograph of this infamous Tet event will help our students appreciate the importance of context, perspective, and asking additional questions. All of these lessons will benefit them in their work as students and citizens.

Conclusion

The Tet Offensive was many things and, as such, perhaps best represents the multifaceted nature—the even schizophrenic nature—of the Vietnam War. Tet was at once a major US–South Vietnamese military victory and a corresponding devastating defeat for the North Vietnamese and VC. Tet, however, was also the blow that effectively derailed the US war effort and led to ultimate communist victory. To Westmoreland and the Johnson administration Tet was the chance for which they had been waiting—a chance to deal a devastating blow to their elusive enemy. To the US public, however, Tet, as seen through the eyes of media reporting of events, was anything but a victory. Tet was instead the moment when the government's excessive optimism and outright lies came home to roost. But, as is the case with most historical events, Tet was not simply black or white, as it is often portrayed. Instead Tet was made up of myriad shades of gray. Indeed, even what should be the most obvious case of simplicity in judgment—one of a general executing an unarmed man on a street corner in Saigon—in retrospect also stands as a testament to the complex narrative that was and is the Tet Offensive.

NOTES

1. Quoted in Edward Murphy, *Semper Fi Vietnam: From Da Nang to the DMZ, Marine Corps Campaigns, 1965–1975* (Novato, CA: Presidio, 1997), 37–38.
2. James Willbanks, "The Battle for Hue, 1968," in *Block by Block: The Challenges of Urban Operations*, ed. William Robertson and Lawrence Yates (Fort Leavenworth, KS: US Army Command and General Staff College Press, 2003), 123. Also see James Willbanks, *The Tet Offensive: A Concise History* (New York: Columbia University Press, 2006).
3. Willbanks, *The Tet Offensive*, 10.
4. Ibid., 11.
5. Don Oberdorfer, *Tet! The Turning Point of the Vietnam War* (New York: Da Capo, 1971), 161–70.
6. For more on how to prepare for an oral history project, see Andrew Darien's essay in this volume.
7. William Hammond, *Reporting Vietnam* (Lawrence: University Press of Kansas, 1998), 121–22.
8. *Time*, July 27, 1998.

KEY RESOURCES

Adams, Eddie. "The Pictures that Burn in My Memory." *Parade*, May 15, 1983, 4–6.
Allison, William. *The Tet Offensive: A Brief History with Documents*. New York: Routledge, 2008.
Braestrup, Peter. *Big Story: How the American Press and Television Reported and Interpreted the Crisis of Tet 1968 in Vietnam and Washington*. Boulder, CO: Westview Press, 1977.
Hammel, Eric. *Fire in the Streets: The Battle for Hue, Tet 1968*. Chicago: Contemporary Books, 1991.
Lung, Col. Hoang Ngoc. *The General Offensives of 1968–69*. Indochina Monographs. Washington, DC: Center of Military History, 1981.

Nolan, William Keith. *The Battle for Hue: Tet, 1968.* Novato, CA: Presidio, 1983.
———. *The Battle for Saigon: Tet 1968.* New York: Pocket Books, 1996.
Oberdorfer, Don. *Tet.* New York: Doubleday, 1971.
Prados, John, and Ray W. Stubbe. *Valley of Decision: The Siege of Khe Sanh.* Boston: Houghton Mifflin, 1991.
Smith, George W. *The Siege at Hue.* Boulder CO: Lynne Rienner , 1999.
Warr, Nicholas. *Phase Line Green: The Battle for Hue, 1968.* Annapolis: Naval Institute Press, 1997.
Wiest, Andrew. *The Vietnam War, 1956–1975.* New York: Osprey, 2002.
———. *Vietnam's Forgotten Army: Heroism and Betrayal in the ARVN.* New York: New York University Press, 2008.
Willbanks, James. *The Tet Offensive: A Concise History.* New York: Columbia University Press, 2006.

Teaching the Collective Memory and Lessons of the Vietnam War

DAVID FITZGERALD and

DAVID RYAN

The US collective memory and the lessons of the Vietnam War remain highly contentious. This essay advances suggestions on how to teach and generate learning experiences that capture the diversity of opinion and argument on these phenomena. It is important, at least from our perspective, that the teacher eschews didactic engagement with the students. We consider it far more pertinent to explore and discuss the sources and agency behind the construction of both the memory and the lessons. Despite President George H. W. Bush's 1989 admonition to put the war behind them, because "no great nation could long afford to be sundered by a memory,"[1] we consider it important to remember the past and to draw certain lessons from it. We are all familiar with George Santayana's well-known dictum that those who cannot remember the past are condemned to repeat it. Yet we argue that it is important to recognize the constructed and fluid nature of historical memory and the lessons of the past. Therefore, we emphasize considering memory and lessons within the appropriate time and context. In addition, it is important to clearly identify the individuals and creative forces behind the construction of memory and consider their particular agendas or objectives. Of course an artifact of historical memory, whatever its form, will be received, interpreted, and articulated by various and diffuse audiences, so audience reception is crucial as well. Overall, there is much in play here, so trying to pin down *the* lessons or *the* memory of the war is futile; President Obama's administration, for instance, saw and used such lessons in a very different way from that of President George W. Bush.

The Collective Memory of Vietnam and US Intervention

Like most of the issues concerning the Vietnam War, the US collective memory of the war is a highly contested subject. It provides a fruitful area of study and can be considered alongside, but not necessarily integrated into, the history and historiography of the war. It is also vital to consider the memory of the war beyond the "collective"; with the historiographic turns to postnational and international histories, it is worth considering the memories generated in Vietnam and elsewhere, from Managua to Baghdad, which are constructed to affect their encounters with the United States. Comparative memory and the teaching of American memory need to integrate the interactions between how societies remember and how and what they forget.[2] When President Bill Clinton visited Vietnam in 2000, he made reference to the "other side of the Wall," to the three million Vietnamese killed during the war.[3] Such references and reflections within the United States are a comparatively rare phenomenon.

As a constructed phenomenon collective memory exists in time and space.[4] Collective memory reflects the way in which society remembers the past. Of course it is based on some elements of reality, but crucially it is constructed and represented within the temporal period of those who remember.[5]

Memory changes and is reconfigured over time. Similar to the "lessons" section below, it is necessary to emphasize the fluidity and constructed nature of collective memories. David Thelen writes that the "struggles over the possession and interpretation of memories are deep, frequent and bitter."[6] It is important in the teaching of collective memory to emphasize the social agency behind the creation of the sites and artifacts that stimulate and train memory. Vietnam veterans are not always central to its creation and preservation. Over time other actors get involved: editors, directors, sculptors, curators, textbook writers, poets, novelists, documentary makers, presidents, and other politicians. The memories are constructed by individuals in constant communication and negotiation with the wider social and cultural fields of production.[7]

Collective memory is constructed by groups and individuals. Steven Rose uses the term *re-membering*, with the hyphen, to emphasize this constructed condition.[8] Contemporary media forms ensure frequent repetition, which limits the discourse and field of memory.[9] The images and sounds of the Vietnam War immediately invoke a feeling and situate the audience. Iconic images permeate US culture: the Eddie Adams assassination shot, Kim Phuc and others on the road after a napalm strike, the bodies on the path killed at Son My/My Lai, the Buddhist monk immolated in stoic protest, the more generic images of the helicopters, the payloads beneath the broad stretch of the B-52 bombers, or Hugh van Es's helicopter on the rooftop.[10] These images reverberate through time.

After 1975 collective memories of the Vietnam War arose with the most ferocity when US military intervention was actively considered, especially if US troops might be involved. Presidential campaigns also invoked memories of Vietnam. Wartime credentials were considered and debated. Dan Quayle, Bill Clinton, and George W. Bush were scrutinized and set against those who had served in World War II, or in Vietnam, as did John Kerry. In short, the Vietnam War, its memory, lies close beneath the surface. At times the memory serves as a metaphor for inhibition. Politicians and pundits asserted an understanding of what the "American people" think. Yet the "Vietnam syndrome" was also juxtaposed with questions of leadership, resolve, and credibility.

There is little space in this essay to explore the workings of memory and the Vietnam War in the necessary detail. We hope that the following endnote and the examples of teaching options presented later might stimulate further reading and curriculum development.[11]

So, for instance, consider these three examples of a time when the memory of the Vietnam War surfaced in contested ways. These are short examples of numerous opportunities to teach on the memory of the war. In the late 1970s, Jan Scruggs and the Vietnam Veterans Memorial Fund pushed to construct the Wall as the memorial to those who had been killed in the field. Not only was the process of selection and construction highly contentious, but it created deep and bitter acrimony and extensive media commentary on the memorial design and the war. A figurative statue, flagpole, and flag were added. Some within the Reagan administration not only played interference but also worried about the impact the memorial might have on their faltering policies in El Salvador and Nicaragua. The media revived Vietnam in their

The Vietnam Veterans Memorial. (photo by David Ryan)

discussions on Central America. The administration considered the issue and penned a document titled "Why El Salvador Isn't Vietnam."[12] The Reagan Doctrine was crafted to avoid the rejuvenation of certain memories and lessons. When in April 1983 President Reagan appealed to Congress for more funding in Nicaragua, he argued, "[L]et me say to those who invoke the memory of Vietnam: There is no thought of sending American combat troops to Central America."[13] One decade after America's defeat in the Vietnam War, as the White House prepared for its tenth anniversary in 1985, it directly linked the memory with the operations in Nicaragua.[14] These policies were deeply affected by the legacy and the memories of the war.

When President George H. W. Bush was inaugurated in 1989 he argued that the statute of limitations on the war had passed and enquired whether any great nation could be sundered by a memory. If Reagan largely avoided direct confrontation, Bush was intent on demonstrating the US capacity to intervene militarily. The memories of Vietnam influenced both tactics and strategies. The Powell Doctrine (discussed further in the "lessons" section below) ensured overwhelming victories in both Panama in 1989 and Iraq in 1991. Afterward Bush declared that the United States had "kicked" the Vietnam syndrome. Airpower ensured that the ground troop engagement could be kept limited. The judicious decision not to push on into Baghdad to capture or topple Saddam Hussein in 1991, in line with the defined objectives of the war, provided the United States with a temporal exit.

Finally, and tragically, it seems that the George W. Bush's administration—like that of his father—was also haunted by the war. In part because the Vietnam War served as a symbol of weakness and defeat, the administration moved to expand the opportunities presented in the aftermath of 9/11 and the inconclusive war in Afghanistan to move into Iraq.[15] Once again the country became locked in a seemingly interminable war, which quickly drew comparisons to Vietnam. The media, political rhetoric, and cartoonists drew parallels. By 2009 there were twenty-three books dealing with both wars.[16] Increasingly the political impact of casualties and casualty phobia, objectives, popular support, and exit strategies were widely discussed. Iraqi protagonists from Saddam Hussein and Moqtada al-Sadr invoked Vietnam to taunt the United States.

Memory, the frequently used aphorism, suggests a potential to avoid the condemnation of repetition. In 1968 Albert Wohlstetter pondered the consequences of the potential impact of such memories and lessons on the powers of the executive branch. He concluded that "of all the disasters of Vietnam the worst may be the 'lessons' that we'll draw from it."[17] If the Vietnam syndrome did inhibit executive power, did it not also provoke a democratic inclination to avoid unnecessary wars?

The Changing Lessons of the Vietnam War

The historiography of the Vietnam War is still strongly contested, so it is little wonder that the "lessons" of that war are equally disputed. The variety of lessons drawn from Vietnam range from criticisms of the fundamentals of the American system of government to the Earl Tilford's sarcastic remark that "the United States must never again become involved in a civil war in support of a nationalist cause against communist insurgents supplied by allies with contiguous borders in a former French colony located in a tropical climate halfway around the world."[18] Secretary of State Henry Kissinger echoed Tilford's sentiment in a memorandum to President Gerald Ford on the lessons of Vietnam. Reflecting the common establishment view of the time that it would be dangerous to draw sweeping lessons from defeat in Vietnam, Kissinger wrote, "It is remarkable, considering how long the war lasted and how intensely it was reported and commented, that there are really not very many lessons from our experience in Vietnam that can be usefully applied elsewhere despite the obvious temptation to try. Vietnam represents a unique situation, geographically, ethnically, politically, militarily and diplomatically. We should probably be grateful for that and should recognize it for what it is, instead of trying to apply the 'lessons of Vietnam' as universally as we once tried to apply the 'lessons of Munich.'"[19]

Indeed, Kissinger's critique was echoed by scholars such as Samuel Huntington, who also argued for the uniqueness of the Vietnam experience.[20] The first academic publication on the lessons of Vietnam, the conference publication *The Lessons of Vietnam*—which contained contributions from figures such as Paul Nitze, William Westmoreland, Robert Thompson, and Robert Komer—did not so much reject outright the possibility that Vietnam offered lessons for American policy makers as focus on the small-scale, tactical things the United States could do better next time. Kissinger and the contributors to the *Lessons of Vietnam* implicitly accepted that there would be a next time.[21] However, avoiding a "next time" was perhaps one of the few lessons that diverse groups—from the White House to Congress to the military to various critics—could agree on. What "no more Vietnams" meant in practice was much more contested.

The first efforts to avoid another Vietnam came from the Nixon White House. At a press conference in Guam on July 25, 1969, President Richard Nixon declared that, while the United States would honor all treaty commitments and continue to offer its nuclear shield to allies or countries whose survival was deemed vital to US national security, in the future it would expect the nation under threat to provide the manpower for its own defense.[22] This essentially meant that the United States would no longer commit ground troops to conflicts in the third world but would instead provide financial and advisory assistance.

Conservatives, however, were not long in pushing back on lessons that emphasized caution. This reaction to the lessons of Vietnam was rooted partially in a broader opposition to Nixon and Kissinger's *détente* policy of easing tensions with the Soviet Union and partially in a desire on the part of some on the right to *transcend* such reluctance to intervene, which they called a "Vietnam syndrome." As a presidential candidate, Ronald Reagan had argued that "for too long, we have lived with the 'Vietnam Syndrome'" and that "it is time we recognized that ours was, in truth, a noble cause." Reagan's embrace of the "noble cause" also meant acceptance of a set of lessons from Vietnam that decried a lack of US resolve in prosecuting such wars: "There is a lesson for all of us in Vietnam. If we are forced to fight, we must have the means and the determination to prevail or we will not have what it takes to secure the peace. And while we are at it, let us tell those who fought in that war that we will never again ask young men to fight and possibly die in a war our government is afraid to let them win."[23]

Richard Nixon, who as president had offered caution, exemplified this revisionist approach in his 1985 book *No More Vietnams*. Nixon railed against the post-Vietnam reluctance to use military force, as he saw the American defeat in Indochina as an aberration: "Our defeat in Vietnam was only a temporary setback after a series of victories. It is vital that we learn the right lessons from that defeat. In Vietnam, we tried and failed in a just cause. 'No more Vietnams' can mean that we will not try again. It should mean that we will not fail again."[24] Nixon's changing lessons of the war were tied to an attempt to reshape the collective memory of the war in such a way as to enable future interventions.

For all the Reagan era pushback against the Vietnam syndrome, Reagan remained cautious as president, largely eschewing direct military intervention even while providing indirect assistance to the Contra insurgents in Nicaragua and the military regimes in El Salvador and Guatemala. This caution found ready support in the military, for which "no more Vietnams" meant a marked reluctance to commit military forces to foreign interventions unless very specific circumstances held. These circumstances were codified by the Reagan administration's secretary of defense, Caspar Weinberger. In a speech delivered at the National Press Club titled "The Uses of Military Power," Weinberger laid out what he called six "tests" that would have to be applied when the United States considered the use of force abroad.

> The United States should not commit forces to combat overseas unless the particular engagement or occasion is deemed vital to our national interest or that of our allies. . . .
>
> If we decide it is necessary to put combat troops into a given situation, we should do so wholeheartedly, and with the clear intention of winning. If we are unwilling to commit the forces or resources necessary to achieve our objectives, we should not commit them at all. . . .
>
> If we do decide to commit forces to combat overseas, we should have clearly defined political and military objectives. . . .
>
> The relationship between our objectives and the forces we have committed—their size, composition and disposition—must be continually reassessed and adjusted if necessary. . . .
>
> Before the U.S. commits forces abroad, there must be some reasonable assurance we will have the support of the American people and their elected representatives in Congress. . . .
>
> The commitment of U.S. forces to combat should be a last resort.[25]

Weinberger's military aide, Colin Powell, had helped to draft the speech and was such a strong advocate of the doctrine in the Bush administration that it was rechristened the Weinberger-Powell Doctrine. Powell essentially restated and simplified the Weinberger Doctrine. If there were to be an explicitly stated Powell Doctrine, then its central tenets would be that military action is the last resort, to be used only when national interests are clearly at stake; force, if used, must be overwhelming; strong support from Congress and the general public is necessary before intervention; and a clear exit strategy is essential.[26]

Powell's determination to avoid another Vietnam bore fruit with the widespread acceptance, at least within the military, of his doctrine in the 1990s. While interventions in Somalia, Haiti, Bosnia, and Kosovo were not in defense of vital national interests, the strictures placed on the use of force by both the Vietnam syndrome and the Powell Doctrine ensured that none of these interventions, even if unsuccessful, would end up dragging the United States into a prolonged war it had not planned for. Its importance as a lesson can be gauged by the comments of then governor George W. Bush at the August 2000 Republican National Convention: "A generation shaped by Vietnam must remember the lessons of Vietnam. When America uses force in the world, the cause must be just, the goal must be clear and the victory must be overwhelming."[27]

Ironically, the Powell Doctrine's ultimate vindication—US victory over Iraq in the 1991 Gulf War—was also a cause of its downfall. Operation Desert Storm seemed to restore the utility of US military power; a jubilant President George H. W. Bush declared that "the specter of Vietnam has been buried forever in the desert sands of the Arabian Peninsula."[28] The renewed capabilities of the US armed forces offered the country a chance to "try again," this time with perhaps a great chance of success. The temptation to use such an effective force to accomplish broad foreign policy goals was apparent in the George W. Bush administration's decision to invade Iraq in 2003. Critics of that war did not take long to invoke the ghosts of Vietnam. Senator Robert Byrd, one of the few senators who voted against the war, used the analogy in the prewar debate in Congress: "Let's go back to the war in Vietnam. I was here. I was one of the Senators who voted for the Gulf of Tonkin resolution. Yes, I voted for the Gulf of Tonkin resolution. I am sorry for that. I am guilty of doing that. I should have been one of the two, or at least I should have made it three, Senators who voted against that Gulf of Tonkin resolution. But I am not wanting [sic] to commit that sin twice, and that is exactly what we are doing here. This is another Gulf of Tonkin resolution."[29]

Ultimately, Byrd's warnings were ignored. In ignoring dissenters who invoked Vietnam and Powell's lessons, which urged caution, the administration of George W. Bush would again conjure up the ghosts of Vietnam, from the very "desert sands of Arabia" in which the first Bush administration thought it had buried them forever.

Teaching Suggestions

In our selection of four teaching exercises we have tried to combine a concern with a variety of learning outcomes and experiences with a range of different media and temporal contexts.

The Wall: The Vietnam Veterans Memorial

The learning outcomes associated with this exercise directly engage issues of memory, the politics of memorial construction, and the temporal context. Therefore, by the end of the session students should be able to:

1. Identify the motivations to construct the Vietnam Veterans Memorial
2. Consider and explain why the selected design by Maya Lin was so controversial
3. Identify and analyze the various interests and social agents of memory and analyze their interpretation of the Vietnam War and their desired form of its memory
4. Situate and describe the controversy within the period in which it took place

Given these learning objectives, provide students with access to the website and extracts from the writing of Jan Scruggs, the founder of the Vietnam Veterans Memorial Fund. Scruggs's book, written with Joel L. Swerdlow, *To Heal a Nation*, not only provides a good discussion point about a central protagonist's reflections but also includes numerous photographs, letters, a good chronology of events, and a roll call of honor. Consider the reflections and narrative provided by this central protagonist. Crucially, the memorial and this narrative conclude in 1982. Ask students to investigate why the Reagan administration was reluctant to accept the memorial until 1984. This exercise focused on Scruggs and the Reagan administration provides a good transition to the next section on Maya Lin's design.

The Vietnam Veterans Memorial. (courtesy of Sarah Thelen)

Gather a range of visual and textual sources on the initial design. Have students think about the design and its potential meanings. Read Maya Lin's reflective writings. Explore her intentions and aesthetic ambitions. Discuss her design within its space on the National Mall, the Wall(s) of the chevron shape, referencing and encompassing the Lincoln Memorial and the Washington Monument. What was Maya Lin trying to achieve? What does its location and surrounding monuments tell us about US national histories and stories? The traditional narratives could be juxtaposed with historiographic alternatives.

Vietnam veteran Tom Carhart, who originally worked with Scruggs on the Vietnam Veterans Memorial Fund, and others objected to the design. Why? Draw student attention to the controversy. Set them the task of investigating the contemporary commentary, the op-eds, the multitude of newspaper articles on the memorial. Why did the different protagonists differ on the design and the war so vehemently? Deconstruct and interpret their opinions and the responses. Investigate how a compromise was reached. Did the Frederick Hart figurative statue, the flagpole, and the flag add or detract from the memorial? What did this mean in political terms? In cultural terms? In aesthetic terms?

Explore these questions through the primary sources, media, visuals, and reflections.

Finally, perhaps examine the controversy of 1980–82 within the foreign policy context of the period. What connections can be made between this memorial and President Reagan's policies on Central America? The connections are there. Have your students examine them through the media, through Reagan's speeches that connect both war and potential intervention, particularly his April 27, 1983, speech to Congress or his speeches delivered on Veterans and Memorial Days during these years. Remember he did not officially accept the memorial until 1984.

The Lessons of the War:
Kissinger's Draft Memorandum to President Ford

The learning objectives related to this exercise directly address historical skills in document analysis, interpretation, and contextualization. Beyond that students could situate the elite and official lessons within a broad range of alternatives.

By the end of this session students should have the ability to:

1. Analyze the content of the memorandum
2. Interpret its content within the context in which it was written, trying to ascertain the intentions of this author at that time
3. Compare the lessons summarized by Secretary of State and National Security Adviser Henry Kissinger to a range of other reflections from officials, the media, and persons in other academic or policy and cultural circles
4. Consider the fluidity of the "lessons" by comparing them to other lessons generated by administrations across the 1980s onward

The Gerald R. Ford Presidential Library has a very good online collection of documents.[30] In the first instance the class could engage in traditional forms of document analysis centered on content and authorial intent. Students could enumerate and discuss the various lessons that Henry Kissinger drafted. The discussion could also consider the drafting process and the input from numerous agencies and studies within the executive branch. The editorial process of selection of "the lessons" as Kissinger saw them provides a good basis for further discussion.

The Vietnam collection online at the Ford Presidential Library provides an invaluable context within which to consider these lessons. Moreover, one might also look at the date of the memorandum and consider it within the immediate context of the *Mayaguez* incident. All of the National Security Council minutes are online, and the discussion of the appropriate US response to the capture of US seamen by Cambodian forces could be examined within the context of the identified lessons. What connections can be drawn? The "lessons" document might also be considered within the broader context of a foreign policy concern with the struggles for independence in Angola, the deployment of Cuban troops (and many others), and the prospects of Soviet and Chinese influence and the appropriate US response. Media searches on Angola and Vietnam and the examination of White House–congressional relations set up another discussion on the lessons of the war. Compare and contrast the lessons on Vietnam in the *Congressional Record* and congressional hearings with those of the Ford administration and its agencies. Identify the objectives of different political actors. Examine the editorials and op-ed pieces on lessons from 1975.

Finally, by making reference to the sources in the "lessons" section above, compare and contrast these to the lessons delineated in the Weinberger speech and the Powell *Foreign Affairs* article. In that context, it is useful also to examine differences among the instrumental, strategic, proportional, and fundamental lessons drawn from the Vietnam War. Set an open-ended assignment to ascertain how these are reflected in US culture and discourse.

The Lessons of the War: The Weinberger-Powell Doctrine

The learning outcomes associated with this exercise engage with the ways in which personal memories of the Vietnam War can influence the lessons drawn from it, and—conversely—the ways in which contemporary challenges can influence the construction of such lessons. By the end of this session students should have the ability to:

1. Articulate the tenets of the Powell Doctrine
2. Understand how Colin Powell's Vietnam experience and his personal memories of the war influenced the lessons he drew from it
3. Analyze the extent to which the debate over American intervention in the Yugoslav wars influenced Powell's *Foreign Affairs* article

4. Discuss how the doctrine influenced subsequent debates over US intervention

Provide the class with copies of Chairman of the Joint Chiefs of Staff General Colin Powell's 1992 *Foreign Affairs* article, "US Forces: Challenges Ahead." Students can discuss whether adherence to the tenets of the Powell Doctrine might have prevented US intervention in Vietnam. If you wish to further debate the appropriateness of the doctrine, then introduce students to critiques of Powell, such as those of President Bill Clinton's secretary of defense, Les Aspin, and United Nations ambassador and later secretary of state Madeleine Albright.[31]

What is perhaps most interesting about the "lessons" of Vietnam, however, is how they are constructed and contested. Ask students to research Powell's Vietnam experience and question how his service in Indochina might have affected the lessons he drew from the war. Focus particularly on the sometimes emotive tone of the *Foreign Affairs* piece. The lessons of Vietnam are, of course, not only drawn from personal experience but also modified to speak to contemporary challenges. Have the students research the Yugoslav wars of the 1990s and discuss how the debate over US military intervention there might have affected which lessons of Vietnam Powell chose to emphasize. Contrast the caution of Powell with the frustration Albright and Aspin showed toward that caution and ask what lessons they might have drawn from the Vietnam War that would have helped them make their case.

Finally, discuss whether or not Powell has strongly influenced subsequent decisions on US military intervention. Provide students with speeches from presidents and military leaders that echo the Powell Doctrine (such as President George W. Bush's announcement of Operation Enduring Freedom in October 2001 or some of the many statements by military leaders repeating Powell) and ask them to consider the extent to which this rhetoric has affected decisions to intervene. Newspaper editorials on these conflicts may help the students in their assessments. Throughout the exercise, emphasize the fluidity of the lessons and the role contemporary circumstances had in their construction.

"Vietnam" in Iraq and Afghanistan

The learning outcomes associated with this exercise relate to an understanding of how commentators "use" the past by invoking historical

305

analogies in contemporary debates and the variety of lessons different actors can still draw from the war. By the end of this session students should have the ability to:

1. Understand how the debate over Vietnam was repeated in the debates over Afghanistan and Iraq
2. Interpret why a particular author might want to invoke or reject the Vietnam analogy
3. Compare and contrast the Vietnam War with the wars in Afghanistan and Iraq
4. Interpret how the lessons of Vietnam are seen *outside* the United States by analyzing foreign news sources

For this exercise, rather than assigning specific pieces for students to analyze, ask them to conduct a search through sites such as the Google News Archive and LexisNexis (if available) to find newspaper editorials and op-eds that discuss both the Vietnam War and the wars in Iraq and Afghanistan. Be sure to ask them to search a wide variety of news sources encompassing national, regional, and—crucially—foreign newspapers. This should provoke a discussion among the students as to how the Vietnam War compares to the wars in Afghanistan and Iraq. Tease out the similarities and differences and pay close attention to issues of context, scale, and strategy. There have been formal studies comparing Iraq and Vietnam, and you may want to read them to prepare for the exercise or make them available to students to further inform their discussions.[32]

An example of the different ways writers invoke the memory of Vietnam can be seen in contrasting opinion pieces from *Foreign Policy* and *Newsweek*. In *Foreign Policy*'s "Obama's Indecent Interval," Thomas H. Johnson and M. Chris Mason invoke Vietnam in order to argue *against* withdrawal,[33] whereas John Barry's *Newsweek* article "Obama's Vietnam" presents a more conventional Vietnam comparison, arguing that the similarities between the wars in Afghanistan and Vietnam were strong enough for President Obama to consider pulling US troops out of Afghanistan.[34] Ask the students to interrogate the reasons these writers invoke the Vietnam analogy. In many ways, the "Vietnams" described by Johnson and Mason on the one hand and Barry on the other are incompatible, despite the fact that both strongly criticize Obama for ignoring the Vietnam analogy. Considering the material presented earlier on the fluidity and contested nature of the lesson, ask students to discuss how the debate over the war in Afghanistan reflects an ongoing dispute over the lessons of Vietnam.

Use these discussions of how the Vietnam analogy can operate within US politics and society to compare the American lessons of Vietnam with the lessons that others took from the war. Direct students to assemble editorials and op-ed pieces from non-American sources. English-language European news sources are abundant,[35] but make sure they select sources from the Arab world as well (Al Jazeera would be an obvious example).[36] Do the ways these sources employ the Vietnam analogy differ from what US publications do? The issue of timing is important here: were these non-American sources quicker to invoke Vietnam with regard to Afghanistan and Iraq than Americans were? If they did invoke Vietnam, how did their vision of the war differ from US narratives?

Conclusion

The lessons of history and the collective memory of the past are constructed phenomena. Both change and need to be located and considered in time and place. It is essential to conduct research and try to discover what particular people are trying to convey through their invocation of a memory or a particular lesson. Despite the vast amount of evidence now readily available, only fractions of these traces of the past are used at a cultural level or through political rhetoric and media discourse. Awareness of the agency behind the process of construction is vital. What groups or individuals were involved? What agendas were they pursuing? In that sense we have argued that the construction of both the lessons and the memories are purposeful and useful for certain and particular ends.

In the examples we discussed, it is also essential to keep two things in mind. First, how is the "collective" being defined and considered? If it is at the national level, what forces dominate the discourse? What cultural fields of production facilitate and disseminate these views or memories? Who speaks? And who and what are the issues that are side-lined or forgotten? It is not that issues are literally disremembered; rather, they are not used, invoked, and reconstructed and therefore do not figure in the ongoing discourse. Second, we have noted that lessons are closely related to certain types of power. In part they relate to the tactics and strategies of avoiding another "Vietnam." At various times this has meant that it will be done better next time or that the United States will avoid defeat. The intersection of memory and lesson is also instructive because it provides opportunities to explore the impact and legacy of the war through a broader spectrum, that is, to consider the popular impact and resonance of the Vietnam syndrome, construed as a positive phenomenon. Moreover, it facilitates an exploration of a broader set of lessons that relate to fundamental lessons of the war on questions of military intervention and the impact and costs of such decisions.

NOTES

1. George H. W. Bush, Inaugural Address, West Front of the US Capitol, January 20, 1989, http://www.yale.edu/lawweb/avalon/presiden/inaug/bush.htm.

2. See, for instance, Paul Connerton, *How Societies Remember* (Cambridge: Cambridge University Press, 1989); Paul Connerton, *How Modernity Forgets* (Cambridge: Cambridge University Press, 2009); Jay Winter, "Thinking about Silence," in *Shadows of War: A Social History of Silence in the Twentieth Century*, ed. Efrat Ben-Ze'ev, Ruth Ginio, and Jay Winter (New York: Cambridge University Press, 2010), 3–31.

3. President Bill Clinton, Remarks by the President to the Vietnam National University, Hanoi, Socialist Republic of Vietnam, November 17, 2000, http://clinton4.nara.gov/WH/New/november 2000/speeches11_17.html.

4. Jay Winter, *Remembering War: The Great War between Memory and History in the Twentieth Century* (New Haven: Yale University Press, 2006), 138.

5. Lewis A. Coser, introduction to Maurice Halbwachs, *On Collective Memory* (Chicago: University of Chicago Press, 1992), especially 22. There are numerous approaches to collective memory. For good theoretical overviews, see Patrick H. Hutton, *History as an Art of Memory* (Hanover: University Press of New England, 1993); and Michael Rossington and Anne Whitehead, eds., *Theories of Memory* (Edinburgh: Edinburgh University Press, 2007). For good readers on the subject, see James McConkey, *The Anatomy of Memory: An Anthology* (New York: Oxford University Press, 1996); Harriet Harvey Wood and A. S. Byatt, eds., *Memory: An Anthology* (London: Chatto and Windus, 2008); and Jeffrey K. Olick, Vered Vinitzky-Seroussi, and Daniel Levy, *The Collective Memory Reader* (New York: Oxford University Press, 2011).

6. David Thelen, "Introduction," *Journal of American History* 75, no. 4 (March 1989), 1117–29.

7. Hutton, *History as an Art of Memory*, 6–7.

8. Steven Rose, extract from "The Making of Memory," in James McConkey, ed., *The Anatomy of Memory: An Anthology* (New York: Oxford University Press, 1996), 55–59; Steven Rose, *The Making of Memory: From Molecules to Mind* (London: Bantam, 1992). "Recollection occurs consciously through association: one finds or hunts out the stored memory-impressions by using other things associated with it either through a logical connection or through habit . . . the sort of associations taught by the various *artes memorativa*." Mary Carruthers, *The Book of Memory: A Study of Memory in Medieval Culture* (Cambridge: Cambridge University Press, 2008), 23.

9. Rose, *The Making of Memory*, 57.

10. James W. Loewen, *Lies My Teacher Told Me: Everything Your American History Textbook Got Wrong* (New York: Simon and Schuster, 1995), 239–53.

11. Marita Sturken, *Tangled Memories: The Vietnam War, the AIDS Epidemic, and the Politics of Remembering* (Berkeley: University of California Press, 1997), 44. The literature on the Vietnam Veterans Memorial and Vietnam and memory is extensive. See, for instance, Patrick Hagopian, *The Vietnam War in American Memory: Veterans, Memorials, and the Politics of Healing* (Amherst: University of Massachusetts Press, 2009); Robert D. Schulzinger, *A Time for Peace: The Legacy of the Vietnam War* (Oxford: Oxford University Press, 2006); Jan C. Scruggs and Joel L. Swerdlow, *To Heal a Nation: The Vietnam Veterans Memorial* (New York: Harper, 1985); Arnold R. Isaacs, *Vietnam Shadows: The War, Its Ghosts, and Its Legacy* (Baltimore: Johns Hopkins University Press, 1997); Myra MacPherson, *Long Time Passing: Vietnam and the Haunted Generation* (Bloomington: Indiana University Press, 2001); Charles E. Neu, ed., *After Vietnam: Legacies of a Lost War* (Baltimore: Johns Hopkins University Press, 2000); Fred Turner, *Echoes of Combat: Trauma, Memory, and the Vietnam War* (Minneapolis: University of Minnesota Press, 1996); Richard Morris and Peter Ehrenhaus, eds., *Cultural Legacies of Vietnam: Uses of the Past in the Present* (Norwood: Ablex, 1990); Kristin Ann Hass, *Carried to the Wall: American Memory and the Vietnam Veterans Memorial* (Berkeley: University of California Press, 1988); H. Bruce Franklin, *Vietnam and Other American Fantasies* (Amherst: University of Massachusetts Press, 2000); and Katherine Kinney, *Friendly Fire: American Images of the Vietnam War* (Oxford: Oxford University Press, 2000).

12. Richard V. Allen to Ed Meese and James Baker, "Why El Salvador Isn't Vietnam," February 25, 1981, El Salvador, volume 1, OA 91363, Ronald Reagan Library.

13. Reagan, "Central America," April 27, 1983, El Salvador, volume 1, OA 91363, Ronald Reagan Library.

14. See David Ryan, *US Collective Memory, Intervention and Vietnam: The Cultural Politics of US Foreign Policy since 1969* (London and New York: Routledge, forthcoming).

15. See David Ryan, "'Vietnam,' Victory Culture, and Iraq: Struggling with

Lessons, Constraints, and Credibility from Saigon to Falluja," in *Vietnam in Iraq: Tactics, Lessons, Legacies, Ghosts*, ed. John Dumbrell and David Ryan (London: Routledge, 2007), 111–38.

16. David Ryan and David Fitzgerald, "Iraq and Vietnam: Endless Recurrence or Stirrings Still," *Critical Asian Studies* 41, no. 4 (2009): 621–53.

17. Albert Wohlstetter, quoted in Andrew J. Bacevich, *The New American Militarism: How Americans Are Seduced by War* (New York: Oxford University Press, 2005), 157–58.

18. Earl Tilford, quoted in H. R. McMaster, "The Human Element: When Gadgetry Becomes Strategy," *World Affairs Journal*, Winter 2009, http://www.worldaffairsjournal.org/article/human-element-when-gadgetry-becomes-strategy.

19. Henry Kissinger, letter to President Gerald Ford on the lessons of Vietnam, 12th May 1975, Folder "Vietnam (23)," National Security Adviser, Presidential Country Files for East Asia and the Pacific, Gerald R. Ford Library, http://www.fordlibrarymuseum.gov/library/exhibits/vietnam/750512a.htm.

20. Stanley Hoffmann, Samuel P. Huntington, Ernest R. May, Richard N. Neustadt, and Thomas C. Schelling, "Vietnam Reappraised," *International Security* 6, no. 1 (Summer 1981): 3–26.

21. W. Scott Thompson and Donaldson D. Frizzell, *The Lessons of Vietnam* (New York: Crane Russak, 1977).

22. Richard Nixon, *Public Papers of the Presidents of the United States: Richard Nixon, Containing the Public Messages, Speeches, and Statements of the President* (Washington, DC: US Government Printing Office, 1971), vol. 1, 544–56.

23. Ronald Reagan, "Peace: Restoring the Margin of Safety," address delivered at the Veterans of Foreign Wars Convention, Chicago, August 18, 1980, http://www.reagan.utexas.edu/archives/reference/8.18.80.htm.

24. Richard Nixon, *No More Vietnams* (New York: Arbor House Publishing, 1985), 237.

25. Caspar Weinberger, "The Uses of Military Power," address delivered at the National Press Club, Washington, DC, November 28, 1984, http://www.pbs.org/wgbh/pages/frontline/shows/military/force/weinberger.html.

26. Colin Powell, "US Forces: The Challenges Ahead," *Foreign Affairs* 72 no. 5 (1992): 32–45.

27. "Governor Bush Delivers Remarks at the Republican National Convention," CNN, August 3, 2000, web posted at 11:20 p.m. EDT (0320 GMT), http://www.cnn.com/ELECTION/2000/conventions/republican/transcripts/bush.html.

28. President George H. W. Bush, Radio Address to United States Armed Forces Stationed in the Persian Gulf Region, March 2, 1991, George H. W. Bush Presidential Library, http://bushlibrary.tamu.edu/research/papers/1991/91030200.html.

29. Robert Byrd, quoted in Jeff Millar, "Iraq Debate: 'This Is Another Gulf of Tonkin,'" *Albion Monitor*, October 4, 2002, http://www.albionmonitor .com/0210a/iraqdebate.html.

30. See, for example, W. R. Smyser memorandum to State Department, "Lessons of Vietnam," May 12, 1975, NSA [National Security Agency], Presidential Country Files for East Asia and the Pacific, Country file: Vietnam, (23), box 20, Gerald R. Ford Library.

31. Aspin's criticisms are quoted in Michael G. MacKinnon, *The Evolution of US Peacekeeping Policy under Clinton* (London: Frank Cass, 2000), 47. Albright famously asked Powell, "What's the point of having this superb military you're always talking about if we can't use it?" Powell later recounted in his memoirs that his reaction was "I *thought I would have an aneurysm* [emphasis in the original]. American GIs were not toy soldiers to be moved around on some sort of global game board." See Colin Powell, with Joseph E. Persico, *My American Journey* (New York: Ballantine Books, 1996), 576.

32. Jeffrey Record and W. Andrew Terrill, *Iraq and Vietnam: Differences, Similarities, Insights* (Carlisle, PA: Strategic Studies Institute, 2004).

33. Thomas H. Johnson and M. Chris Mason, "Obama's Indecent Interval," *Foreign Policy*, 10 December 2009, http://www.foreignpolicy.com/articles/2009 /12/10/sorry_obama_afghanistans_your_vietnam?page=full.

34. John Barry, "Obama's Vietnam," *Newsweek*, January 30, 2009, http:// www.thedailybeast.com/newsweek/2009/01/30/obama-s-vietnam.html.

35. Lawrence Bartlett, "Vietnam War Question Haunts Afghanistan," *Agence France-Presse*, January 21, 2012, http://www.google.com/hostednews /afp/article/ALeqMjzJsxk1fBavSgDgKHWpmCLcVQ?docId=CNG .eaa270b659c4d892693aeb96cfa4f.471.

36. Richard Falk, "The Tet Offensive's Parallels in Afghanistan," Al Jazeera, August 23, 2011, http://www.aljazeera.com/indepth/opinion/2011/08 /201181813345646060387.html.

KEY RESOURCES

Hagopian, Patrick. *The Vietnam War in American Memory: Veterans, Memorials, and the Politics of Healing*. Amherst: University of Massachusetts Press, 2009.

Isaacs, Arnold R. *Vietnam Shadows: The War, Its Ghosts, and Its Legacy*. Baltimore: Johns Hopkins University Press, 1997.

Kinney, Katherine. *Friendly Fire: American Images of the Vietnam War*. New York: Oxford University Press, 2000.

May, Ernest R. *"Lessons" of the Past: The Use and Misuse of History in American Foreign Policy*. New York: Oxford University Press, 1975.

Morris, Richard, and Peter Ehrenhaus, eds. *Cultural Legacies of Vietnam: Uses of the Past in the Present*. New York: Ablex, 1990.

Neu, Charles E., ed. *After Vietnam: Legacies of a Lost War*. Baltimore: Johns Hopkins University Press, 2000.

Record, Jeffrey. *Making War, Thinking History: Munich, Vietnam, and Presidential Uses of Force from Korea to Kosovo*. Annapolis: US Naval Institute Press, 2002.

Ryan, David, and John Dumbrell, eds. *Vietnam in Iraq: Lessons, Legacies, and Ghosts*. London: Routledge, 2006.

Schulzinger, Robert D. *A Time for Peace: The Legacy of the Vietnam War*. New York: Oxford University Press, 2006.

Sturken, Marita. *Tangled Memories: The Vietnam War, the AIDS Epidemic, and the Politics of Remembering*. Berkeley: University of California Press, 1997.

Young, Marilyn B., and Lloyd C. Gardner, eds. *Iraq and the Lessons of Vietnam, or, How Not to Learn from the Past*. New York: The New Press, 2008.

Teaching the Vietnam War in Secondary Schools and Survey Classrooms

STEPHEN ARMSTRONG

The Vietnam War continues to be a favorite topic for many high school students and teachers alike. A number of students have seen at least part of some Vietnam movie even if it is only the Vietnam-related scenes of *Forrest Gump*. Some students are still fascinated by the overall subject of the 1960s or have heard an uncle or other relative discuss his (or in some cases her) involvement in the Vietnam War. Despite the many other responsibilities placed on high school teachers, in some schools the amount of time allocated to study Vietnam has actually increased; more high schools start their US history courses chronologically later than before, thus allowing more time for the analysis of post–World War II events such as Vietnam. Many students read some fiction from the Vietnam era in one of their language arts courses (Tim O'Brien's *The Things They Carried* is a part of many high school language arts curricula). Many of the veterans that come to speak to students during special Veterans Day assemblies are members of the Vietnam era generation; messages given by these veterans often-times have a different tone than messages presented by the World War II or Korean War veterans who spoke at these events in prior years.

It should be also noted that Vietnam is often taught in very different ways than it was in the twentieth century. For a number of high school students, the Tet Offensive has no more personal relevance than the Battle of the Bulge or the sinking of the USS *Maine*. More important, more and more high school students are being taught by teachers who were also too young to have been touched by the social and political conflicts of the Vietnam era. Many would argue that this is a good thing; these teachers do not carry the personal memories of living through the 1960s with them and might teach subjects like the Vietnam War in a more objective manner. Except for those few grizzled veterans of the 1960s that remain in the classrooms, events surrounding the Vietnam War are being taught as historical events and not as a part of historical memory.

When teachers taught the Vietnam War in the 1980s and the 1990s almost all emphasized the critical impact the war had on the military and cultural mind-set of the United States. We now live an era in which 9/11 and the wars that followed did much to shape the identity of contemporary America. However, this essay will argue that Vietnam is still a subject that is very worthy of attention in a US history or world history classroom. As students grapple with issues surrounding more recent conflicts in Iraq and Afghanistan, students and teachers can make worthwhile comparisons between these wars and the conflict in Vietnam, even though they were separated by several decades. Teachers should emphasize to their students that the Vietnam War, like these other conflicts, was in many ways a young person's war, and that many of those who fought and died were roughly the same age as the students in the classroom. For many young people, this is the "hook" that gets them interested in studying the Vietnam War.

This essay is designed to assist the beginning teacher who wants his or her students to explore the Vietnam War in more detail than the somewhat scanty summary that is included in most contemporary textbooks. I will focus on approaches that are most appropriate for US survey classes at the high school or college level; the Vietnam War is certainly a subject very worthy of discussion in any modern world history class, but in a somewhat different context than would exist when studying US history. The essay will first analyze how to approach the Vietnam War in a "big picture" context before moving to a review of the expectations concerning the teaching of the Vietnam War as found in a cross section of national and state history/social studies standards. Finally, it will analyze some of the resources that can be used when teaching the Vietnam War.

Looking at the Big Picture

Before students investigate various aspects of the war itself, it is essential that they grapple with the question of why America became entangled in the Vietnam War. Literally hundreds of books have been written on this subject. Obviously, the students should investigate numerous primary and secondary sources that will allow them to carefully analyze this and other questions related to Vietnam and other topics in their study of American history. There are numerous explanations for why America entered Vietnam; as you provide primary and secondary source materials for your students to study, make sure they have the resources to carefully consider the following possible explanations for the American entry into Vietnam (remembering that other explanations, and combinations of explanations, also exist):

1. Expansion into Southeast Asia was a continuation of American imperialist urges that began in the late nineteenth century and commenced in earnest with the acquisition of the Philippines. The motives for American imperialism were complicated; political, economic, and cultural factors were all involved. Students should consider whether more recent American conflicts in the Middle East were a product of these same imperialist desires.

2. The American entry into Vietnam was a "logical" extension of the containment policy that dominated American foreign policy in the post–World War II, Cold War era. "Containment" meant that America had to be present whenever communism showed up anywhere in the world; the assumption of the containment policy was that communist movements everywhere were supported by either the Soviet Union or Communist China.

3. The Vietnam War was a result of the "military-industrial complex" that President Dwight Eisenhower warned against as he was leaving the presidency. Eisenhower warned that a combination of the American military and massive defense contractors would have the power to have a large influence on American foreign policy. Did this military-industrial complex push American political leaders toward greater involvement in Vietnam?

As you prepare materials for your students to analyze, be sure to include resources on why America was not successful in Vietnam. Again, dozens of reasons exist to explain the American "defeat"; have students focus at least on the following.

1. American leaders felt that the Vietnam War was part of the international war on communism. In reality it was a civil war

that became entwined with global geopolitics. As a result American forces were never welcomed by many South Vietnamese. American and South Vietnamese goals were oftentimes at odds, and American forces in Vietnam became resentful of their South Vietnamese "allies."

2. American military strategy in Vietnam was misguided. For much of the war, American civilian and military leaders felt that if American and South Vietnamese soldiers simply killed enough of the enemy the opposition would eventually be defeated. American officials underestimated the resilience and will of their North Vietnamese enemies.

3. Economic factors in the United States would have made the continuation of the war very difficult. President Johnson engineered the Great Society programs of the mid-1960s, which were costly. To fund these programs and the continuation of a major armed conflict would have placed a major strain on the American economy.

4. America could have won the Vietnam War if military force had been employed quickly and decisively. According to this theory, by the time America was finally on the course to victory in the late 1960s the press and antiwar protesters at home had caused Americans to sour on the war. Proponents of this theory state that the 1968 North Vietnamese/Viet Cong Tet Offensive was actually a victory for American and South Vietnamese forces, yet it was pictured as a defeat in the American media, further poisoning support for the war at home.

The Vietnam War
in Social Studies Standards Documents

It is almost guaranteed that your state social studies standards document includes some mention of the Vietnam War, usually in the description of the content of your state's high school US history curriculum. Of course, you should check your own state social studies standards for specifics.

National standards for US history were published in 1996 by the National Center for History in the Schools. In its model curriculum, the topic of Vietnam comes in "United States Era 9: Postwar United States." In this document, the goal of Standard 2C is that "The student understands the foreign and domestic consequences of U.S. involvement in

Vietnam." The specific expectation of this standard is that the student is able to:

> Grades 7–12: Assess the Vietnam policy of the Kennedy, Johnson, and Nixon administrations and the shifts of public opinion about the war. (Analyze multiple causation)
>
> Grades 9–12: Explain the composition of the American forces recruited to fight the war. (Interrogate historical data)
>
> Grades 5–12: Evaluate how Vietnamese and Americans experienced the war and how the war continued to affect postwar politics and culture. (Appreciate historical perspectives)
>
> Grades 7–12: Explain the provisions of the Paris Peace Accord of 1973 and evaluate the role of the Nixon administration. (Differentiate between historical facts and historical interpretations)
>
> Grades 9–12: Analyze the constitutional issues involved in the war and explore the legacy of the Vietnam War. (Formulate a position or course of action on an issue)[1]

An example of how Vietnam is contained in a state standards document can be found in the recently revised Ohio social studies content standards. In the high school US history curriculum, Content Statement 26 is "The Cold War and conflicts in Korea and Vietnam influenced domestic and international politics." Under "Content Elaborations" it is stated, "The Vietnam War divided the country and sparked massive protests. Spending for the war came at the expense of domestic programs launched by President Johnson. This led to urban unrest in the 1960s. The Vietnam War was a dominant issue in the presidential campaigns of 1968 and 1972. The difficulties and eventual withdrawal from Vietnam led to concerted efforts on the part of the U.S. to find allies in future conflicts."

The "Expectations for Learning" for this standard are than students should "analyze how the Cold War and conflicts in Korea and Vietnam influenced domestic and international politics between the end of the World War II and 1992.[2]

The Ohio standards actually provide more background than many state standards do about what is expected to be taught about the Vietnam War (and other historical topics). More typical are the California standards for grade eleven US history, which under the expectation "Trace the origins and geopolitical consequences (foreign and domestic) of the Cold War and containment policy, including the following" simply lists "The Vietnam War" and seven other topics. The only other mention of the Vietnam War in the grade eleven expectations is "List the effects of foreign policy on domestic policy and vice versa (e.g., protests during the war in Vietnam or the 'nuclear freeze' movement)."[3]

So, if you as a teacher are wondering if national standards and your state standards promote the teaching of the Vietnam War, the answer is, in almost every case, yes. As noted above, however, the guidance you will get from these documents on what to teach about Vietnam will vary widely from state to state.

The Vietnam War in US History Textbooks

There are more and more teachers who are teaching US history without the aid of a standard textbook. These teachers should be commended: they are having their students analyze both primary and secondary source documents without the "filter" of a textbook. These students are not being provided with a single "grand narrative" of history that a textbook almost always provides: students are allowed to create their own narratives and interpretations of historical events. Nevertheless, the majority of teachers still utilize a textbook with the obvious benefits that a textbook brings (including the mountain of teaching materials that textbook companies now provide).

All of the high school US history textbooks have sections on the Vietnam War (the same cannot be said for several of the textbooks used in modern world history courses). In many of these texts the Vietnam War is either discussed in the chapter that outlines the struggles of the Cold War or analyzed as one of the conflicts of the 1960s (along with the civil rights movement, the counterculture, etc.). Many veteran teachers continue to debate which approach works best in making the war understandable to students.

By its nature a textbook is not going to be able to present an exhaustive view of any period or event in American history; textbook writers often lament what they are forced to leave out. What is troubling to some scholars of the Vietnam War is the omission in high school textbooks of absolutely critical topics that would help to change students' thinking about the war. Christopher R. Leahey's 2010 text *Whitewashing War: Historical Myth, Corporate Textbooks, and Possibilities for Democratic Education* describes how and why high school textbooks seldom include controversial or antiestablishment views. A focus of Leahey's book is to point out major omissions about the Vietnam War found in many of the US history textbooks utilized. These include:

1. American military actions against the North Vietnamese before the Gulf of Tonkin Resolution and the specific events that led to the resolution. Leahey points out that few textbooks critically analyze American actions during this period.[4]

2. Most textbooks state that the Tet Offensive was the "turning point" in America's support of the Vietnam War, and press coverage of Tet was the beginning of the large-scale erosion of public support for Lyndon Johnson's Vietnam policies. Leahey points out that American textbooks largely ignore American intelligence failures leading to the Tet Offensive, the fact that the American public began to turn against the Vietnam War prior to Tet, and that press coverage of the war remained largely positive in the aftermath of Tet.[5]

3. Textbooks generally treat the My Lai massacre as an isolated event, and they usually minimize the horrific treatment of Vietnamese civilians by some American soldiers. A number of textbooks fail to mention that there were concerted efforts to cover up the My Lai massacre and similar events. Textbooks generally fail to mention the connection between these events and the "war of attrition" policy that guided American military actions at this time.[6]

These omissions can actually be used as a teaching tool. We ask our students to critically analyze any reading that we assign them; we should ask them to do the same with their textbook. Provide students with documents related to the Gulf of Tonkin Resolution, the Tet Offensive, and the My Lai massacre, carefully analyze these documents, and then have the students do a close reading of the textbook passages concerning these events to see how historically accurate the textbook actually is.

Additional Teaching Resources

On both the web and in print there are mountains of additional materials for both teachers and students who teach and study the Vietnam War. The purpose of this section is to provide suggestions to teachers who might be just beginning to teach the Vietnam War. What are some key resources to start with? All of those mentioned in this section have been used successfully by classroom teachers at the secondary and college levels.

Hundreds of websites address various aspects of the Vietnam War. One place where someone might start is the Vietnam Center and Archive (www.vietnam.ttu.edu/teachers). Found at this site are resources for teachers, college students, and secondary school students. There is also information on approaches to researching the Vietnam War. Another excellent place to begin is the Wellesley College site on the Vietnam War, Vietnam War Internet Links (www.wellesley.edu /PoliSci/wj/Vietnam/vietlink.html). A multitude of sites on the Vietnam War can be accessed from this site.

Simulations, while sometimes tricky to develop from scratch, can provide many teachable moments. Readers are especially encouraged to read Kevin O'Reilly's essay in this volume for information on designing effective simulations. The beginning teacher wanting a simulation on the Vietnam War might also consider several of the excellent simulations that are commercially available. All of the materials discussed below ask students to carefully analyze primary sources. Many teachers are familiar with the excellent materials put out by the Choices Program from Brown University (www.choices.edu). The Choices simulation "The Limits of Power: The United States in Vietnam" is an excellent activity. While analyzing primary source documents students engage in activities on the roots of American involvement in Indochina, on the Gulf of Tonkin Resolution, and on songs of the Vietnam War and engage in role-playing activities on other aspects of the war.

The Social Studies School Service (www.socialstudies.com) has produced an excellent simulation booklet entitled *The 1960s and the Vietnam War: Decision Making in American History*. This booklet provides primary source documents and suggested student activities for the presidential election of 1960, the Cuban Missile Crisis, the civil rights movement, and the war in Vietnam. Students take part in debate activities on whether Americans should use bombing to aid the French at Dien Bien Phu, whether the United States should actively participate in the overthrow of South Vietnamese president Ngo Dinh Diem in 1963, and whether the United States should intensify the bombing of North Vietnam to achieve victory. Background materials are available to assist students as they make these historical decisions. A booklet containing a unit of study published by the Organization of American Historians and the National Center for History in the Schools, University of California,

Los Angeles, entitled *The Vietnam War: A National Dilemma* allows students to analyze a number of primary source documents concerning the war; many are included in their original form. If the goal of a teacher and student is to look at a number of primary source documents, this is the activity to utilize; this booklet actually has all the documents a teacher would need to teach the Vietnam War in a survey class.

Countless documentary films have been made about all aspects of the Vietnam War. Many students of the Vietnam War still consider the PBS series *Vietnam: A Television History* to be the best retelling of the Vietnam War ever made. This eleven-hour series covers all aspects of the war, including the American home front and, most important, the war from the perspective of the North Vietnamese and Viet Cong. It would be impossible to show the entire series to any class, but segments of it would be invaluable. In addition the series has a very valuable website, www.pbs.org/wgbh/amex/vietnam/. In 2011 the History Channel produced another exceptional series, *Vietnam in HD*. This six-hour series focuses on the actions of thirteen soldiers and their experiences in the war; rarely seen footage serves as the backdrop as they tell their stories. Unlike the PBS series, which gives an overarching history of the war, the History Channel series attempts to use the views of those thirteen soldiers to reflect on the larger events taking place around them. This series also has an extensive website, including teacher and student materials, www.history.com/shows/vietnam-in-hd.

The documentary that is most popular with instructors teaching the Vietnam War is *Dear America: Letters Home from Vietnam*. This HBO film, originally produced in 1987, hits home for many students as they listen to letters written by soldiers to girlfriends, friends, and family back home. Students are touched when they hear a letter writer expressing hope about coming home soon and then are informed that the writer died in battle two weeks later. The use of music from the 1960s and early 1970s perfectly matches the tone and message of this film. If there is one documentary that a beginning teacher should consider using, this is it. A book of the same title contains all the letters included in the film and many others.[7] In addition HBO Films has also produced a documentary centering on letters sent home by soldiers from Iraq; several teachers report having powerful lessons when students compare and contrast letters sent home from Iraq and Vietnam.

A book that can be valuable for advanced students is *In Retrospect: The Tragedy and Lessons of Vietnam,* by Robert S. McNamara, the secretary of defense during the Kennedy and Johnson administrations and the man responsible for many of the decisions related to the Vietnam War.[8] In this fascinating book McNamara analyzes what he feels were, in retrospect, the tragic mistakes made by the United States in Vietnam. Segments of a film by Errol Morris, *The Fog of War: Eleven Lessons from the Life of Robert S. McNamara*, can allow students to better understand the thinking of American leaders as they formulated American foreign policy in the Vietnam era. I would suggest that if you are not going to show this film to students, watch it yourself! You will be much better prepared to discuss the Vietnam War with your students. Two other invaluable documentary films are *Why We Fight* (2006), which explores the impact of the military-industrial complex on American foreign policy in the twentieth century, and *Hearts and Minds*, a controversial (and admittedly one sided) film on the disastrous nature of American involvement in Vietnam.

Books continue to be published for students and teachers on the Vietnam War. One that advanced high school students could find useful is *America and the Vietnam War: Re-examining the Culture and History of a Generation*.[9] Chapters in this book summarize findings by historians on the origins of the Vietnam War, the role of women in the war, the Black Panthers and the war, and the impact of post-traumatic stress disorder. Two very interesting chapters discuss "The Legacy of the Vietnam War for the US Army" and "Iraq as 'The Good War' Compared to Vietnam, the Bad War." Teachers and students looking to expand their knowledge of the war should consider this text.

Additional Resources for the Survey Classroom

Teachers who only have a few short weeks (or less) to devote to the war can still enrich their students' learning experience by going beyond the lecture and textbook. For example, time constraints may seem to preclude using literature to teach history, especially at the high school, advanced placement, or college level survey. However, teachers planning their unit on the Vietnam War should know that there are many novels, short stories, and poems devoted to the Vietnam War. Some, though not all, were written by individuals who actually served in Vietnam. In addition to the ideas shared in Maureen Ryan's essay in this volume, secondary teachers can use literature effectively by working with their English colleagues. Unfortunately, in countless schools, while the Vietnam War is taught in social studies classes, Tim O'Brien's *The Things They Carried* is taught in English classes, and there is no effort whatsoever to coordinate instruction (there are many cases, in fact, in which social studies teachers are not even aware that books of this nature are being taught by their language arts colleagues).

Language arts and social studies teachers in many states are facing the challenges of new common core standards. Teachers of both disciplines will be working more closely together to teach literacy skills; in some schools teachers have realized that an effective way to do this is to teach history-related nonfiction accounts, novels, short stories, and poems in each discipline at the same time, with the history teacher providing the historical background for the literature being studied. Since *The Things They Carried* is already being taught in so many language arts classes, this might be the perfect short story collection to utilize for interdisciplinary study. Many resources exist that can assist both the language arts teacher and the social studies teacher in the teaching of this book.[10] The social studies teacher must remember that this is indeed a work of fiction; by the author's own admission some of the stories are "made up." At the same time, this book more than many others "gets at the heart" of the American experience in Vietnam. That factor will allow history students to explore the difference between "history" and "memory" and to analyze the importance of each, both for the individual and for a nation as a whole. An interesting discussion with students in a social studies class would be to analyze whether it might be possible for a work of fiction to get closer to the "truth" than a work of nonfiction can.

One of the highlights of the Vietnam unit for many students is when Vietnam veterans come into the classroom to discuss their participation in the war. Students are often fascinated by the memories Vietnam veterans are willing to share; many are also quite candid in their opinions of American military activities in the Middle East. Two factors are critically important when you are bringing veterans (from any war) into your classroom. First, students should have a thorough knowledge of the conflict the veteran was involved in before he or she comes in to speak; veterans should be invited into classes at the end of the unit on Vietnam, not at the beginning. This will allow for more intelligent questions from students, which almost always provokes more thoughtful responses from veterans. Also, students should be reminded that in most cases Vietnam veterans are not "experts" on the Vietnam war in an academic sense, despite the fact that a few may consider themselves to be. Veterans can discuss in great detail what they saw, experienced, and felt when they were in Vietnam; this may or may not be similar to the experiences of other veterans who were there. In addition the passage of time may have shaded the views (and altered the memories) of the veteran who is speaking to your class. These comments are meant in no way to disparage the importance of having veterans speak to your classes or the contributions made by those veterans when there were in Vietnam; they are simply to remind you and your students that the observations and memories of any individual who comes into your classes should not be taken as historical fact. Andrew Darien's essay in this volume contains additional ideas on to make the veteran visit rewarding for your students.

Using Films to Teach the Vietnam War

As a teacher you probably already know about the power that movies can have over students and American society as a whole. Far more Americans know about details (true or not) surrounding the Kennedy assassination from the Oliver Stone film *JFK* than from the hundreds of books that have been written about that event. Likewise, the image of the unhinged Vietnam vet remains in the minds of many because that is how Vietnam veterans have been portrayed in countless movies; in fact, many vets returned home to normal lives. Movies can be powerful things and in many cases do not depict historical reality; students must constantly be reminded of that. There is a Russian roulette scene in the Vietnam film *The Deer Hunter* that may have a very powerful impact on students that view it; there is no evidence, however, that such an event ever took place in Vietnam.

New teachers should remember that many students think that because you, the teacher, are showing them a movie, it has to be true. As a result, it is incumbent on the teacher to tell students which scenes or characters are true, and which are not, in films that are viewed in class. The real value of using movies in the history/social studies classroom is that they help us to understand the cultural values and beliefs of the era in which they were made. A critical point to discuss with your classes is that movies made about historical events are very often as revealing about the period during which the movie was made as they are about the period being depicted in the film. One example is the 1967 film *Bonnie and Clyde*, which for much of the film glorifies the actions of these famous bank robbers of the 1930s. Many critics note that the film is about the 1930s, but isn't the movie also about the many young Americans who began to rebel against traditional society in the late 1960s, just like Bonnie and Clyde did in the 1930s? Does *The Hunger Games* also make some connections to the attitudes and values of American society in the present day? When you use historical films (and please be sure to consult Scott Laderman's essay in this volume), use them to inform students of the historical past, but also use them to inform students of the values and beliefs of the period or era in which the movie was made.

Using Music to Teach the Vietnam War

There are numerous songs that can be used to teach the Vietnam War; every documentary on Vietnam (or the Vietnam era) contains at least a few Vietnam era songs as background music (Creedence Clearwater Revival's "Fortunate Son" seems to be included in virtually every documentary film on the war). This section will contain some suggestions for the beginning teacher who may not be familiar with the music of the era (my apologies to those teachers who remember the 1960s for the songs that are left out of this list). Readers should consult Hugo A. Keesing's essay in this volume for a wider selection of songs and for more information about each one. This list is designed for teachers who are just adding music in the their classrooms for the first time.

Songs from the Folk Movement

Many folk singers of the 1960s sang antiwar folk songs. The darling of the folk movement was Bob Dylan; a place to start would be Dylan's "Masters of War," which denounces the builders of military machinery. A somewhat forgotten folk singer of the era is Phil Ochs; his "I Ain't Marching Any More" was an anthem for many, and "Draft Dodger Rag" describes various methods one could use avoid being drafted. Pete Seeger is a folk singer from the 1940s and 1950s who was blacklisted during the McCarthy era but still singing in the 1960s. Teachers should play his classic "Waist Deep in the Big Muddy" for their students; it is a song that was originally about World War II, but most who heard it in the late 1960s made the connection between the "big fool" depicted in the song and Lyndon Johnson. Some students wonder what folk songs Bob Dylan sang about Vietnam. By 1965 Dylan had left the folk movement and was singing rock 'n' roll; by this point his "protest era" was over.

Antiwar Songs

There are many songs the teacher could choose. As noted above "Fortunate Son" is one of them. "I-Feel-Like-I'm-Fixin'-to-Die," by Country Joe and the Fish, is a deeply cynical view of domestic America's attitude toward the war. The version from the *Woodstock* soundtrack is the best version to play for your students, although you should NOT play the "Fish Cheer" at the beginning of the song (unless being fired is not a concern for you). "Volunteers," by the Jefferson Airplane, depicts the demonstrations in the streets that were commonplace in America by the end of the 1960s; the Beach Boys even came out with "Student Demonstration Time" during this era. "War," by Edwin Starr, asks what war is good for; Marvin Gaye's "What's Goin' On" asks what is happening to America in 1970. Of course, John Lennon's "Give Peace a Chance" was sung at countless antiwar rallies of the early 1970s (and at some rallies protesting American intervention in the Middle East some forty years later). "Ohio," by Crosby, Stills, Nash, and Young, was recorded immediately following the 1970 Kent State massacre. A song that a teacher might play for his or her students was one of the most popular songs among the troops in the late 1960s: "We Gotta Get Out of This Place" by the Animals.

The Impact of the Vietnam War

Many songs depict the impact of war on American soldiers, civilians, and families. Teachers unfamiliar with the song "Still in Saigon," by the Charlie Daniels Band, should search it out. Another powerful song to use is "Born in the USA" by Bruce Springsteen. Despite what some politicians initially thought, this is not a pro-war song.

Songs from "The Other Side"

If a teacher wants to play "hits" that presented a pro-war viewpoint, they are few and far between. "The Ballad of the Green Berets," by Staff Sergeant Barry Sadler, was number one on the national charts for several weeks in 1966; that fact alone demonstrates that most Americans still supported the war then. Merle Haggard's "Okie from Muskogee" and "The Fightin' Side of Me" demonstrate the disgust felt by at least a part of the "silent majority" toward hippies, the counterculture, and antiwar protesters during this era.

Conclusion

This essay is designed to give the beginning teacher some ideas about how to approach the teaching of the Vietnam War and some resources that might assist that teacher as he or she begins to interact with students on the topic. There are many more subjects related to the war a teacher can explore with his or her students, for example, the role and attitudes of blacks and other minorities in the military, the role that women played in Vietnam, and the evolution of the student protest movement. A topic that films and many other resources ignore is the impact of the Vietnam War on Vietnam and the Vietnamese people; included in many anthologies about the war are poems and short stories concerning the war written from the Vietnamese perspective. When Americans think of prisoners of war in the Vietnam, most immediately think of American soldiers captured by the North Vietnamese; should American students also know what happened to North Vietnamese or Viet Cong prisoners captured by American or South Vietnamese forces? From a military perspective, planners of American military efforts in the Middle East were determined to avoid the "mistakes of Vietnam"; students should be encouraged to study what these mistakes were and whether the planners of the American wars in Afghanistan and Iraq were able to avoid them. The Vietnam War has played a major role in shaping the identity of America in the past forty-five years; teachers should impress this fact on students and help them analyze what America learned (and didn't learn) from the Vietnam War.

NOTES

1. http://www.nchs.ucla.edu/Standards/us-history-content-standards/us-era-9-1.

2. http://www.ode.state.oh.us.

3. http://www.cde.ca.gov/be/st/ss/documents/histsocscistnd.pdf.

4. Christopher R. Leahey, *Whitewashing War: Historical Myth, Corporate Textbooks, and Possibilities for Democratic Education* (New York: Teachers College Press, 2010), 45–65.

5. Ibid., 67–80.

6. Ibid., 85–92.

7. Bernard Edelman, ed., *Dear America: Letters Home from Vietnam* (New York: W. W. Norton, 2002).

8. Robert S. McNamara. *In Retrospect: The Tragedy and Lessons of Vietnam* (New York: Vintage Books, 1996).

9. Andrew Wiest, Mary Kathryn Barbier, and Glenn Robins, eds., *America and the Vietnam War: Re-examining the Culture and History of a Generation* (New York: Routledge, 2010).

10. Barry Gilmore and Alexander Kaplan, *Tim O'Brien in the Classroom: "This too is true, stories can save us"* (Urbana, IL: National Council of Teachers of English, 2007).

KEY RESOURCES

Davidson, James West, and Mark Hamilton Lytle. *After the Fact: The Art of Historical Detection*. 6th ed. Boston: McGraw-Hill, 2010.

Drake, Frederick D., and Sarah Drake Brown. "A Systematic Approach to Improve Students' Historical Thinking." *History Teacher* 36, no. 4 (August 2003): 456–85.

Lesh, Bruce. *Why Won't You Just Tell Us the Answer? Teaching Historical Thinking in Grades 7–12*. Portland, ME: Stenhouse Publishers, 2011.

Wineburg, Sam. *Historical Thinking and Other Unnatural Acts: Charting the Future of Teaching the Past*. Philadelphia, PA: Temple University Press, 2001.

Wineburg, Sam, Daisy Martin, and Chauncey Monte-Sano. *Reading Like a Historian: Teaching Literacy in Middle and High School History Classrooms*. New York: Teachers College Press, 2011.

www.teachinghistory.org. This is an excellent website for history teachers, with teaching resources, history content, best practices, and reviews.

Contributors

KARÍN AGUILAR-SAN JUAN is associate professor of American studies at Macalester College in Saint Paul, Minnesota. Her book *Little Saigons: Staying Vietnamese in America* (University of Minnesota Press, 2009) looks at the relationships between community and place for Vietnamese in Boston, Massachusetts, and Orange County, California.

STEPHEN ARMSTRONG is the president of the National Council for the Social Studies. A longtime secondary teacher, he is also Social Studies Supervisor at William H. Hall High School, King Phillip Middle School, and Bristow Middle School in West Hartford, Connecticut. He has conducted workshops on using film and music in the social studies classroom across the nation. He teaches world history and modern European history at Central Connecticut State University and is the author of *5 Steps to a 5: AP U.S. History* (McGraw Hill, 2011).

BRAD AUSTIN is professor of history at Salem State University, where he teaches modern US history and coordinates a nationally accredited teacher education program. He has served as the chairperson of the American Historical Association's Teaching Prize Committee and has worked with hundreds of secondary school teachers as the academic coordinator of Teaching American History grants in Massachusetts and as the codirector of a National Endowment for the Humanities Landmarks of American History program. He is the author of numerous book chapters and articles on pedagogy and on American sports history. He was 2012 recipient of the Northeast Association of Graduate Schools Master's Teaching Award.

ANDREW DARIEN is associate professor of history and Graduate Coordinator at Salem State University where he teaches courses in modern US and oral history. He writes on the politics of oral history and produced a documentary on the history of the World History Association titled *World Historians Speak Out: Pedagogy, Politics, and Perspectives*. His book *Becoming New York's Finest:*

Race, Gender, and Integration of the NYPD, 1935–1975 will be published with Palgrave Macmillan in 2014.

BRIAN C. ETHERIDGE is associate professor of history and director of the Helen P. Denit Honors Program at the University of Baltimore. He is a previous winner of the Stuart L. Bernath Scholarly Article Prize from the Society for Historians of American Foreign Relations and is the coeditor of *The United States and Public Diplomacy: New Directions in Cultural and International History* (Brill, 2010). He received his PhD in the history of American foreign relations from Ohio State University in 2002.

DAVID FITZGERALD is a lecturer in international politics in the School of History, University College Cork, Ireland. Formerly a post-doctoral fellow at the Clinton Institute for American Studies, University College Dublin, he is the author of *Learning to Forget: US Army Counterinsurgency Doctrine and Practice from Vietnam to Iraq* (Stanford University Press, 2013).

GEORGE C. HERRING is Alumni Professor of History Emeritus at the University of Kentucky. He is the author of many books, including *America's Longest War: The United States and Vietnam, 1950–1975* (4th ed., McGraw Hill, 2001) and *LBJ and Vietnam: A Different Kind of War* (University of Texas Press, 1994). He has taught classes on the Vietnam War for more than three decades.

TUAN HOANG is visiting assistant professor at Pepperdine University. His areas of research are South Vietnamese intellectual history and Vietnamese American history.

HUGO A. KEESING has a PhD in psychology. He presented his first research paper on music and the Vietnam War in 1979. He is the reissue producer/ author of *Next Stop Is Vietnam: The War on Record, 1961–2008* (Bear Family Records, 2010). The anthology has been critically acclaimed both in the United States and abroad. It was recognized as one of 2010's best by, among others, the *New York Times*, *USA Today*, *The Nation*, and *Rolling Stone*.

SCOTT LADERMAN is associate professor of history at the University of Minnesota, Duluth. He is the author of *Tours of Vietnam: War, Travel Guides, and Memory* (Duke University Press, 2009) and the coeditor, with Edwin Martini, of *Four Decades On: Vietnam, the United States, and the Legacies of the Second Indochina War* (Duke University Press, 2013). His research articles have appeared in publications ranging from the *Pacific Historical Review* to the *American Indian Culture and Research Journal*. He is currently completing a political history of surfing for the University of California Press. In 2008 he was the recipient of an excellence in teaching award from the College of Liberal Arts, University of Minnesota, Duluth.

MITCHELL B. LERNER is associate professor of history and director of the Institute for Korean Studies at the Ohio State University. He has held the Mary Ball Washington Distinguished Fulbright Chair at University College Dublin and has been an officer of the Society for Historians of American Foreign Relations. He is the author of *The Pueblo Incident: A Spy Ship and the Failure of American Foreign Policy* (University Press of Kansas, 2002), which won the John Lyman Book Award, and editor of *Looking Back at LBJ* (University Press of Kansas, 2005) and *A Companion to Lyndon B. Johnson* (Wiley-Blackwell, 2012).

MATTHEW MASUR is associate professor of history at Saint Anselm College in Manchester, New Hampshire. His publications on the Vietnam War include "Historians and the Origins of the Vietnam War," in *America and the Vietnam War: Re-examining the Culture and History of a Generation* (Routledge, 2010), edited by Andrew Wiest, Mary Kathryn Barbier, and Glenn Robins; "Exhibiting Signs of Resistance: South Vietnam's Struggle for Legitimacy, 1954–1960," published in *Diplomatic History*; and "Falling Dominoes: The United States, Vietnam, and the War in Iraq," in *Vietnam in Iraq: Tactics, Lessons, Legacies, and Ghosts* (Routledge, 2006), edited by John Dumbrell and David Ryan. He is codirector of the Center for Teaching Excellence at Saint Anselm College and a member of the Teaching Committee of the Society for Historians of American Foreign Relations.

KEVIN O'REILLY is History Department Chair at Hamilton-Wenham Regional High School in Massachusetts. He is the author of the twelve-volume *Decision Making in United States History*, the four-volume *Critical Thinking in United States History*, the film *Vietnam: A Case Study for Critical Thinking*, and the web-based simulation on the Vietnam War *Escalation*. He has won a Teacher of the Year Award from the National Council for the Social Studies, the NASDAQ Educational Foundation's national prize for Excellence in the Teaching of Economics, the Beveridge Family Teaching Prize from the American Historical Association, and the Paul Gagnon Prize from the National Council for History Education.

DAVID RYAN is professor of history and vice-head of the College of Arts, Celtic Studies and Social Sciences at University College Cork, Ireland. He has published extensively on contemporary history and US foreign policy, concentrating on the interventions in the post-Vietnam era. His recent books include *US Collective Memory, Intervention and Vietnam: The Cultural Politics of US Foreign Policy since 1969* (Routledge, 2014), *Frustrated Empire: US Foreign Policy from 9/11 to Iraq* (University of Michigan, 2007), and the coedited (with John Dumbrell) volume *Vietnam in Iraq: Tactics, Lessons, Legacies, and Ghosts* (Routledge, 2006).

MAUREEN RYAN is professor of English at the University of Southern Mississippi, where she teaches and writes about modern and contemporary American literature. Her publications include *Innocence and Estrangement in the Fiction of Jean Stafford* (Louisiana State University Press, 1987), *The Other Side of Grief: The Home Front and the Aftermath in American Narratives of the Vietnam War* (University of Massachusetts Press, 2008), and articles on Marilynne Robinson, Willa Cather, Bobbie Ann Mason, Barbara Kingsolver, and Lillian Hellman, among others. At Southern Miss, she has served as dean of the Honors College and associate provost for institutional effectiveness. She was the sixth Charles W. Moorman Distinguished Professor of the Humanities.

KATHRYN C. STATLER is professor of history at the University of San Diego. She is the author of *Replacing France: The Origins of American Intervention in Vietnam* (University Press of Kentucky, 2007) and coeditor (with Andrew Johns) of *The Eisenhower Administration, the Third World, and the Globalization of the Cold War* (Rowman and Littlefield, 2006). She is currently at work on a history of Franco-American cultural diplomacy.

DAVID STEIGERWALD is professor of history at Ohio State University and teaches courses that cover the range of modern America, from the Gilded Age to the present, including courses on the Vietnam War and the Sixties. He is the author of *The Sixties and the End of Modern America* (Bedford, 1995) and coauthor of *Debating the Sixties: Liberal, Conservative, and Radical Perspectives* (Rowman and Littlefield, 2007). He is finishing a study of American thought in the age of affluence, which will appear as "Lost in the Land of Plenty: Affluence and Alienation in Post-war America, 1945–2001." He is a recipient of Ohio State's highest recognition for teaching excellence, the Alumni Distinguished Teaching Award.

JOHN DAY TULLY is associate professor of history at Central Connecticut State University, where he teaches courses on the Vietnam War and the history of American foreign relations. He served as the founding director of the Harvey Goldberg Center for Excellence in Teaching at Ohio State University. He currently serves as the president of the Connecticut Council for the Social Studies and has been the academic director of multiple Teaching American

History grants. His first book, *Ireland and Irish Americans, 1932–1945: The Search for Identity*, was published by Irish Academic Press. In 2009 he won the Board of Trustees Teaching Award for the Connecticut State University System.

CHIA YOUYEE VANG is associate professor of history at the University of Wisconsin–Milwaukee. She is author of *Hmong America: Reconstructing Community in Diaspora* (University of Illinois Press, 2010). She has published articles on the politics of ethnic minority involvement in the Vietnam War and is currently working on a book about war memories among ethnic minorities who lived in Laos during the Second Indochina War.

RICHARD HUME WERKING is Professor of History and Library Director, Emeritus, at the US Naval Academy in Annapolis, where he taught classes in the history of US foreign relations and US naval history. He earned his BA at the University of Evansville, his MA and PhD in American history at the University of Wisconsin–Madison, and his MA in librarianship at the University of Chicago. He is the author of *The Master Architects: Building the United States Foreign Service, 1890–1913* (University Press of Kentucky, 1977) as well as journal articles and book chapters in the fields of American history and academic librarianship. He has served as a founding member of the Teaching Committee of the Society for Historians of American Foreign Relations, a member of the board of editors of the SHAFR website (www .shafr.org), and the elected chair of the College Libraries Section of the American Library Association.

ANDREW WIEST is Distinguished Professor of History at the University of Southern Mississippi, where he is also Founding Director of the Center for the Study of War and Society. He has published widely on the Vietnam War, including the recently released *The Boys of '67: Charlie Company's War in Vietnam* (Osprey, 2012) and the award-winning *Vietnam's Forgotten Army: Heroism and Betrayal in the ARVN* (New York University Press, 2008).

MARILYN B. YOUNG received her PhD from Harvard University in 1963. She taught at the University of Michigan before joining the faculty at New York University in 1980 where she is professor in the Department of History. She is the author, editor, or coeditor of numerous books and anthologies, including *Rhetoric of Empire: American China Policy, 1895–1901* (Harvard University Press, 1969), *The Vietnam Wars, 1945–1990* (Harper Collins, 1991), and, with A. Tom Grunfeld and John Fitzgerald, *The Vietnam War: A History in Documents* (Oxford University Press, 2003). More recently, she and Lloyd Gardner put together a collection of essays entitled *Iraq and the Lessons of*

Vietnam or How Not to Learn from History (The New Press, 2008). She has served as an elected member of the Council of the American Historical Association and the Board of the Organization of American Historians. She was awarded a Guggenheim Fellowship and an American Council of Learned Society Fellowship in 2000–2001, directed the NYU International Center for Advanced Studies Project on the Cold War as Global Conflict from 2001 to 2004, and served as president of the Society for Historians of American Foreign Relations in 2010. She is currently codirector of the Tamiment Center for the Study of the Cold War. Her abiding interest has been to analyze the American way of war and how to put an end to it.

Index